CAMBRIDGE COMMONWEALTH SERIES

General Editor: Professor E. T. Stokes

DEVELOPING THE THIRD WORLD: THE EXPERIENCE OF THE NINETEEN-SIXTIES

CAMBRIDGE COMMONWEALTH SERIES

Toward 'Uhuru' in Tanzania: G. ANDREW MAGUIRE
Developing the Third World: The Experience of the Nineteen-Sixties:
RONALD ROBINSON (ed.)

These books are published by the Syndics of
the Cambridge University Press in association
with the Managers of the Cambridge University
Smuts Memorial Fund for the advancement of
Commonwealth Studies

DEVELOPING
THE THIRD WORLD:
The Experience of the Nineteen-Sixties

Edited by
RONALD ROBINSON
Fellow of St John's College
Smuts Reader in Commonwealth History, Cambridge University
and Beit Professor Elect of Commonwealth History, Oxford University

CAMBRIDGE at the University Press 1971

Published by the Syndics of the Cambridge University Press
Bentley House, 200 Euston Road, London N.W.1
American Branch: 32 East 57th Street, New York, N.Y.10022

This collection © Cambridge University Press 1971

Library of Congress Catalogue Card Number: 74-138379
ISBN: 0 521 08079 7

Printed in Great Britain
by The Eastern Press, Ltd.
London and Reading

Contents

Preface

Although the Third World developed impressively during the 1960s, it often did so in ways that threw existing theories into disarray. At present there may be as much to be learned from the dilemmas of planners and administrators as from the elegant models of social scientists. In these selected Cambridge conference papers, practitioners discuss some crucial problems of development policy empirically. They are concerned with what might be called the 'practical politics' of the task – the art of correlating economic priorities with political needs in competition for scarce resources.

If the papers are to be appreciated fully, some explanation is required of the conferences which produced them. Their members were a mixture of general administrators and technical specialists in many different fields. At each of them about a hundred and fifty ministers, senior officials, planners, scholars and businessmen came together in a college for a fortnight to examine a particular problem in development strategy. Public executives from Commonwealth Africa and South Asia, from Aid-giving countries and international agencies were in a majority; but Latin American, Middle Eastern and Caribbean planners also attended in small numbers. These annual gatherings were organised by the University Overseas Studies Committee with the help of the Ministry of Overseas Development at the instigation of the late Sir Andrew Cohen; and incidentally, the publication of these papers is one more tribute to his imaginative contribution in this field. Intimately abrasive debate was intended to serve three purposes: to exchange experience between different countries, agencies and professions, so that compartmental orthodoxies were tested against each other; to review the successes and failures of development in practice, and to assess the implications for future policy.

Naturally, the papers reflect the procedure and limitations of such a conference. When specialist officials in different fields of action from different countries discuss issues that require all of them to combine operationally, their standpoint is neither technical nor academic, but governmental. They are bound to communicate in non-technical language and in general terms. There is little hope of success if economists can talk only to economists and administrators will talk only with God. If occasionally the points made seem a little rough-hewn or too generalised to a specialist reader, they are none the less the common sense of a craft which is necessarily less sophisticated in action than it is in the study – in which experts in one branch or country are laymen in all the rest.

The papers are of two different kinds and significance. Some are individual statements of an issue. They were written usually from a technical point of view before a conference, to indicate briefly topics for discussion. Their authors were expressing personal opinions and were not representing those of their agency or government. The remaining papers are extracts from the ' Argument' of the conference, written by its chairman who also edits this volume. Here he sums up personal impressions of consensus and dissent arising from the conference's plenary debates on individual papers and study group proposals. For what are in effect conclusions of the conference, this form of report may seem somewhat eccentric. Its object was partly to prevent study groups from turning into drafting committees, chiefly, to secure for officials speaking privately and personally on contentious subjects a measure of freedom from their official capacities. In the ' Argument', therefore, the entire conference looks at a problem from many angles, taking broader political, administrative and human considerations into account. It reveals the liturgical in-fighting between administrator and planner, politician and theorist, between different agencies and roles that goes into the making of development strategy and pin-points its deepest dilemmas.

Altogether the volume offers a glimpse of the official thinking behind the drive for development in the sixties. Sometimes it suggests a critique of that thought and has implications for the seventies. There is here a rare insight into the anxieties of men who weigh the economic chances against the political and human risks.

The editor would like to record his best thanks to Professor E. A. G. Robinson for valuable suggestions and advice, and similarly to Professor Eric Stokes, the general editor of this series of publications on Commonwealth affairs.

RONALD ROBINSON

St John's College
Cambridge

Acknowledgements

The Cambridge Conferences on Development are supported by the British Ministry of Overseas Development. All the papers in this volume, with the exception of the appendix to Lord Balogh's paper, have previously appeared in the Cambridge Conference on Development Reports published on behalf of the Cambridge University Overseas Study Committee by Her Majesty's Stationery Office.

A version of Stanley Please's paper has also appeared in *Finance and Development*, **4** No. 1, 1967. A version of Professor G. M. Meier's paper appeared as 'Progress and Problems of the Development Decade' in *Social and Economic Studies*, **15** No. 4, 1966. Khalid Ikram's paper has also appeared in *Readings in Economic and Social Development*, edited by Chandrasekar, Sripati and Haltman (Heath), and in *International Development Review*, **6** No. 4, 1964. A version of Professor Hollis B. Chenery's paper appeared in *Capital Movement and Economic Development*, edited by Adler (Macmillan–St Martin's Press). Lord Balogh's paper also appeared as 'Multilateral *v*. Bilateral Aid' in *Oxford Economic Papers*, **19** No. 3, 1967. The appendix to his paper appeared as 'Pearson and Jackson' in *Venture* for January 1970.

The Editor and the Publisher appreciate the support given by the bodies and publications mentioned above in facilitating the publication of this book.

Biographical Notes

RONALD ROBINSON, who has been chairman of the Cambridge conference on problems of developing countries since 1961, is a Fellow of St John's College, Smuts Reader in Commonwealth History in Cambridge University and Beit Professor elect of Commonwealth History at Oxford.

GERALD MEIER is Professor of International Economics at Stanford University and a leading American authority on international trade.

KHALID IKRAM is a senior government economist who works in perspective planning for the Planning Commission of Pakistan.

V. K. RAMASWAMI was Chief Economic Adviser to the Ministry of Finance in the Government of India.

C. F. SCHUMACHER is Chief Economic Adviser to the British National Coal Board and a leader of the movement for the promotion of intermediate technology.

NUNO F. DE FIGUEIREDO was Director of the Latin-American Institute for Economic and Social Planning and is now Professor of Economics in the University of São Paulo.

SIR JOSEPH HUTCHINSON, a Fellow of St John's College, is Draper's Professor of Agriculture Emeritus at Cambridge. A distinguished plant-breeder in India and Africa, he was president of the British Association in 1965-6.

K. A. BUSIA, who is a Professor of Sociology, was Chairman of the Political Committee and is now Prime Minister of Ghana.

TARLOK SINGH is a leading Indian authority on rural development and was for many years a member of the Planning Commission of the Government of India.

EDMUNDO FLORES is professor at the School of Economics in the University of Mexico and an authority on agricultural development in Latin America.

ERICH JACOBY, research professor at the Institute for Economic Studies, Stockholm, is an expert on agrarian reform, who has for many years worked as an adviser to the United Nations Food and Agriculture Organisation.

STANLEY PLEASE at the time of writing was on the staff of the World Bank.

RASHID IBRAHIM was Financial Adviser to the Military Finance Department in the Government of Pakistan and is now a senior executive in the Development Corporation.

HOLLIS B. CHENERY, who was professor at the Center for International Affairs at Harvard, is now Chief Economic Adviser to the World Bank.

LORD BALOGH, Fellow of Balliol College, and Reader in Economics in the University of Oxford, has acted as economic adviser to the governments of many developing countries. He was Economic Adviser to Mr Harold Wilson's Cabinet from 1964-7 and is a leading British authority on problems of economic development.

1 GENERAL PERSPECTIVE

1 · Practical Politics of Economic Development
RONALD ROBINSON

In theory, when considering ways and means of making a poor country rich, it might seem wise to assume that the processes of economic, political and social change required for the purpose are systematically interconnected. If so, how do they interact? It may be that economic growth itself brings about the socio-political changes needed for its own continuance eventually – but how long is it to the event? Or it may be that if the socio-political context is not changed appropriately in time, it falls apart or stunts economic growth. In different circumstances both processes have in fact taken place. In practice, unhappily, there is no theory of social relativity generally applicable to the problem of generating and correlating these different changes in the Third World. The approach to its development during the 1960s was necessarily economic. Anxious to improve their management of scarce resources, Afro-Asian governments attempted to take the advice of economists – within the limits of political safety. Their leaders, wisely perhaps in face of the implacable continuities of Afro-Asian history, began their development crusade by shifting economic resources, rather than moving existing socio-political structures frontally. A fragile, new nation seemed best levered into modernity gently and indirectly through its economy.

It was thus that an economic plan became the characteristic vehicle of development policy, and the decade, the golden age of the economic planner. A plan was the indispensable passport to foreign Aid, the touchstone of rationality and domestic efficiency. As the 1963 conference recited it, the *credo* ran:

There must be a plan for the whole economy . . . based on analysis of past economic trends and projections of those required for the future . . . , broken down into programmes for the different sectors . . . and these in turn into specific projects. Ideally all the parts should conform to the grand design. Without the broad frame, it is impossible on any rational principles to allocate priorities for investment between different sectors and projects, or to calculate the profit and loss of each in terms of the general good.[1]

Essentially the rationale of the plan was to mobilise economic resources and deploy them on cost–benefit criteria to projects with optimal effects on economic growth rates and structures.

This rigorous, if restricted, logic ruled in principle from the second half of the 1950s onward. Plans so far abstracted from socio-political processes proved hard to carry out completely for lack of political will and public cooperation. Whether they succeeded or failed nevertheless, the attempt probed the resistance and behaviour of non-economic elements empirically. And in policy-making, the planners' aggressive challenge on behalf of economic efficiency provoked others to re-define and re-assert the role of non-economic factors in economic growth. There was as a result throughout the decade a confrontation between economic and socio-political standpoints over the problem of correlating different types of change.

This portentous dialogue of the economic planner with the politician and administrator runs through these papers. They weigh against each other various considerations that govern the making and carrying out of an economic plan. Planning poses such questions as: what share of national income can be squeezed out of consumption into savings? What is, and what is not, 'Developmental' expenditure? How much should be allocated to agriculture, how much to industry, how much to the public, how much to the private sector? On what criteria should Aid be distributed? These are not only economic questions, but political, social and executive problems and must be solved as such, if the economic plan is to have any meaning. Not infrequently, in the short term the several considerations involved prove marginally incompatible. It is the dilemma of adjusting these inconsistencies and deciding which ones should override others that is the crux of development strategy and provides the theme linking the topics in these papers. Basically the issues in contention are either those of reconciling the optimal investment or technology with considerations of full employment, social welfare and political stability; or those of translating into action the planned allocation of resources, through indigenous political and administrative processes.

If the confrontation of factors is too sharp in the papers on industrial development from the 1964 conference, there were good contemporary reasons. Up to the mid-1950s, most economic plans in the Third World had respected the classical formula of a balance between the expansion of the agricultural and industrial sectors, with increased farm output setting the pace of industrialisation. Agriculture, on this view, had to provide most of the foreign exchange, raw material, internal savings and markets required for industrial growth; otherwise the economy would soon run into a balance of payments crisis which might set it back for a decade. By 1963 however, India, Pakistan and other South Asian countries had departed from this prescription. Although their farm output was lagging, they were investing between 25 and 30 per cent of their total plan outlay in industrialisation.[2] What is more, they were defying the old injunction to concentrate in the early stages of industrialisation on consumer goods and agricultural processing, and developing in addition heavy and intermediate capital goods industries.

It was in this context that the memorable encounter between Dr Ikram and Professor Kaldor on the one hand, and Dr Schumacher on the other, took place. Mr Ramaswami and Dr Ikram argue that agriculture in South Asian circumstances is incapable of acting as the leading sector because farm surplus increases too slowly and the rural population too quickly. Therefore industrial expansion offers the only chance of a 'break-through' in the economy as a whole. Advanced technology creates large amounts of capital swiftly and provides the resources necessary for its own development, whereas agriculture produces only a little capital slowly. Capital-intensive industry by import-substitution, moreover, saves foreign exchange in larger amounts more quickly than agricultural exports can earn it. From the standpoint of choosing investments with the best capital–output ratio, these are persuasive economic reasons for making industry the leading sector. The 1964 conference for the most part inclined to accept this radical strategy; but with reservations. One was that it called for more foreign exchange than was likely to be available – a doubt which subsequent foreign exchange crises proved well-founded. Another was that, so long as domestic markets for manufactures remained inelastic as a result of the stagnation of agricultural incomes, many industries would prove inefficient. This also came to pass in some plants, which meant that they had to be subsidised by the rest of the economy, and so retarded overall growth. In particular, the stress on machine-building industries in India promised to be both costly and premature, although they will no doubt pay off in the seventies.

Dr Schumacher, however, stresses the dangers of making industry the leading sector in economic growth from the standpoint of political stress and rising unemployment.

Industrial concentrations based on the latest technology [he writes] may give you the best output for capital invested and the best rate of economic growth; but the political and human costs in unemployment in the countryside, in resentment against a policy that leaves eighty per cent of the nation in rural areas worse off than they were before, are so great that society [may] disintegrate and the economy run down.[3]

If resources are concentrated on developing one or two great bastions of modern technology, the already alarming gap between rural and urban incomes will widen still further. Migration from the countryside to the cities as a result will also increase, and since the imported advanced technology destroys many more jobs than it creates, economic growth will be achieved at the expense of widespread unemployment and political unrest. Dr Schumacher suggests two courses of action to forestall the *Eumenides*: to develop and employ 'intermediate technologies' that require less capital per work-place without being too inefficient economically; and secondly, to adopt a strategy of rural industrialisation, based on small-scale manufacturing using intermediate technology, that would increase rural employment and incomes and offset the damaging effects of capital-intensive industry upon them.

This intermediate concept for industry is criticised strongly in its turn by Professor Kaldor.[4] Employment, he argued, is not essentially a function of the technology selected, but of the volume of wage goods produced. Economically and theoretically, ' there is no conceivable situation in which the use of advanced methods of production and organisation will not pay for more employment and social improvements than the intermediate varieties '.[5] By implication, maximum employment is to be attained through investing scarce capital in advanced and concentrated technology which gives the optimal capital–output ratio, rather than in inefficient, small-scale manufactures scattered throughout the countryside. A poor country, it is said, cannot afford to divert scarce resources from investment in maximum production to meet the needs of social welfare. Admittedly, capital-intensive manufacture will widen the rural–urban gap and swell urban migration; but these problems cannot be solved by selecting an inefficient technology, but only by government redistributing wealth from city to countryside once the extra wealth has been produced. Professor Kaldor, however, would be the first to admit that as a matter of practical politics this is easier said than done.

In 1964 it was still possible to be reassured on these economic principles that the application of the most efficient technologies to industry and agriculture would automatically maximise employment and social well-being, so that no special provision for them needed to be made. Conference opinion accepted the optimal capital–output ratio as the overriding consideration in the choice of technology, and maximum economic efficiency as the decisive test for the location of industry. By 1968 however, as the papers on rural development show, experience had redressed the balance of the argument on Dr Schumacher's side. The best of plans based on maximum productive efficiency may yet make bad economic policy. At the end of the decade the divergence of means of relieving unemployment from means of maximising economic growth became inescapable. In many cases it now seemed wiser to accept a slower rate of advance in the one direction in order to make more progress in the other.

It must be allowed that the inconsistencies between the different criteria for allocating resources are sometimes deliberately sharpened in these papers to clarify issues and provoke debate. Nevertheless, if the industrialisation controversy of 1964 assumed that the most effective means of industrialisation, economic growth, fuller employment, social integration and political stability were substantially compatible in the long run, it also suggested that in the short run, the inconsistency would sometimes be far from marginal.

In retrospect it is evident that the industrialisation papers reflected the end of an era in development planning which had opened in the mid-fifties. They forestall perhaps the coming amelioration of the imperious, economic approach in which economic stages and models, economic factors and economic criteria reigned almost unchallenged in principle, as arbiters of development strategy. The tendency of the style was too optimistic. It exaggerated the actual power of economic over non-economic factors, of industrial technology and institutions to invade and conquer the massive bulk of pre-industrial society, and of comparatively tiny, modernising elites to control its political reactions at a time when they were as much its prisoners as its masters. After 1964 the thinking became less confident, the mood more pessimistic. Focus shifted from the economic means of growth to the non-economic obstacles encountered by them.

Gerald Meier's appraisal of experience during the first half of the Development decade reflects the opening of a new era which asked old questions in new forms. His anxious enquiry might serve as text for the years 1964 to 1968. 'Does economic growth', he asks, 'run into increasingly severe, even intractable institutional barriers as it proceeds?'[6] At the time there were signs enough in the lag in agricultural output, the tightening demographic constriction, the increasing political instability and over-burdening of executive capacity, that institutional settings and time-lags enter more profoundly into economic growth than earlier plans had taken into account. Economic inputs had not always reached the production targets expected of them. It was time to fix more attention on socio-political factors. In Meier's words,

The more advanced . . . the economic analysis, the less is it capable of incorporating non-economic elements. But the less developed the country, the more does planning depend on non-economic factors . . . When these strategic non-economic factors have been ignored, the implementation of policies designed to remove the economic barriers has remained limited. For, regardless of the economic logic of the development plan, its success in gaining popular support and participation must depend on attitudes, values and institutions.[7]

Although the implications of this more 'institutional' approach may be disputed, they cannot be ignored. In abstracting the economy too far out of its socio-political context, earlier plans had tended to pursue economic optima mechanistically, without inducing the economic and political behaviour required to achieve them. A rising concern with the socio-political risks of the method, if not with its economic results, is evident in these papers. The more institutional approach is based on rather different assumptions; and obviously, it calls for much closer and continuous collaboration between politician, economist, administrator, political scientist and sociologist, if economic planning is to take non-economic factors fully into account. It stresses the fact that a plan must be a programme of political and executive as well as economic action. This much has been a commonplace of these conferences since 1965, although once again, it is easier said than done to match economic needs to political choices. But the fundamental implication of the institutional approach is perhaps a denial of the idea that the economy is basic and the rest of the society simply superstructure determined by it, and an insistence that in reality socio-political structure bears at every point upon economic growth no less than economic change impinges at every point upon socio-political structure. If this is true, an agriculture-based economy cannot be expected to grow into an industrial one without corresponding innovations in attitudes and institutions; nor can social structure be reformed without corresponding changes in economic organisation. On these assumptions the original problem of developing the economy turns into a far more complicated endeavour to correlate interacting sequences of change on three planes. By 1969, Paul Streeten had carried the point to an almost too logical conclusion. 'Development' he wrote, 'requires not so much the study of economic forces within social and political constraints, as the study of political and psychological forces within economic limits.'[8]

In 1965, as for decades past, it was in agriculture that the problem of correlation and social resistance seemed critical for the Third World as a whole. Famine was widespread in parts of South Asia which became increasingly dependent on United States food-Aid. The population increase eating into meagre increases in farm output per head seemed alarming because, even if by some magic, control measures could be instituted universally at once, they could not remove the demographic drag on economic growth for a generation to come. There were also too many new industrial plants operating below capacity for lack of rural spending power, or standing idle for lack of foreign exchange for imported spares. In these circumstances planners turned their attention more than they had done hitherto from designs for industrial revolution to the humbler tasks of energising the basic, rural economy.

All experience showed that this was the hardest of all jobs of economic engineering; for here industrial technology at its weakest seems to grapple with pre-industrial institutions at their strongest. Economic inputs in the rural sector have to be distributed in small parcels over thousands of villages, and millions of small farmers living in custom-bound communities have to be persuaded to work harder and adopt better methods of cultivation. Peasant conservatism, which Professor Busia examines in an African context, had long seemed the adamant social obstacle to economic growth. There had long been, in addition, a political constraint on rural progress. Over-ambitious governments tended to take too much out of agriculture to put into urban industry[9] and so had strengthened the peasant's social disincentive to take up better methods and respond to market opportunity. If the institutional gaps between urban market and rural producer, combined with urban bias in income distribution policy, are the primary cause of agricultural lag, the remedy is in the hands of government. If, on the other hand, the critical disincentives arise from the nature of traditional institutions in rural society, government can do little to remove them, short of radical social reform at high political risk. In 1965 therefore the crucial question was: is the power of economic inputs to change rural society greater than the power of rural conservatism to reject or frustrate them? Since it was in the rural sector that institutional obstacles seemed intractable, it was there that the institutionalist criticism of the earlier economic approach to development had seemed most justified.

Surprisingly enough, considering the forebodings of the 1965 papers, those of the 1968 conference on the rural basis of national development express confidence that rural social resistance presents no great barrier to modern economic inputs and rural economic growth. By that time a dramatic improvement in farm technology was being made, and higher-yielding varieties of wheat, rice and maize, improved fertilisers, pesticides, pumps and wells, promised a 'green revolution' in the Third World. An unpredicted dawn was brightening the economic sky in Pakistan and parts of India, of Kenya and Uganda, of Mexico and the Philippines, Ceylon and Malaysia. If promise is fulfilled, development may be reaching that historic turning-point at which agriculture ceases to act as a brake on industrialisation and begins to drive it forward.

It was harder than it had been to play the institutional Job's comforter to frustrated economic planners in these circumstances. The conference in 1968 believed, writes Dr Desai, that 'institutional change in traditional rural society is not required to create the desire in the peasant to improve his lot, once he is offered the opportunity'. On the contrary, 'the extension of modern institutions supplying techniques and credit, market and storage facilities is required on a massive scale once the economic incentives are working in full flood'.[10] As sociologists have often insisted, so-called traditional societies prove to be as flexible as any others, given sufficient economic incentive, and as adamant as any others when it is lacking. Evidently peasant farmers conform to this rule. Few of them will accept the offer of new techniques that increase their income marginally; and it is then that tradition seems the intractable obstacle. But they cheerfully throw tradition to the winds and scramble for modern techniques with alacrity if they will double, treble and even quadruple their income. In this sense the experience of the second half of the sixties shows that rural economic growth does not run increasingly into this particular institutional obstacle. It suggests rather that the institutional resistance of traditional society is inversely proportional to the size and efficiency of modern inputs.

There remain, however, social and political threats to rural advance more formidable than peasant conservatism, as the 1968 papers indicate. And they arise from the disruptive effect of modern farm technology on existing social organisation. 'You cannot get big increases in agricultural production', William Allan remarked, 'without increasing social inequality and destroying the security of subsistence once provided by the traditional social and economic order.' [11] As better farming technique spreads, economic and social differentiation, unemployment and political tensions in rural society increase. It means more production from fewer farmers and labourers. Green revolution combines with population increase to swell rural unemployment. The rewards go to a minority of enterprising land-holders while the majority may be worse off than they were before. An increasing proportion of labour formerly occupied in traditional farming is driven into the cities. There will be no jobs in office or factory for most of them there. No rate of industrial growth ever achieved in history, the 1968 conference noted, could conceivably employ the labour surplus displaced from the land, if plans do not provide alternative occupations to keep people in the countryside. Hence modern farm inputs promise eventually to dispose of the spectre of famine and the obstacles of traditionalism and agricultural lag, only to raise up the curse of widespread unemployment in their place. By 1968, Dr Schumacher's worst predictions were being fulfilled.

Large proposals for intermediate technology and rural industry, which earlier found little favour on grounds of economic inefficiency, seemed vitally necessary four years later on grounds of employment and social stabilisation. By the end of the decade, the need to temper the pursuit of economic maxima with provision for employment and social integration had emerged strikingly. It is vital both politically and economically to keep masses of unemployed and under-employed out of the cities, producing, however inefficiently, on the land. Reflecting this change of head and heart, the 1968 conference accepted a 'Two-tier' principle for rural investment which corresponds in aim and method to Dr Schumacher's intermediate principle for industry.

A strategy of maximising the marketable and investible surplus to be obtained from agriculture, Professor Yudelman argued, is likely to reduce work-places in agriculture. But industrial employment will not grow fast enough to absorb the rural labour displaced. On the other hand, a strategy of spreading economic inputs thinly over the entire agricultural population would minimise rural unemployment, but it would also conflict with the surplus-maximisation objective. Therefore agriculture should be planned in two tiers – the upper devoted to maximum, productive efficiency, and the lower of poorer productivity, to maximum employment. Investments in the upper tier should be selected on the principle of maximum capital–output ratio, while in the lower tier, projects would be chosen on the principle of maximising employment. Hence the lower tier is conceived of as a vast holding operation to keep people on the land until they can be absorbed into rural services or urban industry.[12] No other scheme could illustrate so vividly the 1968 conference's conviction that at this point in development, the thraldom of the economic optimum must be curbed in the interest of employment and social equilibrium. An intermediate and evolutionary strategy appears to be as necessary to mop up the disruptive social effects of modern farm technology in agriculture, as it is to offset the disruptive social effects of computer age technology in industry.

Once again on the subject of land reform – which Professor Jacoby discusses – the emphasis in 1968 was not on traditional, institutional resistance to modern economic inputs, but on the new socio-political obstacles that modern economic inputs themselves create. In 1968 traditional systems of land tenure were no longer regarded as the serious obstruction to increased farm output that they had been earlier. Like the rest of rural social organisation, they now seemed flexible enough if economic rewards proved sufficiently attractive. Normally, it was agreed, redistribution of land and reform of tenure is not essential to the task of expanding rural productivity. Rather, tenure systems from this standpoint can be regarded as ' neutral '; and the effect of reforming them on production has often proved disappointing.[13] Land reform, none the less, remains in some areas a powerful means of multiplying rural work-places and of redistributing rural incomes. What is more, it has immense possibilities as a political instrument, as Mexican experience indicates. Land redistribution from big landlords to small peasants, it was said, enables government to win economic cooperation from the peasantry, political control over it, and to exploit it in the interests of industrialisation for several generations to come;[14] if, it should be added, the political resistance of rural elites can be overcome.

It was not the problem of stimulating agricultural output or of overcoming rural conservatism that dominated in 1968, but that of providing employment in face of the labour-saving spread of modern farm technology. Professor Flores insists in his paper on the need to expand rural industry, rural services and rural public works on a large scale, corresponding stage by stage with structural changes in agriculture, to absorb the labour they displace; Sir Joseph Hutchinson in his, also insists on them as the institutional links with the urban sector needed to combine agriculture with industry in reciprocating growth. The 1968 conference also believed that, to provide more work-places, labour-intensive techniques in agriculture should be preferred to capital-intensive ones, provided the loss in productive efficiency involved is not prohibitive; and that for the same reason, it would not be wise, when introducing modern farming methods, to destroy the subsistence basis of rural society. Hence the dilemma of correlating technological, economic and socio-political factors in rural development emerges only too clearly. It seems as essential for socio-political reasons to plan for the absorption of labour and peasant cooperation in raising agricultural production, as it is for economic reasons, to plan the raising of production itself.[15]

The implications of the rural papers are at once disturbing and reassuring. If, during the fifties and most of the sixties, traditional attitudes and institutions seemed the chief constraint on rural economic growth, those predicted for the seventies are unemployment, urban migration, the rural–urban gap and the strains imposed on emergent, national systems of political integration. It is a commonplace, as Professor Flores observes, that the road to economic growth in the early stages runs over the backs of the peasants. Industrialisation and urbanisation stem from agricultural savings in the beginning. Government in some countries is squeezing the peasant too hard in indirect tax and cheap food policies, to invest in city industry and city social services; and the more ambitious the industrialisation, the more the cultivator is squeezed. 'The gap in earnings between town and countryside', Dr Godfrey reported in 1968, 'is much greater . . . than the supply-demand situation would warrant.'[16] This is the essence of the rural–urban gap. It may be that the urban workers' trade unions, or the urban interests and character of ruling political elites imparts this urban bias to public investment.[17] The fear of urban riot, perhaps, drives government to insist on cheap food for the cities and makes it loath to hold down urban wages and salaries. Whatever the causes they are as much political as economic. Unless government helps the small farmer more, it was argued in 1968, with easier credit, fairer prices and incomes policies, and better social services, to cut his costs as he expands production, he will not uphold the development road. A policy of cheap food and high wages for the city not only threatens the advance of green revolution; it invites the political protest in the countryside that it seeks to avoid in the towns. And the higher the rewards in the cities, the greater is the rural–urban migration; and the more urban unemployment, the higher the head of urban discontent.[18]

In Latin-American and Chinese, if not in African, experience, there may be good historical grounds for thinking that the fate of an emerging political system which depends upon an alliance between tiny, modern urban elites and neo-traditional, rural elites, is decided by the politics of the countryside. 'The countryside', writes Samuel Huntington,

plays the crucial swing role in modernising politics . . . If the countryside supports the . . . system, the system itself is secure against revolution . . . If the countryside is in opposition, both system and government are in danger of overthrow. The role of the city is constant; it is the permanent source of opposition. The role of the countryside is variable; it is either the source of stability or the source of revolution.[19]

If the reality is not quite that simple, there is some truth in this principle. It serves to underline the political risks inherent in early economic growth.

The political dimension of the problem is implicit rather than explicit in these papers, for obvious reasons; and as a result the vital question of winning peasant cooperation and keeping rural control is not given its due. Apparently, however, the development argument in the rural as in the industrial sector, returns to its unavoidable crux in the necessity to compromise between the marginally incompatible ends and means of political integration, social stability, employment and economic growth. The obstructions standing in the way of a steady unilinear advance of the modern sector out of two or three industrial agglomerations to engulf the rural sector seem forbiding. The implications of a two-tier strategy as a vast rural holding operation emphasise the difficulty and take some of the gusto out of cheers for green revolution. From the beginning, it seems, agro-industrial economic growth may have to be loaded with the burden of a huge welfare state in South Asia if not elsewhere, if the frame of political integration is to be secured and extended. Otherwise, as the increasing political instability of the Third World during the sixties may indicate, economic growth may be purchased at increasing, and perhaps, eventually, prohibitive political cost.

The wealth or poverty of a country, Professor Kaldor told the 1965 conference, is determined more than anything else by the existence over long periods of good or bad government.[20] Especially is this true of underdeveloped countries where the state generates and organises modern economic activities for lack of private institutions to do so. At its simplest, the government problem in economic development is one of creating the executive capacity to manage it, which Mr Rashid Ibrahim examines. Official managerial resources throughout the decade were outrun by the ever-extending range of public sector activities. In Mr Nottage's metaphor, the administrative swan, serene and unruffled above the water-line, paddled frantically underneath it, in an effort to keep up.

One solution, it is often argued, might be to leave more economic management to the private sector; but, it is objected, if official capacity for managing business is short, that of the private sector is shorter still in many countries. Private enterprise, which often tends to be alien in origin, is not always congenial to national ideology; and wealth in private hands does not always contribute as much to income redistribution or political integration as it would in the hands of government.

Another solution, in the conference paper on administrative difficulties,[21] is to rationalise and expand the bureaucracy to meet the executive demand of the development plan. Practical administrators, however, complain that although this is necessary, ' too frequent and radical alterations of administrative structure . . . tend to produce not more capability, but more chaos '.[22] Experience shows that the fashioning of this vital agency of development is not simply a question of importing modern managerial institutions and procedures, or of stamping out corruption. That traditional ways of doing things survive the most thorough-going rationalisation of the forms of administrative organisation, is not perhaps surprising. A bureaucracy is to a great extent imprisoned in the philosophy of the society which it serves; and if it does not work through indigenous socio-political processes, it is unlikely to work at all.[23] What is more, the bureaucracy, particularly in a developing country, is a political as well as an executive institution. And since political security is prior to economic growth, it tends to give priority to political needs over economic opportunity if it comes to the choice, in its management of economic resources. Here once again, therefore, the spider of economic growth spins deeper into the institutional web.

Inevitably the more economic resources are channelled through political institutions, the more the marginal incompatibility between economic and political criteria in their deployment widens. The extent of this effect in practice is debated between Mr Please and Professor Kaldor from a domestic standpoint, and between Professor Chenery and Lord Balogh from the standpoint of international Aid.

The Third World extracted public savings to invest in nation-building quite heroically during the first Development Decade, and it should be remembered that it paid for about four-fifths of the costs of development in this way. Mr Please contends that too much of these savings were spent on government and social services, and too little invested in economic projects with a direct economic ' pay-off '. However, since it is hard to quantify the economic output of investment, for example, in a university college, a dispensary, or a police barracks, it is also hard to classify in budgets what is legitimate ' developmental ' expenditure or investment and what is not. Mr Please also implies that if fiscal policy had left more resources in private hands, they would have stood a better chance of being invested in economic growth than they had in government hands. Professor Kaldor's reply on this issue of relative scope for the public and private sector is classic: ' It would be difficult to contend ', he observed, ' that any item of public expenditure, however wasteful . . . could have a lower social priority than say, the sixteenth Cadillac of a Latin American millionaire.' [24]

Whether the expenditure of developing countries on social infrastructure in the sixties was disproportionate or not may be debatable on grounds of economic efficiency; actually it was more often than not the inevitable result of politics distorting the optimum pattern of investment. When a large proportion of a country's economic resources and most of its international Aid are managed by a government striving to unite a variety of ethnic, elitist and regional groups politically, the rule of maximising production bows to the necessity of pulling the nation together. Earlier economic planners criticised bitterly this political distortion of optimal investment patterns. It has come to be regarded much more sympathetically on institutional grounds. It is obviously as important to pursue economic development in ways that integrate the nation politically as it is to pursue it in ways that will maximise economic growth. Once again, it is necessary to go more slowly in the economic direction for the sake of making more progress politically. Everybody agrees that resources must be directed more specifically to increase productivity; at the same time it must be remembered that they are also in the form of political patronage, one of the few reliable building materials available for constructing and stabilising a modern state.

The marginal incompatibility of practical politics and maximum economic growth is illustrated again in the 1966 conference papers [25] which study means of improving the impact of foreign Aid through better international cooperation. What seemed to be lacking then was order and purpose. Much of the existing organisation of Aid had accreted from the layered 'ad hockery' of individual donors and recipients with little coordination or design, so that Aid channels had become labyrinthine, its forms and conditions multifarious. Recipient countries were finding it difficult to match external Aid to their internal resources in a consistent plan.

Professor Chenery, as an economic planner, contends in his paper that too much Aid is allocated on the criterion of its political and commercial 'fringe' benefits to the donor; and too little on that of expanding the long-run productive capacity of the recipient. Since each donor in giving Aid makes provision for his own self-interest, the provisions in effect probably cancel each other out – chiefly at the recipient's expense. Therefore, Chenery argues, the sooner the bulk of Aid is allocated on economic performance criteria, through international agencies, to projects which will bring about maximum structural change in the recipient's economy, the better it will serve the universal interest in the economic growth and political order of the Third World.

If indeed international Aid operations were controlled by technocrats, and governments were rational enough to allocate Aid on strictly apolitical, economic criteria, the advantages would be great. It would take the politics and much of the neo-colonialist taint out of giving and taking Aid; and it would turn irrationally competitive national operations into rationalised and neutralised international cooperation.

Lord Balogh in his paper points out that in the real world, such good economics may prove bad practical politics. If Aid were distributed on economic performance criteria, the richer developing countries would get more of it at the expense of poorer. Such a policy is likely to affront and perhaps alienate political support for Aid programmes in donor countries, much of which is inspired by popular response to the appeal of simple, human need. Donor governments again, find it more difficult to persuade their taxpayers to give through international agencies than bilaterally from one government to another. Parliamentary purses are opened more generously for bilateral Aid to countries with which there are close historic, cultural and commercial connections, or in which there are large national interests, than they would be opened for multilateral Aid to be given clinically to the best economic performers. Too heavy insistence on strict economic criteria, it is argued, and the denigrating of bilateral to the greater glory of multilateral Aid, cut across the political processes which produce it, and so tend to be self-defeating. They could easily bring the axe down on the total volume of Aid made available. Compromise between economic criteria and political ends and means thus seems essential in the field of Aid, as it is in most other fields of development strategy.

What these discussions of the practical politics of Aid and public investment show is that in practice these two commodities are political as well as economic resources. They also imply that the two aspects are hard to separate from each other in fact, so that the element of economic input cannot easily be divorced from the political motivation, for purposes of allocation on objective economic principles. Aid, for example, is not the homogeneous commodity that it appears to be in the statistical aggregates. Rather it is a variety of things given from a variety of motives. The resources available cannot well be separated from the humane and political motives that make them available. Aid for this reason can be governed like a standard commercial product by the rules of cost–benefit analysis and the play of the market, only to a limited extent. Much of it is not available – it does not exist for that purpose. Attempts to bend it too far in that direction may make it vanish into thin air.

Nor is it safe politically to treat public savings as homogeneous aggregates of economic resources, equally available for economic or non-economic purposes. In this case also, the economic resource is not easily separable from the political motivation of the taxpayers contributing it. If they demand schools when, according to the economic planner, they ought to have a rural development scheme, it is hard politically to deny the schools; if the demand is for industrial revolution, it is not easy to insist on rural development. Being controlled by political rather than economic institutions, public savings will tend to be invested in social infrastructure, politicisation and integration at the expense of efficiency in economic growth. Even so much of the so-called waste that comes from political distortion of the optimal pattern of investment is not permanent. Most of it is waste only in the sense of making premature provision for eventual need. It is just as important to develop modern attitudes and institutions for the purpose of economic growth, as it is to achieve economic growth for the purpose of developing modern institutions. Far too often in this decade, public investment in social infrastructure – and even in long term economic assets – has been decried as wasteful, because it does not produce the kind of short term dividends in economic production that the same amount of capital should have produced in some utopian economy insulated from all human and political considerations. Much unnecessary damage had been done thereby to the cause of world development.

Hence the development planner emerges from the social explorations of the decade with dilemmas not unlike the maritime discoverer of the fifteenth century. Economic latitude he can measure fairly well, but his social and political longitude is subject to a much wider margin of error. More than that, he has no reliable means of telling the time at sea, so that plotting the sequences in which different kinds of change should be brought about is bound to be highly experimental. The strategist as a result is usually able to obtain only crude fixes on the combined movement of economics and politics in the society as a whole.

Obviously it is unsafe to assume that the economy is basic, and that institutions and attitudes are merely infrastructure determined by it; or even if they are, that time-lags in the adjustment of the one to the other are not critical for production and stability alike. In reality, economy, polity and social organisation interact, constricting and expanding each other. Politicians and administrators normally act on this assumption. If they forget it, they do not stay long in practice. That assumption has been the bone of their contention with many economic planners. ' The function of government and party ', Professor Huntington writes, ' is to organise participation and aggregate interests. In performing these functions they necessarily reflect the logic of politics not the logic of efficiency. Those who pursue modernity at the expense of politics . . . fail to achieve the one because of their neglect of the other.' [26] Equally, it is the function of the economic planner to uphold the logic of economic efficiency. Those who pursue modernity at the expense of economics will also fail. The conflict of the two types of consideration is the crux.

What light then do the experiments of the sixties in economic development shed on the problem of correlating the factors represented by these two kinds of logic? Evidently the power of modern industrial and agricultural technology to generate change which is immense has been established beyond question. Technology and economics remain by far the most powerful levers for modernisation available; and this implies that economic plans must still hold sway. The resistance of so-called traditional society to technological innovation as a result is becoming little more than a myth. It is the disruption that modern technology and institutions only too eagerly imported, wreak upon the indigenous social order that now confronts the advance to modernity. The complexities of these effects implied in the papers may be summed up for the sake of brevity in the form of a neo-Parsonian model.

Every economic input of modern technology and institutions appears to have a constructive, and a corresponding destructive output in terms of political and institutional change. Hence every decision to allocate economic resources is in effect a decision to mobilise new political support at the expense of old, and to strengthen modern institutions at the expense of indigenous ones. Every allocation, moreover, involves more people in politics for or against the government, and is thus an instrument of politicisation. New sources of political support are created as more modern economic interests are expanded. On the other hand, there is usually an economic 'backlash' in the form of unemployment, migration or differentiation from modern economic inputs, as well as a political reaction from existing socio-political interests which they damage.[27] If all these plus and minus effects of modern economic inputs were quantifiable, their total effect on social equilibrium would be easy to calculate mathematically.

Fortunately or unfortunately, such calculations cannot be put into a computer. The crudities of the model merely indicate the kind of calculation that inspires the recommendations for intermediate technology, two-tier strategy, land reform, employment, and a balance between industrial and agricultural growth recommended in these papers. They are in effect all attempts to compromise between the constructive and destructive effects of modern economic inputs. What they imply is that the political and institutional output of economic inputs is every bit as critical as their economic output. They also suggest why the overriding consideration in allocating resources cannot simply be that of maximum economic efficiency. It is rather whether the economic and political pluses in an allocation exceed the negative ones and contain its political backlash.

The model merely demonstrates the delicacy and complexity of the balance. It is easy enough to get too many minuses and too few pluses in one sector or region at the same time. Unavoidably it seems, economic growth in the Third World tends to destroy employment faster than it creates it, to deepen social cleavages faster than the political system can contain and integrate them. Inequality in income distribution tends to outstrip the equalising power of government; while old and new social and regional divisions tend to widen more swiftly than national sentiment and common economic interest extend to span them. The practical politics of economic development is to contain these negative trends and reverse them in the direction of economic growth and political integration.

It appears to be easier to do this with some kinds of economic investment than it is with others. Modern industrial technology, for example, often tends to produce its maximum economic pluses in the city, its maximum socio-political minuses in the rural areas. If this is so, it has comparatively less built-in capacity for containing the social tension and political strains which it creates than rural investment, which seems to produce its plus and minus effects in the same sector, so that the one offsets the other. Modern farm technology, it is true, also has negative social and political effects in rural society and intensifies political antagonism there, but on a far smaller scale than industrial technique does. But rural investment also creates there its positive economic and institutional effects and mobilises new political interests to contain the reaction of the old.

The reality of course is nothing like so simple. Nevertheless, for purposes of integration and stability combined with a fair rate of economic growth, it seems essential to invest in the rural economy increasingly to make up the damage that industrial and farm technology do there. If it is good economics to insist that industrialisation depends upon improved farm output, it is equally good politics to insist that economic growth depends upon integrating rural and urban sectors politically. Almost everything hangs on politicising and modernising the rural population quietly and keeping it quiet.

It is not surprising, therefore, that development strategy in the course of this decade should have shifted emphasis from urban industrial to rural development; or that the yardstick of economic efficiency has had to be increasingly tempered with considerations of employment and income redistribution, as an uncompromising economic approach uncovered the ramifications of non-economic factors. The experience of the sixties suggests that development is a continuing race between inputs of modern technology in pursuit of optimal economic growth on the one hand, and on the other, the processes of political unification struggling to contain their corrosive sociopolitical effects. It is a race between modern innovation and the implacable continuities of Afro-Asian history. It is still touch and go and it will be all the way until the race is won. It is now certain, however, that it can be won.

The decade was not without glories, which are by no means fully indicated in statistics of increased gross national product and income per head, good though these were. One glory of the times, seen in the century-long perspective of international relations between the industrial and pre-industrial world, has reference to the past. Afro-Asia consolidated a hazardous transit from imperialism and *laissez faire* to independence and governmental Aid. A greater glory may yet be revealed to those who come to look back on the unprecedented experiments in social and economic engineering set on foot in this period. Based though these experiments were on trial and error and the partial social analysis of the economist, it may yet be said of the sixties that it was then men first began to fix position by political longitude as well as economic latitude, learned to tell sociological time, and fashioned an applied science for navigating societies on a path of discovery far more momentous for human happiness than the farthest vision of a Columbus or an Einstein.

2 · Development Decade in Perspective[1]

GERALD M. MEIER

Half a decade counts for little, of course, in the long sweep of development; but when viewed against the perspective of the two post-war decades, the first five years of 'The United Nations Development Decade' (1960–5) do raise some fundamental questions about the progress, formulation, and implementation of development planning. This paper explores these questions.

PROGRESS OF ECONOMIC DEVELOPMENT

The aim of the decade is 'to attain in each underdeveloped country a substantial increase in the rate of growth, with each country setting its own target, taking as the objective a minimum annual rate of growth in aggregate national income of 5 per cent at the end of the Decade' (General Assembly Resolution 1710 (XVI)). What has been the record in attaining this objective?

Although any such calculation is fraught with statistical ambiguities, it would appear that for the countries of Asia, Africa, and Latin America taken together, economic development has proceeded in the last twenty years at a rate close to 4 per cent per annum. This has meant a doubling in the total income of the underdeveloped areas of the world – certainly a major accomplishment compared with the long preceding period of relative stagnation. Nonetheless, a number of factors make the progress much less impressive.

When we relate the aggregate growth rate of 4 per cent to population growth which has in recent years been about 2 to 2½ per cent in the underdeveloped world, we come down to a rate of income growth *per capita* of only 1½ to 2 per cent on the average. At this rate, personal living standards will not double for another 35 to 47 years – a period somewhat longer than most countries wish to contemplate. Generally a rate of increase in *per capita* income of 2½ to 3 per cent would be considered more adequate, so that *per capita* income doubles within the life span of a generation. Although this has not yet been achieved on the average, actual performance has been fairly respectable in approaching it, and the record of some countries has been even better. But there still remains the distressingly hard core of underdevelopment in many countries which have fallen below this rate; and in some countries, it is even doubtful whether the pre-war level of *per capita* national output has yet been regained. Moreover, there is some indication that the aggregate rate of growth has been slowing down for many poor countries in the first half of this decade as compared with the 1950s. Average annual rates of growth in the gross domestic product of less developed countries were 4·6 per cent in 1950–5, 4·5 per cent in 1955–60, and 4·0 per cent in 1960–3. Gross domestic product *per capita* increased at an average annual rate of 2·5 per cent in 1950–5, 2·1 per cent in 1955–60, but only by 1·5 per cent in 1960–3 (United Nations, *World Economic Trends : Economic Progress during initial years of Development Decade*, June, 1965). This poses the important question whether the development process is now running up against increasingly severe or even intractable problems.

The record of achievement is also tempered by the heavy reliance on foreign assistance. Public and private grants and loans from all sources to the underdeveloped countries have been in recent years about $8 to $9 billion annually. At the same time, a generous estimate of total gross investment in these countries would be roughly $35 billion a year. Thus, the flow of foreign capital has accounted for approximately one-fourth of the investment resources of the underdeveloped world. If it had not been for external assistance, the ratio of net saving to domestic product would actually have fallen in many countries. And in some countries, no increase in *per capita* income would have been realised if there had not been a capital inflow.

We must also realise that the course of development has been highly uneven and has perpetuated or accentuated a number of inequalities. Even within those countries that have good overall records, there has been relatively little progress in removing the inequality of income between the employed and the unemployed, the inequality of income between the agricultural (rural) and the industrial (urban) population, and the inequality of income and wealth between the very poor 95 per cent and the very rich 5 per cent of the population. Such differing economies as India and Mexico both attest to this.

Industrial output *per capita* increased in the developing countries during the 1950s at a rate equal to or even slightly higher than that achieved in the more advanced countries. Nonetheless, manufacturing industry still accounts for less than one-fifth of the output of the underdeveloped nations, and its employment-creating capacity remains insufficient to prevent growing unemployment and underemployment.

At the same time, agricultural output has in general increased only a little faster than population. In a number of countries, agricultural output per head is even lower than it was ten or fifteen years ago. In Latin America, food production per head has been at a standstill for the last decade. South Asia for several years has been increasingly changing from a surplus to a deficit region in food. In Latin America and the Far East, agricultural production per head still remains below the level of the 1930s. For all less developed countries, the average annual rates of growth in agricultural production have been 3·5 per cent in 1950–5, 3·2 per cent in 1955–60, and 2·2 per cent in 1960–3 (Food and Agriculture Organisation, *The State of*

Food and Agriculture, 1964). This weak performance of the agricultural sector has been pervasive and is one of the most difficult of developmental problems.

As distressing as the lag in the agricultural sector, and not unrelated to it, has been the lag in the export sector. Over the last two decades, world trade has expanded at a higher rate than ever before, but most of this expansion has been in trade between the advanced countries and in exports from the advanced countries to the less developed countries, while the export earnings of the underdeveloped countries have risen only slowly.[2] At present, about a half of all world trade is carried on between the developed countries themselves, and over the past decade the value of exports from the developed countries rose about twice as fast as those from underdeveloped countries (77 per cent, as against 36 per cent, between 1952–4 and 1962). The ratio of exports from underdeveloped countries to total world exports has declined steadily since the early 1950s and was less than 25 per cent for the years 1960–3 the lowest at any time since the war.[3] In contrast with the slow growth of exports, development programmes have induced a sharp rise in import requirements for most of the less developed countries.[4] From 1952–4 to 1962 exports from developed to underdeveloped areas rose by $6·3 billion while, in the reverse direction, the exports from underdeveloped countries increased by only $2 billion if petroleum and other fuels are excluded (by $5·4 billion including petroleum and fuels). Export earnings have thus been able to cover only a relatively small proportion of the import expansion in developing countries other than the petroleum exporting countries. The major part of the rise in imports has been financed by foreign borrowing and economic assistance. This is, of course, but a corollary of the earlier point that a substantial portion of total investment in the developing countries has depended upon external resources: the import surplus has permitted a rate of capital formation in excess of domestic saving.[5]

The unevenness of development also appears in the more rapid expansion of the public sector relative to the private sector. Since development plans have concentrated on public investment, and foreign aid has also been directed mainly to the public sector, private investment has lagged behind public investment. As will be argued below, development planning has tended to give too much attention to the public sector and too little to the private sector. Indeed, if in the affluent societies there has been a starving of the public sector to the benefit of the private sector, there has been just the opposite tendency in many poor countries: it can be contended that there has been an excessive diversion of scarce resources from directly productive investment in the private sector to public works and social overhead.

Finally, the new centres of growth within the developing countries have tended to be geographically concentrated. The economies of conglomeration may rationalise this; nevertheless, it has resulted in growing regional inequalities within many countries. The problem of 'enclaves' remains as acute as it was for the historical development based on foreign capital.

From the foregoing, we may conclude that notable as has been their accomplishment in doubling total income during the past two decades, poor countries have still generally failed to realise the other objectives that are commonly sought in a development programme. As conveniently outlined in a recent United Nations document, these objectives are: (i) a rapid increase in *per capita* income, (ii) a high level of employment, (iii) a relatively stable price level, (iv) equilibrium in the balance of payments, (v) a reduction of inequalities in income distribution, (vi) the avoidance of marked disparities in the prosperity and growth of different regions within a country, and (vii) a diversified economy (U.N., E.C.A.F.E., *Programming Techniques for Economic Development*, 1960). Although the record of development has earned fairly high marks for the rate of growth in aggregate income, it can still receive only low marks for the progress made towards the fulfilment of these other objectives. The Development Decade still faces the overriding problems of how an increase in aggregate income is at the same time to carry along with it a higher rate of increase in income per head, less dependence on foreign assistance, and a removal of inequalities.

FORMULATION OF DEVELOPMENT PLANS

Turning now to the methods by which the goals of development have been sought, what can we single out as outstanding features?

The widespread conviction has clearly been that government must be the primary agent in producing economic modernisation, and that development efforts must be coordinated within a national development plan. Given the criticisms of the price system, the intermixture of a desire for social reform along with development, and the character of the obstacles to development, it is readily understandable why central planning has been more attractive to the governments of poor countries than was ever true in the historical experience of the presently advanced western nations.

For the attainment of their development objectives, newly developing countries have been reluctant to follow the dictates of the price system. In many countries the price system may be considered ineffective in its presently rudimentary form: market imperfections, inflexibilities and rigidities may give no play to market forces, or they may be too weak to provide the necessary incentives and price–income inducements for a transformation of the economy. The price system is also considered unreliable when market prices of goods and factors do not truly reflect the social opportunity costs of these goods and factors: abundant factors are generally overpaid, scarce factors are underpaid, and external benefits and costs – which are so important in the development process – lie completely outside the market mechanism. It is also thought that the price system must be superseded in order to approach more closely the optimal amount and composition of investment: instead of relying on a multitude of individual investment decisions based on current market prices, government decisions are necessary to raise the level of saving and to allocate investible resources in accordance with criteria other than those provided by the market. Moreover, it is believed that the market mechanism is at best only relevant for coping with marginal adjustments in the present period – not with the large structural changes over a long period ahead which is the very essence of the development process. For these reasons, planning has had an extensive appeal throughout the underdeveloped world, and efforts have been made to coordinate from within a development programme the variety of interdependent activities involved in the process of development, instead of placing major reliance on the market system for such coordination.

Beyond this distrust of the price system on economic grounds, the appeal of planning has also stemmed from ideological considerations and the pressure for social reform. The demand for social services, a redistribution of income, a diminution in the concentration of economic and social power, freedom from foreign control, and a removal of dependence on the 'inferior' activity of primary production have all reinforced the case for active governmental intervention.

Perhaps even more persuasive has been the argument that since the obstacles to development are now more pervasive and more intense than they were for western countries in their pre-industrial period, the scope for private calculation and individual action is accordingly much less. The very level of *per capita* real income from which development must now proceed is much lower than it was in the presently advanced countries before they entered their phase of active industrialisation. The ratio of savings to national income also tends to be lower. And in a number of countries (especially in Africa) the market-oriented monetised sector of the economy is also smaller. Another basic contrast is the failure of many of the poor countries to have yet experienced a sufficient increase in agricultural productivity to provide a favourable base for industrialisation. Population pressures are also now more severe, in so far as population growth is associated mainly with a declining death rate due to medical advances and is therefore independent of the rate of economic development, unlike the situation in western countries during the nineteenth century when it could be maintained that population growth was induced by development. Further, the latecomers to development are now surrounded by more advanced nations. The 'gap' between the industrial and underdeveloped countries measured in terms of *per capita* incomes has been increasing absolutely and also probably relatively; industrial countries have a more entrenched position in international trade; and the 'cost of catching up' to more advanced countries has undoubtedly increased. Finally, a most important difference is that the institutional structure, value system, and social environment that prevail in less developed countries are now much less conducive to development. Social and cultural traditions place less value on the individual, and the core institutions of the family, religion, and education have yet to encourage the mobility and adaptability of economic agents to the extent necessary for a sustained developmental effort.

For all these reasons, the government of many an underdeveloped country has turned to the adoption of a national development plan as if this were itself a precondition for development. But while the case for planning was *prima facie* strong, the early post-war attempts at formulating a development plan proved quite inadequate. During the first plan-period in many countries, the so-called ' plan ' was little more than a list of discrete projects on which the government proposed to spend its financial resources—at most, a public expenditure programme. Or else many emerging countries thought it sufficient merely to follow the depression and wartime examples of Keynesian aggregate planning and to add to their economies the missing component of capital through foreign aid in a manner equivalent to Marshall aid.

With the experience of the second or third five-year plan, however, the formulation of development plans improved markedly. The governments of newly developing nations have fairly rapidly attained an understanding of what developmental measures might be undertaken, and progress in the formulation of development plans has been substantial. Over the past two decades, this has been a most encouraging aspect of development planning. Successive plans have progressed from the simple listing of public sector projects to a balancing of outlays and resources in the whole economy; with a recognition that decisions in the public sector cannot be made in ignorance of the private sector, plans have given greater attention to projections and targets for the private sector as well as the public sector; macro-plans have been filled in with sector plans and project appraisals; the usual five-year medium term plans have been supplemented on the one side by long term perspective plans and on the other by annual operational plans; and increasing emphasis has been placed on the consistency and coordination of decisions.

If we were now to review current development plans and appraise their formulation, we would have to conclude that most of the developing countries have arrived at the point of approximating the elements of a well-formulated plan in a creditable fashion. And yet, we are left with two disconcerting questions that detract from this accomplishment.

First, what really is the merit of achieving consistency and coordination in a development plan? This is, of course, a necessary characteristic of a well-formulated programme, but it is equally essential to recognise that the mere attainment of consistency and the mere act of coordination do not guarantee in any way the quality or merit of the particular decisions that are being taken. We must heed Alec Cairncross' observation that a programme 'is a focus, not a substitute for decision-making . . . it is nonsense to think that a programme settles everything and that no sensible decisions can be taken without one . . . Although unco-ordinated decisions may be bad or costly, so also may co-ordinated decisions: there is no magic about a programme that transforms the quality of decisions beyond the virtue that co-ordination lends.' (A. K. Cairncross, 'Programmes as Instruments of Co-ordination', *Scottish Journal of Political Economy*, June 1961, p. 90.)

Regardless of improvements in the formulation of planning models, the policy-maker still cannot escape from the rendering of value judgements, and political decisions are still required. Logically prior to the attainment of consistency and coordination is the fundamental question of *what* is to be planned. What decisions are to be centralised and what is to be left for decision-making by firms and households? Nor does the attainment of consistency and coordination within a particular development programme remove the ambiguity that is inherent in the establishment of objectives and the selection of policy instruments. A conflict among multiple objectives is frequently encountered in development programming, and it is then necessary to decide which objective should receive precedence in planning. Thus, instead of a single development programme, there are in reality any number of alternative programmes according to the values given to diverse objectives and to various policy instruments. The attributes of consistency and coordination cannot disguise the fact that the ultimate decision is political.

Our second question refers not to the quality of the decisions being coordinated, but rather to the capacity to implement these decisions. Has the ability to implement a development plan grown *pari passu* with the ability to formulate a plan? The record of development planning reveals that problems of implementation now need to receive more attention than problems of formulation. Why is it that a development plan may meet all the tests of a good plan on paper, only to fail in practice?

IMPLEMENTATION OF DEVELOPMENT PLANS

Miscalculations and unforeseen changes alone do not account for the wide divergence between what has been planned and what actually realised. We must look to more fundamental reasons.

One such reason is that there is no analytical model of development that can be readily translated into a development programme. It is difficult to think of another area of economic policy in which the distance between theory and policy tends to be as great as it is for developmental problems. All the theories of development – classical, Marxian, Schumpeterian, Neo-Keynesian – are simply ways of looking systematically at the general development process. They relate to the 'economics *about* development' –

the way an economist looks at the development process in the abstract and from the outside, but they do not immediately constitute the ' economics *for* development ' – the pragmatic way that the local practitioner must use economics in the daily administration of a development programme within a particular environment. Only too often, however, a development theory has been misread as if it revealed a recipe for successful development, and access to the teachings of modern economics has been thought to have some new magical quality. In spite of the shortcomings of such a naïve approach – to which the past two decades give ample testimony – the mystique still persists. And instead of utilising more operational concepts and empirical constructs, development economists are still prone to resort to ' empty stages of growth ' or empty phrases such as ' a big push ' or ' balanced growth '.

If the literary economist has allowed slogans to substitute for analysis, the mathematical economist has moved on to a much loftier view of development – but without the caution and restraint which should come from a realistic awareness of the especially acute limitations of mathematical programming in an underdeveloped economy. Whether it be due to the operation of an international ' demonstration effect ' among governments or the dominant influence of intellectuals on planning commissions, there has been in many developing countries an overly keen receptivity for the most refined model, the newest technique, the latest element of expertise. When the ultra-sophisticated technique has been allowed to shape the development plan, its implementation has become unduly difficult. In many cases, the solutions to immediate and crucial needs have been ignored through the over-reaching for more complex techniques of analysis and highly formalised models. In this connection, we may question whether much of the effort devoted to the use of econometric models and linear programming in framing a development programme is not premature.

Attraction to the highest style of analysis has also weakened the planning effort by divorcing the economic analysis from the contributions of other social sciences. The more advanced and more rigorous the economic analysis, the less is it capable of incorporating non-economic elements. But the less developed the country, the more does the efficacy of planning depend on non-economic factors. Before concentrating on the purely economic factors, attention should be given to those social and organisational characteristics of the economy that have been critically important in impeding growth. When these strategic non-economic factors have been ignored, the implementation of policies designed to remove the economic barriers has remained limited. For, regardless of the economic logic of the development plan, its success in gaining popular support and participation must depend on attitudes, values and institutions.

It has sometimes been thought that linear programming models of development provide a set of ' decision rules ' that can serve as specific guides to action for the policy-maker. This may be true for some types of business and military operations, but it cannot do so for a process that is as complex and qualitative in character as the modernisation of an economy and the transformation of a society. Such a broadly humane undertaking cannot be viewed as a mechanical process, and its diagnosis cannot be reduced to a matter of pure technics. A good deal of the disparity between the theory and practice of planning can only too often be traced to an excessive reliance on the pure mathematics of an 'optimum' or a 'maximum' that has distilled the life out of the development process and left the development plan without operational significance. In order to institutionalise and sustain developmental forces, we cannot adopt the approach that 'a maximum is a maximum regardless of the maximizing agent'. In spite of – or rather, because of – the efforts of mathematical economists and linear programmers, we need to be reminded that economics is still a social study, and that the loss of some rigour and precision in analysis may be worth the production of a more workable plan. Given the present circumstances in most of the developing countries, the cause of development might be better advanced by a sound application of some basic elementary principles of economics instead of by borrowing and imitating at too high a level.

Other reasons why development plans may be big on paper but small in result have received more attention and need only be summarised here. The implementation of development planning has been clearly handicapped by the lack of requisite data and the imperfect character of such statistics as are available. In many countries, development plans have become obsolete before they were completed because they were not initially based on adequate and accurate current information. Economic policy measures necessarily assume quantitative estimation for their formulation and for the evaluation of their effects, but knowledge of the future can only be derived from that of the past and present. When the existence of historical statistics is negligible and the measurement of key variables is deficient, it is difficult to make realistic projections and estimate the probable results of changes in the means of policy needed to meet the aims of the development plan. A more comprehensive and rational collection of data is indispensable if those responsible for development policies are to be able to assess the benefits and costs of alternative measures before the decisions are taken instead of only afterwards. What has been lacking in development planning is not only factual knowledge, but even more the knowledge of fundamental regularities and relations among economic magnitudes. As long as a country remains underdeveloped statistically, its capacity for effective planning will be limited.

Another shortcoming involves the failure to arrive at a proper ordering or sequence in policy-making. In its formulation, a development plan must provide a comprehensive view of the economy and recognise its interrelationships. But when it comes to implementation, a simultaneous solution of the plan is not possible. In the operational realm, planning cannot be comprehensive but is necessarily only partial and phased over time. It is then essential to arrive at some effective chronological order of decision-taking.

This problem has both an 'horizontal' and a 'vertical' aspect. Horizontally, the very interdependence of the obstacles to development requires the policy-maker, when he is attempting to remove a given obstacle, to go beyond this particular obstacle and determine how, by causing specific changes elsewhere in the economy, additional pressure can be brought on the obstacle to make it give way. It is not difficult to arrive at a list of obstacles to development, but it is extremely difficult to determine the sequence of events for removing these obstacles. This entails a detailed analysis of sequences in policy-making, so that an effective combination of pressures (à la Hirschman) can be brought to bear over a period of time. Vertically, the implementation of a development plan implies some effective procedure by which decision-making can proceed down from the macro- to the micro-level. Thus, the aggregate plan must be backed up with the preparation and evaluation of specific investment projects, and there must be some procedure by which the totals of the plan that preoccupy the central planning agency can be 'filled in' with the specific decisions of other governmental agencies, firms, and households.

Finally, implementation of a plan has been difficult because of the familiar deficiencies in political and administrative requirements. Plans have often been prepared without attention to the actual operations of administrative agencies and departments. The planning commission itself is usually in merely an advisory position without executive functions or operational powers, and other operational agencies and ministries may be unwilling or unable to act upon the plan, especially when they lack sufficient political leadership and authority. At the other extreme, there have been instances in which the government has overestimated its political power, only to realise later that it cannot enlist sufficient popular support to accomplish its aims. In many cases, political interests have also run counter to the economic rationale of the development plan: the political party in power has too often been concerned only with the immediate or very short run of time, has been willing to settle for 'showcase' projects, has succumbed to sectional interests, or has tried to prevent a loss in social status or political power for certain groups in the society at the expense of effective implementation of the plan.

Deficiencies in administrative and managerial procedures have been especially severe impediments to planning in practice. To the extent that the organisation of public administration in many poor countries has been limited to the 'law and order' kind of administration, it has not had the competence for the administration of economic controls which is a sensitive art that cannot be practised in a routine fashion, or subjected to indecision and delay. Nor can economic enterprises be operated as if they were administrative departments. In many countries, a neglect of administrative and management considerations has allowed the development plan to envisage a public investment sector larger than is capable of effective administration and to rely on imposition of controls that are beyond the implementing capacity of existing public administrative services.

In sum: the overreaching for the highest level of theory in preparing a development plan, the under-supplying of the plan with needed data, the under-emphasising of the pattern of sequential decision-making, and the overtaxing of administrative competence and managerial capacity have all combined to thwart the practical implementation of the plan.

IN LIEU OF PROGNOSIS

It is almost impossible to prognosticate the progress of development during the rest of the Development Decade. In concluding this paper, we can only set forth the major policy problems that now confront developing countries.

At this juncture in the Development Decade (1965), a primary problem is whether or not to expand the role of the private sector. For reasons akin to those outlined above, a greater number of development economists now subscribe to the conclusion that the comprehensive heavy type of central planning, based on an elaborate and complex development plan, is premature for most countries. Many believe that in conformity with their present needs and capabilities, the majority of poor countries should retrench to a lighter type of planning that would rely more on decentralised decisions operating through the market mechanism, and that governmental policy should shift in emphasis towards the devising of policies that might make private action more effective. There is now wider receptivity to the view that if an ongoing momentum is to be built into the development process, it is necessary to have multiple centres of initiative based upon a greater diffusion of individual opportunities and individual activities.

The case for a high degree of planning, with a large amount of public investment and deliberate industrialisation constituting the core of the plan, may remain strong for countries that suffer seriously from the pressure of population on the land but have the potential for large domestic markets (such as India or China). For other countries, however, in which there are under-utilised natural resources but only small internal markets, it can be persuasively argued that the basic problem is one of creating a favourable social and economic environment which will lead to expansion of private activity, more effective use of the under-utilised resources, and capitalisation on the existing opportunities for international trade (as is being done in the Philippines, Thailand, Malaya, and some Latin American countries).

If the private sector is to be enlarged, how is this now to be accomplished?

Instead of allowing any economic resource to be left unemployed, governmental policies must try to mobilise through positive economic incentives and inducements the latent skills and capital in the private sector. This can be done in a number of ways. Fundamentally, the stimulation of private activity depends on the establishment of markets and encouragement of market institutions. Economic and social overhead capital can help to establish the physical conditions for a market to exist and can support the interdependence of markets. The government also has a crucial role in building institutions such as a banking system, a money and capital market, agricultural cooperatives, labour organisations, rural credit institutions, training institutes, etc. It must also be recognised that many of the policy measures that can affect individual action by altering the economic environment are not of the usual monetary or fiscal type of policy, but rather those involving the legal and institutional framework, such as land tenure legislation, commercial law, property rights, etc.

Once market imperfections are removed and the structure of markets is improved, the market mechanism can itself be used as an instrument of development. Instead of relying on comprehensive and detailed economic controls, governmental policies can work through the market and provide price and income stimuli for an expansion in private output, an increase in exports, and a widening of domestic markets.

A more immediate way to stimulate private activity is through tax concessions and subsidies. Subsidy and tax schemes may be especially significant in inducing firms to value inputs according to their social opportunity costs, or to exploit external economies, or to introduce new techniques of production.

More can also be done by way of providing public foreign capital to the private sector through development corporations and banks. Foreign investment laws may also be devised to encourage a greater inflow of direct foreign investment, while channelling the investment in accordance with development objectives. Although the traditional opportunities in public utilities, mining, and plantations are foreclosed, there is a new potential for private foreign investment in import-replacing activities and the expanding industrial sector. In this connection, joint international ventures may facilitate a desirable partnership between domestic and foreign enterprises or even between the government and foreign enterprise. Various contractual arrangements for the transfer of technical and managerial skills (management contracts, technical services agreements, engineering and construction agreements) may also be useful in securing the equivalent of the 'technical assistance' component of direct foreign investment without incurring the cost of granting its supplier a controlling or even any equity participation in the recipient enterprise.

Finally, and presently of considerable importance, it would be possible to induce more effective private activity by removing the distortions in internal price relations which result from the use of numerous specific controls. A more realistic price structure could lead to both greater total investment and the avoidance of detailed investment planning. To this end, there may be merit in the adoption of flexible exchange rates to avoid currency overvaluation, the removal of price controls on foodstuffs, and the liberalisation of foreign trade controls with the substitution of domestic subsidy and tax schemes.

A second set of major policy problems pertains to the inadequate growth rate of the agricultural sector, referred to earlier. There is evidence that the development process is now severely hampered in many countries by deficient production of foodstuffs and raw materials and by the failure of productivity to rise in agriculture. The growth base for other sectors must be expanded by increasing the marketable surplus and investible surplus from the agricultural sector. To do this, more attention must be given to devising a tax system that will exploit the saving potential in the rural sector without restraining agricultural output, to the adoption of new techniques of production, and to assistance for small farmers beyond the large schemes such as irrigation, flood control, and land clearance as in the past.

The foreign exchange bottleneck gives rise to a third set of policy problems. Import demand is much greater than the capacity to import based on exports. A United Nations study estimated in 1962 that, on the assumption of a 5 per cent a year growth rate in underdeveloped areas and a continuation of current trends and policies the international payments gap on current account of the underdeveloped areas would be some $20 billion by 1970 – an increase of $15 billion during the first Development Decade. Even if the net flow of long-term capital and official donations from developed countries continued to rise at then current rates, the payments gap by 1970 would still be as much as $11 billion. (United Nations, *World Economic Survey*, 1962, Part I. It was estimated that between 1959 and 1970, imports would rise from $21 to $41 billion, net payments for investment income from $4 to $8 billion, exports from $20 to $29 billion, and the net capital inflow from $5 to $9 billion.)

To the extent that the payments gap is not met, the import requirements of the development programme cannot be fulfilled, and countries are forced to adopt less than optimal import-substitution policies or to reduce their growth rates. Avoidance of this requires policies to expand exports, improve the terms of trade, and increase the inflow of capital and aid. Given the limited prospects for a sufficiently large increase in the flow of capital, there will have to be more concerted efforts to increase export earnings.

Directly related to the foreign exchange shortage is the fourth major policy problem – the serious external debt-servicing problem. At a time when exports are growing only slowly and foreign economic assistance has become static, the ratio of debt service to exports is rising rapidly. Between 1956 and 1962, amortisation and interest payments of developing countries in respect of public and publicly guaranteed debt increased about two and a half times (*Economic Growth and External Debt : A Statistical Presentation*, I.B.R.D. Report No. Ec-122, 12 March 1964). For the developing countries as a whole, debt-service payments were then estimated at about $3.5 billion, amounting to some 12 per cent of the export earnings of all developing countries. For some countries debt-servicing already absorbed more than 25 per cent of their export revenue. Moreover, several of the major international debtors had concentrated their debt structure in short- and medium-term maturities.[6] As a result, from 1965 onwards, an increasingly large proportion of their foreign exchange earnings was absorbed by debt service. It was estimated that between 1965 and 1970, gross foreign aid would have to increase by at least 5 per cent a year in order to yield merely the same net inflow. The proportion of grants and soft loans in the total capital flow would also undoubtedly have to increase if foreign capital was in the future to make as large a net contribution to development needs as it had in the past, while external obligations were kept within the developing countries' debt-servicing capacity, without forcing these countries to compress imports unduly.

For their effective solution, the foreign exchange and debt-service problems should really be treated as part of the wider problems of reform of international economic institutions. The international saving-investment mechanism is at the centre of the international development process. But if domestic policy has finally become effective in coping with the saving-investment problem, the same is not yet true for international policy. Lagging exports and the discipline of the balance of payments now exercise under the gold-exchange standard a drag on international development, just as lagging investment and the discipline of a balanced budget once exercised a fiscal drag on domestic expansion. In the decade of the great depression we had to rid ourselves of misconceptions about 'fiscal deficits'; now in the Development Decade we must also do so for 'balance of payments deficits'. For accelerated development more elasticity in the international monetary system may be necessary to remove the 'gold-exchange standard drag' so that capital outflow and a deficit in the balance of payments of a reserve currency country can be more readily tolerated. Modifications of the I.M.F. may be required to meet the problems of reserve currency countries, as well as to provide more generous compensatory financing by the Fund to offset shortfalls in export earnings of developing countries.

The international saving-investment problem may also be eased by having the I.B.R.D. assume that leading role in foreign assistance. It is particularly distressing that when many developing countries are reaching the point where they could now absorb more aid, foreign assistance is flattening out when it should be rising and offering the assurance of greater continuity.

Instead of bilateral aid, the argument is strong for an increase in the sub-scribed 'capital' of the I.B.R.D. and its subsidiaries and for the Bank expanding and liberalising its lending activities in the fields of agriculture, industry, education, and the general support of development programmes.

Although less developed countries constitute two-thirds of the contracting parties of the G.A.T.T., there is a widespread belief that G.A.T.T. places too heavy a burden of commitments upon these countries. At the United Nations' Conference on Trade and Development of 1964, the dominant contention was that more exceptions should be extended to the less developed countries: special preferences should be granted on their exports of semi-manufactures and manufactures; they should be enabled to extend tariff preferences to each other without being bound to offer such preferences to other G.A.T.T. members; they should not be required to bind their tariffs; and subsidies on their exports should be allowed. In advocating these changes in G.A.T.T. rules, the less developed countries are challenging the values of full reciprocity of bargaining and non-discrimination when development is the primary objective of international policy. The new chapter on Trade and Development, now being submitted for approval to member govern-ments, does not squarely meet this issue. The challenge remains, and the rules of G.A.T.T., along with those of the I.M.F. and I.B.R.D., will con-tinue under pressure as a new code of international trading conduct is advocated to meet the external needs of national development planning.

A final set of policy problems relates to the need for social development. In view of what has been said earlier, these are now among the most critical of all development problems. It has become increasingly apparent that an improvement in the quality of human life cannot be simply awaited as an objective of development, but is necessarily an instrument of development. Development policies must ultimately merge into a common strategy that combines an increase in the quantity of economic factors with an improve-ment in their quality. The basic theses of the first Development Decade can truly be expressed by saying that 'the problem of the underdeveloped countries is not just growth, but development. Development is growth *plus* change; change, in turn, is social and cultural as well as economic, and qualitative as well as quantitative.' (*The U.N. Development Decade : Proposals for Action*, pp. 2–3.)

But to explore the implications of this thesis calls for another paper – which the mere economist cannot write!

Table 1 *Growth of output and population in selected countries*

Country	Growth in output (compound % annual rate at constant market prices)		Population growth (compound % annual rate)
	Fifties [a]	1960–4/5	
Argentina	1·5	0·8	1·8
Bolivia	0·2	n.a.	2·4
Brazil	n.a.	6·0	2·4
Burma	6·1	3·5	1·1
Ceylon	3·2	3·4	2·8
Chile	3·3	3·4	2·5
Colombia	4·6	3·9	2·8
Costa Rica	5·0	3·8	4·3
Ecuador	5·0	4·2	3·1
Ghana	n.a.	5·0	3·0
Honduras	4·7	5·1	2·6
India	3·5	3·4	2·4
Korea	4·4	3·6	2·7
Malaya	n.a.	4·5	3·1
Mexico	4·9	4·6	3·1
Morocco	1·5	0·7	2·7
Nicaragua	3·6	3·9	3·5
Nigeria	3·9	2·1	2·0
Pakistan	1·6	n.a.	2·2
Philippines	5·0	4·0	2·3
Thailand	5·0	6·2	3·1
Tunisia	n.a.	3·0	2·1
Turkey	6·1	6·4	2·9

Sources: I.B.R.D. Reports and U.N. *Yearbook of National Accounts Statistics*.
[a] Generally 1950–60.

Table 2 *World trade flows in 1962, and changes from 1952–4*

	Exports in 1962 ($ billion)				Change from 1952–4 (per cent)	
	Developed countries	Under-developed countries	Soviet area	Total	Developed countries	Under-developed countries
Food, beverages and tobacco	13·6	8·4	2·4	24·4	+57	+11
Crude materials	10·9	7·4	2·4	20·6	+47	+18
Fuels	3·8	8·8	1·9	14·5	+30	+87
Total, primary products	28·3	24·5	6·7	59·5	+49	+33
Manufactures	64·7	4·2	10·4	79·3	+92	+59
Total	94·4	28·9	17·3	140·6	+77	+36
of which, to:						
Developed countries	67·3	20·8	3·1	91·3	+96	+36
Underdeveloped countries	21·1	6·3	2·0	29·4	+43	+18
Soviet area	3·4	1·5	11·7	16·5	+282	+305

Source: *Monthly Bulletin of Statistics*, United Nations.

Table 3   *Trends in exports from developed and underdeveloped countries*

	1928	1938	1950–1	1952–4	1958–9	1960–1	1962–3
	($ billion)						
Value of exports							
Developed areas	22·6	15·2	44·6	53·3	73·3	87·8	98·1
Underdeveloped areas	9·1	5·9	21·6	21·3	25·2	27·5	30·4
Total	31·7	21·1	66·2	74·6	98·5	115·3	128·5
Underdeveloped as per cent of total	29	28	33	28	26	24	24
	Index numbers, 1952–4 = 100						
Volume of exports							
Developed areas	76	67	84	100	140	165	181
Underdeveloped areas	87	92	98	100	128	142	161
Total	80	74	88	100	136	158	176
Unit value							
Developed areas	56	43	100	100	98	100	102
Underdeveloped areas	49	30	103	100	93	91	89
Total	53	38	101	100	97	98	97

Sources: *Statistical Yearbooks*, United Nations; *Monthly Bulletin of Statistics*, United Nations; International Trade, 1958, G.A.T.T., Geneva, 1959; *Review of World Trade*, 1938, League of Nations, Geneva, 1939; and estimates by N.I.E.S.R.

Table 4   *Growth rates of export volume and ratios of export, to import growth*

Country	Growth in export volume		Export growth relative to import growth	
	Fifties	1960–4	Fifties	1960–4
Argentina	1·3	3·9	2·17	1·08
Ceylon	1·9	1·5	0·41	0·39
Chile	6·9	4·1	n.a.	0·67
Costa Rica	3·6	7·9	0·52	3·95
Ethiopia	6·9	2·6	n.a.	0·54
Ghana	3·2	7·6	0·34	0·88
India	1·4	1·5	0·40	n.a.
Israel	16·3	19·0	4·29	2·68
Malaya	3·5	5·0	0·83	0·77
Mexico	4·8	3·0	2·40	0·67
Nicaragua	7·4	1·5	0·79	1·88
Nigeria	3·7	4·3	0·31	0·60
Sudan	4·5	5·2	0·90	0·73
Thailand	4·4	6·4	0·5	0·9
Tunisia	4·4	7·3	1·69	1·59

Source: I.B.R.D., 'Economic Growth and External Debt – An Analytical Framework', U.N.C.T.A.D., E/CONF. 46/84, 16 March 1964, p. 59.

Table 5   *Investment, savings and trade 1957–62*

(Averages in millions of 1962 $U.S.)

Country	(1) Gross national product	(2) Gross investment	(3) Gross national savings	(4) Net foreign capital inflow	(5) Trade in goods and services Imports	(6) Trade in goods and services Exports
Near East						
Cyprus	250	52	35	17	132	115
Greece	3,861	777	547	231	704	474
Iran	4,610	705	654	50	1,070	1,020
Israel	2,107	635	229	405	854	448
Jordan	339	52	−45	97	141	43
Turkey	6,082	968	770	198	699	501
U.A.R.	3,692	575	312	263	1,002	739
South Asia						
Ceylon	1,454	223	196	27	447	420
India	37,211	6,423	5,584	839	2,529	1,690
Pakistan	7,551	922	683	239	756	517
Latin America						
Argentina	12,166	2,956	2,625	331	1,656	1,326
Bolivia	470	61	20	41	104	62
Brazil	14,053	1,912	1,494	418	1,792	1,374
British Guiana	149	50	26	23	100	77
Chile	3,458	468	271	197	765	568
Colombia	1,259	909	759	150	722	572
Costa Rica	467	74	52	22	130	108
Ecuador	857	138	112	26	180	154
El Salvador	527	64	56	8	144	136
Guatemala	1,077	112	81	31	161	130
Honduras	418	60	63	−3	81	83
Jamaica	737	137	98	39	296	257
Mexico	14,175	2,180	2,039	141	1,639	1,498
Nicaragua	369	60	51	9	103	94
Panama	478	90	57	34	186	153
Paraguay	233	18	6	12	59	47
Peru	2,444	500	525	−24	595	620
Trinidad-Tobago	558	177	117	60	479	419
Venezuela	5,741	1,085	1,812	−726	1,801	2,527
Africa						
Algeria	3,680	560	156	404	1,207	804
Ethiopia	881	91	64	28	133	105
Ghana	1,513	298	195	103	577	474
Kenya	718	99	87	12	297	285
Liberia	139	93	13	80	159	79
Mauritius	167	32	13	18	86	67
Morocco	1,977	209	150	60	515	455
Nigeria	3,434	564	381	183	738	555
Rhodesia-Nyasaland	1,505	268	245	23	795	773
Sudan	1,237	177	139	38	283	245
Tanzania	597	67	40	27	223	196
Tunisia	739	185	64	121	296	175
Uganda	454	44	30	14	182	167

Table 5   *Investment, savings and trade 1957–62—continued.*

(Averages in millions of 1962 $U.S.)

	(1) Gross national product	(2) Gross investment	(3) Gross national savings	(4) Net foreign capital inflow	(5) Trade in goods and services Imports	(6) Exports
Country						
Far East						
Burma	1,405	209	231	−22	248	270
Indonesia	8,348	745	486	259	1,206	947
Korea, South	2,178	315	82	233	393	159
Malaya, Federation of	1,896	347	419	−72	941	1,013
Philippines	3,789	479	404	75	762	687
China (Taiwan)	1,805	401	273	128	371	243
Thailand	2,879	455	414	41	572	530
South Vietnam	1,381	157	−50	207	305	98

Source: Agency for International Development, Statistics and Reports Division and Office of Program Coordination, data as of September 1964.

G.N.P. and gross investment data used for preparing the 1957–62 trends were largely taken from the 1963 edition of the United Nations' *Yearbook of National Accounts Statistics.* Modifications were made in a number of instances where revisions to a country's national accounts had not yet been incorporated in the published U.N. estimates or where independent A.I.D. estimates were believed superior to the official figures. Dollar estimates were derived by converting national currency values to constant 1962 prices and then converting the values for all years through a 1962 dollar exchange rate. In choosing dollar exchange rates a few adjustments were made to approximate more closely 'equilibrium' rates (especially when devaluations had occurred in 1962 or 1963). No adjustments, however, were made on the basis of internal purchasing power comparisons of the national currencies.

Dollar values of exports and imports of goods and services were either taken directly from the I.M.F., *Balance of Payments Yearbook*, vols 14 and 15, or else converted from *Yearbook* national currency estimates at annual exchange rates suggested by the I.M.F. The difference between imports and exports corresponds, therefore, to the I.M.F.'s 'balance on goods and services' and includes net merchandise, net freight, insurance, tourist, and other services, and also net factor income (dividends, interest, but not transfers of capital) to or from abroad. No attempt was made to change the imports and exports to a 'constant' dollar basis on the grounds that there was little perceptible change in the international purchasing power of the dollar during the period 1957–62.

Estimates of gross national savings were derived as residuals by subtracting the balance on goods and services (or foreign savings) from gross domestic investment. The definition of savings corresponds to the pre-1961 usage in that no adjustment was made to reduce foreign savings by the amount of current account transfers from abroad. The revised U.N. procedure is to treat some transfers not as foreign 'savings' but as foreign contributions to current consumption.

Table 6   *External debt structure*

Country	Scheduled amortisation over the next 5 years as percentage of outstanding debt as of 1962	Public debt service as percentage of exports of goods and services, 1962
Brazil	n.a. (extremely high)	20
Argentina	n.a. (extremely high)	22
Philippines	58	3
Israel	51	29
Spain	50	2
Mexico	49	16
Turkey	48	17
Taiwan	47	5
El Salvador	45	3
Chile	44	25
Nicaragua	44	5
Ethiopia	42	4
Costa Rica	41	9
Burma	40	n.a.
Colombia	40	11
Peru	40	7
Iran	38	9
Thailand	36	3
Ecuador	35	8
Korea	33	n.a.
Sudan	33	9
Nigeria	30	2
Bolivia	25	n.a.
India	25	9
Pakistan	23	7
Ceylon	22	1
Honduras	17	3
Malaya	16	1

Source: I.B.R.D., 'Economic Growth and External Debt – An Analytical Framework', p. 30.

3 · Obstacles to Progress[1]

CAMBRIDGE CONFERENCE REPORT

It might seem at first sight that the more the developing countries have tried to advance, the less they have succeeded, for the statistics of growth for the 1960s look slightly disappointing. On the credit side, the Third World has made remarkable progress with economic planning, increased tax revenues and national savings for investment, and produced and exported more year by year. Moreover, on paper at least, the poorer countries have also had more capital and technical aid. On the other hand, fall in world prices have robbed them of the reward that their increased export effort deserved, and unfavourable terms of trade have deprived them in real terms of much of the benefit expected from increased aid. As a result, they have made present progress at the cost of piling up heavy foreign debts and mortgages on their future. They may not unreasonably claim further increases of foreign aid to compensate for these undeserved misfortunes. Again, their people have paid more taxes; but the Parkinsonian propensity of governments to spend extra revenue on social services and prestige, instead of investing it in economic production, has disappointed those who expected higher savings to produce more wealth.

What is more, although the rise in gross national product is encouraging, the gains in income and output per head are much less so. True, more wealth is being produced, but, especially in Asia, more people are born to consume it; and everywhere, population increases brought about by modern medicine are checking the hoped-for rise in standards of living. As the distribution of wealth between modern and traditional sectors is notoriously uneven in developing countries, it cannot confidently be claimed that 'development' has made the average man better off than he was before. Worse still, the growth of agricultural output (upon which everything else depends) has lagged behind. Altogether, if statistics are to be believed, the pace of economic progress has been slower in the Development Decade so far than it was in the 1950s.

These are by no means rosy impressions and they raise some searching questions. Are the statistics believable? Do they tell the whole story? Is the disappointment to be blamed on too much planning or too little, too little government intervention in the economy or too much? Is there something in the socio-political make-up of these countries that raises more and more intractable obstacles as they attempt to advance economically? Is it easy enough to initiate growth but increasingly hard to sustain it? As one speaker put it:

When we look at the comparative stagnation in the agricultural sector, the mounting burden of external debt, we wonder whether all this effort in the past five years has really added to the long term productive capacity of these countries, or whether the increases in national product achieved, represent a 'phoney' and artificial leap forward, only made possible by increased foreign aid and foreign borrowing that will lead to stagnation hereafter?

In other words (but tell it not in Gath) is there something radically wrong with our economic theory of development?

Inevitably, such questions divided the conference into those of great and those of little faith; and perhaps there was more faith among international civil servants and recipient countries than among economists and representatives of donor countries.

THE MEANING OF THE STATISTICS

It should be said at once that we all agreed to take the average statistics of development in the sixties with a pinch of salt. As a Nigerian speaker pointed out, it would be hard to find an 'average' developing country whose economic behaviour complied with the average figures! Some countries have done much better than that – though many have done worse. Some of the statistics are interim measurements and allowance must be made for a considerable margin of error. Warned by a wise Turk's saying, we resolved not to use statistics as a 'drunk' uses lamp posts – to stagger from one maudlin conclusion to another!

An altogether more optimistic interpretation of the figures than that of Professor Meier emerged from our discussion and the case for it is given in the words of its chief protagonist:

It has been suggested that development is petering out . . . that obstacles previously submerged . . . are now fully asserting themselves; and we are being asked to discuss this problem, not exactly in a crisis atmosphere, but from the point of view of alarm. In my own mind this general framework is too pessimistic and I would like to say why.

My first point concerns the facts of the matter. We have been given valuable statistics by Gerald Meier and I do not question the statistics as such. But from them we have been asked to conclude that the total, overall rate of growth in G.N.P. in underdeveloped countries during the sixties has been less than during the previous decade. We are not justified in drawing such a conclusion yet. The difference in growth rates between the two periods is small enough to be well within the possible range of statistical error.

Secondly, the figures have suggested to some of us that it is easier to initiate development than to carry it on; and that the alleged slowing down of aggregate growth is due to radical defects in underdeveloped societies or to basic fallacies in the economic theory of development. I believe that the facts run to exactly the opposite conclusion. If you go through the statistical exercise of converting the production and export performance of the nineteen sixties into terms of the world prices and terms of trade prevailing in the fifties, you will find that the physical growth rate has not fallen. In other words, the apparent slowing down can be shown to be due, not to internal causes, but to external circumstances in world trade. In terms of export volumes there is no evidence that expansion in the present decade has slackened. And the physical increases in production and export already achieved would have been more than sufficient to reach the target growth rate of 5 per cent in G.N.P. per annum in the conditions of the 1950s. Hence the problem reduces itself very much to a matter of prices, and monetary and commercial constrictions in world trade.

Thirdly, the figures of performance so far do not tell anything like the whole story. A great deal of money and energy has been poured into infrastructure and social overhead capital: into health, education, housing, communications. It will take some time before the dividends from these investments in human resources appear in the balance sheets of production and particularly agricultural production. But all the evidence shows that there is a critical level; and once you have achieved a certain advance in social improvement, these social inputs combine with the economic inputs and make something like an economic breakthrough. Our present figures give no indication of how far towards that point the development effort has brought us.

Fourthly, one of the things that Gerald Meier found unsatisfactory about current development in his paper was that it relies so much on external aid. This is a valid argument but it is open to us to put forward the opposite, and equally valid view, that it is highly satisfactory. For the international movement for cooperation between rich and poor countries in aid of development – whether as a matter of human concern, or of political re-insurance or pure self-interest – I do not care what motives – brings a 'touch of healing' to world affairs and promises a better future.

Most of us agreed that it would be foolish to make more than a tentative assessment of prospects on the basis of performance figures for the first quinquennium of this decade. The question of success or failure is still open. We believe wholeheartedly that the investment in human resources will pay off many times over in the next decade and the next. In discussing the obstacles to further progress, nevertheless – perhaps because that is a gloomy way of looking at the subject, perhaps because the nearer we get to the difficulties to be overcome, the more formidable they seem – a less sanguine mood overtook us. There is indeed still a case for thinking that the road of development gets harder the farther one travels it.

OBSTACLES TO DEVELOPMENT

That road seemed easy enough so long as we could reasonably suppose – as all development planning has done hitherto – that economic advance was simply a question of economics. So long as we could believe that the chief obstacles were to be found in shortages of economic resources such as capital, foreign exchange, skills and entrepreneurship, all that had to be done was to inject the missing factors of production. During the past fifteen years this has been done to an increasing extent. Now, we were told, it has been discovered that it is not as simple as that. Experience shows that it is not so much the economic shortages but the entire institutional, social and psychological setting in which they occur, that stands like a giant in the way of long term economic growth.

Shortages of capital for development have not turned out the insuperable obstacles that they were once expected to be. Since the war, although some countries would not have had any capital for internal investment if they had not received foreign aid, others have increased domestic savings and invested them at a rate exceeding expectation. Secondly, more foreign capital aid has been received than could have been hoped for in the fifties, so that aid in the past quinquennium has provided between a fifth and a quarter of the developing countries' total investment. Thirdly, they have extracted more production per unit of capital invested than planners foresaw: and as a result, capital–output ratios of between two and three have often been achieved. From all this it was argued that shortages of capital are not a serious bottleneck in many countries.

If the agricultural economists are to be believed, not very much capital is required to increase output in the vital agricultural sector. What is needed there, it was argued, is only little capital but a much better deal for the peasantry – through land reform, agricultural credit facilities, the diversion of more resources from conurbations to improving life in villages, the encouragement of small rural manufacturers and entrepreneurs and a different type of primary education that keeps people on the land instead of driving them to unemployment in the towns.

We needed no persuading that by far the biggest obstacle to progress is the almost universal stagnation in agriculture and the rate of population increase. If this is not overcome there is no hope of maintaining the present rates of industrialisation and economic growth. But, it was suggested, it is not essentially shortage of capital that holds agriculture back; it is often the political preference for investing large amounts of scarce capital in a few spectacular industries and public works or political alliance with the wrong kind of landlord. It is not essentially shortage of schools and schoolteachers; it is the social preference for literary over technical instruction in hopes of white-collar jobs that do not exist. It is not essentially shortage of rural entrepreneurs and credit – the landlord and moneylender are common enough – it is a question of persuading them somehow to take up a creative, in place of a parasitic, role in the rural economy. Hence, according to this argument, the formidable problems in this key sector are not simply economic. There seems to be no simple economic solution to them short of radical social, political and institutional reform.

The second argument of this 'socialistic' school of thought about obstacles to development was no more optimistic than the first. It begins with the premise that what decides the poverty or prosperity of a country above all else is the prolonged existence of good or bad government; and ends by suggesting that unless the sacrifices and rewards of development are more justly distributed between the rich 5 per cent and the poor 95 per cent of the population, the advance will run into economic stagnation and political crack-up.

In some countries, especially in Latin America, the Middle East and the Mediterranean, and to a lesser extent in Asia and Africa, the ruling élite is said to be still partly 'feudal' and partly modern. Traditionally, the 'feudal' landowners have always used their governing power to extract wealth from the productive classes and spend it on prestige, power, status symbols, land speculation and luxurious living. So also does the modern or westernised élite which from taste and education imitates the standards and status symbols of its cosmopolitan counterpart in the richer countries. Maybe this is a caricature of the facts. But for the purposes of the argument, it suggests that ruling élites in the developing countries have a strong propensity to consume national income rather than to invest it. Certainly, complaints of conspicuous consumption on grand public buildings, air lines, Rolls Royces, political patronage and corruption are not unheard of, though they may not always be justified. Here once again therefore, the formidable obstacles to increasing productive investment and distributing wealth and employment more evenly throughout society seem to be not simply economic, but socio-political. Nor, it was suggested, are they likely to be removed by supplying the missing economic factors of capital, education and entrepreneurship from outside. Unless the social and political structure is liberalised indeed, more aid could conceivably increase inequalities and political instability without strengthening the internal forces working for economic growth. Hence in some countries, it was said, it is not easy to see how obstacles to internal capital formation and increased investment are to be removed without social and political reformation; and in many more it will be very hard to find ways of expanding agricultural output without removing the glaring inequalities in sacrifices and rewards between those who farm the land and those employed in the modern sector. After all, the peasant has no incentive to produce more when, either through taxation or low prices, too much of his surplus is taken from him to be spent on conspicuous consumption or invested in industry or services from which he gets precisely nothing in return. Under these circumstances the small farmer might be forgiven for thinking that 'development' is a new name for highway robbery.

'SOCIAL' VERSUS 'AID AND PRIVATE ENTERPRISE' APPROACH TO DEVELOPMENT

Implicit in what has been said so far are the two poles of theory about which the compass of argument fluctuated throughout our discussions. On many of the particular issues, the conventional 'Aid and private enterprise' approach was confronted directly or indirectly with a radical 'social' or 'socialistic' critique. Whereas the 'Aid' school of thought puts more blame for disappointing results on external trading and monetary influences, the 'socialistic' critique gives more blame to internal defects of social, political structure and the maldistribution of wealth. There are, as a result, two different opinions on the question of whether economic progress in developing countries is now running into increasingly intractable obstacles. The 'Aid' school is more optimistic in believing that a return of favourable external conditions will make the conventional prescription for injecting increased amounts of the missing economic factors work. The 'socialistic' school, on the other hand, doubts whether this formula will succeed, however much the dosage is increased, without drastic internal social and political reforms. One speaker indeed carried this approach to its logical conclusion and suggested that we should postpone attempts at economic growth for fifteen years so that society could be adapted to make it possible! Naturally this idea was rejected out of hand.

It should be made clear at once that the word ' socialistic ' here has no Marxist connotation; indeed the reverse is the case. For paradoxically in this discussion, the ' Aid and private enterprise ' school shows more faith in the power of purely economic factors to promote economic growth and alter society than the so-called ' socialists ' who hold that traditional social and political structure has the power to determine and frustrate economic growth. The two different approaches lead to corresponding differences of opinion about the nature of the obstacles to development. As one of the more socially-minded contributors put it :

The main obstacles cannot be formulated in conventional economic categories such as lack of capital, skills, entrepreneurship or foreign exchange. The real long-term obstacles to growth are linked with these economic deficiencies but they cut across them. Indeed they are not essentially economic difficulties at all. But they are institutional and psychological difficulties of a social kind. They are also to a great extent political obstacles – questions of policy, of political patronage, of administrative capacity and, sometimes, of religion.

In itself this analysis is enough to make this conference memorable. To everyone's surprise except their own, economists are now saying that the secrets of economic growth are not after all contained in their science. They have yet to come to light through empirical trial and error. But they are to be found apparently not in economic abstractions, but in the unexplored interactions of the politics, sociology and administration with the economics of a country. The amount of scientific knowledge about these mysterious interstices is tiny at present. So far as planning consists in abstracting the economics of a society, planning it and assuming that the socio-political context will automatically fall into line, it is an unlikely way of working miracles. It was said that planning is a ' confidence trick ' in the sense that in itself a good plan encourages state and private business to think and act expansively. But the trick is in danger of wearing thin soon unless these inter-actions are taken into account more than they have been hitherto. The ' Aid ' approach to obstacles, on the other hand, would not in principle deny the essential inter-action of economic, social and institutional factors in the development process. But its belief in the efficacy of supplying the missing economic factors puts more stress on too little external aid as a major obstacle and advocates big increases to remove it – a solution which its critics feel puts the cart before the horse. But everyone agreed that economic growth could not be induced by external stimuli, however powerful, without complementary, internal structural changes.

TOO MUCH STATE CONTROL AND TOO LITTLE SCOPE FOR PRIVATE ENTERPRISE?

Finally, in this review of progress we faced the question of whether too much state control and too little scope for private enterprise had, or had not, proved a major obstacle. Certainly, in most developing countries the expansion of the public sector has dwarfed that of the private sector during the past decade. Their attempts at economic planning have almost everywhere led to intensified central control of economic activity of all kinds. A threefold case for thinking that this was helping to strangle growth was made by advocates of liberating the energies of private men. First, higher taxation and rising public expenditure mean that too many resources are being diverted from the private sector (where they might have been invested in projects with an economic pay-off) and spent on improving administrative and social services and public works with no direct economic pay-off – luxuries that the economy cannot yet afford. Secondly, in many countries, in attempting to control the economy directly and to run an unnecessarily large public sector, the state has bitten off more than it can chew and far exceeded its administrative capacity. Thirdly, there has been too much 'heavy' state planning and control and too much reluctance to rely on the mechanisms of the market and the price system. Private initiative as a result has been stifled by lack of incentives and resources, and embalmed in red tape. As one speaker put it:

The essence of development behind all these economic abstractions is simply making people in the mass better off. Whatever the scope of government planning and controls, this cannot be achieved except as a result of millions of individuals deciding that it is worth working harder and using better methods, whether in industry, trade or agriculture. From this point of view the economy is like a centipede. Government may be able to persuade him to move six or seven of his legs forward by kicks and controls. But that is not enough. Too many governments have been planning and controlling as if they had the managerial capacity and economic wisdom to move each of the centipede's hundred legs bodily for him and coordinate the whole of the resulting movement into the bargain. Obviously, the state cannot be expected to do everything.

Therefore the state needs to devote itself, to a much greater extent than hitherto, to the business of providing incentives and disincentives for the mass of the people, particularly for the peasant on the land, to take these decisions to work harder and better. Development plans, especially in agriculture, will never get off the drawing board until they are conceived as projects that can only be carried out through the decisions of millions of individuals.

In reply, the more socialist-minded argued that, in the poorer developing countries, to advocate more private enterprise and less state control, is to mistake the problem for its solution. Private sectors capable of taking their own investment and management decisions, and market price mechanisms to regulate economic growth effectively, only emerge at a comparatively advanced stage of development and often after a preparatory period of state control, as in the case of Japan. But in less advanced countries, where the private sector is weak, internal markets undeveloped and capital scarce, it was argued, government must take overall control of investment decisions. But the chief objection to relying on the play of the market from the socialist standpoint, was that it could not be relied on to bring about the necessary alterations in social and institutional structure, and that more equitable distribution of wealth which is the object of development.

2 INDUSTRIALISATION

4 · Role of Industry in Pakistan's Development Plan[1]
KHALID IKRAM

Pakistan is one of a growing number of countries which have become dissatisfied with their traditional planning horizon of five years or so. This dissatisfaction emanates from both political and economic causes. On the political side the Government is committed to equalising *per capita* incomes in East and West Pakistan, eliminating dependence on foreign aid and providing full employment to the entire labour force. It is frankly recognised that these aims can be concretely planned for only over the long run. On the economic side, the most compelling factor was the long gestation period of projects in the vital fields of education, transport, heavy industry, irrigation and power. Decisions taken during the usual Five-Year Plan will thus have their most potent effects in the post-Plan period. If the long-run implications of these decisions are not explicitly considered, there is a danger that later Plans may have to be devoted to removing imbalances and bottle-necks unwittingly created by earlier ones. In other words, in order to ensure consistency between a number of consecutive short-term plans it is essential to work out a strategy for the long-run development of each major sector, fitting them all into an overall Plan which is geared to the attainment of some specified national objectives.

This paper discusses the strategy adopted for the industrial sector in Pakistan's Perspective Plan and shows how this fits in with the total Plan objectives. The discussion has been confined to Pakistan's experience but the argument does not apply uniquely to her. The same factors would weigh heavily in the formulation of a long-term industrial strategy for any country which is at roughly the same stage of development as Pakistan or which has a comparable set of long-range objectives. The chief reason for restricting the discussion to Pakistan is that since perspective planning is of very recent origin, more can be learnt from the detailed examination of an actual instance than by considering a number of generalities.

The Perspective Plan will span the period from 1965 to 1985, and provide a framework for the preparation of the Third, Fourth, Fifth and Sixth Five-Year Plans. A quinquennial revision of the Plan is provided for, both to incorporate changes in its basic objectives and to reassess the assumptions of the long-term model in the light of the actual behaviour of the economy.

Specific social and economic goals have been laid down for the Plan. For our purpose the most relevant of these are the following:

(a) a tripling of the Gross National Product from the forecast of Rs.4,400 crore[2] in 1965 to about Rs.14,500 crore in 1985 (at 1965 prices);

(b) the provision of full-employment to the entire labour force;

(c) the elimination of dependence on foreign assistance.

We shall consider, in turn, the role of industry in promoting each of these ends.

The tripling of Gross National Product over a twenty-year period implies an annual compound rate of growth of about 6·3 per cent (from the 4·4 per cent expected in the Second Plan). The planners have pinned their faith upon the industrial sector to act as the spearhead of the thrust to achieve these higher growth rates. Table 1 shows the projected behaviour of the manufacturing sector:[3]

Table 1   *Projected gross value added, share in G.N.P., and average growth rate of manufacturing sector, 1965 and 1985. (Rs. crore in 1964–5 prices)*

	1965		1985		
	Gross value added	Percentage of G.N.P.	Gross value added	Percentage of G.N.P.	Average annual growth rate (%)
Total manufacturing	562	12·8	3,186	22·0	9·1
(a) Consumer goods	392	8·9	1,632	11·3	7·4
(b) Intermediate products	140	3·2	1,054	7·3	10·6
(c) Investment goods	30	0·7	500	3·4	15·0

Source: Planning Commission, 'The Outline of the Third Plan', Karachi, August 1964.

There are many reasons for this reliance on industry as the leading sector. First, it is due to the performance of this sector to date. Over the last fifteen years the value added by large-scale manufacturing increased at an average annual rate of about 14 per cent, while its share in the composition of the G.N.P. rose from less than 2 per cent to over 8 per cent. Even if one includes the much slower growing contribution of small-scale industries, the average rate of growth of the total manufacturing sector over the last fifteen years works out at over 8 per cent per annum. Thus it does not appear an impossible task to raise the growth rate of the sector to about 9 per cent a year over the next twenty years, especially as the much faster-growing component (i.e. large-scale manufacturing) will be rapidly increasing its weight in the total.

Secondly, the growth of the industrial sector, coupled with the relative decline in the contribution of agriculture from about 60 per cent of the G.N.P. in 1949–50 to 48 per cent at present, has reduced the sensitiveness of the economy to fluctuations in agricultural output caused by the weather, floods, etc. In other words, a certain firmness has been imparted to the growth rate. A natural corollary of this development is that in devising a strategy for future growth the planners have sought to further diversify the economy, reducing the relative contribution of the most vulnerable sector (i.e. agriculture) and relying chiefly on such activities as have demonstrated a capacity for continuous and stable growth. Table 2 shows the contribution of the different sectors to the rate of growth during the Second Plan. The year 1962–3 is particularly interesting, because in that year the value of agricultural output fell in absolute terms, yet because of the rapid growth of the non-agricultural sectors (to which industry made a handsome contribution) the G.N.P. actually rose at about the same rate as the population, so that *per capita* incomes did not suffer.

Table 2 *Contribution of major sectors to economic growth 1959/60 to 1962/63. (Percentage points of increase in G.N.P. attributable to various sectors)*

	1960/1 over 1959/60	1961/2 over 1960/1	1962/3 over 1961/2	1962/3 over 1959/60
1. Agriculture	1·3	2·8	−1·1	3·0
2. Non-agricultural sectors	2·5	3·4	3·7	10·2
(a) Mining and manufacturing	0·7	1·0	1·1	2·9
(b) Construction	0·3	0·7	0·8	2·0
(c) Transport, trade	0·8	1·0	0·7	2·6
(d) Other services	0·8	0·7	1·1	2·7
Total G.N.P. at factor cost	3·8	6·2	2·6	13·1

Note : Totals do not add up exactly because of rounding.
Source : Planning Commission, ' Mid-Plan Review ', Karachi, May 1964.

A third reason for the planners' stress on the manufacturing sector stems from the rates of saving and investment required to furnish the growth rates of the Perspective Plan. The projections indicate that the rate of investment will have to rise from a current level of about 16 per cent of G.N.P. to almost 24 per cent by 1985. (These rates have been calculated after assuming both a rising ratio of capital to output and a considerable time-lag between investment expenditures and consequent changes in output.) This investment will have to be met from the country's own resources, for one of the main objectives of the Perspective Plan is to eliminate the dependence on external finance. Thus the rate of domestic savings is projected to increase from somewhat over 9 per cent of G.N.P. at present to about 23 per cent in 1985. The marginal rates of saving implicit in these figures rise from 20 per cent in the Second Plan to 30 per cent in the Sixth. Clearly, therefore, if these higher rates are to be obtained the planners must emphasise those sectors in which the marginal savings rate is much higher than the average. The main such sector is large-scale industry, which in recent years has been saving and investing almost 75 per cent of additional profits (which have been kept high through generous tax concessions, tariff protection and shortages in the domestic market). Thus a prime element in the attempt to raise the savings rate is a strategy of rapidly increasing the contribution of this sector.

A second element in this strategy relates to the composition of industrial output. Within the industrial sector, relatively more emphasis will be given to the manufacture of capital goods (see Table 1). The reasons for this shift are connected chiefly with the Balance of Payments and the objective of eliminating Pakistan's external dependence and are discussed below, but this is also an implicit strategy for obtaining a higher rate of savings. It has proved very difficult in the past to obtain a high rate of savings by manu-facturing consumer goods and trying to trade these for capital goods imports from other countries. The difficulty has arisen not so much from a lack of world demand for Pakistani products, as from domestic pressures for higher consumption which pre-empt the exportable surplus. As one planner has observed, ' It is far easier, politically and institutionally, to limit the expan-sion of capacity in the consumption goods sector in the very first instance and to deny the economy the temptation of an unplanned increase in its consumption. The argument rests more on institutional feasibility than on any inherent logic.' [4]

Let us turn now to the employment objective. The labour force is esti-mated at about 37 million workers by 1965, of whom over 20 per cent would be idle if the rest were to be fully employed. The actual number of persons affected is, of course, even larger, since unemployment chiefly takes the form of an under-utilisation of the available manpower. This under-employment occurs mainly in the agricultural sector. On the basis of figures for the agricultural labour force, the cropped acreage and the numbers of different kinds of livestock on the one hand, and data on manhours required per acre of land under each crop and per unit of livestock on the other, it is esti-mated that there would be full-time employment for less than 75 per cent of the agricultural labour force. Clearly, therefore, given the full-employment objective, a planned increase in the agricultural labour force can be postu-lated only on the basis of explicit policies to extend the area under cultiva-tion, increase the cropping intensity and shift the cropping pattern in a more labour-intensive direction. All these are provided for in the Perspective Plan, but even then it is estimated that agriculture will be able to offer full employment only to the existing agricultural labour force, plus perhaps another couple of million workers. The overwhelming majority of the new entrants into the labour market will have to seek employment in other sectors (see Table 3).

Table 3 *Employment by sectors, 1965, 1985 (million man-years)*

	1965	1985
1. Agriculture	18·0	26·3
2. Manufacturing	3·2	8·1
(*a*) Consumer goods	(2·5)	(6·0)
(*b*) Intermediate goods	(0·5)	(1·4)
(*c*) Investment goods	(0·2)	(0·7)
3. Services [a]	8·0	22·1
Total employment	29·2	56·5
Labour force	37·2	59·7
Of which: Agricultural labour force	24·5	27·9
Non-agricultural labour force	12·7	31·8
Unemployment as a percentage of labour force	21·6	5·4

[a] Including construction and transport.
Source: Planning Commission, ' The Outline of the Third Plan ', Karachi, August 1964.

Thus it will be seen that agricultural employment falls steeply from over 60 per cent of total employment in 1965 to about 45 per cent in 1985, and as a proportion of the total labour force it falls roughly from 50 to 44 per cent. Industrial employment, on the other hand, is projected to increase from approximately 11 per cent of all employment to 14·3 per cent over the Perspective Plan period, while the proportion of the labour force employed in industry rises more impressively, from roughly 8·5 per cent to 13·6 per cent of a much bigger total.

These projections depend, of course, on the choice of assumptions regarding increases in productivity. In general, after comparing the elasticity of labour productivity to output for different sectors of the Pakistan economy over the past fifteen years with the values of similar coefficients for relatively more advanced countries, it was assumed that the increase in productivity over the Perspective Plan would be almost two and a half times that between 1950 and 1965.

It is clear that in providing additional employment industry plays an important, albeit not a dominant, role. The bulk of the new workers will have to be accommodated in the traditionally labour-intensive sectors like construction and other services. There is a reason for this. As was discussed earlier, in order to achieve the higher growth rates required, the planners had to emphasise the fastest growing sectors, in particular that of large-scale manufacturing. Moreover, within this sector, a major shift towards heavy industry is planned. Therefore, the pattern of industrialisation that is envisaged will become increasingly capital-intensive. It is estimated that at present it costs about Rs.20,000 to employ an additional worker in large-scale industry. This is the average; in particular industries, e.g. oil-refining, the cost may go up to Rs.100,000 per worker. With the increasing emphasis on heavy industry the average may also be expected to rise. Thus, although successive Five-Year Plans will make substantial allocations for industry, its impact on employment will be less than proportionate.

This raises another interesting question of strategy. It is often argued that underdeveloped countries should not adopt the latest technology which, because of the relative scarcity of labour in the country of its origin, is generally very capital-intensive, but should go in for an earlier version, when the relative availabilities of capital and labour in the now developed country were more in line with those prevailing in underdeveloped countries. Thus a technique which has become obsolete in an advanced country because it uses too much of the factor (i.e. labour) that now is relatively the more expensive may still be economical in a less developed country, where this factor is relatively the more abundant.

This argument, of course, does possess some merit, and indeed there has been a small inflow into Pakistan of second-hand machinery from the developed countries. However, it is unlikely that this strategy can be adopted on a significant scale. First, Pakistan is committed to a considerable export effort and the bulk of the additional exports will have to come from the manufacturing sector. (This is discussed below.) Thus the increasing competitiveness of Pakistani industry in international markets is vital to the success of the Plan and a large-scale policy of adopting a relatively 'inefficient' technology must be viewed with considerable caution.[5] (In almost all industries save textiles, Pakistani costs are higher than those of her competitors.) Secondly, the relative abundance of labour in an underdeveloped country merely means that the prevailing *wage-rate* is lower than in the advanced countries. However, its productivity is also much lower in the developing countries so that the amount of labour required to produce a given output is more, and consequently the total *wage-bill* per unit of output may not differ markedly between the developed and underdeveloped countries. Thirdly, it is not possible to assure a steady supply of spares and replacements for equipment that has become obsolete and is not in use in the country where it was developed. Fourthly, when expansion is desired, it is seldom possible to obtain additional plants of the obsolete technology, hence a different type must be obtained. And the multiplication of plant-types only intensifies the maintenance problem. Actually, what this argument *does* suggest is that if the underdeveloped countries want to adopt a technology more appropriate to their factor-endowments, they will, very largely, have to develop it themselves. And this, incidentally, brings us back to the importance of the capital-goods sector in a strategy of industrialisation.

Let us try now to assess the contribution of industry to the achievement of the third main objective listed above, namely, the ending of independence on external assistance. The inflow of external resources in 1965 is estimated at Rs.275 crore. This, of course, serves a dual purpose in that it augments both the supply of domestic savings and the pool of available foreign exchange. We have already seen the contribution of industry to the strategy for mobilising higher savings; here we shall only be concerned with the foreign exchange aspect.

The strategy for the Balance of Payments rests very heavily on two main elements, and industry will play a decisive role in the success of each. First, the strategy envisages a vigorous policy to increase export earnings. (The changing composition of exports over the past fifteen years is shown in Table 4 below.) The projections imply an average annual growth rate of 7 per cent. This is undoubtedly an ambitious target and to achieve it the country will have to call on all its effort and ingenuity. Moreover, recent studies,[6] which cover about two-thirds of Pakistan's exports, suggest that these traditional exports will be able to grow only at a very slow rate. In fact, they put the maximum expected growth rate at around 2 to 3 per cent a year. The non-traditional exports (especially manufactures) will therefore have to increase at a much faster rate. Over the first four years of the Second Plan these non-traditional exports have grown at an average rate of just under 7 per cent per year, so they do hold out the hope of achieving the export targets if a concentrated effort is made. Moreover, it should be noted that the attainment of the export targets will mean that the ratio of exports to G.N.P. rises only from a current level of about 7 per cent to 8 per cent by 1985, so that the task of devising appropriate policies to push these additional exports into the international markets may be less formidable than appears at first sight.

Table 4   *Composition of exports, 1952, 1965. (Percentages)*

	1952	1965
1. Primary goods	89	52
2. Manufactures	1	30
3. Invisibles	10	18
	100	100

Source: Planning Commission, 'The Outline of the Third Plan', Karachi, August 1964.

A side-effect of the drive to boost the export of manufactures relates to the size of industry. It has been observed that many of the industries established behind a protective barrier of high tariff walls are composed of units that are too small to compete effectively in world markets. The 'infants' have shown no marked desire to grow up. The planners feel that it may be a much better bet to set up industries which from the very beginning are established on a larger scale than required by the immediate (domestic) market. This may orient the industry from its very inception towards the export trade in order to dispose of its surplus. Another factor which tends to keep down the size of plants is the lack of a well-thought-out policy regarding regional specialisation in the location of industry. In sanctioning plants, there has been a tendency towards duplication by establishing the same industries in both East and West Pakistan. The size of the market for each is thus reduced and the scale of the units has perforce to be smaller and economically less viable. A strategy is being considered whereby some industries in which economies of scale are important, e.g. steel and heavy engineering complexes, will be concentrated entirely in one region and some others, e.g. petro-chemicals, in the other. Later on, as the market widens, it may make economic sense to establish the same industrial facilities in both the Wings.

The second prong in the attack on the Balance of Payments consists of a policy of massive import substitution and this hinges even more on the growth of the industrial sector for its success. Over the last fifteen years a policy of replacing imports by domestic manufacture was indeed followed, and, so far as it went, it was most successful. This policy was followed most vigorously with respect to consumer goods, so that the imports of finished consumer goods declined from 46 per cent of total imports in 1951 to an estimated 23 per cent in 1964–5. A similar substitution for raw materials for consumer goods also took place as domestic industry took up the manufacture of intermediate products (see Table 5).

Table 5 *Composition of imports, 1951, 1965. (Percentages)*

	1951	1965
1. Consumer goods	46	23
2. Raw materials for consumer goods	27	14
3. Capital goods	20	47
4. Raw material for capital goods	7	16
	100	100

Source: Planning Commission, 'The Outline of the Third Plan', Karachi, August 1964.

The very factors which made for a rapid increase in the domestic manufacture of consumer goods worked against the early establishment of a capital goods industry. Consumer imports attracted high tariff rates not only because they were considered less essential than capital goods; of equal importance was the aim to raise more revenue. (As in all developing countries, customs duties bulked very large in Government revenues, and even at present they account for nearly 25 per cent of all tax receipts.) The effect, however, was to provide a very high degree of protection to the domestic market and thus offer a big incentive to invest in these lines. The capital goods sector, on the other hand, not being protected, did not hold out the same inducement. One of the threads in the long-term industrial strategy, therefore, is a rationalisation of the tariff structure to bring it into line with the objectives of the Plan and the economic realities of today.

Over the Perspective Plan, however, the main substitution will be that of capital goods. The domestic manufacture of machinery and equipment is projected to rise sharply from about Rs.30 crore at present to Rs.500 crore by 1985, implying an annual growth rate of 15 per cent. A number of reasons for this emphasis on the development of heavy industry have already been discussed; in the present context the aim, of course, is to save foreign exchange in the long run. At the moment the import of capital goods accounts for nearly half of total imports and this proportion will increase rapidly as the economy moves on to higher growth rates. Unless something is done about replacing some of these imports by domestic manufacture, the long-run foreign exchange problem will become unmanageable.[7] Certainly the objective of eliminating dependence on external finance will become much more difficult to realise. Moreover, since heavy industries possess extremely long gestation periods, it is necessary to begin establishing them as early as possible if this strategy is to pay off fully by the end of the Perspective Plan. Thus for Balance of Payments reasons, too, the planners were led to emphasise the rapid development of the industrial sector.

Before concluding, let us place the foregoing discussion in proportion by considering briefly the role assigned to the agricultural sector for the Perspective Plan. By 1985 agriculture will still be the largest single activity,[8] contributing over 30 per cent of the G.N.P. and employing 45 per cent of the labour force. To do this it will have to grow at an average rate of 4·5 per cent a year, which is considerably more than the rate of 1·5 per cent or so that has actually prevailed over the last fifteen years. Indeed, some of the *biggest questions* concerning the feasibility of the Plan relate to whether it will be possible to move this sector – which in Pakistan has shown all the inertia ascribed to it in discussions on underdeveloped countries – as quickly as the requirements of the Plan dictate. By any reckoning, then, agriculture remains a most important activity and the planners cannot afford to neglect its development.

While the Plan does provide for the rapid development of both agriculture and industry, this should not be taken as an endorsement by the planners of the 'balanced growth' thesis. On the contrary, there is a clear awareness of the concept of a 'leading' or 'strategic' sector whose contribution to a Plan is out of proportion to its size. That is to say, not only does its rapid development contribute directly towards the fulfilment of a Plan's objectives, but a decisive break-through in such a sector acts as a catalyst, accelerating the transformation of several other activities and thus bringing all the Plan targets closer to realisation. There may be many contenders for this title, for instance agriculture, transport, power, etc., and the rational basis of any actual choice would be the aims of the Plan and the stage of development reached by the country.

This paper has tried to argue the claims of industry to be given the role of the leading sector in Pakistan's Perspective Plan, for not only does it contribute handsomely to the achievement of the growth, employment and foreign exchange objectives of the Plan (indeed, it is difficult to see how else these could be attained); equally important are its contributions to the other major sectors. Agriculture, for example, benefits from the provision of fertilisers, pesticides and various kinds of machinery; construction from steel and cement; transport from the manufacture and maintenance of vehicles, rolling stock, ships and river-craft; investment in *every* sector benefits from the foreign exchange earning and saving potential of industry discussed earlier. Finally, industry has shown itself to be a major source for the inflow of modern skills and progressive attitudes which are the *sine qua non* of economic development. There is, thus, a strong case for giving industrialisation the leading role in the economic growth of underdeveloped countries, and this case gains its greatest cogency, as in Pakistan, when it is related to some explicit objectives and seen in a long-term perspective.

5 · Promotion of Indian Industrial Development[1]

V. K. RAMASWAMI

This paper is based on my experience as an official economist concerned with problems of industrial development in India. Much of what I have to say may not be applicable to other developing countries, or may be applicable only with qualifications. The conclusions that can be drawn from Indian experience may, however, be of some general interest, in view of the considerable industrialisation that has taken place in India over the last decade.

The existence of a large surplus labour force in agriculture is the main reason for industrialisation in India. Whether or not the labour force in agriculture is so large that the removal of some workers from the land will have no effect at all on output, it is clear that reasonably productive employment cannot be provided for additions to the labour force without a rapid expansion of industry.

Industrialisation is also called for in India on balance of payments considerations. Exports cannot be a leading growth sector. The rate of increase of population is such that agriculture cannot contribute large surpluses for export even allowing for improved productivity per acre. The world demand for the major export items – jute, textiles, cotton textiles and tea – cannot be expected to increase rapidly. Iron ore is the main commodity which is being exported in substantial quantities and has a good growth potential. Indian planning has therefore been directed primarily to the production of the articles on which increased incomes will be spent. The additional consumption from higher income is directed largely to industrial products, such as textiles and bicycles. The expansion of agricultural output requires larger quantities of industrial inputs such as fertilisers and pesticides. As incomes rise, the proportion saved will increase; and the investment goods bought with savings such as tractors, implements and machinery of various kinds must again be provided by industry. The growth rate of industrial output has therefore to be well above the rate of increase of national income as a whole.

In Indian planning, there are fairly detailed projections of the pattern of industrial development for a period of years. Such projections have been found to be of value in securing the right investment decisions, as they point up the areas of growing demand. Forward estimates for a number of years do, of course, require periodic revision, and there is an elaborate machinery for consultation between industry and Government to review progress and revise investment programmes from time to time. The existence of a detailed programme is nevertheless of considerable value; when the pattern of demand is changing rapidly, individual businessmen cannot foresee requirements with certitude in the absence of such an overall picture.

The industrial programme also provides the basis for planning of basic facilities, such as power, water and rail transport. Careful matching of supplies and demands is necessary to avoid significant under-utilisation of capital equipment either in power plants and the railway system or in industry. Another objective of industrial planning is to match the expansion of capacity in processing industries with the growth in supplies of basic materials, such as steel; with a difficult balance of payments situation, expansion of imports to make up for short-falls in domestic supplies of raw materials may not be feasible.

When imports are severely restricted, it is easy for high-cost industrial capacity to be established. Businessmen may assume that protection will continue indefinitely. They may, for example, set up unduly small units, because of lack of finance and a desire to avoid the risks associated with trying to secure too large a share of the market. The political desire to avoid monopolies and to distribute industry regionally may also lead to pressures on official licensing authorities to promote the setting up of unduly small units. Monopoly cannot, of course, be effectively countered by these means; if the total demand for a product is limited there can be only a few units even if each one is small and there will not be effective competition between them. The claims of regions for a share in industrial development of each single industry can be met without setting up uneconomic units. It is now generally agreed in India that capital must be used in the most effective way, and that industrial licensing policy must be directed to secure this.

The charging of an adequate interest rate for capital is one way of ensuring that it is put to the best use. Over the last few years, interest rates have been steadily raised in India. Even so, market prices may not adequately reflect the shortage of capital in relation to labour. Prevailing wage rates probably exaggerate the social cost of labour. It is therefore sensible to use labour rather than equipment for many construction jobs even if costs at market prices will be lower with the mechanised technique. The weaving of cotton textiles is another field in which labour-intensive methods are extensively employed for this reason.

Not only costs but also prices must reflect the scarcity of capital. It is sometimes believed that essential products, and particularly the services provided by public utilities, must be cheap. There is little to be said for this view. The low pricing of essential products can only retard the expansion of supplies, as a result of lack of resources for re-investment. Such supplies as are available are liable to be used in wasteful ways. The extent to which a system of direct controls can secure the allocation of scarce supplies of essential materials to priority uses is limited. Such direct controls will be necessary in temporary situations of imbalance between demand and supply; but the expansion of output on the basis of a price which will secure an adequate return can be the only long-run answer consistent with efficiency.

If industrial projects are to be undertaken at least cost they must be well conceived. The shortage of properly prepared projects is a major limit to development. Quite often, the absence of adequate knowledge about natural resources hinders the preparation of investment plans. The first step is to have reasonably complete surveys of geological resources, meteorological records, etc. Public sector investment in the proving of limestone deposits is a prerequisite for the rapid growth of the cement industry, and the mapping of iron ore areas must precede the growth of a steel industry or of export of ores. The rapid expansion of these activities is being given high priority in India.

The next step is the preparation of feasibility studies, covering both economic and technical aspects. The working up of detailed project reports will follow the evaluation of the feasibility studies. The lack of facilities for undertaking work of this kind limits the pace of industrial development, and results in the wrong projects being taken up. Foreign firms can, of course, be commissioned to do individual studies. This is, however, expensive, and costs foreign exchange. A foreign firm may also not take fully into account the special circumstances of the economy of the developing country; for example, it may not be able to identify fully local sources of equipment supplies and it may tend to recommend unduly capital-intensive methods. The development of skills within the developing country for the preparation of feasibility studies and project reports will therefore be of considerable value. This is a field in which foreign collaboration can be useful. A foreign firm could set up business in the developing country on the understanding that it will employ and train local men. The larger private industrial undertakings in growing industries might set up their own units, and so could the public sector departments or undertakings concerned not only with industry but also with irrigation, mining and transport.

The financial institutions of aid-giving countries have done much to raise the standards of project preparation, by insisting on properly worked up project reports before granting loans. A problem that has, however, arisen in this context is that a financial institution in a developed country normally insists on a project report prepared by its own nationals. A degree of internationalisation may be helpful. The detailed work on equipment supplies must naturally be tailored to the source of equipment; but this need not apply to all the stages of the preparation of the detailed project report.

The local financial institutions in developing countries have also, by insistence on properly worked up projects, done much to improve standards. When such a local institution works in cooperation with a lending institution in a developed country, the task of project appraisal can be handled primarily by the former agency on behalf of both, with considerable saving in time and effort.

The financial institutions can often actively help businessmen to prepare a worthwhile project, and an application which is initially unacceptable may be put into proper shape as a result of such assistance. However, the institutions are primarily concerned with the appraisal of projects submitted to them; and other agencies must assist businessmen in preparing the projects.

Both international and national assistance could usefully be devoted to a somewhat greater extent than in the past to the development of facilities for the preparation – and the appraisal – of worthwhile industrial development schemes in the developing countries.

The easy availability of suitable sites is necessary for the speedy implementation of projects. The supply of developed sites, with buildings, water and power laid on, has been a useful means of stimulating small industry development in India. For the larger industrial units, some fairly quick means of securing land at reasonable prices is essential. The compulsory acquisition of land by Government, at somewhat more than the value for agricultural purposes, and its transfer to industrial undertakings can provide a solution. If this is not done, the need to negotiate with a large number of small landowners can seriously delay the setting up of industrial projects. Even if negotiations are successfully completed, there can be doubts with regard to titles to land, which may impede the creation of mortgages to secure loans. The compulsory acquisition of land by Government can eliminate these difficulties; for this to be politically acceptable, there must be not only adequate compensation but also resettlement of those affected.

It may be difficult for industry to secure a stable labour force, even if there is considerable unemployment. Industrial centres often draw labour from far away, though there is surplus labour in the surrounding countryside; social and cultural factors may account for the unwillingness of the local population to take up industrial employment. The textile mills of Bombay, for example, have a considerable number of workers from north India. The immigrant workers may not bring their families with them and may keep their connections with their villages. The consequence of this is likely to be a considerable turn-over of the labour force. While labour of this kind may be nominally cheap, it is difficult to develop skills and raise productivity. The provision of housing, of fringe benefits related to length of continuous service such as pensions and provident funds, and security of employment can help to reduce turn-over. The assurance that the employment will not be terminated, except for reasons of proved misbehaviour or closure of the unit, provides a modern substitute for the security of the joint family. It can have the disadvantage of impairing industrial discipline; whether this happens will depend on the good sense of the unions and of the conciliation and arbitration machinery.

The supply of skilled labour, particularly of the foreman type, can be a major bottleneck. The traditional educational systems introduced by colonial powers in developing countries have often not paid adequate attention to this need. There is likely to be anyhow strong preference on the part of parents and pupils for the more general type of education which can lead up to white-collar jobs rather than for training in technical schools. The persistence of relatively high wages for skilled workers can do much to break down this resistance. On the side of supply, the provision of adequate training facilities for craftsmen, based on an estimate of industrial requirements, must have high priority in the educational programme.

Foreigners may often provide the first industrial managers. In India, British firms introduced modern management in the jute mills and tea gardens of Bengal. The managing agency system provided a means of using a limited supply of foreign managers to run a large number of relatively small enterprises.

Within the developing country, there will often be classes with considerable trading experience. The more enterprising among them – the Parsee and the Marwaris provide Indian examples – may take up industrial ventures. At a later stage of development, the shift to industry of the indigenous trading classes may be more widespread. Traders handling imports may take up manufacture of the products which they distribute, perhaps in collaboration with foreign suppliers. Traders in agricultural produce may set up processing units; the man who instals a rice mill consolidates his hold on the supplies of paddy and the movement of rice from the area. The larger landowners may also take part in this activity.

To a limited extent, men with professional training, such as engineers, may set up small industrial units. Whether they can do so will depend largely on the availability of finance from institutions: professional knowledge, the desire to set up industrial units and possession of capital may not go together.

The main source of managerial ability is likely to be the large or medium corporate enterprise. The growth of such enterprises results in a supply of professional managers from among the educated who want salaried employment. Traditionally, such men would enter the public service or the law. Careers with companies can become an acceptable alternative, if selection and advancement are recognised to be on the basis of merit.

Initially, it may be the foreign companies which provide such openings. They offer greater security, being well established, and their salary levels are likely to be higher, as these need to be attractive to expatriate personnel. Foreign firms may be under political pressure to reduce the number of expatriate officers. It is in any case cheaper to employ local personnel and while foreign firms will naturally wish to have a limited number of expatriate managerial staff, apart from technicians, a steady increase in the proportion of posts held by the nationals of the developing country can be expected.

Many of the locally owned firms may be family businesses, which do not provide careers for able outsiders. As industry expands, however, some of these firms may change their character. There may be considerable public holding of the equity, and while members of the controlling families may continue to hold directorships and some of the top managerial posts, it may also be possible for others to rise to the highest positions.

The public services may provide a useful source of managerial talent. A considerable number of Indians were employed in senior managerial posts in the railways long before similar opportunities were available in industry, and railway officers have played a useful part in the management of some of the new industrial undertakings. Some general administrators may also have the aptitude for industrial management. In general, however, the public sector enterprises will need to build up cadres of managers by providing the requisite training and experience on the job.

The development of a large professional managerial class is critical for successful industrialisation. Persuading foreign firms to train nationals, encouraging indigenous enterprise to rely more and more on professional executives, and appointing specialists rather than general administrators to run public sector undertakings can be useful measures of public policy.

Capital is scarce in developing countries, relative to labour and possibly land. The proportion of incomes saved is low, and the mobilisation of savings for productive purposes is difficult. This can be partly achieved through taxation. Industrialisation itself helps the process. Additional incomes are more likely to be spent on industrial than on agricultural products, and indirect taxes on industrial consumer goods are a very convenient means of taxing the income increases resulting from development. Direct tax yields are also likely to be related more to industrial output than to the national income, and if industry grows faster than output as a whole, tax revenues may rise steadily as a proportion of national income without any increase in rates of tax. In addition an effort should be made to tax specifically those farmers who benefit substantially from development expenditures, through the imposition of betterment levies, for example.

In Indian experience, both life insurance and small savings can be expanded very rapidly, not only in the towns but also in the rural areas. The setting up of organisations for this purpose is well worthwhile, as widely dispersed savings cannot otherwise be mobilised for productive purposes.

The supply of equity capital to industry presents special problems. Personal savings invested in family businesses may suffice for small industries. The large and medium industrial units, however, need a well-established stock market. Initially, the middle classes may be unwilling to assume the risks associated with industrial investment, and even if there is a stock market, the shares of joint-stock companies may in fact be held by controlling families. As, however, there is experience of industrial undertakings making profits and providing capital appreciation on shares, a wider public may be interested; and the new managerial class engaged in industry will be a major source of finance. The available evidence indicates that, over the last decade or two, there has been a very considerable increase in India in the number of people investing in equities.

As prevailing interest rates are generally high, dividend rates must be in line, and the proportion of profits ploughed back may be less than in developed countries. The tradition of relatively liberal dividend distributions can set a limit to the financing of expansions from the industry's own funds. Discrimination in the tax system in favour of ploughed back profits can be of help. Such a provision can also be defended on the ground that while the taxation of consumption must be high and progressive on grounds of equity, there must be incentives for investment and savings.

Specialised financial institutions will be needed to supplement the stock market. They can serve as agencies for the transfer of Government budget surpluses, or of Government borrowings, to private industrial purposes. They can also raise capital from other financial institutions, such as banks, which may not be willing to lend long-term to industry. Unit trusts can make it possible for the small investor to invest in equities while spreading his risk.

There is room for specialisation as between financial institutions according to the type of activity financed. Lending to small units may usefully be decentralised, and undertaken by small institutions meeting regional requirements. In India, this type of lending is handled largely by State Finance Corporations. The recipients of loans are often likely to be proprietary concerns or partnerships not maintaining systematic accounts. A close degree of supervision over the operations of the borrowers may be called for, and personal knowledge of the borrower may be essential. There is also in India a central corporation lending to small-scale industries, which has concentrated largely on the supply of equipment on hire purchase. Such centralised lending must necessarily be confined to a part of the value of fixed assets, with legal provision for resumption in the event of non-payment of instalments. The lending institutions covering smaller areas can provide assistance more flexibly.

The *modus operandi* of institutions lending to large and medium-scale enterprise will be different. Here it is possible and desirable to insist on properly prepared project reports. The borrowers are likely to be mainly joint-stock companies, and the extent of supervision of operations can be less. These institutions may undertake not only lending but also underwriting, the provision of guarantees, etc.

In the operations of financial institutions, proper prudence must be combined with some risk-taking. New entrepreneurs cannot be encouraged unless the institution is reconciled to accepting a loss now and again. Institutions not subject to direct parliamentary control may be more able and willing to adopt such an approach than those which have to defend individual transactions. A major Indian financial institution, the Industrial Credit and Investment Corporation of India, is entirely private, though Government lent it a substantial sum and has a Director on the Board. The Industrial Finance Corporation of India had a large Government holding of its equity till recently, and was subject to detailed parliamentary scrutiny of its operations. A Development Bank has, however, now been established under the control of the Reserve Bank, and this has taken over the Government holding in the Industrial Finance Corporation. The charter of the Development Bank provides for much greater flexibility of operations than was possible for the Industrial Finance Corporation.

A method by which financial institutions can provide flexible assistance is investment in equity. This can help the undertaking to meet its requirements while maintaining a reasonable debt-equity ratio. If all goes well, the institution can secure a return considerably higher than on a fixed interest loan, while if the enterprise is not successful, it will not have to carry a heavy burden of debt servicing. This has not been attempted so far by Indian financial institutions, except to the extent that shares have been taken up in pursuance of underwriting obligations. The International Finance Corporation and the Commonwealth Development/Finance Corporation do, however, invest in this form.

Reference was made earlier to joint evaluation of projects by institutions in the developing and the developed countries. Such joint evaluation can result in the foreign exchange requirements of the project being made available by the foreign institution. The financing institutions in India have also taken foreign exchange loans against foreign official assistance, and therefore they are able to finance both the rupee and foreign exchange cost of a project in a single operation.

There is an important distinction between the terms suitable for lending to individual industrial undertakings and those on which a developing country can afford to borrow abroad. Any really worthwhile industrial undertaking should be able to repay a loan in anything up to twenty years; if it cannot do so, it should not be started at all. On the other hand, the balance of payments outlook for a developing country may be such that the repayment of external debt must be spread over a much longer period, if massive borrowing merely to cover debt servicing obligations is to be avoided. When, therefore, official assistance is made available direct to industrial units in developing countries, or to these industrial units through financial institutions, ways and means have to be found of reconciling these conflicting requirements. That part of official aid which goes to this purpose may be short or medium-term, and the balance of aid may be made available to the Government of the developing country on much more liberal terms. Alternatively, the industrial undertaking may repay in local currency over a relatively short period, but the repayment to the foreign lenders in foreign exchange by the Government may be according to a different schedule.

Not all industrial undertakings need loans to finance their programmes. There may, however, be a requirement of imported equipment; and the imports may have to be financed against foreign assistance or not at all. In such a case, the technique of evaluation and lending by a financial institution is not appropriate. The Government will need to take a loan abroad, against which foreign exchange can be sold to the undertaking against payment in local currency. The Government will need to have its own arrangements for scrutiny of the project, to ensure that it makes a worthwhile contribution to the development programme. Such official scrutiny, where provided for under the normal legislative and administrative procedures, would naturally apply also when a financial institution provides a loan.

Private investment from abroad has the advantage of bringing with it the foreign exchange needed to pay for imported equipment. It can thus not only supplement domestic savings, but supply the additional scarce resource of foreign exchange. The returns on private investment must naturally be substantially higher than on official lending. Foreign investment may, however, strengthen the balance of payments if a substantial part of it is used for the production of exports or for import substitution. Also, to the extent that profits are ploughed back, there will be no current burden on account of remittances.

The attitudes to foreign investment in developing countries are greatly influenced by the pace and pattern of development. When there is little growth, particularly in industry, the image of foreign investment is one of exploitation of limited natural resources, resulting in a remittance burden which is difficult to bear and in foreign domination of economic and perhaps political life. The indigenous business classes may be opposed to foreign investment as taking the cream off a limited market. On the other hand, foreign investment which forms only a part of a rising level of investment in industry, and which assists the local businessmen in taking up new lines of manufacturing and catering to expanding markets, may be welcomed.

While the wholly foreign firm will have a role to play in industries with very new techniques, the joint enterprise of local and foreign businessmen is likely to secure greater acceptance in the developing country, and also contribute more to the raising of managerial and technical standards. The association of the general public with joint ventures, or for that matter with industrial units wholly controlled by foreign firms, through participation in the share capital, can do much to promote acceptance and to encourage the habit of investment in equity.

The straight technical collaboration agreement, without any financial participation by foreigners, must necessarily be far more widespread than investment. The technical assistance provided by international institutions and Governments can meet only a small part of the need, and the primary reliance must be on commercial arrangements. Governments of developing countries can play a part in ensuring that the terms of these agreements are not unduly onerous. There may be scope for somewhat greater effort than in the past by Governments and organisations of industries in developing countries and by international institutions to assist industrial units in developing countries to secure the kind of collaboration arrangements that they really need. The small businessman in a developing country, with perhaps no industrial experience or knowledge of foreign industrial concerns, is at a handicap in negotiating worthwhile arrangements. Investment centres or similar bodies set up by developing countries can be of some help in this regard.

The application of new techniques from abroad will be called for also in the field of marketing. The organisation of distribution of traditional products in the developing economy may be both efficient and cheap. The foodgrains trade, for example, is often remarkably well organised. The sale of industrial consumer goods in rapidly increasing quantities, in order to monetise the economy and secure larger supplies of agricultural products for urban consumption, will on the other hand involve considerable effort. To be successful, the effort will have to be based on detailed study of how incomes are spent and of the reactions of the consumer to additions in income. Sample surveys of consumer expenditure have been made use of for the purpose in India. While these can provide valuable basic information, there can be no substitute for effective marketing organisations which undertake distribution down to the retail level and continually test the market. The big successes in promoting sales of manufactured consumer goods have been achieved by the firms which have invested heavily in such distribution arrangements.

6 · The Role of Industry[1]

CAMBRIDGE CONFERENCE REPORT

It goes without saying that everybody in developing countries wants to industrialise swiftly. Industry glitters with promise. Nothing else seems to hold out much hope of fulfilling the expectations of new nationalism, winning economic independence and raising average prosperity dramatically; nothing else seems drastic enough to cast off the millstones of population increase and falling prices for primary producers that, in spite of their doubled efforts, have made them worse off than before. But have they got what it takes to make a policy of 'Industrialise or bust' go? For many years throughout the world, the economists' advice has been 'caution; probably not'. Our main task was to see whether this orthodox doctrine still holds good.

Would it pay new states to invest most of their money and brains in crash programmes for industrial revolution here and now? Or would it be wiser to give priority to contriving agricultural revolutions first? Obviously the question of whether industry or agriculture is the cart or the horse in economic development over-simplifies the actual problem. Nevertheless, opinion is sharply divided about the proper role of industry in the overall strategy of development; for one school of thought backed the agricultural horse to pull the industrial cart; the other, more radical, school backed the industrial horse to draw the agricultural cart.

AGRICULTURE FIRST?

A text which most economists would inscribe over the door of every planning department, sums up the case for agriculture: 'The most certain way to promote industrialisation . . . is to lay the foundation it requires by taking vigorous steps to raise food production per person engaged in agriculture. This is the surest way of producing the large and ever-increasing demand for manufactures without which there can be little industrialisation.'[2] In mainly agrarian economies, it is said, the rate of industrialisation is decided first and foremost by the rate of expansion in agriculture. Its purchasing power mainly determines the size of the home market for manufactures. Its food surpluses decide the numbers of workers that can be employed outside agriculture. It has been, and must be, the main source of capital and foreign exchange required for industry. And agriculture is the main chance of employing the majority of people for a long time to come. Paradoxically, therefore, the quickest way for most countries to industrialise in the early stages is to concentrate their resources on developing their agriculture.

These well-known arguments suggest a model of 'Balanced growth', working on the principle that overall expansion depends upon the action of an expanding agriculture on industry, with the drive coming initially from agriculture. The same principle sets the pattern for industrialisation itself. When, at the end of the first stage, agriculture has been expanded to produce sufficient surpluses, industrialisation begins with those manufactures that are most closely connected with supply and demand from the land; i.e. those processing food and raw materials, and those making agricultural tools, machinery and fertilisers. At the same time, suitable consumer-goods industries are set up to substitute for imports and save foreign exchange. Only in the final stage is the economy considered ready to expand into heavy, capital goods industries. So much for the agriculture first model.

There may be much in the economic history of developed countries like

Japan and the U.S.A. during the nineteenth century that conforms to it. Unfortunately there is less evidence during the past fifteen years to show that it will work in developing countries now. Two vital factors have changed, making Rostovian historical models of doubtful use. In the nineteenth century, the capital needed to create one work-place in industry was of the order of hundreds of pounds. Today, with the advance of technology, it takes thousands; and so the countries developing industry now need much more capital than the developed countries did. Secondly, thanks to science and social services, population is rising much more rapidly than it did when the developed countries were being industrialised. The Malthusian brakes that held population in check on the land have been taken off. So the new states trying to cross from an agrarian to an industrial economy today are faced with demographic obstacles that the rich countries never encountered.[3] It is much harder to squeeze capital out of agriculture at present rates of population increase; yet much more capital is needed to industrialise.

The population problem is already so bad in many Asian countries that agriculture cannot possibly boost industry through the early stages. Far too many people are on the land. Too many are eating and reproducing without producing. There is little new land that can be brought under cultivation. And so agriculture defies all efforts to quicken its growth and remains torpid. In Africa the population–land equation for the time being is much better. The land is not super-saturated with people; there is no shortage of food and more land could be brought into production. But if population keeps growing with agricultural development as it has done elsewhere, may not Africa end up in the same plight as Asia?

Population in developing countries tends to increase more quickly than the agrarian economy can be developed to produce surpluses. And so long as population on the land more than eats up increased output, the ability of agriculture to provide capital and expanding markets for manufactures is at best marginal, at worst nil. This was the heaviest spanner that the industry first school found to throw into the agricultural school's works. Admittedly the criticism has more force for Asia than for Africa. Maybe it suggests that priority should be given neither to agriculture nor to industry, but to checking the population increase that is strangling economic growth at birth. Population increases to the agricultural school, however, seemed all the more reason for concentrating on the agrarian economy in order to feed people. And they continued to insist that industrialisation depends upon producing large food surpluses. Their opponents, on the other hand, implied that the more food produced, the more people there would be on the land to eat it up. If industrialisation had to wait for the development of agriculture, it would never get off the ground. Agriculture is never likely to be able to supply the main drive for industry; on the contrary, industrialisation is the only hope of releasing agriculture from the stranglehold of population to pull its weight in development.

INDUSTRY FIRST?

So the industry first model was demonstrated, with Asian conditions mainly in mind.[4] Its principle is that industry as the leading sector will drive the development of agriculture and the rest of the economy faster than any other sector can. Industry alone can draw the hidden unemployed off the land into production; and so long as they are left on the land, agriculture cannot increase its efficiency. Farmer and peasant will not be stimulated to produce more until industry provides enlarged markets and better prices for their food and raw materials. Industrialisation must jerk the agrarian sector out of its deep sleep. What is more, manufactures, and especially large-scale, heavy industries, save foreign exchange, raise output per head and create investment capital much faster than any other sector possibly can. Lastly, the more swiftly the industrial community grows, the more swiftly modern attitudes and enterprise will spread through the nation. So much for the industry first model.

Revolutionary in character and not without risks, this theory was sharply criticised. Obviously agriculture can never be much more than a carthorse. Industry, if it is successful, is certainly a racehorse. But to breed and train this racehorse and coax him to the starting post under Afro-Asian conditions could be as big a gamble as putting your shirt on the carthorse to beat him home. The industrial model will work if – and it is a big 'if' – large-scale, heavy industry proves something like economic. If much of it turns out to be really inefficient, the development of the entire economy may be set back many years.

Critics pointed out that in large Asian countries like India and Pakistan, agricultural output is rising at about 1 per cent annually, while population is growing at something over 2 per cent. The short-fall in food production has had to be made good with foreign aid. How can these countries develop large-scale industry on so feeble an agrarian base? Who can afford to buy the output of manufactures when internal buying power is so low? The advocates of industry first admitted these weaknesses. How is a country on this policy going to earn enough foreign exchange to pay for the high imports of capital goods and technical know-how required for large-scale industries? A crash programme for industry with a poor home market would have to rely heavily on export markets to sell its production and earn foreign exchange. But there is scepticism about these prospective world markets. Asian heavy industry is unlikely to be able to compete with already industrialised countries, at least in the early stages; and so countries with this plan soon run into severe balance of payments difficulties that bring industrialisation, and economic development as a whole, grinding to a standstill.

So much for the battle of the models. The two theories seemed absolutely opposed. With an eye to Africa, the one proposed a gradual evolution from developing agriculture into industries processing its products and relying mainly on the home market; the other, with Asia in mind, proposed a revolutionary plan for heavy industry, relying on foreign markets. Both models appeared to have something radically wrong with them.

To the layman at least, the contest seemed a little unreal. Models are necessarily simplified, abstracted from reality, and perhaps that is why economists are able to construct them to do almost anything; or to make the same model – with slight adjustments – work to opposite conclusions; or to throw enough spanners to wreck any conceivable construction! What was left after the crunch when we tried to put the pieces together again, proved none the less instructive.

RECIPROCAL ACTION BETWEEN INDUSTRY AND AGRICULTURE

One side had asserted that the quickest way to industrialise is to concentrate on agriculture; but it had also admitted that industrialisation is the sharpest spur to agrarian development. The other side had asserted that the quickest way to develop agriculture is to concentrate on industry; but it also admitted that torpid agriculture is a heavy drag on industrialisation. Basic differences of emphasis remained, but most of us wondered whether in principle the two theories were not two sides of the same coin. Upon one thing at least, the two schools seemed to be at one: that swift economic growth depends upon reciprocal action between expanding industry and expanding agriculture. At one stage of development the key may be agriculture, at another, industry. The emphasis changes from time to time without inconsistency in the theory. According to the principle of interaction, both agriculture first and industry first are half truths without these qualifications.

An Asian speaker drew the popular conclusion thus:

The point is really that both industrialisation and agricultural development have to go on simultaneously, creating a cycle of exchange between them at any one point in time. The farmer will grow more, the better prices for his products are in urban markets, and the cheaper he can buy consumer goods. The townspeople must be able to get enough food at cheap prices and at the same time sell their manufactures. So I think it is wrong to think of industrialisation and agricultural development as alternatives, or as different stages in the process. They must grow in parallel. What we do want to say is that there must be a continuing balance between growth in agriculture and growth in industry; and from plan to plan and from year to year, governments must see that this balance is struck.

We had come into the subject of industrialisation through the same door by which the 1963 conference had left the subject of agriculture.

Our belief in the fundamental importance of agriculture, by no means implies that it should, as such, always be given priority over industry in development plans. The two are not alternative courses of development. *Agriculture is no substitute for industry; and industry is no substitute for agriculture. The development of both has to be planned and phased so that each complements the other in balance and sequence.*[5]

If the previous conference was impressed by agriculture's contribution to economic growth, this one was more impressed with the contribution that industry could make to agriculture. Perhaps this shift of emphasis is most marked in Asia; but many African speakers also stressed industry's role and rejected the idea that Africa has to go through a further phase of agricultural development before attempting industrialisation seriously.

' I have been somewhat shaken ', one of them admitted,

by this very categorical assertion that you must have this agricultural development *before* industrial development. I am also rather shaken by my good friend's categorical assertion that we must now produce more food before we do anything further . . . The majority of countries [in Africa] are over-all producing more than enough food . . . I should have thought that that was a very early stage in the development of a country – almost a primitive stage – and that you move over this rapidly, not into a stage of producing agricultural surpluses, and afterwards into the stage of industrialisation, but into the stage when you develop them both in parallel. Africa is ready – is in fact already moving into import-substitute industries like textiles, brewing, distilleries, shoes, pots and pans etc., for which there is a local market right now. *Surely industry and agriculture go hand in hand*, though not in the sense that one must move at the same rate as the other. *But you cannot have agricultural development without industrial development; nor can you have industrial development without agricultural development.*

' For Africa ', another speaker put it,

it is not a question of agriculture today; tomorrow, industrialisation. That is not what we are thinking about at all. *It is a question of how you really make them mix.* There was this categorical statement that as of now, African countries should concentrate on agriculture. We take issue on that. We are trying to bring in as much industry as possible and industry is really moving in. So I think the proposition which our friends are trying to sell us is slightly academic, because what is actually happening is that African countries *are* trying already to make industry their leading sector. I do not think that you have to do this at the expense of agriculture. The trouble at present is that African agriculture is not fully productive. Half the time the farmers are not working and they produce only enough for their families. Once you produce the cheap manufactures they want, they will work full time to earn enough to buy them. There is no point in training college graduates to go round and persuade farmers to produce more and better, when your real problem is to produce the manufactures which the peasant will grow more to buy if they are cheap enough.

In principle therefore, the role of industrialisation in development is not a question of industry first or agriculture first. It is a question of finding the right mix for a particular country at a particular time. Any generalised, absolute priority for either sector is theoretically nonsense. Countries that have attempted crash programmes for industry have run into recurring food shortages and agricultural crises which have forced them to go back and attend to their agriculture, before going on with their industrialisation. Moving from crisis to crisis, advancing by fits and starts in this way slows down economic growth and it is better to recognise the actual principles of interaction in the first place.

The mixture of development in industry and agriculture that will give the quickest rate of expansion all round differs from country to country according to its factors of production and stage of development. And the stress will alter as development goes forward. Depending on size and density of population, internal buying power and competitive advantages in export, range of natural and human resources, the available capital, power, communications, skilled cadres and institutions, foreign aid and many other things – the correct mixture is entirely relative. With all the variables, there cannot conceivably be a universal formula either for economic growth or for industry's role in bringing it about. That is why industry first and agriculture first, as universal prescriptions, are both silly answers to a silly question. The two sectors have to be developed to complement each other in a way that suits the unique array of factors in each country.

One high authority criticised this conclusion:

It may create some peace, Mr Chairman, between the gentlemen to your left and those to your right – but agriculture is not a singular and neither is industry. There are so many different kinds and branches of industry and so many different kinds of agriculture. A decision in favour of an industrial project is not necessarily good; a decision for an agricultural project is not necessarily bad. Decisions which are right for one country may be wrong for another. And some decisions may be bad today but may be worthwhile tomorrow. We have to start with the situation in a particular country at a particular time.

We did not agree upon the complementary nature of industrial and agricultural development for the sake of compromise, but because it seemed to be written in the iron code of economics. In applying the principle for practical purposes to cases, the two schools of thought in fact differed as sharply as ever. But the cut and thrust between them now spread to the issues in more practical form. The 'right mix' is also a question of finding the most suitable types of industry to develop. It is a question of finding profitable markets for them. It is also a matter of deciding the best kind of technology for industrialising developing countries.

THE NEED FOR MORE INDUSTRIALISATION

The conventional doctrine that progress depends upon the play of multiple interactions between sectors, especially upon the right balance between industry and agriculture, had been re-stated. What was new to the discussion was the belief that for many countries, the agricultural side of the equation had been stressed too much for too long; that it was time to shift the emphasis on to the industrial side to redress the balance and achieve a better rate of expansion. This is the plan of the larger, more advanced, Asian countries like India and Pakistan. There are risks in such a plan as there are with every other plan; but then if every development risk predicted by economic theory had been taken seriously, the world would still be looking for a single example of industrial revolution. Yet the shift of stress to the industrial side at this conference was not restricted to India and Pakistan. It was said that this ought to be the plan in Malaysia and Nigeria – even for small countries like Malawi. The cry for much more, and much swifter, industrialisation to balance previous agricultural development and drive it forward in Africa as well as Asia, was perhaps the most striking trend in our discussion.

WHICH INDUSTRIES FOR WHAT MARKETS?

What kinds of industry are most profitable in the earlier stages and where are markets to be found for the output? Here the argument ran inevitably into the thick of balance of payments difficulties which is one of the four major obstacles to industrialisation: shortage of capital; even more serious, lack of managers and technicians, and of the institutional setting for manufactures; the low buying power of home markets; and acute shortages of foreign exchange.

Criteria for selection

In selecting which branches of manufacture to set up, as in deciding between projects generally, the crucial test is that of the best 'pay-off' for the economy as a whole. Much more than other forms of development, industrialisation makes heavy demands on scarce capital, foreign exchange and trained manpower; so the penalties paid by the rest of the economy for its inefficiency are very high. To shorten the odds, the branches of manufacture chosen should give firm expectations of becoming competitive in the long run; they ought to have comparative advantages over similar industries in neighbouring countries, if they have to depend partly on export markets. More than that, planners have to take special care that the projects chosen do not run the country into catastrophe in its balance of payments. Ideally, the industries chosen should produce more extra wealth for the country than any alternative use of the resources invested in them could possibly do.

And they should stimulate the rest of the economy more than any alternative project would. By these tests, what manufacturers are most likely to succeed?

Export markets for manufacturers?

Heavy industry of large scale relying on export markets may, or may not prove feasible for large Asian countries like Pakistan. It is an unlikely starter for most African countries at this stage. In world markets, the competitive advantages are all in favour of developed countries. As one expert put it:

The prospects of competing in overseas markets in basic manufactures, where the overseas markets themselves are producing the same things, are really pretty remote. We have to accept that in the first instance, most countries will depend largely on domestic markets for industrial development, unless they are processing raw materials for export; and will use a moderate degree of protection, if they are to get industries going at all.

There are of course exceptions, such as Hong Kong's spectacular successes and the Swiss watch industry, both of which relied on foreign markets from the beginning. Some of us were more hopeful than the quoted speaker, although we all saw the comparative disadvantages facing the developing countries' manufactures in world markets – their lack of research and technical know-how, of the needed entrepreneurs and commercial and financial institutions, their high comparative costs. Possibilities of expanding manufactured exports do nevertheless exist, given enough ingenuity to break out into new export patterns. New styles and types of consumer goods may be developed. High labour costs in developed countries may encourage manufacturers to move capital into developing countries with lower labour costs. By exploiting the very latest technology, developing countries may have a chance of gaining the lead over some developed countries using obsolescent plant and bearing capital losses in replacing it. But the main chance is for developing countries to create protected regional markets in which they can sell their uncompetitive manufactures to each other. One part of Africa can exchange its high-priced steel or cement for its neighbours' high-priced fertilisers or textiles. But for all the possibilities, it is still unlikely at this stage that African or Asian countries will be able to sell steel to developed countries more cheaply than, say, Luxembourg, or outcompete German cement or chemicals in world markets.

Import-substitute industries for the home market

'For most countries in the earlier stages of industrialisation, manufacturing should be geared mainly to internal, and if possible, regional demand, and to indigenous raw materials.' Selling in the home market and using home-produced materials, this sort of industry should enjoy competitive advantages; it can be protected by tariffs; and it places least strain on the balance of payments.

The manufacturers most likely to succeed are first of all the industries processing agricultural products and metals. 'Basic materials which a country exports in crude form should be exported as far as possible in processed form. Here is one type of industrialisation that is not in any way dependent on internal markets.' It is also a good way of earning more foreign exchange. 'Secondly, consumer goods manufactures with a fairly sizeable internal market that do not require a very high or complex technology.' Substituting for imported products, these industries will eventually save foreign exchange. They have a powerful multiplying effect on the economy. They are a good way of introducing industrial training and techniques; and industries which have first trained their muscles in the home market get fit to compete for export business later.

'A country is much more likely', an economist suggested,

to develop an industry efficient enough to be able to export, if it has a sizeable home market . . . To become efficient an industry needs to reach a certain level of activity. It needs experience. It has to exploit economies of scale. All these are most easily achieved first in the domestic market. The simpler textiles are a good starter for these reasons. All over the world the process has usually started with local cotton and textile manufactures. The machines have to be imported, it is true; but the trained men to operate them do not require such a high degree of skill as, say, those required for an engineering or chemical industry. Later, when we think of moving into those industries, the same principle applies. The simpler processes should be introduced first. Instead of buying the completed motor car abroad, you import the parts and assemble them at home. When you have trained men and managers to do that, you can gradually introduce the manufacture of more and more of the parts – and so on.

Though manufacturing for the home market at first was stressed, we did not thereby exclude planning them from the beginning to export a proportion of their output abroad. What we doubted was the wisdom of developing manufactures which rely mainly on export markets in the early stages of development. The consensus for beginning with processing and import-substituting manufactures mainly for the home market, was a victory for those who stressed the agricultural drive in industrialisation. It was not conceded by the more radical industrialisers who felt that their opponents were too pessimistic about export possibilities. The home market, moreover, is not necessarily limited to the buying power of the agricultural sector. Cannot the industrial sector provide its own market and sell its manufactures mainly to itself? Certainly this is possible – once industrialisation has gone far enough. In Asia perhaps that point is now within reach; in Africa, it is for most countries much further away; but in Zambia for example, it may be nearer than elsewhere.

Obviously the possibilities for manufacturing differ from country to country, according to its existing industrial base, the size of its home market, its raw materials and trained manpower.

The order in which the various branches of industry can be introduced will also vary. In Africa, the size of the home market covers a wide range. Much more buying power for example is to be found in west, than in east Africa. Eleven countries have a population of less than two million, twenty-two less than five million and there is only one, Nigeria, with fifty-five million. It may be economic to equip every one of them with a textile mill and some processing plants. Even with regional markets in mind, it would be wildly uneconomic to set up a steel mill, a cement factory and a petro-chemical plant in each of them now. On the other hand in Nigeria, with its huge domestic market and raw materials, it may well be economic to develop some heavy industries as well as processing and consumer goods manufactures all at once.

'Catches' in the balance of payments

Import-substituting industries mainly for home markets is a more cautious prescription than some of us would have liked, but the balance of payments limitations even on this line of advance discourage higher ambition. There are many 'catches' here that could set back economic growth. Catch number one is simple. How do you earn enough foreign exchange to pay for the setting up of import-substituting industries that rely mainly on the home market, and so earn none themselves? You are unlikely at first to earn much from exports of manufactures to world markets; you may be able to save foreign exchange by buying and selling manufactures in a regional market, but you will not thereby earn more foreign exchange to buy the capital goods and know-how from the developed countries required for industrialisation. So you run into a balance of payments crisis that brings industrialisation to a halt, unless you can cover the import–export gap by other means: either with more foreign aid, or increased exports of agricultural staples. It is here on the balance of payments question, that the agricultural developers play their highest trump. Industrialisation is pinched most severely into the limits of agrarian production at this point. But can primary production be increased quickly enough when agricultural growth is so painfully slow, world prices uncertain and balance of payments crises strike fast? There is no other escape from catch number one, except into the arms of catch number two – the limits of foreign benevolence.

If developed countries were generous enough in a good cause to give preferences to developing countries' manufactures in a small part of their home markets, industrialisation of course need not be restricted by the expansion of agriculture. We were told that a mere 10 per cent share in rich countries' consumption of textiles would be a tremendous fillip to industrialisation in poor countries. Without preferences, their manufactured exports will not sell. Most of their industries at first cannot compete with foreign manufactures even in their own home markets, except behind tariff walls; and the more protected they are at home, the less they are able to compete abroad. So unhappily the new states are asking developed countries to give them preference in foreign markets at the same time as they are shutting their own markets to foreigners. The bulk of foreign aid moreover, is tied to the donor's exports. How long will it be before donor countries compensate for their loss of exports by cutting the amount of aid? It may happen long before most developing countries have reached take-off.

Catch number three is the depressing effect of badly inefficient industrialisation on the whole economy. Suppose a smallish country, regardless of the limitations already mentioned, puts its resources into indiscriminate manufacturing. Suppose it can borrow sufficient loans from well-wishers to set up all kinds of plants, whether there are markets or not, whether they are competitive or not. The more inefficient they are, the higher the tariff protection they need to survive against foreign imports; the more protected they are, the less able to compete in export markets they become. In order to keep them going, government subsidises the manufacturers to lower their prices and expand the home market; and subsidises the export of surpluses abroad at knock-down prices. By those subsidies in effect, the rest of the economy is taxed to support industry. But even subsidies cannot save wildly inefficient manufacturers from the penalties laid down by the ' dismal science '. Under the strain of subsidising too many of them too much, the entire economy slides into a depression from which it will not soon recover. But before this Ruritania has slithered very far it would have hit the inevitable balance of payments crisis, showing that indiscriminate industrialisation cannot pay. Worse than that, it sets back the cause of industrialisation itself.

This hypothetical road to ruin is simply a caricature of the difficulties that most countries have actually encountered when setting up import-substitute industries. As one eminent authority said:

The experience of all countries engaged in this policy has been that they are pretty soon confronted with a very acute balance of payments crisis. Imports rise. Exports are stagnant, and they become increasingly dependent on foreign assistance. Now this at first sight seems paradoxical because after all, the substitution of home for imported manufactures should have improved, not worsened the balance of payments. So it does; but not quickly enough, and not enough. What happens is that the new industrial activity raises national and personal incomes inside the country; and this in turn raises the total demand for imports to such a level that it more than cancels the savings on manufactured imports achieved by the new industries. So, as happened in many Latin American countries, import-substitution reduces the proportion of imports in total consumption but increases the total consumption so much that it increases imports absolutely.

Imports rise rapidly for three reasons: partly because the industrial machinery for construction, repair and maintenance has to be imported; partly because industrial raw materials and perhaps fuels have to be imported; and partly because there is an import element in rising standards of living.

At the same time in the early stages of industrialisation, developing countries are severely handicapped in expanding their exports to cover this rise in imports. This is because industry has to be subsidised – because the money costs of manufacturing are so much higher than the social cost. In effect a country that pursues import-substituting industrialisation creates an artificial internal price structure which is different from the world price structure; and this makes it very difficult for its manufacturers to compete in world markets. They find it hard because, while protected by high tariffs in the home market, their domestic costs are so much higher in relation to the rate of exchange and the prices of staple exports than those of their competitors.

Subsidies for manufacturers

These are some balance of payments difficulties which limit import-substituting industrialisation. They teased some of us into suggesting certain forms of subsidy to expand manufactured exports and so help pay for rising imports and debt charges. Ideally, from the balance of payments angle, the principle should be that a manufacture's exporting capacity ought to increase with the increased imports it needs for its development. One speaker qualified our stress on production for home markets thus:

My own thesis is that a country while developing industries mainly for the home market ought from the very beginning to aim at developing export markets as well . . . There are very bitter lessons to be learnt from the experience of countries such as Brazil, Argentine, Chile and many others, that have got into tremendous tangles because they have industrialised without succeeding in exporting enough of their manufactures. If they had developed their industries in such a way that their export capacity had risen *pari passu* with their import needs, they would have had a far healthier and sounder economic development.

A neat – possibly too neat – form of subsidy was suggested to help achieve this.

If a manufacture is only profitable on account of the protective duty laid on the foreign product, then the protected industry should receive an export subsidy equivalent in value to the import duty. If it is worth while from the country's point of view to give that industry tariff protection – which amounts to taxing the rest of the economy to give it a subsidy – then it is also worth while to subsidise its exports to the same extent. Moreover if that were done, then from the point of view of world markets, you would not get that distortion of price structure between manufactured goods and primary products which handicaps manufactured exports from developing countries so harshly.

A charge of 'dumping' was laid against this suggestion; and dumping could provoke counter-action from other countries. On the other hand, its advocate hoped that developing countries would be benevolent enough not to regard it as such.

The conference however did not dissent from three propositions about subsidies and tariffs to ease balance of payments and other difficulties in the early phases of industrialisation:

1. Government should consider subsidising, so as to compete at world prices, the export of surpluses produced by industries whose optimum working capacity is more than can be absorbed in the domestic market.
2. Subsidised prices for manufactures may be necessary and worthwhile to expand internal demand for them at first.
3. Some basic industries on a large scale can only be developed on a regional basis, for example in West Africa. They could be encouraged by a three-tier differential tariff on manufactured goods; the lowest rate would apply to goods manufactured within the region; the medium rates to manufactures from countries with special relations with the regional partners; and the maximum rate against imports from all other countries.

Does industrialisation depend on increased agricultural exports?

The best of economic arguments seem to go round in a circle and the conference's argument so far is no exception. We had concluded that import-substitute industries mainly for home markets were the best bets for most developing countries at this stage. We had been told that this policy usually runs straight into catch number one – balance of payments crisis; and the intrinsic difficulties facing manufactured exports in world markets had become plain. How then are developing countries going to pay for the rapidly increasing imports they require to industrialise? Manufactured exports cannot do much for some time to come. Foreign aid will pay for some, but not all of them, and much foreign aid has to be repaid eventually. Manufactured exports to regional markets will not earn much foreign exchange for purchases in developed countries. So primary exports must be increased to fill the gap. We are thrust back to square one with those who argue that the agricultural horse must be strengthened to pull the industrial cart – this time out of balance of payments difficulties. Like the 1963 conference we felt that agricultural exports would have to go on carrying the load in earning foreign exchange for industrialisation, as they have done in past decades.

There were the usual protests against this hard saying. What is the use of trying to expand primary exports when world prices are discouraging and part of the crops are left to rot unsaleable on the ground? The usual reply to the objection was sustained. World demand for most of them may be expected to rise in fits and starts as living standards rise in different parts of the world. Western Europe would drink a lot more coffee if revenue duties were reduced. Wool prices have risen 30 to 40 per cent over the past few years now that every Japanese can afford a woollen as well as a cotton suit. If every Russian ate one bar of chocolate a day, the world demand for cocoa would double. World markets for primary products are never saturated for long and in the past two years prices have been picking up again. And after all, an unsaleable surplus of steel or petro-chemicals will cost a developing economy far more in scarce capital and foreign exchange than an unsaleable surplus of cocoa, groundnuts or palm oil. For Africa and Asia to escape from catch number one – balance of payments difficulties – the verdict went in favour of the agricultural developers.

Regional industries for regional markets
Although in the short term regional arrangements cannot be expected to solve the problem of earning enough foreign exchange for industrialisation, they will in the long term provide the markets for manufactured exports which developing countries need. They must feed increasingly on each other's markets, so long as they cannot compete in world markets. To develop regional markets for manufactures and to develop regional industries to supply them therefore, seems to be a must.

Most small countries will obviously not get very far with industrialisation without joining some larger economic group. Their internal resources and buying power are too limited in narrowly national terms. This is true of many West Indian islands. It is also true of most African states – so much so that the Economic Commission for that continent considers regional cooperation to be prerequisite to its industrialisation.

Regional partnerships obviously enlarge markets for manufactures, making it possible to set up large-scale, basic industries which for any single country would be uneconomic and could not otherwise be introduced at all. Regional industrialisation means more manufactures and swifter growth; it also means more efficiency. One large plant for a region in some branches of manufacturing, though not in all, produces more at less cost than several small works, each serving one country. The gain is in economies of scale in operation, servicing and maintenance, in savings of skilled manpower, communications and many other things. Regional partnerships may also save scarce capital. One or two large and efficient plants may take less of it than many smaller enterprises scattered about haphazardly. The advantages are plain enough, but here the argument runs into catch number four – national interests standing in the way of industries for regions. Part at least of these economic advantages may have to be sacrificed to make regional arrangements politically practicable.

A vivid impression of the political difficulties facing the regional planner is given in this extract from one of our study-group's working papers:

Location of industry – regional

Approach – for each branch of manufacture:

(a) Calculate size of market as against economies of scale in each member state.

(b) Calculate regional market on existing consumption per head.

(c) Project five years ahead and calculate demand on that base.

(d) Prepare feasibility studies, including several optimum sites for a portfolio of industries.

(e) Leave negotiations as to siting of industries to member governments – political horsetrading.

Snags:

(a) Any project must be politically viable.

(b) To what extent within the region is neglect of less promising areas politically acceptable?

(c) Is the cost of the site with the highest comparative advantages worth the political cost of neglecting other possible locations?

The criterion of comparative economic advantage is not so important in the siting as

1. Getting the project under way:

(a) to forestall the growth of opposing local vested interests;

(b) in view of the long time period before projects begin production;

(c) to anchor member governments' commitment.

2. Setting the correct scale for each industry.

3. Selecting the most advanced technology for each industry.

Politics at odds with economics has rarely been so breathlessly defined in terms of planning procedure!

Industries for regions are a forlorn hope unless the common political will to coordinate development and share its profits is there. To negotiate and work a regional partnership requires give and take between member governments; and they normally feel that they are giving much and taking little. So they often are, particularly when the partners are too unequal in wealth, resources and stage of development. Not even the magic of a regional market will turn Cinderellas into princesses. Industry tends to concentrate inevitably in the most economically favoured parts of a region, in one or two countries, neglecting the rest. It will often advance one member's development at the others' expense; and the losers contribute, perhaps in reduced revenue, increased import prices, disturbance of trade and losses of population, all to no apparent national advantage. Xenophobic fears of domination breed easily in these circumstances and prevent or corrode regional arrangements. Long-term interests of the region as a whole are blocked by short-run national interests. Stresses of this sort are wracking the East, as they have already helped to wreck the Central African commercial association.

If the will is nevertheless there, something can be done to ease the strains. Weaker brethren may be compensated financially for losses of revenue. Those that receive less than their fair share of manufactures may be mollified with more generous grants for other purposes from a regional development fund supplied by the profits of regional industry. They may also share in capital gains and profits by investing in regional industries. Palliatives such as these help but they smack too much of hand-outs and will not usually be enough to make up for lack of industries.

Industrial planning for a region therefore must temper the economics of comparative manufacturing advantage with the politics of something like fair shares for all, if it is to be at all acceptable. Efficiency in manufacturing and marketing will often have to be sacrificed for the sake of distributing industries between countries more fairly. There are of course strict economic limitations on the extent to which this can be done. If the object were simply to achieve the quickest industrial growth and no more, industry should probably be allowed to concentrate on existing sites. What most of us had in mind, however, is not only efficient industries, but industries to stimulate the agrarian economy; and for this purpose, as well as to avoid mutual resentment between partners, industries should be distributed as widely as possible throughout a region. Obviously the balance of advantage between swifter industrial progress and stimulus to agriculture, between concentrating and dispersing manufacturing will differ from region to region.

The short-run difficulties of organising regional industries for regional markets may be formidable; but in the long run they can make all the partners wealthier more quickly than could a set of individual national attempts at the task. The choice for small, developing countries indeed is between a tiny amount of industrial development on national lines indefinitely, and a share in regional industrialisation – in a much larger concern with far better prospects of economic growth all round.

Types of regional organisation

Regional development may be organised in many different forms, varying greatly in the extent of economic and political integration that each requires, and Common markets, like the European Economic Community and the Central American Common Market, are by far the tightest. But there are many looser and more flexible arrangements, such as the European, and the Latin American, free-trade associations, and others, in which member countries exchange preferences over a wide field of trade and plan regional development together. More flexible still, countries in a region may make trade agreements and other *ad hoc* arrangements to fix tariffs and quotas mutually.

The more closely-knit the arrangement, the more powers have to be transferred from national to regional authority; the more give and take is required between partners; the more it will tend to work to the disadvantage of weaker members. On the other hand, the greater will be the political appeal, and the attraction to investors, assured of the permanence of the regional market. It was not our business to discuss the relative merits of these possibilities for any one region, but some points were impressed upon us. Regional organisation at first need not be more than an *ad hoc* system of preferences for manufactures and raw materials. These should not be all that difficult to achieve and they would speed up industrialisation immensely. We do not have to wait for the millenium of a full-scale common market in order to begin regional cooperation. Secondly, ' Member governments have to agree together upon the sharing and location of regional industry, and be prepared to sacrifice a degree of economic efficiency to reach agreement, if regional arrangements are to be politically viable.' Tribute was paid to the international agencies, like E.C.A., E.C.L.A., and E.C.A.F.E., for their technical studies and advice on planning regional associations. Lastly, the potential regional markets will never be realised unless regional communications are developed. Existing links join each developing country to the industrial economy of its former colonial ruler, not to its neighbours. A massive investment in regional communications is therefore required to create regional markets for regional industries.

Location of industries

' Unless governments attempt to control the location of industry, manufacturing tends to concentrate in one or two urban centres within each country (except when location is determined by the supply of a particular raw material – e.g. sugar milling, cotton ginning, etc.). In extreme cases (e.g. India) this leads to the creation of very large urban concentrations. Is this a good thing, or should there be a deliberate policy of dispersing industry more widely? '

Advantages of concentrating industry

' The establishment of a number of industries in one centre can lead to " external economies ". For example, there can be a local pool of skilled manpower; industrial servicing facilities can be supplied; there can be economies in the supply of infrastructure services (power, water, communications). Cities are places where an exchange of ideas can occur and where there is the steady fertilisation of new concepts and thoughts. Industrialisation, especially in developing countries depends on innovation, and this may be easier to achieve in cities than in rural areas. On the whole, industrial entrepreneurs (or their wives) prefer to live in cities rather than in rural areas.'

Advantages of dispersing industry

'Underdeveloped economies tend to be "dual economies", in which a small advanced sector co-exists with a large backward sector. As a result, the benefits of development are confined to a narrow section of the community. Clearly this dual feature will be accentuated if industrial development is concentrated in one or two centres. Moreover, these concentrations can lead to the depopulation of areas which, for various reasons, have not benefited from development.

The establishment of very large urban areas involves heavy social costs (e.g. transport, an increase in crime, etc.) which are not experienced to the same degree in smaller centres. Sometimes it may be economic to develop new centres rather than to expand existing towns.

The larger the numbers in a city, the greater distances its food and supplies must travel. In a large country with poor communications this involves high costs, and the benefits of industrial development to the rural population in outlying areas in providing an increased market for their foodstuffs can be reduced by this cost of transport. In such circumstances, an industrial centre may find it cheaper to rely on imported foodstuffs even though outlying areas of the country may have the potential to increase food production. If, however, industries are established within reasonable reach of the food-producing areas, this can stimulate agriculture by increasing local markets for foodstuffs.'

Concentration versus dispersal

'The answer depends on the stage of development of the economy. A country which is just starting to industrialise may well find it economic to concentrate the bulk of its industries in one or two centres. The provision of services over a number of centres would probably be uneconomic, and the attempt to disperse industry prematurely could well discourage industrial development and waste scarce resources.

But for other countries a range of possibilities exists. These may be listed as:

(*a*) "*Megapolis.*"
(*b*) Other large industrial centres.
(*c*) Smaller (dispersed) industrial centres.
(*d*) Rural and craft industries.

It was generally agreed that (*a*) is undesirable, but is hardly an immediate problem in most African countries; (*d*) has its place in industrial development programmes, but this is likely to be limited in view of the high price and specialised markets of many of its products. The effective choice, then, lies between (*b*) and (*c*).

There was some feeling in favour of (*c*), on condition that the industrial centres so established were large enough to be economically viable (e.g. could provide external economies and make the provision of infrastructure services worthwhile). Such a policy of moderate dispersal could increase the impact of industrialisation on the rest of the economy (e.g. provision of local markets, use of local raw materials, local labour, etc.).

The first need is for governments to assess the potential for industrial development in different parts of the country, and to decide where to build up industrial centres, according to the advantages of the places considered (e.g. access to markets, supply of water, communications, etc.). There is no case for trying to build up industrial centres in unfavourably situated places, but it may well be that, within any particular country, there are a few places whose advantages are not substantially less than those of the centre to which industry would naturally go without government interference.

Government measures to promote industry in the centres it selects include :

(*a*) the provision of communications and other infrastructure services;

(*b*) the building of industrial estates, possibly including the construction of factories for letting or sale on mortgage;

(*c*) tax advantages for firms going to selected areas (possibly taxing industrialists according to social cost of location);

(*d*) channelling investment applications through a government body, which approves only if the firm concerned is willing to accept government's location;

(*e*) where government (or a government-controlled body) is a participant in the enterprise concerned, there is more effective control over location. There is, however, a danger here that industries may be located in unsuitable places for political reasons;

(*f*) the location of technical training institutions at the proposed industrial centres.

In general, we considered that some movement of people from the rural areas into towns is inevitable and not wholly undesirable. It is possible to sentimentalise rural life. But at the same time it should be possible for developing countries to avoid some of the worst excesses of urban development such as are to be found in Western countries and India. Urban drift is partly the result of the lack of many basic amenities in the rural areas, and any serious policy to arrest it must tackle the development of the countryside on a large scale. But resources are limited and the rate of rural advance may well be slower than governments hope. Planning in most countries must assume that more people will come to the towns; to attempt to stop the flow would in many cases be fruitless and merely have the effect of perpetuating poverty and under-employment in the rural areas.'

7 · Industrialisation through 'Intermediate Technology'
E. F. SCHUMACHER[1]

An immediate cause of much misery and frustration in many developing countries is undoubtedly unemployment, particularly in rural areas. This generally gives rise to mass migration into metropolitan areas. It is possible to speak of a 'process of mutual poisoning'. The establishment of modern industry in a few metropolitan areas tends to kill off competing types of traditional production throughout the countryside, thus causing widespread unemployment or under-employment. The countryside thereupon takes its revenge by mass migration into the metropolitan areas, causing them to grow to a totally unmanageable size.

Current forecasts on the growth of metropolitan areas in the developing countries suggest that few people expect this destructive process of mutual poisoning to be stopped or mitigated. Very few people indeed appear to expect that even the most ambitious 'rates of economic growth' could suffice to cope with the problem of unemployment during the foreseeable future, exacerbated as this problem is by the so-called population explosion. Fifteen and even twenty-five year 'perspective plans' have been published in various developing countries which appear to hold out no hope of economic integration for the majority of people in those countries. In fact, the longer the forecast, the more desperate the situation appears to become, with towns growing to a size of 20, 40, and even 60 million inhabitants, a prospect of 'immiseration' for multitudes of people that beggars the imagination.

It may be mentioned in passing that the trend towards 'megalopolis', towards vast conurbations, coupled with the denudation of the countryside, has recently been recognised as a serious problem even in the most highly developed countries, such as the United States, Britain, France, and Italy. These countries may be able to shoulder the colossal economic burdens arising therefrom, although the question remains whether developments of this kind really represent a rational and desirable employment of economic wealth. Whether or not the economy and the social fabric of the wealthy countries can carry these burdens, it seems abundantly certain that the developing countries cannot recover economic health along this road. No doubt, national incomes can grow and will continue to grow; but statistics of this kind do not necessarily signify a nation's 'standard of life': they may merely give evidence of its rising 'cost of subsistence'. It is undeniable that a man's 'cost of subsistence' rises significantly the moment he moves from a rural area into a big town where he becomes dependent upon a multitude of costly public services which the rural environment provides free of charge.

'Economic growth', a purely quantitative concept without any qualitative determination, cannot be accepted as a rational objective of policy. The problem is how to obtain healthy growth. Experience shows that there are types of economic growth which spell increasing misery for ever more people and destroy all social cohesion. Many developing countries already suffer from internal economic divisions which are euphemistically called the 'dual economy', where there are in fact two different patterns of living as widely separated from one another as two different worlds. It is not a question of some people being rich and others being poor, both being united by a common way of life: it is a question of two ways of life existing side by side in such a manner that even the humblest member of the one disposes of a daily income which is a high multiple of the income accruing to even the hardest working member of the other. The social tensions arising from the 'dual economy' are today evident in many, if not all, of the developing countries.

Again in passing, it may be mentioned that tendencies in this direction are recognisable even in the 'richest country in the world', the United States, which have moved President Johnson to declare a 'War on Poverty' to rescue from misery some 38 million Americans. It appears therefore that immensely strong forces of a disruptive kind are being let loose by certain modern developments of the economy. America may deploy massive wealth to cope with them; but how are the developing countries to master them without massive wealth?

The experts rarely refer to the twin evils of mass unemployment and mass migration into towns in the developing countries. When they do so, they merely deplore them and treat them as 'transitional'. Yet there is no evidence at all that time alone will be the great healer. In case after case unemployment is greater at the end of a Five-Year Plan than it had been at the beginning. India is a case in point, and so is Turkey. Developing countries 'cannot include the goal of full employment among their immediate planning targets', says a recent study published in the International Labour Review. They cannot, so it is argued, because they are short of capital. As they cannot conquer unemployment, so they cannot conquer mass migration, and as their towns grow to an ever more monstrous size they tend to absorb what little capital there is just to maintain more people in misery.

There is need, it seems, for some fresh thinking. It might help to remember certain fundamental truths, such as the undeniable fact that 'capital' consists primarily of tools and machines, the purpose of which is to save work, or to lighten it, or to enable people to accomplish more through it. A lack of capital, therefore, should not mean less, but on the contrary, more work for people – more work, albeit less productive work. Even work of low productivity is more productive than no work at all. Why should we accept that 'lack of capital' makes unemployment inevitable? Lack of capital today means lack of modern machinery. Was there mass unemployment before the advent of modern machinery? Was there a mass flight from the land in the now-developed countries before the industrial revolution? To pose these questions does not mean to solve the problem as it faces us today, but it may help to make a constructive solution visible.

It would seem that the primary task of the developing countries – and also of the givers of foreign aid – is to go straight into battle with the twin evils of mass unemployment and mass migration into cities. This means:

first, that workplaces have to be created in the areas where the people are living now, and not primarily in metropolitan areas into which they tend to migrate;

secondly, that these workplaces must be, on average, cheap enough so that they can be created in large numbers without this calling for an unattainable level of savings and imports;

thirdly, that the production methods employed must be relatively simple, so that the demands for high skills are minimised, not only in the production process itself but also in matters of organisation, raw material supply, financing, marketing, and so forth; and

fourthly, that production should be largely from local materials for local use.

These four requirements can be met only (*a*) if there is a 'regional approach' to development, and (*b*) if there is a conscious effort to develop what might be called an 'intermediate technology'.

A given political unit is not necessarily of the right size as a unit for economic development. If vast and expensive population movements are to be avoided, each 'district' with a substantial population needs its own development. To take a familiar example, Sicily does not develop merely because Italian industry, concentrated mainly in the north of the country, is achieving high rates of economic growth. On the contrary, the developments in the north of Italy tend to increase the problem of Sicily through their very success, by competing Sicilian production out of existence and draining all talented and enterprising men out of Sicily. If no conscious efforts are made to counteract these tendencies in some way, success in the north spells ruination in the south with the result that mass unemployment in Sicily forces the population into mass migration. Similar examples could be quoted from all over the world. Special cases apart, any 'district' within a country, if it is being by-passed by 'development', will inevitably fall into mass unemployment, which will sooner or later drive the people out.

In this matter it is not possible to give hard and fast definitions. Much depends on geography and local circumstances. A few thousand people, no doubt, would be too few to constitute a 'district' for economic development. But a community of a few hundred thousand people, even if fairly widely scattered, may well deserve to be treated as a development district. The whole of Switzerland has less than six million inhabitants; yet it is divided into more than twenty 'cantons', and each 'canton' is a kind of development district, with the result that the tendency towards the formation of vast industrial concentrations is minimised.

Each 'district', ideally speaking, would have some sort of inner cohesion and identity and possess at least one town to serve as the district centre. While every village would have a primary school, there would be a few small market towns with secondary schools, and the district centre would be big enough to carry an institution of higher learning. There is need for a 'cultural structure', just as there is need for an 'economic structure' within any country, be it even so small as Switzerland. This need for internal 'structures' is of course particularly urgent in large countries, such as India. Unless every district of India is made the object of development efforts, so to say: for its own sake and in its own right, all development will concentrate in a few places with devastating results for the country as a whole.

It is obvious that this 'regional' or 'district' approach has no chance of success unless it is based on the employment of a suitable technology. We have already alluded to the disruptive forces, stemming from modern technology, which are making themselves felt even in the most highly industrialised countries today. The trend to 'megalopolis', noticeable all over the world, is simply the effect of modern technology, in transport as well as in industrial production, which lives under the law of 'nothing succeeds like success'. Unfortunately, the inevitable concomitant of this law is its opposite: 'Nothing fails like failure', and this gives rise to the twin evils of unemployment and mass migration in the developing countries. The only chance of counteracting these baneful laws would seem to be the conscious development of an 'intermediate technology'.

Here again, it is not possible to arrive at any simple and clear-cut definition. 'Intermediate technology' must be appropriate to the country in question. It is surely an astonishing error to assume that the technology developed in the West is necessarily appropriate to the developing countries. Granted that their technological backwardness is an important reason for their poverty; granted, too, that their traditional methods of production, in their present condition of decay, lack essential viability: it by no means follows that the technology of the richest countries is necessarily suitable for the advancement of the poor. It must never be forgotten that modern technology is the product of the countries which are 'long' in capital and 'short' in labour, and that its main purpose, abundantly demonstrated by the trend towards automation, is to substitute machines for men. How could this technology fit the conditions of countries which suffer from a surplus of labour and a shortage of machines?

If we define the level of technology in terms of 'equipment cost per workplace', we can call the indigenous technology of a typical developing country (symbolically speaking) a £1-technology while that of the modern West could be called a £1,000-technology. The current attempt of the developing countries, supported by foreign aid, to infiltrate the £1,000-technology into their economies inevitably kills off the £1-technology at an alarming rate, destroying traditional workplaces at a much faster rate than modern workplaces can be created and producing the 'dual economy' with its attendant evils of mass unemployment and mass migration. The gap between these two technologies is so enormous that a tolerably smooth transition from the one to the other is simply impossible, even if it were desirable.

It is obvious that the high average income of the developed countries derives primarily from the high level of capitalisation of the average workplace. But the development planners appear to overlook the equally obvious fact that such a high level of capital per workplace itself presupposes the existence of a high level of income. 'Income per man' and 'capital per workplace' stand in an organic relationship to each other, a relationship that can be 'stretched' to some extent – for instance with the help of foreign aid – but cannot be disregarded. The average annual income per worker and the average capital per workplace in the developed countries appear to stand in a relationship of roughly 1 : 1. This implies, in general terms, that it takes one man-year to create one workplace, or that a man would have to save one month's earnings a year for twelve years to be able to buy his own workplace. If the relationship were 1 : 10, it would require ten man-years to create one workplace, and a man would have to save a month's earnings a year for 120 years before he could make himself independent. This, of course, is an impossibility, and it follows that the £1,000-technology transplanted into a country the bulk of which is stuck on the level of a £1-technology simply cannot spread by any process of normal growth. It cannot have a positive 'demonstration effect'; on the contrary – as can be observed all over the world – its 'demonstration effect' is wholly negative. The vast majority of people, to whom the £1,000-technology is totally inaccessible, simply 'give up', while there remain small 'islands' of an alien world which can in no way blend into the economy as a whole, and the extra income generated by these 'islands' is immediately absorbed by the cost arising from mass migration.

It is of course admitted that there are certain sectors and localities in every developing country which are irrevocably committed to the employment of the most advanced technology available in the world. In a typical developing country, these would account for perhaps 15 per cent of the population, and as there is no possibility of putting the clock back they will continue to exist. The question is what is to become of the other 85 per cent of the population. Simply to assume that the 'modern' sectors and localities will grow until they account for the whole is utterly unrealistic, for the reasons given. The task is to re-establish a healthy basis of existence for these other 85 per cent by means of an 'intermediate technology' which would be vastly superior in productivity to their traditional technology (in its present state of decay), while at the same time being vastly cheaper and simpler than the highly sophisticated and enormously capital-intensive technology of the West. As a general guide it may be said that this 'intermediate technology' should be on the level of £70–£100 equipment cost per average workplace. At this level, it would stand in a tolerably realistic relationship to the annual income obtainable by an able worker outside the westernised sectors.

These few indications must suffice, as space does not permit me to deal with the matter in the detail which it certainly would deserve. The question now to be considered is whether the development of such an 'intermediate technology' is realistically possible. It is unfortunately the case that many people are totally unable to imagine anything they are not already used to. There are countless development 'experts' who cannot even conceive the possibility of any industrial production unless all the paraphernalia of the Western way of life are provided in advance. The 'basis of everything', they say, is of course electricity, steel, cement, near-perfect organisation, sophisticated accountancy (preferably with computers), not to mention a most elaborate 'infrastructure' of transport and other public services worthy of an affluent society. Gigantic projects to provide this 'base' form the hard core of 'development plans' the world over. They are, of course, fairly easily arranged and carried out with the help of foreign aid and foreign contractors. This mentality, one is bound to insist, is perhaps the most destructive force operating in the developing countries today. In the blind pursuit of an in itself highly questionable utopia, these 'experts' tend to neglect everything that is realistically possible. More than that, unfortunately, they denounce and ridicule every approach which relies on the employment and utilisation of humbler means.

It is, none the less, precisely in these humbler means that the only hope for real progress appears to lie. The countries counting as 'developed' today attained a fair level of general wealth long before the Industrial Revolution – a level far higher than that of the developing countries today. They did this without electricity, steel, cement, computers, or an elaborate 'infrastructure'. Apart from the direct effects of war, pestilence, or occasional famines, they never had any appreciable part of their populations living in the kind of misery which is now the fate of countless millions the world over. Poverty, of course, has always been the lot of the majority of mankind: but misery, a helpless condition of utter degradation, as a permanent feature of life in town and country, associated with and promoted by the twin evils of unemployment and limitless urbanisation – this is a new phenomenon in the history of mankind, the direct result of modern technology thoughtlessly applied.

The 'intermediate technology' will not reject any, not even the most modern, devices, but it equally does not depend on them. It will use whatever is handy, insisting only on one thing: that the average equipment per workplace should not cost more than something of the order of £100. This is an average to be applied to every ordinary process of production, leaving out those special sectors, already mentioned, which are irrevocably committed to the Western way of life. On the basis of this stipulation any competent engineering firm can get to work and design the appropriate implements and methods to convert (mainly) local materials into useful goods for (mainly) local use. The types of industry to be tackled immediately would be

    (*a*) every kind of consumers' goods industry, including building and building materials;

    (*b*) agricultural implements;

    (*c*) equipment for 'intermediate technology' industries.

It is only when, so to say, the circle is closed, so that, on the whole, the people are able to make their own tools and other equipment, that genuine economic development can take place. In a healthy society which employs an appropriate technology the argument that unemployment cannot be conquered for want of capital could never be true, because there would always be the possibility of turning unused labour to the production of capital goods.

Design studies for a small number of production processes on the suggested basis have already been made in India, with proper cost and price calculations. They relate to agricultural implements, food processing, and various consumer goods. The results, as a matter of fact, are nothing short of sensational. The products of 'intermediate technology' are found to be fully competitive with those of Western technology. The modern prejudice that the best equipment is the best, irrespective of circumstances, is shown up – as might have been expected – as a gross error. It is the circumstances that decide what is best, and it is the principal task of every developing country to apply a technology that is really appropriate to its circumstances. That a technology devised primarily for the purpose of saving labour should be inappropriate in a country troubled with a vast labour surplus could hardly be called surprising.

A remark of a general nature may be fitting at this point. It is generally assumed that the achievement of Western science, pure and applied, lies mainly in the apparatus and machinery that have been developed from it, and that a rejection of the apparatus and machinery would be tantamount to a rejection of science. This is an excessively superficial view. The real achievement lies in the accumulation of knowledge of principles. These principles can be applied in a great variety of ways, of which the current application in Western industry is only one. The development of an 'intermediate technology', therefore, does not mean a return to an outdated system, something that is a mere 'second best'. On the contrary, it means a genuine forward movement into new territory: that some fundamental rethinking of the applications of modern science will be necessary before long is being recognised today even in the West. There are many 'neuralgic points' which can already be identified without difficulty, where further technological developments in the established direction are certain to produce 'negative returns' – motor traffic in cities is merely the most obvious case in point. Only slightly less obvious, albeit more controversial, is the critical situation that may develop during the next twenty years or so on account of the steep and accelerating rise in world energy demands. Developing countries which are committing themselves in their forward thinking to the wholesale adoption of present-day Western technology might do well to undertake a study of their long-term energy needs and consider the likelihood or otherwise of these needs being met. Industrialisation as conceived by the majority of development 'experts' is in any case like a long, dark tunnel; they believe that a marvellous light will be found at the end, no matter how long it takes to reach it. But if energy supplies should become a limiting factor, one might get stuck in the middle of the tunnel where it is very dark indeed.

However that may be, the case for 'intermediate technology' rests on the solid basis that there is no other means of fighting the twin evils of mass unemployment and mass migration in the developing countries. It also is the only way by which these countries can achieve genuine economic independence and recover the kind of social cohesion which the dual economy is in the process of destroying. It should not be assumed that the development of 'intermediate technology' is a task of exceptional difficulty. On the technical side, there exists already a wealth of usable material; but it is extremely widely scattered and needs to be brought together. In India, for instance, the Khadi Commission and a multitude of other organisations have been working on this very subject, although perhaps in a somewhat half-hearted way. The primary lack, it would seem, has been of down-to-earth business sense. This is not surprising, because in most cases the immediate need seemed to be to protect and keep alive the activities of helpless people who, without protection, would have become utterly destitute. The spirit of protection is rarely one conducive to enterprising business management.

But 'intermediate technology' is not in this sense protectionist. It is not concerned with keeping alive activities which lack essential viability: it is concerned with creating a new viability. The question has been raised whether this 'intermediate technology' is to be attained by upgrading the traditional technology or by downgrading Western technology. Either of these approaches may be feasible in some cases; but it is more likely that a new approach would be more promising: a new design derived from a sound knowledge of basic principles and conceived as a business venture. The kind of talent needed for this approach is available in many countries; the price of employing it would be merely a small fraction of the money now poured out on giant schemes which, even if successful, cannot lead to a real mitigation of the misery caused by mass unemployment and mass migration into cities.

Finally, a word might be said about raw material supplies. The 'intermediate technology' is of course far less sensitive to the quality of raw materials than a more sophisticated technology. As mentioned already, it will have to rely mainly on local materials, and these will be just the same as those on which all pre-industrial generations have had to rely. It is a remarkable fact how much of the traditional knowledge of local materials has been lost during the last two or three generations. People will have to learn again that it is possible to have a highly productive agriculture by means of 'green manure' and other organic methods and that chemical fertilisers may not be the real answer at all. They will have to remember how their forefathers built without modern cement and yet extremely durably; how much they relied on trees, not merely for the supply of food and materials but also for the improvement of soil and climate. With the help of modern knowledge they should now be able to do even better in these respects than their forefathers did. Tree planting, indeed, deserves to be singled out for special emphasis in this context, because the world is full of cases where the neglect of trees is one of the chief causes of misery and helplessness, while the recovery of a realistic sense of man's dependence on trees would be a most fruitful move in the right direction. No high technology or foreign aid is needed for planting and looking after trees; every able-bodied person can make his contribution and benefit from it; a wide range of useful materials can be obtained from trees – some species being very fast growers in tropical and semi-tropical climates – and these materials lend themselves exceptionally well for utilisation by 'intermediate technology'. Yet there are few developing countries where trees do not suffer from heedless neglect. (To mention only one significant example, the half-term report on India's Third Five-Year Plan shows that it is precisely the planned activity in forestry which is most seriously behind schedule.) In most places there is no excuse for any alleged shortages of building materials. The planning experts should study how much has been built without modern cement throughout the ages.

The idea of 'intermediate technology', since it was formulated two years ago, has attracted a good deal of attention in many developing countries. Highly important work has been done at the S.I.E.T. Institute at Hyderabad, and the Indian Planning Commission held a seminar on 'Intermediate Technologies' at that Institute in January, 1964. One of the papers submitted came from Professor D. R. Gadgil, the doyen of Indian economists, and some passages from it may form a fitting conclusion to this paper:

Everything [he says] thus points to the desirability, nay, urgency, of initiating widespread industrial development in all regions of the country which will prevent accentuation of dualistic features within the economy and make for concerted and uniform economic progress . . . The scientists and the technicians must be made fully aware of what is expected out of the adoption of 'intermediate technology'. Their efforts must be directed towards the selection and development of those techniques which can serve the given aims . . . The process of evolving and adopting intermediate technology is a dynamic process which should be the centre of interest of the plan of industrialisation of the country. It should claim the attention, in an important way, of the ablest scientists and technicians in the country, and planning in relation to it should be undertaken through integrated planning of whole aspects and fields of industrial development.

Foreign aid will be fruitful, instead of destructive, only if it recognises these paramount needs and makes Western intellectual resources available to serve them. In closing, it might be mentioned that the United Kingdom is well placed to give assistance of the right kind. Its 'Rural Industries Bureau', for instance, established some forty years ago, may have only a minor role to play within the British economy, but it has a fund of accumulated experience (and literature) which could be invaluable for the developing countries. Similar organisations exist in many other countries. What is immediately needed is a concerted effort of design.

8 · Technology, Employment and Culture[1]
CAMBRIDGE CONFERENCE REPORT

Bold though he would be who suggested it, the whole idea of planning economic development rests on partly false assumptions. To be aware of them is the best insurance against losing faith in its possibilities altogether. Economists, like other social scientists, abstract a single aspect of society and tend to assume thereafter that all others are included or determined in it.

Yet everybody knows that man is a political and social, as well as an
economic, animal, that the part is not the whole, and that the whole is
more than the sum of parts. Economics is not the whole story and economic
models are not the real thing.

Industrialisation has been looked at hitherto as a short cut to economic
growth, to raising national income statistics. We were challenged now to
consider it from the standpoint of giving people full employment, of making
them happier, wiser, better. After all, development planning is also about
people, and the question here is: what are the costs to society of setting
up one or two monstrous bastions of industrial technology in the midst of
traditional, agrarian societies? It was asserted that the costs are mass unemployment, mass misery in cities, the gutting of agrarian communities and
the disruption of entire societies – and that they are not worth it. Others,
especially from Muslim countries, are anxious to count the cultural
costs of industrialisation. How much of tradition and religion has to be
sacrificed to Mammon? How much do Africans and Asians need – how
much are they willing to alter their national personalities for the sake of
industry? What shall it profit them if they lose their own souls? Or can
modern technology and economic institutions be grafted on to native traditions? All these far-reaching problems crowded in at once when Dr Schumacher pleaded against concentration of manufactures using advanced
technology in big cities, and advocated instead a humbler concept of industrialisation, using 'Intermediate' technologies, dispersed throughout the
countryside to give new economic life to agrarian communities.

The case for this thesis is disquieting enough. Urban unemployment is
already acute – in Asia, due to population supersaturating the land, in
Africa, due to the swollen streams of school-leavers supersaturating jobs
in the modern sector. If we set up more large-scale manufactures using
advanced, labour-saving machinery, still more people will be drawn off
the land into the cities and, proportionately, there will be even fewer jobs
for them, and still greater numbers of unemployed. 'In case after case',
writes Dr Schumacher, 'unemployment is greater at the end of a Five-Year
plan than it [was] at the beginning. India is a case in point and so is
Turkey.' Statistics may show that national income has been raised: but
this does not necessarily mean that the national standard of living has
improved. Much of the rise reflects the increased cost of subsistence for
vast numbers of people who have moved into cities where they are dependent
upon a multitude of costly public services that the countryside used to provide free of charge. At this rate developing countries will never conquer unemployment. 'As their towns grow to an ever more monstrous size they tend
to absorb what little capital there is just to maintain more people in [urban]
misery.' The effects of advanced technology and urbanisation are equally
disastrous for the agrarian economy, according to Dr Schumacher. Rural

areas lose their younger, more enterprising, people to the cities; their traditional handicrafts are killed off by competition from modern industry, and unemployment spreads throughout the countryside. 'A process of mutual poisoning' is set off in which the agrarian economy decays while Megalopolis receives its people into unemployment.

His theory, from the standpoint of employment and social integration, is a version of interaction between industry and agriculture, alarmingly different from that reached from the viewpoint of economic growth. We had assumed, for example, that in drawing surplus population off the land, industrialisation would be a good thing for agrarian development in Asia; Dr Schumacher sees it as a disaster. We had supposed that industrialisation using modern techniques would speed agricultural development; Dr Schumacher presumes that it would kill it. The conference as a whole stuck to its thesis – and Dr Schumacher stuck to his! Most of us felt that it was wrong to blame the drift to the towns and urban unemployment entirely on advanced technology. For all kinds of other reasons it has always been difficult to 'keep 'em down on the farm, now that they've seen Paree', probably since the days of Sodom and Gomorrah. Given the fact that people insist on coming into towns and will not go back to the land, the more industry there is, the more employment for them there will be, though still more arrive to fill the unemployed ranks. But happily, while doubting Dr Schumacher's idea that advanced technology as such causes industrial and agrarian sectors to kill each other off, we did not throw away the main point wrapped up in it. Here he emerged as the agricultural developer *par excellence*. We had all complained about the painfully slow progress in agriculture and hoped that industry would stimulate quicker results. Dr Schumacher's enthusiasm for dispersed manufacturing, using intermediate technology to revitalise agrarian economies, suggested how this might be done.

THE CASE FOR INTERMEDIATE TECHNOLOGY

Modern technology is obviously designed to suit rich-country conditions of full employment, labour shortage and capital surplus. Does it make sense when imported into poor-country conditions of massive unemployment, labour surplus and capital shortage? On the face of it, the probability would seem to be that it does not. To quote Dr Schumacher:

If we define the level of technology in terms of 'equipment cost per workplace', we can call the indigenous technology of a typical developing country a £1-technology while that of the modern West could be called a £1,000-technology. The current attempt of the developing countries to infiltrate the £1,000-technology into their economies inevitably kills off the £1-technology at an alarming rate, destroying traditional workplaces at a much faster rate than modern workplaces can be created.

What is proposed instead is to design a special technology halfway between computer-automation and traditional handicrafts which uses much less capital and much more labour, more men and fewer or simpler machines than the production techniques used in developed countries. There is reason to believe that intermediate techniques of this kind will be feasible and efficient in some manufactures, although they may be impossible in others. They should in the main use local raw materials and produce for home markets. Although some were sceptical, the consensus was that intermediate technology has big possibilities and advantages. Simplified production methods should minimise industry's demand for highly skilled manpower. Lowered cost per workplace in industry should make it possible to create much more employment without calling for an unattainable level of savings and imports. More than that, these intermediate manufactures can be widely distributed throughout rural areas and help stem the costly immigration into cities, at the same time as they stimulate the development of agriculture. It is of course impossible now with so little experience to say exactly what importance should be attached to this comparatively new approach, and we were divided in our guesses; but at least it promises to help a good deal with the unemployment problem, save capital and speed up industrialisation.

Developing countries tend to feel that the most up-to-date machinery must always give the best rate of development, that anything simpler must be second best. It is emphatically not the case that intermediate techniques of manufacturing are necessarily less efficient than advanced methods. It may sometimes be just the reverse. In technical jargon, the simplified production may be the optimum technique, given the characteristics of the market, the factor availability and the state of skills. Where it is the optimum technique it will be cheaper in terms of social cost than any other production technique – though for reasons discussed later, it may not be cheaper in terms of cash costs to the manufacturer himself. Intermediate methods of production, moreover, may well prove competitive in some branches with capital-intensive industries in developed countries. It is not competition in highly-capitalised production that advanced countries fear, but production based on intensive use of lowly paid labour. Intermediate technology can be scaled upwards progressively into advanced technology as more capital becomes available. Developing countries could do better with their rate of industrialisation and all-round economic growth, if they avoided over-capitalising a few branches of manufacturing based on computer-automation, and used their capital so as to minimise the social cost of production and maximise the use of labour.

THE CASE AGAINST INTERMEDIATE TECHNOLOGY

Intermediate technology seems more likely than the advanced variety to bring about the reciprocal action of agriculture and industry which is the mainspring of development. It might be expected, therefore, that the whole conference was converted to it, and the agricultural developers especially. Many of them in fact were sceptical, a few opposed the idea entirely. Second best is obviously difficult to sell to developing countries; and in developed countries the notion is easily mistaken for a piece of romantic conservatism. Perhaps because they have lived in industrial cities longest and lost their peasant communities long ago, 'Anglo-Saxons' have been peculiarly prone to idealise and preserve peasant life in other countries. Reaction against this prejudice was not, however, the objectors' main ground. They accepted intermediate technique as a social welfare measure – as a policy of 'philanthropy plus five per cent' – but they doubted whether it would produce the five per cent which advanced technology certainly would. Would it in fact give a much slower rate of overall economic growth than advanced technology? If so, it was argued, it would also mean more unemployment and urban misery, not less.

Theoretically, the case for advanced technology against the intermediate alternative is this.

It is nonsense to advocate a technology that requires much less capital per employee, without also considering how much it will produce per unit of capital invested. Research has shown that the most modern machinery produces much more output per unit of capital invested than less sophisticated machinery which employs more people. If you want to achieve the quickest rate of economic growth – which means maximising output per head of population, you should therefore invest scarce capital in advanced techniques, not waste it on inefficient ones. In other words, methods of production with the best capital–output ratio give the most economical use of capital which you most need when you are short of it.

Admittedly the latest techniques will give much less employment in industry than more labour-intensive methods; but, it was said, by producing more goods for the capital invested and making more capital out of higher profits, they will create more jobs elsewhere than simplified techniques will do. As one critic put it:

The amount of employment created outside agriculture looked at *in toto* is not primarily a matter of technology at all. What are the limits on wage employment in any country at any given time? As many people as will not create an inflation. As many as you have wage goods to pay for their work. So the total employment capacity of a country depends simply and solely on the supply of wage goods. The latest technology will produce more manufactured wage goods than labour-intensive techniques and so you will be able to pay more wages to more people. But it is food that is the primary need and the size of the agricultural surplus is the vital factor that limits the wage labour force. That decides the amount of wages a country can afford. When you realise this, then you see immediately that all this tremendous discussion about technology is really rather beside the point.

If we can employ only a limited number of people in wage labour, then let us employ them in the most productive way, so that they make the biggest possible contribution to the national output, because that will also give the quickest rate of economic growth. You should not go deliberately out of your way to reduce productivity in order to reduce the amount of capital per worker. This seems to me nonsense because you may find that by increasing capital per worker ten-fold you increase the output per worker twenty-fold. There is no question from every point of view of the superiority of the latest and more capitalistic technologies.[2]

Logically the case for them is impressive and leaves the discussion in a dilemma. Intermediate methods of production offer minimum social costs, employ more labour in industry, stimulate agricultural growth more directly and so enlarge the wage fund in that way. On the other hand, the latest methods produce more manufactured wage goods, create more capital and give more output for capital invested, but with much higher social costs and less employment in industry. Since the advocates of advanced technology agree that the vital element in the wages fund is the agricultural surplus, and intermediate technology promises to quicken the agrarian economy most, maybe they should concede their case. But it is not as simple as that. The balance of advantage between the two will be different for each branch of manufacturing and for each country.

THE SCOPE FOR INTERMEDIATE TECHNOLOGY

Developing countries should seriously consider the possibilities of evolving intermediate technologies. There may be much scope for them and they offer many advantages, provided they achieve an efficiency somewhere near that of the latest methods of production, and yet manage to use less capital and employ more people. Research may discover new intermediate methods which achieve almost as good a capital–output ratio as advanced techniques without increasing the capital–employee ratio too much. Improvisations and modifications of existing methods may do the same. Second-hand machinery retired from other countries may be bought at prices which will give capital–output ratios in developing countries as low as the latest machines, and at much lower capital–employee ratios, although difficulties about spares arise here.

Its critics complained that it was easy enough to make such claims for an intermediate technology that had yet to be invented! The charge, however, was denied, although we were hard put to it to gather experience of actual examples. Hong Kong's industrial success was credited largely to its ingenuity in applying labour-intensive methods without losing efficiency or raising the capital–output ratio; it was claimed that Indian research with proper cost and price calculations had discovered intermediate methods of producing some thirty types of agricultural implements, processed foods and consumer goods which were actually cheaper and more efficient than the latest machinery. The industrial museums of the advanced countries, it was said, are full of more labour-intensive types of machinery, the principles of which could be adapted to manufacturing in developing countries; and engineers could easily design intermediate techniques for many branches of industry if only they were asked.

Discussion of examples of 'medium capital' methods showed that they ranged from improved traditional handicrafts, primped up for the tourist or export trade, such as Nandi wood carvings and Hebridean hand-weaving, through hand-powered oil crushers, hand-powered sewing machines for cheap clothing and plants assembling metal beds, on up to second-hand textile mills, first-hand cement and ammonia plants with reduced outputs and lower capital costs, and kinds of machinery yet to be invented. From Indian and Pakistani experience,

it is certainly sensible to use persons rather than equipment for many construction jobs, even if costs at market prices are lower for the mechanised technique. The weaving of cotton textiles is another field in which labour-intensive methods pay for this reason. The optimum technique may be obtained either by scaling down advanced techniques, or by scaling up handicraft methods, or by evolving entirely new methods. The latest machinery can often be simplified so that it costs less and requires more operator attention; the product itself can often be simplified. Development up from traditional handicrafts requires the introduction of new tools and simple machines, new methods of organisation and modifying and standardising the product design. With either of these approaches, study and experiments are needed. A much greater effort in research is required to evolve intermediate techniques *de novo* from basic principles. But cost should not be a serious obstacle and foreign aid should be able to provide technical help.

DIFFICULTIES IN THE WAY OF INTERMEDIATE TECHNIQUES IN INDUSTRY

There are many sides of the institutional set-up in developing countries which favour excessive capitalisation in industry and discourage the widespread use of intermediate techniques. Is not the appeal of the most up-to-date refinery or steel plant as a status symbol irresistible? Normally, intermediate technique enthusiasts have no money and those who control the money have no enthusiasm for the technique − or for investing scarce capital in small doses all over the country where it is difficult to administer safely. Foreign aid agencies seem especially chary of shouldering this kind of risk. More than that, industrial development is often in the hands of expatriate companies and consultants who naturally favour the advanced types of technology with which they are familiar, as do indigenous advisers who have been trained abroad. Dr Schumacher's *cri de coeur* is understandable :

many people are totally unable to imagine anything they are not already used to. There are countless development 'experts' who cannot even conceive the possibility of any industrial production unless all the paraphernalia of the Western way of life are provided in advance. The basis of everything they say, is of course, electricity, steel, cement, near-perfect organisation, sophisticated accounting . . . not to mention a most elaborate infrastructure of transport and other public services . . . Gigantic projects to provide this base form the hard core of development plans the world over . . . In the blind pursuit of an, in itself, highly questionable Utopia, these experts tend to neglect everything that is realistically possible.

Nevertheless it is true that modern factories cannot work efficiently unless they are provided with the necessary institutional setting – but that perhaps is one more point against advanced technology.

No less than the administrative set-up, the economic situation in developing countries favours excessive capitalisation in industry. Institutional factors tend to raise the cash cost of labour higher than the social cost and to depress the cash cost of capital lower than its social cost. Trades unions and minimum wage legislation, for example, often require wages to be much higher than the cost to society of employing unskilled labourers, given a large pool of unemployed and under-employed people. On the other hand, development agencies often lend capital at 6–7 per cent when on the open market the rate is 12–15 per cent. Tax incentives for investors also help to lower the effective cost of capital artificially. These difficulties of capital and labour costs may not be easy to overcome. For purposes of analysis they can be by-passed, using the system of 'accounting prices' or 'shadow prices' as a measure of social cost in designing the make-up of a project and evaluating its pay-off.

The difficulty that the enterprise must pay market prices and maintain its cash solvency however remains. Some arrangement for off-setting high labour costs against low capital prices might be found to deal with this, but in some cases direct subsidies will be needed.

Many doubts about the feasibility and competitive efficiency of intermediate technology remain. Will the total cost per unit of output in these labour-intensive factories be more, or less than in a capital-intensive industry producing the same goods? We do not really know the answers for most manufactures. But the majority felt that intermediate techniques might well be the rational path to industrialisation, if only because the possibilities of introducing advanced technology with the extremely costly infrastructure it needs, are so limited in many countries. Much of the highly capitalised industry being introduced now may prove to have been a waste of scarce resources. Deliberate efforts towards new thinking and a new approach are needed because the conventional approaches are not working at all well. An important place in this reappraisal should be given to exploiting the advantages of methods of production which use less capital and more labour and yet remain efficient enough to compete with the output of high-capital producers.

It has been pointed out that during the early phases of industrial revolution in Europe, the technical skills required to make, maintain and operate manufacturing machinery were so little advanced upon existing handicrafts that any intelligent craftsman or farm labourer could master them without further education or training. Today in developing countries the gap between the two has widened immensely. An enormous investment is required in education and training. This is also true of the managerial, entrepreneurial, research and financial skills and organisations needed for the success of advanced technology. Can the developing countries hope to leap up to the levels of technique and organisation needed all in one bound? Or will they have to go step by step up the evolutionary staircase of intermediate technologies which the developed countries themselves had to climb in history?

There must be a middle way, for both economic and cultural reasons. There is, on the one hand, a need deliberately to adapt those traditional technologies, attitudes and institutions which can be of service to economic growth; and on the other hand, a need to scale down Western technologies, economic attitudes and institutions so that they work effectively in Afro-Asian social settings. If this middle way could be developed in practice, it could revitalise agrarian communities by adding an industrial dimension to them. Through the dispersal of industry in small units it might also save countries from one or two giant industrial centres swallowing them whole. In this way the conference glimpsed a vision of intermediate technology serving the emergence of intermediate cultures, somewhere half-way between Afro-Asian tradition and Western industrial civilisation.

TECHNOLOGY AND CULTURE

At first sight it seems slightly eccentric that a discussion of economic planning should end up talking seriously about culture; yet whoever has followed the argument this far, will not think it quite so odd. There is even a certain logic in it. For throughout all the previous discussion, two diverging tendencies of thought and prejudice emerge. One of them runs towards concentrations of large industrial units using the latest technology in big cities, on grounds of maximum economic efficiency and fastest rate of economic growth. The other, which may be called the ' middle way', runs towards industrial units dispersed through the agrarian economy, organised in institutions and using a technology ' intermediate' between advanced foreign practice and native tradition. Admittedly, this approach by way of ' industrialising the agrarian economy' may not give maximum efficiency in the use of capital for production. But, it is argued, this road to industrialisation is cheaper and more practicable if political risks and costs in unemployment and human misery are balanced against losses in economic efficiency. An intermediate approach, it is claimed, is slow but sure – and slowly and surely will prove quickest in the end. It was upon the question of the cultural costs of industrialisation in the broadest social sense, that the final dispute between these two different approaches took place.

Mr Rashid Ibrahim of Pakistan has asked whether Western technology could be imported on a large scale without bringing with it the whole apparatus of Western culture, and bulldozing the traditional cultures of agrarian Asia and Africa into oblivion; or whether in fact, Western technology and economic institutions can be grafted on to native tradition. For practical as well as psychological reasons, some middle way must be found for the peoples of developing countries. ' It is true ', one of them put it,

that in a way we are very anxious to improve our standard of living, and in that struggle, we may forget at times the importance of our religion, our customs, our social traditions. But in the long run, the essential elements of one's culture must be dominant. Technology alone and higher material standards of living will not suffice. One wants to be oneself. Each nation wants to be different. Not all of us would like to be affluent and rich at the expense of our traditional religion, our national identity and personality . . . Changes there must be, and we are prepared to accept those that are essential. Not everything that is traditional or old is as good as gold. But it is imperative to preserve the cultural essentials at the same time as we promote economic advances. There is a vital need to adjust imported processes of industrialisation and imported technologies to suit the economic factor endowments of developing countries. But there is an even greater need, which the economist rarely allows for in his statistical calculations, and that is the need to adapt traditional social values and institutions, so that they promote economic growth, and to adapt modern industrial organisation so that it fits into and works in non-European cultural settings. These traditional settings are normally regarded by Western economic man, in the light of his peculiar cultural experience, as bars to economic growth. But if we can find out how to utilise them properly and set them to work for economic progress, they would put more power behind development than all the imported capital and institutions in the world. This is the great challenge to planners from developing countries, who may otherwise lazily follow the line of least resistance and go on importing machines and organisations conceived and designed for Western cultural settings.

Another defender of the ' middle way ' stressed the perils of importing advanced technology and Western education from the standpoint of unemployment.

It is I think slightly Utopian to suggest that one can pick and choose which elements in a culture you should retain and which you should give up. The evolving of a culture is largely a sub-conscious process, most of it beyond control. The greatest danger to any culture is mass unemployment, as it was to German culture when Hitler rose to power on the backs of seven million unemployed.

It is quite useless talking about picking and choosing cultural and social values if you are going to industrialise with advanced technologies in huge metropolitan areas, where millions, whose livelihood in the countryside has been destroyed, are going to live on the poverty line in shanty towns and misery belts, completely disinherited of their traditional legacy. It is no use to say that if you concentrate your capital resources in a few efficient workplaces you will then produce enough goods to fob off the mass of unemployed that you have created. The same thing is happening because of over-enthusiasm for Western education. If you really want to ruin a culture, take a lot of people and educate them for jobs which, when they leave the schools and universities and technical institutes, do not exist. This is an excellent recipe for turning everything upside down and creating unemployment. This is the road to bloody revolution, and produces disinherited people with disinherited minds who have lost all sense of identity and sense of purpose. These are the factors that seem to an economist to decide the fate of a culture. If we can adapt education and technology to the Afro-Asian cultural and economic environment, so as not to create mass misery and mass unemployment – if we can find the intermediate and middle way – we shall solve these problems. If we go on importing Western technology and institutions, then everything will go to pieces.

Hence the argument of the middle way is simply this: industrial concentrations based on the latest technology may give you the best output for capital invested and the best rate of economic growth; but the political and cultural costs in unemployment, in resentment against a policy that leaves 80 per cent of the nation in rural areas much worse off than they were before, are so great that the society will disintegrate, its cultural cohesion will crack and the economy will decline.

To this argument the advocates of the latest technology and large-scale industrialisation retorted: 'There is no conceivable situation in which the use of advanced methods of production and organisation, with their higher comparative efficiency, will not pay for more employment and social improvements than the intermediate varieties. There may be some exceptions to this statement, but not enough to destroy the rule.' Those who believed in this doctrine inevitably criticised the intermediate school's attitude to machinery as 'Luddite', their exaltation of virtuous peasantries, their decrying of life in cities, as 'romantic, agrarian conservatism'. On the contrary, it was asserted, 'It is a great and generous thing to bring the impoverished peasant off his leached land into the higher life and better living standards of the city.'

Finally, a distinguished sociologist implied that in the argument of the middle way, the cultural costs of industrialisation with advanced technology, had been exaggerated.

We may possibly be slipping into the error of thinking that social systems must, of necessity be integral wholes, and that if you start changing one section, then the whole system must change. I think this is no longer accepted by sociologists.

[margin note:] But over longer time.

It is perfectly clear that people can and do operate on modern commercial values in one sector of their lives, and on a completely different set of values in others. Secondly, all social institutions have a certain range of tolerance. We cannot assume that just because certain types of industrial technologies have been introduced that traditional societies are going to collapse just because of that. Indeed, innumerable modern commercial and industrial enterprises have been successfully established inside traditional societies, particularly, for example, in Japan, without doing any such thing. Thirdly, this idea of a clear-cut division between traditional culture on the one hand, and Western industrial culture on the other, is a false distinction. If you just open your eyes and see what goes on, you will see people using motor cars to go off and attend an ancestor cult ritual. This juxtaposition it seems to me is not so strange; it is a case of combining two types of a single culture in which, as in all living cultures, there are elements drawn from different origins. Fourthly, it was claimed, the idea that industrialisation can destroy national identity is a bit of a bogey. Has industrialisation made the Frenchman any less French? Or any more like the English?

So the conference brought out clearly the conflict between two different approaches to industrialisation, though it had hardly resolved it. There is an 'evolutionary' or 'agrarian' trend of opinion about industrialisation, over against a 'revolutionary' or 'industrial' tendency of thought. The agrarian school begins and ends with agriculture and stresses the importance of dispersed industries using labour-intensive techniques that will promote agrarian reconstruction. On the other hand, the industrial school presses for concentrated industries and the latest techniques to produce maximum wealth that can then be invested to give more employment and energy to agriculture. For all practical purposes, it is unlikely that the two courses are alternatives, although between the two there is room for enormous differences of emphasis. Perhaps every country's development plan includes some of both types of industrialisation, but all these fundamental considerations have to be taken into account to obtain the right balance.

CONTROLLED CULTURAL CHANGE

A group studying the problem of the impact of industrialisation on culture put up these propositions :

1. The effects of industrialisation on culture are so fundamental that governments should not take up an attitude of *laissez faire*. The possibility of influencing cultural change through policy should be taken more seriously. 2. So far as possible, a deliberate attempt to influence the process should be made, directed towards adapting traditional habits, attitudes and institutions more favourably towards economic enterprise, and discouraging undesirable tendencies arising from the importation of Western technology. 3. Western domination in science and technology gives rise to the belief that all elements of traditional cultures are inimical to economic growth. Careful studies are therefore needed to find out how and where traditional cultures are inhibiting economic progress and how

they should be altered to encourage it. Each country has its own personality and industrialisation must be tailored to its cultural as well as its material environment. 4. The prime criterion in these inquiries is whether or not a cultural element promotes economic enterprise.

One comment on these proposals gives the majority opinion on them :

Now the problem that we have to deal with is this: in what sort of society are economic enterprises so strangled by traditional institutions and activities, that they cannot make progress? It seems that here different types of society have a different range of tolerance, so far as industrial capitalism is concerned. On this it is almost impossible to make a valid generalisation of a broad kind. What happens so far as I can see is that as a rule, people prefer to go on living in the way they always lived until they are forced to change. Governments may try to kill off some customary practice and recommend another because it is better for economic growth; but in the end people decide this sort of question for themselves instinctively and unconsciously. It is almost impossible for us, sitting in a conference like this, to make these essentially moral decisions for people. They have to work it out for themselves. It is always easy to generalise in a subject like this about which practically nothing is known for certain. I always feel terribly humble faced with a question like this one, because frankly – I just don't know.

' Everybody wants to go to Heaven. But nobody wants to die.'

9 · Latin American Industrial Development[1]
NUNO F. DE FIGUEIREDO[2]

The purpose of the following notes is to offer a few remarks about the Latin American experience on two vitally important and closely interrelated problems confronting the Conference: first, the relative priorities of agriculture and industry in a programme for the acceleration of development, and, secondly, the influence of the nature of technology on the level of employment in the developing countries.

The first of these questions was discussed in the contributions made by Dr Arnold Rivkin and Mr Khalid Ikram, while the second was raised in Mr Schumacher's paper on the need to work out an ' intermediate technology ' better adapted to the situation of the under-developed countries.

There are, in my opinion, some features of the experience of Latin America's economic development during the past two decades which should be taken into account in any attempt to generalise on these subjects. With regard to certain aspects of the development process, Latin America's position seems to be roughly halfway between those of Africa and Asia, approaching more nearly to the former in some respects and to the latter in others. Thus, for example, the ratio between the available land resources and the population in Latin America (11 inhabitants per square kilometre) is much closer to that in Africa (8 inhabitants per square kilometre) than to the corresponding figure for Asia (62 inhabitants per square kilometre). On the other hand, in the growth of its internal markets, and the progress of industrialisation, Latin America is far more comparable to Asia than to Africa. Hence, the problems of the relative priorities of agriculture and industry and of the manpower absorption capacity of the development process reveal analogies with both African and Asian responses to these questions.

The next section of these notes reviews briefly some of the features of Latin America's economic development that are relevant to the topics chosen.

The meaning of the Latin American experience can be indicated here in a few words. On the problem of agriculture versus industry, we endorse, on the one hand, Dr Rivkin's point that it is a matter of timing, of relative emphasis and of adaptation to each country's specific conditions, rather than of establishing absolute priorities as between the two sectors of the economy. But, at the same time, the experience of Latin America suggests that normally it is the manufacturing industries that play the dynamic role in the growth process, while the development of agriculture is usually generated and promoted by the industrial sector. The nature of the industrialisation process that is appropriate in each instance, and the extent to which the parallel development of agriculture may be expected to result from industrialisation or must be stimulated by special measures, will differ from one country to another, according to the varying circumstances of the case.

The relations between economic growth and the provision of employment seem to depend essentially upon the vigour of growth and the directions in which the investments that constitute its life-blood are channelled. The 'intermediate technology' which may ultimately be worked out – and which will be acceptable only if it increases the absorption of manpower without decreasing total output per unit of capital invested – seems to offer a necessarily limited (although not negligible) contribution to more rapid economic growth.

THE INDUSTRIAL DEVELOPMENT OF LATIN AMERICA

It is no easy task to give a brief account of Latin America's recent economic development and of the role played in it by industrialisation, since one of the region's most outstanding characteristics is the extremely wide variety of conditions prevailing in the individual countries.

Statistical estimates of the national product as well as of real income show the tendency of economic development to slacken in pace over the last decade. During the second half of the fifties real income per head for the region as a whole rose by 1·7 per cent yearly, i.e., at an appreciably lower rate than in the first half of the decade (2·2 per cent). The decline became more pronounced around 1951–9, with the result that *per capita* income tended to remain stationary or even to fall in the majority of Latin American countries. Brazil was an important exception to the rule, since during that period it continued to develop at a rapid pace, though in more recent years it has also reached a near-stagnation point.

In 1959–61 there was a short-lived recovery, with *per capita* income again at a standstill and showing a tendency to fall in absolute terms in 1963.[3]

In the past, the development of Latin America has been influenced above all by foreign trade. This influence has operated in two ways: first, in determining the overall rate of development, because of the dependence of the economy as a whole upon the agricultural and mining export sectors; secondly, in determining the structure of production and the relative growth of the primary (agricultural and mining) and the secondary (manufacturing) sectors, either as a result of response to the stimuli of world markets or by way of compensating for this dependence on foreign trade.

The relatively rapid development in the post-war period was partly due to the external resources accumulated during the war, but mainly due to the high level of the export quantum and improvement in the terms of trade. These factors enabled imports of capital goods to be considerably increased and the rate of growth of both product and income to rise progressively.

By 1949, however, the Southern-Zone countries were already beginning to feel the effects of the gradual price fall of temperate-climate products in world markets which was by no means offset by the increase in their quantum. In the case of countries exporting tropical products, the corresponding trend began in about 1954.

During the first half of the fifties, the quantum of exports of Latin America as a whole was maintained, on an average, at the same levels as in the early years of the post-war period, but their purchasing power increased by 18 per cent, thus making possible a corresponding expansion of imports. During the period 1955–61 the volume of Latin America's exports was 34 per cent greater than in the preceding period, but in consequence of the deterioration in the terms of trade, their purchasing power rose by only 15 per cent; that is, the negative effect of the terms of trade nullified nearly 60 per cent of the increment in the volume of exports.[4]

Lastly, in the most recent period, the immediate effect of the deterioration in the terms of trade, according to E.C.L.A. estimates, was to reduce the annual rate of growth by over 10 per cent in 1960–3.

Concurrently, the structure of production in Latin America underwent a radical change, with manufacturing industry developing at a steady average rate of 6 per cent during the fifties, under the impetus of an intensive effort at import substitution.

This evolution of the external sectors has strongly influenced national policies in the region towards industrialisation, but this process has taken a number of different courses, depending on the country or group of countries concerned. A broad analysis shows that the Latin American countries have experienced three types of economic growth during the past thirty years. The first, a relatively outward-directed process, can be observed in Central America, Peru and Ecuador. The second, based on an intensive process of industrialisation relying on import substitution, is the type followed in Argentina, Brazil, Chile and Mexico, precisely the four most industrially advanced countries in the region. The third type of economic growth represents a middle course, and is to be found in Colombia and lately also in Venezuela.[5]

Let us briefly consider what has been the role of industrialisation in each category of countries.

The countries whose growth has been outward-directed were able, up to a few years ago, to maintain high import coefficients, thanks to a relatively high export growth rate, together with some diversification of exports, although in primary products which were already traditional Latin American export items. These are mainly the tropical countries, with intermediate and low levels of *per capita* income (in relation to the Latin American average).

The countries in the second group, those which have suffered most in their exports and, consequently, now have the lowest import coefficient, tend to occupy a higher place in the scale of *per capita* income. These countries underwent a more intensive process of industrialisation during the post-war period. Some, like Brazil and Mexico, achieved a comparatively high rate of growth, while others, particularly Argentina and Chile, developed at a much slower rate. In these countries (excluding Mexico, which is a special case because of its very high and steady foreign exchange proceeds from the tourist trade), exports expanded very slowly and for long periods remained at a standstill; moreover, their external purchasing power fluctuated sharply, as a result of changes in the terms of trade. The slower rate of development in Argentina, however, must be viewed against the high level of *per capita* income already reached in that country. The poor growth performance of Chile, on the other hand, is an outcome, mainly, of its limited domestic market combined with an intensive industrialisation policy in this particular country (in comparison with Brazil and Mexico).

Although under different conditions, Colombia and Venezuela have embarked on a process similar to that undertaken some time ago by the countries in the second group. Colombia, with a relatively low *per capita* income, attained high import coefficients in the early fifties and has recently

been reducing them by means of an intensive import substitution industrialisation process and strong restrictive measures made necessary by its
balance-of-payments situation. The drop in Venezuela's import coefficient
in the last few years is even more marked, and, partly as a consequence,
this country is embarking on a far-reaching industrial development
programme.

Broadly speaking, exports (and, therefore, investment in the primary
sector) can be said to have constituted the dynamic factor of economic
growth in the first group of countries, those with smaller populations. In the
second group, comprising the bigger countries, the internal process of industrialisation and import substitution tended to become the factor making
for growth. The intermediate group – those countries that are also intermediate in size – has shown a clearly-marked tendency in the last few years
to join in the process of industrialisation through import substitution. Finally,
the Central American countries too, through their common market scheme,
have recently been adopting the same industrialisation approach, which
nowadays appears as a Latin American common denominator.

However, insufficient external purchasing power obviously limits the
economic growth rate of some countries and makes it difficult for them to
proceed with import substitution. The desire to organise the import-
substitution type of industrialisation in a wider context, making feasible
more complex industrial activities, is the driving force behind Latin
America's economic integration movement.

The points raised above can be summarised as follows:

(a) the countries that have developed most (shown higher rates of
growth) are those which were the first to embark on an intensive
industrialisation process, i.e., those with larger markets;

(b) the smaller and intermediate countries are now also actively pursuing the same policy;

(c) the industrialisation process has taken the form of import substitution, beginning with consumer goods and some relatively simple
intermediate products and moving on to intermediate products
requiring substantial investment and to certain types of consumer
durables and capital goods;

(d) this process has produced a change in the relative magnitude and
composition of imports, with demand for fuel and other intermediate and capital goods increasing substantially;

(e) the import-substitution industrialisation process has been forced
upon the Latin American countries by balance-of-payments difficulties, and was, at its start, a by-product of restrictive measures
applied to imports for payments reasons: only more recently have
industrialisation policies been evolved independently of such motives.

AGRICULTURAL VERSUS INDUSTRIAL DEVELOPMENT IN ECONOMIC
GROWTH

What are the lessons that can be derived from Latin America's experience,
as regards the controversy concerning relative priorities for agriculture and
industrial development as means to economic growth? The dilemma
between industry and agriculture does not seem to be a true one. Both
sectors must be developed, though at different rates. As economic growth is
tantamount to a change in the structure of production and a displacement
of active population from agriculture to manufacturing industry and services,
industry must increase at a higher rate, if the national economy in question
is not to remain stagnant. This does not mean that agriculture will not have
substantial investments to receive and an important role to play, according
to the specific conditions (natural resources, type of export crops, etc.) prevailing in each country. In any case, however, observation of Latin America's
past development, in its large as well as its small countries, suggests that
industrialisation has to perform the dynamic role of pushing ahead the whole
process of growth, creating a surplus for reinvestment, reducing the external
vulnerability of the economy and gradually extending the whole framework
of external economies and interrelationships, without which a self-sustained
process of growth will never start, and primitive farming will never be
transformed into a modern and progressive agricultural sector, closely tied
to the whole structure of the economy.

A process of growth means, basically, intensifying capital accumulation
throughout the economy. The increased supply of capital goods must be
obtained in one of the following four ways:

(*a*) Through an increase in traditional exports (primary products) and
the corresponding increase in the capacity to import capital goods from
abroad, which would mean giving high priority to the primary sector in
the allocation of investment. Latin American experience suggests this to
be a most unwise long-term policy, in view of the continuing reduction of
the purchasing power of exports (deterioration of terms of trade and relative
weakening of demand in the industrialised countries).

(*b*) By starting non-traditional exports (i.e. exports of manufactured goods)
to world markets and thus increasing the capacity to import. This entails
laying the emphasis on industrialisation in the allocation of investment
resources, though on an industrialisation of an outward-directed type. It is
not easy to estimate the results which the Latin American countries would
have achieved in the post-war period had they adopted a vigorous policy of
export diversification, and thus offset the slow growth of commodity trade
by introducing new export items, especially manufactured goods, into the
world market. Though it is recognised that not enough has been done in
this direction and that Latin America will inevitably have to take part in

trade in manufactured goods, it is likewise pointed out that several obstacles stand in the way of this eventuality, which will probably also be present in other underdeveloped countries, though their patterns and incidence will differ according to the country concerned (restrictive and discriminatory practices in world trade in manufactures, as well as some characteristics of the Latin American industrialisation process which have led to relatively high manufacturing costs and prices).

(c) By domestic production of the capital goods needed. This corresponds to an industrial development strategy that plunges almost straight into the most sophisticated forms of industry, without passing through the previous stages of consumer and intermediate goods. This strategy of heavy industry at an early stage of development, which is applied more frequently in the centrally-planned economies, has not been followed strictly in any Latin American country. However, Venezuela is partially adhering to it, in its heavy industry (steel-making, basic chemicals, aluminium and heavy machinery) programme for the development of the Guayana (a newly-opened jungle region). The advisability of this policy for any country, however, suffers from obvious limitations in several respects.

(d) Through import substitution, i.e., starting to produce locally a growing proportion of the consumer goods previously imported and using the resulting savings of foreign exchange to import the capital goods increasingly needed. This implies assigning a high priority to the industrial sector in the allocation of investment, decisions on what to produce being based on the requirements of a balanced industrial structure. Such has been the course most generally followed in Latin America.

I should like to add a few more considerations to support my view that industrialisation, adapted to the special situation of each country, should be the dynamic force of growth. I think a large-scale effort to improve and modernise the agricultural sector has possibilities of succeeding only when two basic conditions are fulfilled:

(a) The previous existence of an industrial sector developed enough to absorb, as its rate of growth rises, a fast-increasing agricultural output, to provide employment [6] for the surplus manpower inevitably released from agriculture as a result of the introduction of up-to-date techniques, and to supply a growing proportion of the inputs a modern agricultural sector (or one in process of modernisation) needs (fertilisers, machinery, etc.).

(b) The existence in the country in question of an enlightened and progressive mentality, without which it would prove impossible to organise and operate efficiently a vast administrative and technical framework of agricultural extension services, training schemes, experimental stations, etc. The same requirement applies when there is need for an agrarian reform as a prerequisite for the modernisation of agriculture, as is the case in nearly every Latin American country; and a progressive mentality of this kind is closely associated with industrialisation and urbanisation. Accordingly, on the basis of Latin American experience, the inception of a self-sustained process of growth, based on industrialisation induced by faster growth in the agricultural sector, appears as a remote possibility.

In other words, even at the risk of over-simplifying the issue, the problem can perhaps be outlined as follows.

In deciding upon the most suitable strategy for accelerating the economic growth of a young country, the first aspect to consider should be the export prospects for primary (agricultural or mining) production in the country concerned. If these prospects are deemed favourable, both as regards the elasticity of the internal supply available for export, and with respect to world market demand and the terms of trade (a decision in which a considerable part is bound to be played by a somewhat subjective evaluation of the efficacy of world market price machinery in a rapidly changing world), it will be possible to base the whole of the development process on the primary export sector, which will then receive a substantial proportion of total investment and will be given priority in the Government's promotional efforts. The expansion of the manufacturing sector will not fail to take place alongside that of exports, but its development will be basically induced by the primary export sector, which means, in essence, two things: first, investment will be financed by the export sector and the requisite capital goods will be imported; and, secondly, the distribution of investment will be a mathematical function of input requirements in the primary sector and of the structure of demand on an open domestic market.

But it is possible that the expansion of exports to world markets may not be a very feasible proposition, either because of limited natural resources or other internal circumstances, or because world market trends in the country's primary exports are unfavourable from the standpoint of price and volume. In this case, which in the writer's opinion is that of the great majority of the developing countries – and certainly of almost all those of Latin America – the expansion of the industrial sector must play the dynamic role in the development process; and this requires a deliberate and energetic policy in which industrialisation based on import substitution must be given top priority over all other claims on investment of resources.

This assertion, however, must be accompanied by two basic reservations. First, an agricultural sector is needed to support the growth of the industrial sector, to feed a rapidly increasing urban population, supply part of the industrial raw materials required to absorb some of the new industrial output. The characteristics of the agricultural sector at the time when acceleration of the development process begins will determine whether it can be left to follow the industrial sector more or less on its own account or whether, on the contrary, it should share public attention (and investment) with manufacturing industry. If the food-producing sector of agriculture, despite its retarded development and low productivity, presents no major obstacles to an expansion of its production for the purposes of feeding the growing urban population (and, in addition, supplying industrial raw materials, such as cotton, etc.), either by means of an increase in the area under cultivation or through more intensive methods of farming, a policy of accelerating development through the mass concentration of the investment effort in industrialisation based on import substitution will be meaningful. In this case, industry will have to be the priority sector, in the sense in which Dr Rivkin uses this term, with agriculture developing alongside industry (although at a slower pace), and independently of special investment and technical assistance incentives or efforts. To the application of such a development strategy a limit is of course set by the real possibilities for agricultural development induced by the industrial sector. A time will come when agriculture will have exhausted its possibilities of developing within the same institutional framework, and under the sole impetus of the market stimuli deriving from industrial and urban development. From then on, special attention will have to be devoted to the task of leading agriculture on to another stage, by introducing the structural changes (agrarian reform, for example) and the basic technical improvements that turn out to be necessary. But at this more advanced stage of development the manufacturing sector will be in a position to furnish a considerable proportion of the agricultural inputs of industrial origin (fertilisers, machinery, etc.) that are needed on a large scale for an energetic move to modernise agriculture.

In the other case to be considered – when the agricultural sector is faced with obstacles to an expansion of production that would be difficult to remove without comprehensive and properly-programmed remedial action – the industrial and agricultural sectors must obviously share top priorities in the allocation of investment and promotion efforts: in what proportions, and according to what specific design, will have to depend upon each individual country's particular situation with regard to natural resources, market size, type of agricultural shortcomings, etc. In any event, it will not be possible to carry industrial development and urbanisation very far, unless as a preliminary – or rather, a parallel – measure such institutional and technological changes are gradually introduced in the agricultural sector as will enable it to respond to normal market stimuli and to feed a rapidly increasing urban population. This could deservedly be termed a balanced development of agriculture and industry.

Lastly, the second necessary reservation to the general assertion of the leading role of the industrial sector relates to the type of industrialisation which is justifiable in each specific case. Here the determining factors are the size of the domestic market, endowments in respect of basic resources for development, and so forth. From careful consideration of all these aspects, within a framework of overall development programming, will emerge the industrial development strategy best adapted to each individual case.

'INTERMEDIATE TECHNOLOGY' AND ABSORPTION OF MANPOWER

The problem to which Mr Schumacher's paper refers – that of the incapacity of the development process in most young countries to provide an uninterrupted supply of productive employment for the new population that reaches working age every year – assumes very serious proportions in Latin America.

For the region as a whole, the annual rate of demographic growth is about 3 per cent, whereas it is not as much as 1 per cent in Southern Europe or 2 per cent in Africa and Asia. Moreover, the fact that the urban areas are growing at a much faster pace than the rural areas implies the concentration of large agglomerations of wholly or partly unemployed population in the bigger towns. During the fifties, the urban population increased at an annual rate of 4·5 per cent, while the corresponding figure for the rural population was 1·5 per cent. The disparity is still more marked if the towns considered are those with over one million inhabitants, where the rate of growth was about 6 per cent.[7]

This intensive urbanisation process is inherent in economic development itself, but in Latin America – as in other developing regions – it also generates increases in the number of persons employed in marginal services, where productivity and remuneration are very low, or in the totally unemployed. Thus it is that the development process in the sense of the steady growth of the *per capita* gross product, is accompanied by increasing unemployment or under-employment and patent disequilibria in the distribution of the product. How far is all this attributable to the nature of the production techniques placed at the disposal of the developing countries, and what role could be played by the gradual development of an 'intermediate technology', of a less capital-intensive type?

This thought-provoking question raised by Mr Schumacher, I should like to suggest, involves the following four factors:

(*a*) the overall rate of economic growth, in relation to the demographic situation;

(*b*) the orientation of industrial development, in each individual country's specific case, with regard to the type of industries to be developed, i.e., the strategy of industrial development;

(*c*) the nature of the technology currently applied, as regards its degree of capital intensity in different industries and the range of alternatives it offers for the performance of one and the same productive operation;

(*d*) the selection of production techniques and equipment from among the
alternatives offered by the existing technology, and the obstacles,
mainly of an institutional character, which make proper selection
difficult in the developing countries.

It seems to me that an opinion on the role of an 'intermediate technology'
in the development process can be formed only when the subject is viewed
in true perspective, in the light of each of these factors. An attempt will now
be made to analyse them briefly.

First comes the overall rate of growth and capital formation, which is the
main factor determining an economy's capacity to absorb manpower into
productive employment. Clearly annual rates of development in the neighbourhood of 4 or 5 per cent, in countries whose population increases at a
rate of 3 per cent, are far too low. And these rates depend essentially upon
capital formation and the evolution of the external sector. On the assumption that the product–capital ratio is about 0·40, it is estimated that Latin
America as a whole would have to make an annual net investment amount-
ing to 7·5 per cent of its gross product in order to achieve an overall annual
rate of development of 3 per cent, which would do no more than keep the
level of *per capita* income unchanged.[8] Such a state of economic stagnation
– which has been the situation prevailing in recent years – necessarily
involves a rapid increase in unemployment, as a result of the inevitable
concentration of each country's limited investment effort. To attain a *per
capita* growth rate of 3 per cent, which may be considered a minimum
target, net investment would have to reach 15 per cent of the gross product,
which implies a tremendous effort,[9] seeing that the present rate is barely
10 per cent. And even so vigorous an activation of the economic development process would probably not suffice to solve the development problem.
To achieve that end, the growth rate of the *per capita* product would have
to be higher – possibly not less than 4 to 5 per cent per annum, and that for
a sufficiently lengthy period. It is worth mentioning here that Pakistan,
following a line nowadays recognised as valid by an increasing number of
countries, has thought it necessary to allow not less than twenty years to
reach the objective of providing productive employment for almost the whole
of its active population (about 95 per cent in 1985, as compared with 78 per
cent in 1965). And if this aim is to be fulfilled, the product will have to
increase at a steady rate of 6·3 per cent, or over 4 per cent per head,[10] over a
period of two decades.

The second point to consider is the effect on unemployment of a given
country's industrialisation strategy as regards the selection of industries to be
developed. Different capital–labour ratios are found in different branches of
industry, and thus, given a specific level of capital formation and a similarly
specific share of the manufacturing sector in the allocation of investment

funds, the absorption of manpower is primarily a function of the branches of industry selected.

Generally speaking, the manufacturing sector, by its very nature and in view of the composition of final demand that characterises successive phases of economic development, accounts for only a relatively small proportion of the employment opportunities offered by the economy, and the attainment of higher levels of development makes but little difference to this limitation. The proportion of the active population employed in manufacturing industry in Latin America as a whole, in the year 1960, was barely 15 per cent, while 'it was estimated that by 1950 the proportion of the urban population employed in manufacturing industry averaged only 5·7 per cent in the region as a whole, and fluctuated between 5 and 8 per cent in the more highly industrialised countries and between 3 and 5 per cent in the countries at less advanced stages of development; and these percentages decreased on the whole during the fifties', as a result of the slackening of the development process and the increase in low-productivity marginal services.[11] Consequently, the influence of different industrial development strategies on the absorption of manpower cannot be other than limited.[12]

In the conditions prevailing in Latin America, there would seem to be two main possibilities for increasing manpower absorption through a reorientation of industrial development, namely, the progressive adoption of an income redistribution policy and the accelerated expansion of export industries. In both cases, industrial development would be rechannelled towards less capital-intensive and more labour-intensive manufacturing lines. Income redistribution policy [13] would spur on the current consumer goods industries to develop faster than more capital-intensive activities such as the manufacture of durable consumer and capital goods, which have hitherto been the dynamic elements in the process of development based on import substitution. The encouragement of export industries, in turn, would likewise imply a relatively more rapid expansion of the manufacture of current consumer goods, processed raw materials and simple intermediate products.

A greater concentration of attention on relatively labour-intensive industries would undoubtedly be a factor of some importance in the elimination of the considerable amount of unemployment still existing in Latin America. However, the Latin American countries' economic development policy is unlikely to veer decidedly in this direction, for two main reasons. In the first place, an income redistribution policy involves the risk of a decrease in the country's overall rate of saving, in view of the higher marginal propensity to consume in the population sectors that would benefit by such a policy. Secondly, in Latin America's circumstances, for the region to export manufactured goods to world markets would seem hardly feasible (save in a very few cases), until it has passed through the intermediate stage of a common market, by means of which its countries will be able to achieve the market dimensions and scales of industrial production, as well as the satisfactory and eventually efficient operational levels which will permit them to compete with the manufactures of the industrialised countries on the latters' own markets.

A third question that should be touched upon in connection with the absorption of manpower is that of the nature of the technological possibilities open to the developing countries and the narrow range of alternatives they offer as regards proportions of capital and labour per unit of output. E.C.L.A. has been concerned with this problem from almost the outset of its activities up to the present day.

The problem for new countries is their inability to develop at the same pace as the industrialized part of the world. At the time when the developed countries were evolving industrially, this problem did not exist. Their industrial development knew nothing of import substitution or of the transfer of production techniques devised in different economic conditions in other regions. Hence the capital intensity adopted for their production processes was the logical and proper culmination of their earlier lines of development.[14]

In carrying out their investment programmes, the young countries find that they must adopt the same techniques and import the same equipment as the countries which have developed over a long period have come to use.

Thus, equipment which represents a high density of capital per gainfully employed person and which is compatible with the high level of *per capita* income in the industrial centres, is equally available to the underdeveloped countries, in which *per capita* income, and therefore the capacity to save, are evidently lower. In other words, it is theoretically possible for the Latin American countries, considering their relative scarcity of capital and abundance of human labour, to have an optimum capital intensity lower than that of the more advanced countries, but in view of the nature of the economic process and its irreversible character, the underdeveloped countries have a very limited possibility of obtaining in fact their optimum capital intensity.[15]

Few as they actually are, the young countries' possibilities of establishing a level of technology suited to their conditions are worth mentioning. In the first place, such countries can resort to less up-to-date production techniques and equipment which, because they correspond 'to a stage of technology and capital intensity that has already been transcended in the industrial countries' are characterised by a lesser degree of automation, 'and therefore allow a larger amount of labour to be absorbed per unit of output. But as equipment of this kind is usually second-hand, it is especially complex and hazardous to choose.'[16] The difficulty of obtaining parts and spare parts is becoming increasingly great, and the amalgamation of processes and equipment pertaining to widely disparate levels of technology, when an expansion of activities becomes necessary, raises extremely thorny problems. Furthermore, technological progress not only alters the proportions in which the factors of production are combined, but also implies, in most cases, an improvement in the quality and characteristics of the article produced.

On the other hand, it seems to be true that there is a possibility – in respect of the nature of technical know-how itself and the limitations inherent in it – of a technological development more appropriate to the stage of growth reached by the young countries. Of course, this would only help to accelerate the economic development of the countries in question provided that production techniques and equipment designed with a view to saving capital did not also imply a commensurate or even greater reduction in the product obtained as a result of their application.[17] That is, the less capital-intensive techniques and equipment should not be less efficient than the more advanced techniques and equipment they were intended to replace, for otherwise the counterpart of the expansion of employment made possible by a given rate of capital formation would be a decrease in the growth rate of the product, and for a young country this seems too high a price to pay for the attainment of the social objective of increasing the volume of employment. The application of more labour-intensive methods should not mean that more capital is used per unit of output, in order to raise total manpower absorption without reducing total production (in relation to a given total investment).

There are signs that an 'intermediate technology' meeting the foregoing requisite could be worked out for a fairly wide range of industrial activities. By way of evidence, I will cite two examples drawn from precisely the field where it would seem most difficult to change the capital–labour ratios prevailing in conventional modern technology: namely, that of the industries producing petroleum derivatives.

The first relates to the recent tendency (fostered by the policy of most African, Asian and Latin American Governments of having oil refineries in their own territories, however small their markets) for international firms to design small petroleum refineries with low capital investment per unit of output and a low total capacity, say from 5,000 to 30,000 barrels daily. These units are as efficient and low-cost as the much bigger and more capital-intensive refineries corresponding to conventional designs. The second example relates to 'package plants' for ammonia production, also recently designed for small markets. According to some provisional data, the investment cost per ton in a 'package plant' with a 60-tons-a-day capacity may be about 30.000 dollars, whereas a conventionally designed unit, with a daily capacity of 100 tons (which is, for a conventional plant, very small) would require an investment of approximately 50.000 dollars per ton.

These two examples, in a critical industrial field where the investment cost for small countries is frequently prohibitive, show that it is technically feasible to go over existing technologies and equipments and redesign them according to the specific needs of underdeveloped regions.

To the important question of how and where to organise this task on a systematic basis, I have no answer. It could provide, obviously, an attractive opportunity for cooperation between underdeveloped and industrialised countries.

Fourthly, there is the possibility of increasing manpower absorption by means of more appropriate selection of production techniques and industrial equipment.

The obstacles impeding or hindering the choice of production techniques and equipment suited to Latin American conditions are of two main types. One stems from the fact that enterprises in Latin America (and, generally speaking, in all developing countries) have neither the technical expertise nor the information needed for evaluating the alternatives existing at the conventional level of technology; and the other from certain distortions in the operation of price mechanisms which systematically lead to entrepreneurial decisions that are right from the private standpoint of rates of return, but wrong from the point of view of the national economy.

The Latin American entrepreneur – who in most cases is at once the owner and the manager of the enterprise – has not the same long experience and tradition behind him as his opposite number in the industrialised regions, nor does his environment offer the vast network of technical assistance, specialised training and technological research organisations which form the vanguard of industry in the United States or Europe. Moreover, such traditions as he has are more closely linked to trade or farming than to industry, and this helps to determine his personality and abilities. Hence the transfer of production techniques and equipment from the advanced countries is often effected heedlessly, without a prior effort to adapt it to the conditions of a region where manpower is plentiful and capital scarce.

The catalogue issued by the European or United States exporter of machinery is still the prime source of technical assistance. The very ease with which the stock of technology accumulated in the advanced countries can be disposed of, as a result of the differences in timing between their development and that of the younger countries, helps to bring about this result, since too often royalties agreements are concluded for the local manufacture of products formerly imported, with the same design and characteristics, and on the basis of the same raw materials (which, having been specified in terms of the conditions prevailing in the advanced countries, have to be imported from these) and the same industrial processes and equipment.

In many cases, of course, highly mechanised production techniques and equipment are adopted deliberately as a means of offsetting some other limiting factor. For example, in some of the metal-transforming industries certain more highly capital-intensive production methods may require less skilled labour than alternative methods calling for less capital. The shortage of skilled manpower in Latin America's metal-transforming industries has in several cases made it imperative to choose methods requiring more capital when the investment concerned was amply justified on other grounds (its external economies creation effect, for instance). Examples of this were frequently met with in the course of the recent establishment of the motor-vehicle industry in Brazil.[18]

Again, decisions as to where to invest and what production techniques to use, even in cases where the entrepreneurs have based them on correct economic calculations, taking into account all the possible alternatives, cannot but lead, in many instances, to an unsatisfactory distribution of available resources, as a result of distortions in the market price system on which these entrepreneurial decisions are grounded.

The basic factors underlying this state of affairs are threefold. First, in nearly all the Latin American countries the distribution of capital resources effected by the banking system is based on a system of quantitative rationing rather than on rates of interest. These rates are often limited by law to nominal levels which in real terms drop sharply in times of persistent inflation. The seemingly high interest rates payable in Latin America are often tantamount to negative if the annual rate of increase in domestic prices is taken into account. At such interest levels, the volume of requests for credit would easily exceed the total amount of funds available, unless a quantitative criterion were applied to limit the demand for investment capital. The interest rates current on the market are therefore appreciably lower than the equilibrium rates that would result from the relative shortage of the capital factor. This completely vitiates the entrepreneurs' estimates of rates of return, from the standpoint of the national economy as a whole, since it conduces to the selection of highly capital-intensive sectors and techniques.

Secondly, the same observation is applicable, although in the opposite sense, to nominal wages, which, as a result of various regulations, are systematically kept at a higher level than is compatible with a state of market equilibrium. For example, in Brazil, there is very little difference between the legal minimum wage in areas with such disparate conditions of employment as the over-industrialised State of Sao Paulo and the poor Nordeste States. This likewise distorts the calculations of rates of return made by private entrepreneurs, and has therefore the same effect on the orientation of investment.

Thirdly, the reservation of markets as a result of high tariff protection in relation to imports and the virtually monopolistic situation resulting from the size of national markets and the economic scales of output in many activities are also conducive to high prices. Consequently, high costs have little effect on the expected rate of return of new undertakings.

Thus, the above-mentioned factors make for a climate that favours the channelling of investment along lines precluding a more intensive use of labour per unit of output (and of investment).[19]

In connection with the absorption of manpower, and in the light of the above comments, I think two points should be stressed: first, the need to use shadow prices in calculating the rate of return on investment, which means in practice that the choice of the sectors to be developed will have to be made within the framework of overall programming of the manufacturing sector; and, secondly, the necessity of systematic technical assistance programmes for various sectors of industry, so that entrepreneurs may be given better guidance in the selection of production techniques and equipment.

All the above-mentioned points have been extensively discussed in recent technical and inter-governmental meetings in Latin America. And the conclusion that is being reached is that the reorientation of industrialisation in the area – essential if the region's economic and social development process is to be given fresh impetus and conducted on more balanced lines – must be based on four elements of key importance :

(*a*) industrial programming within the framework of over-all programming, which first and foremost implies strict coordination of import control policy with the industrial development objectives established;

(*b*) a continuing technical assistance policy to improve operational conditions in the industry installed, which would cover training at all levels, technical and administrative internal organisation, modernisation and rational selection of equipment, and technological research, and would be applied through integrated programmes for each branch of industry, based on previous diagnoses of the existing situation;

(*c*) regional integration of industry, within the framework of a common market, to include not only the new capital goods industries but also the traditional activities producing consumer goods, with the indispensable complement of energetic industrial promotion at the regional level;

(*d*) regional cooperation for technological research orientated towards the reconsideration and redesigning of existing processes and equipments in accordance with the factor proportions prevailing in the region.

3 RURAL DEVELOPMENT

10 · Historic Role of Agriculture in Development
SIR JOSEPH HUTCHINSON[1]

Agriculture developed against a background of resources in land that appeared inexhaustible. This first phase is long past in Western Europe and the United Kingdom, and in most of Asia. It is a matter of recent history in the United States, and it is the current situation in parts of Africa, Latin America and Australia. Where land is abundant, it is not valued, and the demand for more produce is readily met by cultivating more land. Agriculture is exploitive, and little or no care is exercised to ensure the return of fertility to the land under cultivation. Fortunately, at this stage human communities are small, transport and travel are very limited, and the movement of people and of their food supplies is so restricted that there is little drain on the fertility resources of the soil. Agriculture of this type has a devastating effect on the natural vegetation, but except where circumstances are such as to give rise to accelerated erosion under cultivation, there is little permanent damage to the soil.

So long as the population is stable, or if it is increasing there is land available for the overspill, a simple subsistence community remains in balance with the ecosystem within which it lives. When its resources in land are all exploited, and there is a further increase in the size of the population, the rate of exploitation exceeds the rate of regeneration, and there arises a progressive depletion of the natural resources available to the community. This situation has been studied by Allan in *The African Husbandman*.[2] He has defined the size of population beyond which a progressive decline sets in as the 'Critical Population Density'.

Human communities the world over, and over the whole period during which agriculture has been practised, have reached the Critical Population Density, and the course of civilisation that follows depends on whether the community can establish a new balance with the land on which it depends. Where there is no advance in agricultural practice, the population presses increasingly on the land, squatting on the poorer wastes as in England in the fourteenth century, reducing the rest period, as in Zambia today, or fragmenting the holdings into smaller and more inadequate units in successive generations, as in the rice cultures of Asia. This increasing pressure on the land leads in extreme cases to a demographic collapse such as was suffered in Western Europe and the United Kingdom in the fourteenth century.

That this catastrophic adjustment of human numbers to land resources has not happened more often is due to two factors. One was the rate and magnitude of the changes that were brought about in land use, leading to higher productivity. The other was the discovery and exploitation of vast new lands not previously available to the expanding populations of Europe. The changes in land productivity in Europe, and the opening up of America, enabled Europe to avoid the consequences of population pressure on the home-lands for two centuries. Failure to achieve this change in productivity still keeps much of the rest of the world in a state of poverty and low productivity. The extent of the change in productivity in Europe before the impact of American agricultural produce on the British food market is indicated by the change in population, all fed on home-grown food, in Britain in the 250 years from A.D. 1600 to 1850.

Year	Population
1603	3·8 million
1690	4·1 ,,
1740	6·0 ,,
1800	9·0 ,,
1811	10·0 ,,
1820	13·0 ,,
1830	15·0 ,,
1841	16·5 ,,

Successful development of agricultural resources leads to the growth of urban occupations, and of town populations. This is rarely an easy form of growth. Hill, for instance, in his *Tudor and Stuart Lincoln*[3] gives an account of the problems of an urban community defending itself and its craft employment against immigrants from the countryside. In the sixteenth and seventeenth centuries urban employment was not growing, but the growth of rural populations and the changes coming about in farming practice gave rise to an overspill of people who drifted to the towns. The drift to the towns has a modern ring about it, but the shanty towns of Nairobi, Calcutta, Caracas and the rest are symptoms of the same malaise as that which afflicted Lincoln four centuries ago.

This is an age-old situation in agriculture. Since the food requirements of the individual are inelastic, improvements in the ability of the farm population to produce food give rise to a surplus. This can be used to feed people engaged in non-agricultural activities. The farm population also produces a surplus of people. There ensues a migration from the land, and the growth of an urban-based labour force. The growth of urban employment becomes imperative. There is no answer to the shanty towns and unemployment of the urban fringes in developing countries except industrial development that will absorb the productive capacity of these people, and create the demand for agricultural produce that will raise the living standards and increase the attractiveness of the rural areas. Failing an increasing level of urban employment, unemployment on the urban fringe is matched by under-employment in rural areas, together with subdivision of holdings in land, and fragmentation leading to ever lower efficiency in agricultural production.

It is generally recognised that dividing up the land into parcels below the size necessary to give a satisfactory living to a family ought to be avoided; but if a man has two sons and they marry, and one family is replaced in the next generation by two families, what is to be done if there is no more land, and no other occupation than subsistence farming? Farmer [4] has pointed this out in discussing settlement schemes in Ceylon. Legal prohibition of subdivision of holdings cannot be enforced if the population is expanding, and the opportunities for migration to other land or to urban employment are inadequate. Land is divided by subterfuge, or occupied by family partnerships.

The Industrial Revolution altered for Britain this whole pattern of land use. It was not until very late in the industrial era that employment opportunities caught up with population growth, and even now full employment is difficult to maintain. But through industrialisation it has been possible to support a steady migration from the land without overwhelming the towns or draining essential labour from agriculture. Moreover, productivity has been increased at a rate that not only matched population increase, but made possible the release of agricultural land on a grand scale for urban use.

The sequence of events in the agricultural sector of the communist economic revolution was very different. The economic and social policy of the communist revolution involved the creation of an industrial state over a very short period of time. The human resources for this development were drawn, as in the earlier British industrial revolution, from the rural population. This abstraction was made in agricultural circumstances quite different from those existing in Britain at the corresponding stage of development. British agriculture yielded labour to industry in a context of enclosures which improved agricultural structure, and of the developing ‘New Husbandry’, which improved agricultural technology. When the U.S.S.R. began to draw off rural population, the great estates had been parcelled out to peasants – the exact opposite of the enclosures! – and there was no adequate body of educated and imaginative agriculturists to lead an advance in agricultural technology. The urban revolution was for years beset with the problems arising from the inadequacy of the agricultural contribution to development. So a revolution which began by distributing land to the peasants to liberate them from the tyranny of the estate monopoly in land, had shortly to recreate great estates to secure the urban food supply. Only through collectives and state farms was it possible to generate the productivity that would ensure the feeding of a growing urban population by the efforts of a diminishing farm labour force. This was true for two main reasons: first, the very limited supply of management and technological ability had to be deployed over large units if the ground was to be covered, and secondly, labour economies by the use of machinery only became possible if the farming units were designed for efficient machine operation.

This view of the world's great industrial revolutions makes very clear the significance of agriculture in development. The resources for the British Industrial Revolution became available because an agricultural revolution was in progress. To ensure the success of the U.S.S.R. industrial revolution, it became necessary to undertake an agricultural revolution. Having demonstrated this interdependence of agriculture and industry in development, it is possible to look at the problems of the newly developing countries.

The pattern of development of the European industrial revolution was changed during the course of the nineteenth century by the opening up of the New World and of Australasia. At first the impact was outward, on the new lands through the migration of colonists and by the export to them of industrial goods. The colonisation of the New World was mounted on the Industrial Revolution in England, and the feed-back of agricultural produce from the 1860s on depended on the earlier export from this country of steamships, port equipment, steel rails and rolling stock, and of the necessities of the colonist's existence, from pots and pans to farm equipment.

This massive export drive took the industrial products of Britain and Western Europe to other countries as well. The international trade in cotton textiles began with the export of muslins and calicos – note the names – from India to Britain, but the Industrial Revolution established a vast trade in the other direction, from Britain to India, to the ruin of India's textile crafts. Steel rails and rolling stock were exported the world over, and established a system of rural–urban exchange over vast distances, mediated by the railways and ocean liners of the first Industrial Revolution.

It was on this pattern that the development achievements of the first half of the twentieth century were based. British urban communities exchanged their industrial products for foodstuffs and raw materials from all the world and the developing world climbed the first rungs of the development ladder on the exchange of agricultural and mining produce for the industrial goods they needed.

This was the economic foundation of the imperial and colonial era. The end of the era marks not only the rejection of imperialism and colonialism, but also the growing inadequacy of the economic foundation on which they rested. The key to an understanding of the situation is in the interdependence between agriculture and industry that has been set out above. The growing agriculture of the developing countries must release labour for urban development, both to provide the goods on which a higher standard of living is to be based, and to offer a market for the produce of the farms. The urban–rural exchange mediated by railways and ocean liners offers no solution to the problem of the human overspill. Emigration of Pakistanis and West Indians to British industrial centres is wholly inadequate in volume to help the donor countries. Equally, it is beyond the limit of acceptability in the receiving country, which is already suffering from the effects of the size and distribution of a vast urban population on a limited land area.

The long-distance exchange of industrial products for agricultural produce has been an invaluable instrument of development for a hundred years. It will continue to be the means whereby the developing countries obtain many of the essential inputs for their economic growth. But for a broad strategy of development it is now essential to exploit the human flow between countryside and neighbouring town. The flow has begun, but it is silted up in the shanty towns because the industrial intake is inadequate. Industrial capital is scarce and local industries are not competitive with the massive export power of the nations that industrialised first. This is the problem, but this paper is concerned only with the agricultural contribution to its solution.

In Britain, the contribution of an expanding agriculture to the Industrial Revolution was predominantly in food. Wool, flax, oilseeds and some dye-stuffs were also produced, but food was the greater part from the beginning, and became more so as urban populations grew and as the townsmen became rich enough to afford a better diet. In the developing world, two distinct situations must be considered. In the Indian subcontinent, the social structure of a countryside closely related to a neighbouring town has long been established. The impact of the British Industrial Revolution was initially to weaken this natural and potentially hopeful relationship, by linking rural India with urban Britain. Only when British industry began to develop in India was there again a prospect of development on the old urban–rural relationship. In India the structure is right, but development is hampered by the need to make at least some provision for the vast and persistent increase in population.

In Africa and Latin America, the first stages of development came from the association of local agricultural production with the industrial production of Europe and America. Urban growth was from the beginning oriented towards the urban communities with which they traded. And in contrast to India, their urban food supply depended substantially on imports from the same sources as Western industrial communities draw their food supplies. Flour mills in Colombia were built at the ports to mill imported wheat, though there is admirable wheat land at 8,000 feet in the vicinity of Bogota, which is a major consuming centre. Foodstuffs of temperate region origin can be bought in any small township in Uganda, and Sudan spends precious currency derived from the sale of the cotton crop to buy wheat and rice for consumption in Khartoum and Medani. In all these countries, the agricultural emphasis is on crops that can be sold for cash to overseas purchasers, and not on the development of the home market, where the home labour force must seek employment.

It was the economic strength of the Western industrial revolution that made possible the exchange of the produce of farms and mines in developing countries for industrial goods from the distant urban communities of the West. Though it gave a start to development it is not an instrument that can carry development further. Exchange of produce between country-side and town is but half the enterprise. The other half is the migration of labour to the towns. Throughout history the contribution of agriculture to development has been to give up labour to urban enterprises, and with the reduced labour force remaining, to feed the expanding town population. So if the development process is to operate in the emerging countries, the local towns must expand, and the local agriculture must feed them. This calls for a reappraisal of policy. An export–import oriented policy must give place to a home supply policy. The new growing points of agriculture will be dairy and horticultural farming systems in the neighbourhood of the towns, and staple foodstuff farming further out. On these, research, advisory work and development should be concentrated, at the expense if need be of the cash export crops more widely distributed over the country. This will require a complementary change in urban policy. Foreign exchange is needed for capital imports. It cannot be spared for imports of foodstuffs. And since local foodstuffs have not yet been adapted to urban needs, research and development work is needed on transport and marketing, packaging and storage, and most important, on processing and cooking to make of local produce acceptable and nutritionally satisfactory diets.

Thus the pattern of agricultural development can be established in the newer countries. The industrial dominance of the West has been a stimulating and profitable interlude. As it comes to an end, rising productivity in the agriculture of the newer countries must be devoted to feeding the rising population of the new cities with the aid of a falling agricultural labour force.

11 · Social Attitudes to Agriculture

K. A. BUSIA[1]

In most developing countries in Asia and Africa, agriculture has been traditionally pursued for subsistence. The attitude to it has been that it is an inescapable and necessary task. The prime motive has been to satisfy the need for existence.

Everywhere, man meets his need for food by drawing on the resources the habitat provides, using the techniques he knows. Where his technology is simple and rudimentary, and the demands of the habitat are rigorous, as in most of Africa and Asia, his energies have been absorbed by efforts to cope with primary needs for food and water, and protection from an inclement climate or from animals.

In such conditions, the connection between agriculture and survival is vital and obvious, and a high sense of dependence on land is inculcated. This is manifest in ceremonies held to celebrate harvests. In many African communities the most elaborate and cherished annual celebrations are those devoted to harvests, when through prayers and dance and song and ritual the community expresses thanks for the food the habitat has provided. As anthropological studies have shown, a sense of dependence has frequently been symbolically expressed in various concepts of the Earth as Mother and Giver of life to whom prayers are offered at these ceremonies on behalf of those who cultivate the farms so that food may come forth in abundance.

The religious attitude that is consequently developed is noteworthy, for the existence of mystical conceptions has influenced theories of ownership and occupancy of land. In Ashanti conceptions, for example, the real owners are the ancestors; the living have only the right of use, and never the right of permanent alienation by sale. Such concepts come to have a bearing on problems of development. If what is inherited is only the right to use the land for subsistence, it is not difficult to see that the land may be parcelled out in scattered subsistence holdings, without much regard for titles of ownership. When production from the land has to meet more than subsistence, developing countries have to face new problems of land reform, as well as definitions of titles and ownership. If account is taken, for example, of the religious attitude to land, of the mystical values that come to be associated with it, and of the concepts of ownership that derive from it, then it will be recognised that land reform should not be approached in terms of economic returns alone, although these can be powerful incentives to change. Some of the reasons for the well-known conservatism of farmers, and their resistance to innovations may be based on values other than economic.

The conservatism and resistance have sometimes been justified by what has been learnt from ill-considered innovations that have failed to take account of all the factors of a situation, or to consider, as far as could have been foreseen, all the possible consequences of the innovation contemplated.

There have been occasions when farmers have had just cause to resist innovations on economic grounds. They have calculated that the changes will be to their disadvantage economically. Cases could be cited of changes aimed at more productive use of land which have in fact led to unemployment and increased hardship for farmers. Some well-known examples may be recalled. In India, when land reforms were started, some farmers were deprived of their land. They could not find new jobs in industry, because new techniques which were introduced in industry about the same time diminished opportunities for work. The situation was made worse, for the products of European industry put craftsmen out of work, and some of them turned to seek work on the land, increasing unemployment in agriculture, and adding to the misery of the poverty-stricken farmers. Land reforms are not necessarily synonymous with improvements in the lot of agricultural workers, and they have had cause to be wary of them. There is also the lesson of Turkey where land reform and the introduction of machinery into agricultural work led to the worsening of the lot of the farmer. The innovations made it possible for less work to be done for greater returns. This was an attractive incentive which caused some families to emigrate from town to country to invest in agriculture. At the same time, the mechanisation of agriculture displaced many hired labourers in the country. They emigrated to the towns to find work which did not exist. These examples illustrate that, even on economic grounds alone, farmers have had justifiable cause to resist innovation. One may also mention gigantic agricultural schemes that have failed, such as the groundnut scheme of Tanganyika, the egg scheme in the Gambia, or the Damongo scheme in Ghana. Ill-fated schemes like these have been deterrents to the acceptance of innovation. One of the lessons the schemes have taught, to which reference is made below, is the need to consider agricultural and industrial schemes together as parts of a bigger whole.

The attitude to agriculture is not wholly conservative. Farmers, even non-literate ones, learn from experience to appreciate that there are problems which require the application of new knowledge and techniques. There is plenty of evidence to show that in traditional subsistence agriculture, it was recognised that the continuous use of a plot of land exhausted the soil. Where land was plentiful, this problem was by-passed by simply moving to virgin soil to prepare new farms; where land was not plentiful, the growth of the preceding year was burnt to supply ash as fertiliser for the next crop. The attitude to agriculture has not inhibited experimentation or innovation when experience has shown this to be necessary. But in measures aimed at development, it should be admitted that new techniques have sometimes been introduced without proper consideration or circumspection, and farmers have been discouraged. There have been instances where irrigation has been introduced without proper attention to drainage, and the soil has been poisoned by salting; or where fertilisers have been provided without an adequate supply of water, and the crops have failed.

Quite apart from such instances, what has been said above about taking account of the religious attitude to land, or of other values, points to the fact that the economies of societies have a dual character, and that due note should be taken of this by those who are concerned with agricultural development, and consequently with social attitudes to agriculture. Economic activities are not only concerned with the satisfaction of material needs, but also with values like religion, security, prestige, power, or achievement. These also determine social attitudes, and can provide powerful motivations to work.

For example, the religious rites of many African communities emphasise the value placed on the solidarity of the tribe or kinship group. This is also manifest in agricultural activities. Where there was no precedent for paid labour, and seasonal factors demanded many hands at particular periods, the family unit or kinship group was a source ready to hand to turn to for cooperative labour. Agricultural work became a social event, strengthening the bonds of kinship. Obligations to one's kinsfolk to share in agricultural work was a potent means of preserving group solidarity. In many instances the motive to cultivate a farm was provided by the obligation to find the customary exchanges which are expected of one; these exchanges of services or goods validated social relationships and contributed to group solidarity.

The value of social solidarity is still a highly prized one in Africa; it is a sheet anchor of security in the midst of rapid social change, often baffling and confusing. In the political sphere, it is illustrated by the resilience and intransigence of tribalism encountered in the efforts at nation-building; it poses problems in the economic sphere also. With specific reference to agriculture, the question may be asked whether the problem of increasing agricultural productivity can only be solved at the expense of kinship solidarity. Must the transition from tribal or extended family land-tenure or ownership to large-scale, technologically efficient production inevitably proceed through the destruction of kinship solidarity? Can large-scale production and technological efficiency be reached through some form of cooperative system that makes use of the concept of extended family ownership? The recognition of the value attached to kinship or tribal solidarity would give a new dimension to the economic problem; but it also points to the appreciation of a social value which could be harnessed for winning acceptance for new methods to improve agriculture.

The desire for personal prestige, to win approval or stand high in the estimation of one's fellows has also been a powerful motive for the practice of agriculture. It gives satisfaction for one to be able to display one's success through meeting the food requirements of a large group of kinsfolk or dependents. But it is a motive which does not necessarily lead to prudent housekeeping or the rational use of resources. Prestige spending is nevertheless observable in many cultures. Respect is commonly accorded to conspicuous spending or consumption. The desire for prestige has in many developing countries induced governments to invest less in agriculture than its important role demands, and funds which could have been made available have been spent on prestigious projects which have added little or nothing to productivity. Nevertheless, the desire for prestige seems universal in the human psyche, and so where the products of the farm have offered opportunities for winning prestige through conspicuous consumption, to achieve the means for such consumption has been a contributory factor impelling to greater agricultural activity.

Even so, contemporary social attitudes to agriculture, especially among the young in Africa, are marked by aversion. Agricultural work is arduous, for in many countries in Africa, as in some other developing countries in Asia and Latin America, the techniques used are inefficient, and the returns are small, for all the effort put into farming. More money can be earned from other jobs such as clerical or industrial work. Young people are therefore loath to take up agriculture. This attitude tends to persist even when there are increasing opportunities for earning more money from the land. Agricultural work has tended to be assigned a low prestige in job ratings.

The introduction of cash crops has, however, provided a motive that is modifying such social attitudes to agriculture. Whereas, traditionally, farm work was regarded as an inescapable drudgery necessary for survival, with the introduction of cash crops like cocoa, coffee, or cotton, farming is increasingly coming to be regarded as a lucrative occupation; and social attitudes to it are being modified by the desire for wealth. There are other attendant attitudes engendered by this change. Some of the cash crops, such as cocoa, need relatively little supervision. Landowners are able to absent themselves for long periods, and they eventually become absentee owners, leaving the care of the crops to tenant farmers. Agriculture then comes to be regarded as a source of gain for the absentee owner or speculator. In the long run, the new attitude is reflected in the way land and the use of land come to be regarded. The attitude to land and to agriculture becomes more mercenary.

In Ghana, for example, cocoa cultivation has led to the establishment of small, dispersed holdings. Land and boundary disputes have multiplied. Farmers have moved from areas where the crop cannot be easily grown to areas more favourable for its cultivation, and land has consequently become more commercialised, as diverse agreements for various payments, in money or in kind, for farming rights have evolved. Land has acquired larger monetary value, and an evolution from communal to family and even to individual land ownership has begun.

The traditional sense of dependence on land has not been altogether obliterated, but attitudes to agriculture now go beyond subsistence to values like wealth, security, or power.

Discernible, too, is the increasing sense of international interdependence which the production of cash crops for external markets has brought home to the producer. What he obtains for his agricultural produce is determined by the consumers – the rich industrial countries. In the final analysis, these consumers control the standards of living of the producers. The fluctuating prices the producers are offered have engendered a sense of insecurity. This is another reason why agriculture does not attract the young. The insecurity of fluctuating prices also throws light on the urgency the producer countries attach to negotiations to reach agreements with the consumer countries guaranteeing stable minimum prices for their cash crops. Such guarantees would provide incentives for greater productivity.

Within the producer countries themselves, the mercenary attitude of absentee landlords to land-holding may obstruct improvements in the agricultural system. The landlords tend to be more interested in what they get than in improving their lands, and they may resist innovations aiming at better utilisation of their holdings. In such a situation, it is the absentee landowners rather than the tenant farmers who may become obstacles to change.

The developing countries require agriculture to play an important and fundamental role in development. Their populations are growing, from falling death rates and increasing birth rates, and the additional mouths have to be fed. These countries are also embarking on industrialisation. Where, as in most cases, there are no markets readily available to buy their manufactured goods, they have to depend on the workers in the agricultural sector to purchase the goods; and the farmers must produce more in order to increase their purchasing power. Further, most developing countries depend on the agricultural sector for the foreign exchange they need to purchase the capital goods required for industry; as experience in different developing countries has shown, capital formation has largely to be financed from savings in the agricultural sector. Without improvement in agriculture, therefore, the hopes of developing countries achieving industrialisation are slim.

Hence it has become a basic necessity to provide new knowledge, and attractive incentives to the farmer, and to change his attitudes, where this is called for, in order that agriculture may play the important role expected of it. The social attitudes required must be inculcated through education, the reform of systems of land-tenure, the formation of productive cooperatives, and the provision of adequate incentives.

The examples of India and Turkey to which brief references have been made, and the other cases mentioned, point to the lesson that the development of agriculture must be seen within the wider context of the development of society as a whole. Agricultural and industrial development must be seen as complementary, to be planned and worked together as parts of a wider whole. In fact, some economists who have been called upon by developing countries have advised that agriculture should play the leading role in industrialisation, and that industrialisation should be based on agricultural raw materials. This, for example, was the advice given in 1953 to Ghana by Professor Arthur Lewis. But it was not heeded, and the consequences of following a different course have been disastrous. Some countries have based much of their development on industries linked with agriculture, with noteworthy success; as, for example, the timber industries of Honduras based on their hardwood forests, or the paper and packing manufactures of Ceylon based on their softwoods, or the spinning and weaving mills of India, Kenya, Uganda or Tanzania, based on cotton. But prestigious industrial schemes have sometimes been given precedence over such beneficial linkages. Agricultural development needs to be correlated with general economic planning to ensure its success.

In the realm of social attitudes, the lesson to be drawn and emphasised is this: that material development is not the only thing which developing countries are seeking. Bread is desirable, but their concept of the good life includes more than bread, and agricultural development should be seen as part of the quest for a greater whole, the quest for the good life. This may be differently conceived in different cultures, or aspects of it be given different emphasis; it is for governments and planners to be aware of this, and to seek to understand the concepts of the good life which they seek to help their peoples to realise. It is a common experience that there are values for which people are ready to sacrifice material efficiency, as this may be calculated from rationalised economic considerations. The best and most potent incentives to improvement are those that people accept as leading towards the good life as they conceive it; and the best social attitudes to inculcate for agriculture, as for development generally, are those that lead to the realisation of individual and community aspirations towards their conception of the good life. To ascertain this is one of the prime prerequisites of development planning.

12 · Planning the Rural Sector

TARLOK SINGH[1]

Over the past decade, the economies of several underdeveloped countries have expanded in production, income and employment. Frequently, the benefits have been concentrated in a few areas and have been shared mainly by a small section of the population. At the same time, the rural sector as a whole has lagged behind, and the growth of population has pressed more harshly on it. The complex nature and implications for public policy of this situation are not conveyed fully by such expressions as the development of a dual economy or of disparities in the growth of urban and rural areas and of areas of greater or smaller economic change. Indeed, the question how the economy of a nation and of its rural sector can grow in step with one another now lies at the heart of the problem of development in the poorer countries. Though there are common issues, the problem is by no means identical for every country, for factors such as population and area, climate and rainfall, cropping system, the rate and pattern of economic growth, the institutional and political background and the role and direction of planning together constitute much more than a difference in degree in the conditions of development between one country and another. In seeking principles of economic and social change which may have a measure of general validity, it has to be stressed that each country presents a somewhat unique situation in terms of its national economy and even more in its rural sector in which so much of its past is inevitably embedded.

In its economic aspect, an economy can be described as ' national ' if, within its entire range, goods, services, labour and resources can move freely and the prices at which they are available vary within comparatively small limits, as determined by differences in transportation and other costs. This degree of economic integration has been achieved only in the more advanced countries and, among them, to a greater extent in the smaller than in the larger countries. Everywhere, in the more as well as the less developed countries, the process can be seen at work, but there are wide differences in the pace at which economic integration occurs, the areas in which its influence is specially marked, and the relative impact of different factors of change. Consideration of the place of the rural sector in the national economy, therefore, turns into an enquiry into measures and policies for enabling the rural sector to contribute its maximum to economic growth and into conditions under which the rural economy and the economy of the nation as a whole can grow together without developing too great a divergence in productivity, incomes, opportunities for gainful employment and levels of living.

The rural sector may be understood to comprise that part of the output of goods and services and of employment within the economy which depends directly or indirectly on the exploitation of land conceived as a natural resource. Thus, crop production, horticulture, animal husbandry, dairying, poultry, forestry and, by a slight extension of meaning, fisheries, will constitute the rural sector. Within it, we may reckon both primary production and processing up to the final or the intermediate stage as the case may be. A steel plant or a chemical works or an engineering workshop, even if set in the heart of a vast rural area, will form part of the industrial economy falling outside the rural sector as described above. In its composition, the rural sector will include all agricultural and allied production, rural industry, especially household and small-scale industry, trade in what is produced by and what is required for agriculture and allied branches of activity and for rural industry, and services and construction associated with agricultural production and rural industry and trade and rural life generally.

Outside agriculture, precise data corresponding to such a definition of the rural sector are not easy to come by. The size of the rural sector within the national economy has, therefore, to be judged roughly in terms of estimates of (a) the working force and (b) the net domestic product represented by activities included in it. There are conceptual and computable problems in ascertaining the share of the rural sector in small industries, construction and trade, though gradually in many countries new refinements are being introduced.[2] In India, in 1960–1, out of a total working force of 187 million, 137 million or about 70 per cent were accounted for by agriculture and allied activities, 7 per cent by small industries, about 4·5 per cent by trade and allied services and about a million by 'construction'. In terms of contribution to the net domestic product, in that year agriculture and allied activities accounted for over 51 per cent, and small industries, construction and trade for 20 per cent over the entire economy. The significance of these and other similar data is twofold. The growth of the national economy and its inherent strength cannot be far ahead of the sector which accounts for more than three-quarters of the working force and close on two-thirds of the net domestic product. Secondly, important as the modern sector is for the transformation of an economy, agriculture remains at the very centre. Taken as a whole, the national economy will advance in the measure in which, at each step, the growth of the greater part of industry supports and is derived from the growth of agriculture and the rural sector. In other words, in an underdeveloped country, an integrated national economy emerges only towards the end of a prolonged process of integration between the industrial and the urban economy on the one hand and agriculture and the rural economy on the other. To define the place of the rural sector in the national economy and in relation to changes in the composition of output and occupational distribution of the working force is, therefore, to recognise the need to plan consciously and systematically to bring about such integration.

The rural sector has to be seen in its two basic and interrelated aspects –
as a rural society and as a rural economy. As a society, it is composed of:
- (*a*) those who own the land or have permanent rights in it;
- (*b*) those who work on the land as tenants or labourers and are themselves
  landless or nearly so, sometimes combining with field work certain
  menial village services;
- (*c*) those engaged in rural service crafts;
- (*d*) those engaged in trade and allied activities.

In some societies, as in India, caste and the ownership of land have gone
together and the lower castes have remained virtually landless. In the case of
rural artisans, in the past caste was frequently associated with occupation.
To observe rural society as a whole is to realise both the high degree of interdependence and the high degree of divergence which subsists between the
interests and the needs of different groups and the extent to which economic
and social factors are intertwined. The impact of economic and social
changes is, therefore, different for different groups. This is an important
consideration in planning for the rural sector in relation to the national
economy.

The social structure through which, historically and traditionally, the
various economic and social interests have come together, is the village. The
nature of the village differs from country to country and even in different
parts of the same country. The vast majority of villages are small communities. In India, out of about 565,000 villages, 31 per cent have a population of less than 200, 62 per cent of less than 500 and 95 per cent of less than
2,000. Out of a total rural population of 359 million in 1961, 75 million
lived in villages with a smaller population than 500, 173 million in villages
of between 500 and 2,000 and 111 million in larger villages. Whatever the
area of operation for any aspect of rural development, in most regions the
village is a basic social reality to be reckoned with and is either a base for,
or an essential link in, any larger organisation.

On the economic side, the dominant fact of the rural sector is the crucial
place in it of agriculture as an industry. Incomes, productivity, levels of
living and employment, equally with economic and social relationships,
derive mainly from agriculture – from the pressure of population, the
quality of land, the stability of production, depending on whether there is
irrigation or assured rainfall, the manner in which rights in land are distributed, and the level of technology in vogue. In looking at agriculture,
instantly we come face to face with the economic, institutional, technological
and resource development aspects of the rural sector as a whole. For long,
agriculture and, therefore, the rural economy, was static and inward-looking.

Growth of population and of industry and cities and towns extends the
market for agricultural products and creates the basis for the rapid development of agriculture and the rural sector. But this will bear fruit in the

measure in which the central problem of increasing agricultural productivity is dealt with simultaneously in its several aspects. These aspects include: changes in rights in land, extension services, community effort, credit and supplies, technological research and development, strengthening of the resource base through irrigation, drainage and soil conservation, imparting of new skills equally with mass education, the utilisation of rural manpower and the provision of a more adequate infrastructure by way of markets, communications and other facilities. With these, there is need also to reshape and strengthen individual production units in agriculture.

The total task to be undertaken is of such magnitude and complexity that along with a comprehensive and somewhat longer term design of development there has to be concentration at key points and in key areas so as to obtain rapid increases in agricultural production. For lags in agricultural output create a whole range of imbalances within the national economy – in relation to supply of food for the urban areas and for weaker sections in the rural areas, supply of raw materials for industry, and pressures on prices and the balance of payments. Dependence on rainfall, fluctuations in agricultural output and weaknesses in organisation greatly accentuate the effects of even small and marginal shortages. The imbalances may become so difficult to manage as to bring economic development almost to a halt, especially in countries with large populations, rapid urbanisation and industrial growth and heavy import liabilities.

The physical and economic conditions under which agricultural activities are carried out differ enormously from one country to another and indeed within the same country. Therefore, the regional approach forms a necessary intermediate stage in planning for agriculture in relation to the requirements of the national economy. There are areas in which crops are reasonably assured, others in which they are uncertain. From the standpoint of the national economy, the former have special importance and, at any rate, over the short period, a comparatively larger flow to them of resources by way of investment funds, scarce materials and extension facilities would be justified. However, the capacity of an area or of an agricultural community to absorb resources and achieve large increases in output depends only in part on favourable physical factors. Likewise, in areas less favoured in physical conditions, there is no reason to assume that a better economic balance may not be achieved. In addition to whatever can be done to improve the rural environment and provide an adequate infrastructure of services, production units in agriculture which are better organised and equipped than those now existing could enhance the ability of farmers to profit from favourable natural conditions and elsewhere to overcome limitations due to unfavourable natural conditions. To convert the existing farm units into efficient production organisation is an aspect of agricultural planning whose critical importance for the national economy has yet to be fully appreciated.

For the under-estimation of the importance of the organisational factor in agricultural policy, a possible reason may be found in the increases in agricultural output which were achieved in many underdeveloped countries during the first years of their developmental effort. These perhaps created the expectation that steady advances in agriculture could continue to materialise with measures such as were then initiated, especially extension services and community development and the spread of irrigation. The gains in the first phase were due to a large extent to the expansion of areas under cultivation and to the utilisation of knowledge from research results already available. These were factors which could be quickly brought into play with the widening of the market and through the initiative of individual farmers.

In the next phase in agriculture, which has been hastened by the experience of stagnation in recent years in many countries (including India) the major emphasis is on inputs and supplies, especially fertilisers and pesticides. The importance of inputs has been enhanced almost dramatically by the development and spread of high yielding varieties of rice, wheat, maize and millets. In turn, this poses certain new problems, both of organisation and of allocation priorities.

In time, answers to these problems will be found and some of the current limitations in supplies will also be overcome. It will then be seen that there is a third and a more difficult phase in agriculture which underdeveloped countries cannot avoid. The growth of population, the requirements of industry and the need to improve nutritional standards make it obligatory upon them to achieve growth objectives over the next decade or two which are far larger than any envisaged in the past.[3] Although approaches will differ this very fact should compel each country to make a well-considered effort to solve the problems of organisation in agriculture, to rationalise the land system, to establish economic production units, and to diversify the rural economy and expand employment opportunities. These tasks can only be accomplished if structural changes within the rural sector, growth in

Table 1 *Estimates of aggregate demand for selected agricultural commodities in 1970–1 and 1975–6*

Commodity	Unit	1960–1	1970–1	1975–6
1. Foodgrains	million tons	82·0	122·8	152·0
2. Cotton	lakh bales	53·9	89·5	111·5
3. Jute and mesta	lakh bales	51·1	100·0	125·0
4. Oilseeds	lakh tons	66·3	125·5	159·7
5. Sugar cane (Gur)	lakh tons	106·1	135·0	160·0
6. Tobacco	million kg.	311·9	431·5	525·3
7. Milk and milk products	million tons	18·6	34·5	48·2
8. Fruits and nuts	Index	100·0	137·5	163·9
9. Vegetables	Index	100·0	124·8	140·6
10. Meat, fish and eggs	Index	100·0	126·8	344·2

agriculture and rapid development of the national economy proceed side by side as organic elements in the plan of development.

From the first stages in planning, almost all the less developed countries have assigned the 'first priority' to agriculture. However, the precise connotation of this expression and its implications for resource allocation, for organisation and for economic policy have become clear only gradually and as a result of frequent setbacks in agriculture. Since the nature of the agricultural problem itself changes as the economy expands and throws up new tasks, it is to be expected that the demands which agriculture makes on resources, personnel, organisation and policy will become even greater and more pressing in the future. The change occurs both at the level of quantity and quality.

Although over the years, considerable practical experience has been gained in preparing and implementing agricultural plans, there is still much to be learnt. Attempts which have been made to systematise experience in this field have not yet gained sufficient precision; there is need to focus closer attention on ways of resolving some of the key problems which arise. Estimates of agricultural production to be aimed at, which are often misnamed as targets, assessment of levels of production achieved and determination of the contribution of different factors to growth in production are of great importance in agricultural planning. But statistical data in agriculture leave much to be desired and improvements come but slowly. Through crop-cutting experiments carried out by sampling methods, for a wide range of crops, data on yields are now better than they were some years ago, but there are still considerable shortcomings in respect of areas under different crops. Although some experimental work has been undertaken to establish 'yardsticks' of additional production, which could provide a sound basis for estimating physical production possibilities and ascertaining the requirements of scarce resources, the data available so far are essentially illustrative, leaving much of the practical work of planning and estimation to be performed with cruder information and judgement.[4]

Despite limitations of data, efforts have been made in successive Five-Year Plans in India to consider in much detail, with reference to population growth, norms of requirements for industries, *per capita* availability and other factors, the levels of output for different crops which need to be achieved over each plan period. Along with these, with the help of available yardsticks or norms, attempts have been made to estimate the quantities of fertilisers and pesticides and other material inputs needed and the requirements of trained personnel. In proposing production goals, account is also taken of existing and future irrigation from large and small works and the benefits anticipated from soil conservation and other land development programmes.

The resources and programmes envisaged are accompanied by estimates of investment requirements and by corresponding allocations in the plan. In respect of supplies of inputs, such as fertilisers, pesticides and tractors, the expected internal production is noted and the import requirements are incorporated into the foreign exchange budget drawn up for the plan period. For these and other associated steps in agricultural planning the methodology and the work 'drill' have come to be fairly established though doubtless, at many points, improvements in technical programming are still called for.

Planning of such magnitude is only the first step. On the side of plan implementation, certain shortfalls, which had become familiar, yield but slowly to improved administrative action and organisation. Thorough application of modern management techniques and systems analysis could help reduce the gaps and imbalances which occur in practice in so complex a field as agriculture. Much can be done to ensure that budgetary allocations, provision of personnel, supply of fertilisers and other inputs, credit and progress in utilising new irrigation, are in accordance with plan proposals. The operational plans can be made more precise and adjustments can be more orderly. Even so, the hazards and risks to which agriculture is exposed will always leave a large area of uncertainty in giving effect to the best laid plans.

Beyond the problems of planning and implementation, a few other issues of considerable import have come up in recent years to which attention should be drawn. In agriculture, the ultimate decisions are highly decentralised. Yet the average farmer operates under severe limitations in terms of land surface, water resources, supplies, credit and, above all, knowledge and information. Each of these is a field for action in agricultural development and is replete with practical organisational and policy problems to which satisfactory answers are being found only as experience is gained and inadequacies of the effort made at each stage have come to be realised. Secondly, a characteristic of the situation found in many countries is that only a small proportion of the farmers have a surplus to sell and are in a position to pursue 'commercial' agriculture along scientific lines; many more operate only subsistence farms.

With urbanisation and economic growth, the 'commercial' sector in agriculture no doubt becomes larger, and technological developments, such as high yielding varieties and improved extension and credit facilities, may diminish some of the disadvantages of the small farmer. Nevertheless, it is true that in planning agriculture, two separate groups of farmers and two separate interests have to be catered for, namely, those who have holdings large enough to enable them to produce for the market, and those, constituting by far the greater number, who are barely producing enough for themselves and who work against heavy odds. There is an element of conflict in the allocation of scarce resources between these two groups of farmers, which recent technological developments are even tending to sharpen. The approach of intensive area development, which gave priority to the more favourably placed areas but, within these, sought to carry forward the farm community as a whole, is an attempt to resolve this dilemma, and is to be preferred to an approach which picks upon ' surplus ' farmers and does little for the rest.

There are three other important issues in agricultural planning which may be briefly mentioned. The importance of research support for agricultural extension is being increasingly recognised. But the approach to agricultural research is still mainly technological. Much would be gained and farm investments could be more soundly planned if, from the beginning, the study of technical possibilities and economic and financial implications for farms of varying sizes could be conceived of together, as part of the same operation. Secondly, recent technological developments, in their emphasis on inputs and investment, are overlooking the importance of utilising the available labour and manpower resources as an essential ingredient in the strategy of agricultural and rural advance. Thirdly, agricultural planning should embody a clear view concerning tools and implements and the approach to mechanisation. These aspects are for separate consideration. It is, however, necessary to stress, in relation to them all, that, in agricultural and rural development, the production organisation and the manpower base have central significance for public policy and should not be regarded as incidental or merely long-term aspects of agricultural and economic development.

We may turn now to three sets of specific economic issues which arise in the planning of agriculture. These concern (*a*) investment, (*b*) prices, wages and costs and (*c*) finance of agricultural and economic development.

When observers of the scene in underdeveloped countries sometimes plead for concentration on agriculture, with industry and social services relegated to a much lower place, they do not give enough weight to the interrelationships which exist between a wide range of investments in the context of agriculture. Broadly, agriculture needs both direct and indirect investments. The direct investments are those which bear directly on agricultural production. They may be further divided into short-term and long-term, the latter being devoted particularly to resource development and the strengthening of institutional arrangements and production organisations. The indirect investments may be economic or social in content. The former will include the development of industries important for agriculture, such as fertiliser plants, the manufacture of agricultural implements and machinery and the opening up of rural communications. Industrial investments will call for the allocation of foreign exchange along with the domestic resources needed. To the extent that internal production is expected to fall short of requirements, for instance, of essential fertiliser supplies, foreign exchange will also be needed for imports.

Allocation of foreign exchange, in the midst of difficulties which have been encountered repeatedly in recent years, is a good test of the degree of priority given to agriculture in the total plan, specially in the phase of development in which inputs and supplies have a dominant role. Among social investments, the most important are those which facilitate the expansion of education and skills among rural communities. Few would wish to question Schultz's emphasis on human capital as a major source of economic growth from agriculture; but often, in practice, there is failure to appreciate that too narrow an approach to investment in agriculture leads to the same kind of weaknesses as investment which is too small in volume in relation to the needs and the physical possibilities of development which exist in any region or area.

Another aspect of investment in agriculture is the relative contribution of public and private investment to the growth of agriculture. Through farm management studies there is now better knowledge of the nature and extent of private investment in agriculture. Aside from land and cattle, for the vast majority of agricultural holdings, investment per acre is altogether too small. Yet the large sums now devoted to irrigation, rural electrification, roads and other essential projects cannot yield their maximum benefits without at the same time intensifying investment in labour and in capital, such as can be achieved only at the level of the production unit. This is another important reason for stressing the need for reorganising agriculture, so that production units engaged in this industry will have the resources and the capacity greatly to enlarge the quantum of private investment.

In the recent past, the terms of trade for agricultural commodities have improved significantly. The improvement has come partly under the pressure of shortages which have forced up price levels and partly from recognition that without remunerative prices the farmer cannot undertake the investment essential in scientific agriculture. In India, an agricultural prices commission has been engaged in bringing economic and statistical data to bear on the determination of agricultural prices but, by its nature, in this field the prevailing levels of prices, expectations of the future, and judgement on the overall requirements of the economy play a large part. In the past, low prices for farm produce caused anxiety; now, the greater concern is that, because of inadequate machinery for ensuring stability of prices at whatever levels may be considered appropriate, prices of individual agricultural commodities get pushed up and throw out of focus other related prices. Management of agricultural prices has, thus, become a much more crucial area of agricultural planning than it was in earlier periods.

By far the greater part of labour employed in agriculture is family farm labour. Hired workers are required mainly in the sowing and harvesting seasons for supplementing family labour, especially on medium-sized farms. The demand for labour varies with the cropping pattern, intensity of irrigation and the social characteristics of landowners. The larger holdings require hired workers for longer periods. Under legislation enacted in India in the early fifties, minimum wages have to be prescribed for agricultural labourers in different areas according to the prevailing conditions, but it is generally believed that enforcement is poor, and the course of wages mainly follows the circumstances of local supply and demand.

In respect of agricultural labour, the extent and continuity of employment are even more important than the amount of wages paid for days for which work becomes available. A substantial part of the problem of low income and low standards of living is to be found among this section of the rural community. As population increases and those with better-sized holdings take to personal cultivation with more capital intensive techniques and as smallholdings get still smaller, a considerable body of landless agricultural workers find themselves, as it were, cast out of the rural economy without, however, adequate opportunities for work offering in any non-agricultural sector instead. It is obvious that, on a broader view, plans for agriculture must also embody plans for employment for those sections of the rural community who are not directly engaged in cultivation. At this point agriculture and the rural sector have to be seen together as an organic whole.

In view of the relatively small element in production costs of agricultural commodities accounted for by the wages of hired workers, in most under-developed countries, the high costs of production must be attributed to other causes. These include small and uneconomic agricultural holdings, failure to utilise available labour and the work animals which have to be maintained through the year, low levels of technology and low productivity. To the extent to which prices of agricultural produce become more remunerative for the farmer who has a surplus to sell, they become more burdensome to the urban consumer and the agricultural labourer. On the whole, if sudden spurts of agricultural prices, which occur from time to time mainly because of failures in economic management, could be avoided, then levels of agricultural prices which provide for adequate incentives for the farmer could form a basis for steady increase in productivity and eventually for reasonable levels of prices for the consumer. Price policy in agriculture and plans for the raising of labour productivity have, therefore, to be viewed as parts of a common scheme for action.

As at present organised, rural communities can finance only a small part of the investment required in agriculture. The level of rural savings in a country such as India is much too meagre for the situation to be otherwise. According to a comprehensive all-India survey undertaken in 1962, the average net saving of a rural household amounted only to Rs.63 per year. Over 60 per cent of the households returned negative net saving; barely 15 per cent of the households saved more than the average. Among self-employed farmers taken as a group, the average net saving was Rs.101;

agricultural wage earners indicated negative saving.[5] A proportion of the rural savings among the better-off sections tends to pass into urban forms of investment.

Investment in agriculture is, therefore, heavily dependent on public funds and on the flow of credit resources from the financial system into the rural economy. The channels for such a flow of credit finance have yet to be cleared, partly because banks and financial institutions (other than co-operative agencies) operate mainly in relation to industry and trade in the towns and partly because few production units in agriculture are organised to absorb and effectively utilise credit granted on a wholly commercial basis.

The contribution which the rural sector can make through taxation towards the development of agriculture and of the economy as a whole is also limited on account of a number of institutional factors. The situation in most under-developed countries is unlike that in the early period of economic development in Japan. Thus, in the recent past, the large rural vote has induced all parties in India to begin forgoing land revenue. In the past, land revenue has been levied on all holdings on the theory that it was a rent due to the State rather than a tax on income. In giving up traditional systems, no effort is being made yet to devise ways in which the rural economy could contribute more adequately to its own future development. Despite limitations due to the system of land-holding and cultivation and the present pressures, a constructive approach to rural taxation must still be sought.

Irrigation rates, betterment cesses, taxes on commercial crops, increases in the value of land in many favoured areas, investment in the mobilisation of rural manpower to build up productive assets and assets of value to rural communities, and contributions in kind and in the form of voluntary labour, are among the directions in which much more can be done, given the necessary leadership and organisation – particularly at the level of the local community itself. In the main, however, these possibilities will be of value for local capital formation and development, and the greater part of finance and credit will have to come from what is at present regarded as the non-rural sector of the national economy. To the extent to which the financial system is organised so as to channel resources effectively to the rural areas, there will be greater integration between the rural sector and the national economy, the larger flow of financial resources will be matched by larger marketable surpluses, levels of agricultural output will rise faster, and the rural sector will be able to save and invest more in its own development. In areas of greater prosperity, the contribution of the rural sector towards the development of the regional economy as a whole should also increase steadily.

Seen in its wider relationships, as suggested earlier, the rural sector involves much more than agriculture or those engaged in cultivation. But, as an industry, agriculture is the foundation of the rural economy. Important as they are, all other activities as well as measures for solving the economic and social problems of other sections of the rural community flow directly or indirectly from agriculture and are complementary to it. The organisation and development of agriculture has to be, therefore, the main plank in rebuilding the rural economy as a whole.

13 · Priorities in Agricultural Production and Rural Industry

EDMUNDO FLORES[1]

National economic development is a process which requires the growth and modernisation of both the rural and industrial-urban sectors. Whether such growth is more or less balanced during the early stages of development or not depends on the specific history and circumstances of the nation in question. In my opinion, no universal generalisations are valid regarding alternatives but the discussion of the specific conditions that would lead us to choose one alternative instead of the other helps to illustrate the general dynamics of rural development.

DOMESTIC FOOD CROPS OR CASH CROPS?

Categorically both. But it must be quickly added that we are really facing here a matter of degree. Today we can assume neither a closed economy nor a perfect market in the international trade of agricultural products. This means that a degree of self-sufficiency in food supply is highly desirable while, at the same time, increased volumes of agricultural exports are essential to pay for the growing quantities of consumption goods and, above all, capital goods that must be imported during the initial and intermediate stages of industrialisation.

Cuba provides a good example. After Castro took over at the beginning of 1959, the Cubans tried to diminish the importance of their basic export crop, sugar-cane, and tried instead to produce their own food. They had an obsession against their single-crop economy, which symbolised their colonial status, and went to the extreme of destroying thousands of hectares of perfectly good sugar plantings already in production. Naïvely, they thought that industry and domestic food production could take the place of sugar-cane overnight.

After a few sobering years, Cuban planners have moved to a more practical position and are trying to become, in the words of Castro, 'the best producers of sugar-cane in the world'. They are now aware of the need to export sugar in increasing quantities in order to obtain the ever-growing quantities of capital goods and raw materials, such as petroleum and cotton, which they need for their ambitious programme of industrialisation. In fact, they aimed to produce a record ten million tons of sugar by 1970. In addition, they have gone massively into the production of oranges, coffee, tobacco and bananas for domestic consumption and export.

At the same time, however, the welfare and full employment measures instituted by the Castro régime have increased tremendously the demand for food, since, at the very low income levels which prevailed, the income elasticity of the demand for food was high. Thus the pressing need to produce more food led to their determined effort to develop domestic food production: rice, beans, maize, fresh vegetables, fruits and animal products.

Underlying this whole process we find a characteristic feature of underdevelopment: the lack of applied knowledge and previous research, which renders peculiarly difficult the successful establishment, in the short run, of new economic activities whether they be new crops or manufactures. Referring to Cuba again, Cubans knew how to produce sugar, albeit at ridiculously low yields per hectare, and how to produce the best tobacco in the world; but they did not know how and where to grow other products. This they are learning with the assistance of Soviet and Israeli technicians mainly through the time-consuming process of trial and error, since their foreign advisers do not know much about tropical agriculture either.

LARGE OR SMALL SCALE FARMING? MECHANISATION?

Most of the current controversy about farm size is ideological and is carried on without resort to empirical evidence. Professor T. W. Schultz has observed:

Strongly held beliefs about the 'proper' farm size make it difficult to examine this question without incurring the risk of being misunderstood. An appeal to the concept of 'returns to scale' is as a rule barren because the transformation of traditional agriculture always entails the introduction of one or more new agricultural factors, and therefore it gives rise to a process in which the critical question is not one of scale but of factor proportionality.[2]

Empirical evidence shows that the scale of successful agricultural units varies widely not only from country to country but even regionally, and that generally the size of the unit is not the variable that accounts for success. Variations in the location of the unit, changes in the prices of inputs and outputs, obsolescence, and the ubiquitous surge of external economies and diseconomies so typical of contemporary dynamic societies are all reflected in the costs imputed to land, and tend to make its 'optimum area' oscillate widely and continuously.

The seemingly compulsive quest for the optimum size of the agricultural unit must be attributed in part to the erroneous belief that economies of scale in agriculture are as important as in industry – that when agricultural units reach a certain size it becomes possible to introduce mass production methods that lower unit costs and effect considerable savings. In industrial production, in distribution, and in merchandising, economies from enlarged scales of operations are common, but emphatically this is not the case in agriculture.

The really important question in the development of the agricultural sector, I believe, is not the scale of farming of individual or single units, which may vary according to local geography, to tradition, and to political preferences, but rather *the proportion of the labour force productively employed in agriculture* vis-à-vis *the proportion engaged in secondary and tertiary activities.*

There is no ideal answer to this question and its solution in concrete cases lies within the following opposite limits: on the one hand, if a country is going to develop, the proportion of its labour force engaged in agriculture should diminish steadily until it reaches around one-fifth of the total labour force,[3] on the other hand, this shift from agriculture to urban-industrial employment ideally should be commensurate with the increase of the demand for labour outside farming,[4] otherwise it generates urban unemployment and misery as well as a shortage of labour in farming. This is why it is essential to devise, nurture and preserve the institutions and incentives that contribute to anchoring the farm population in rural areas until they can be productively employed elsewhere. This goes a long way to explain the prevalence in developing economies of a dual agriculture: a rapidly modernising, commercial sector, and a traditional, semi-stagnant, subsistence sector. In this particular context, the high concentration of land ownership and the landlessness and poverty of the peasants characteristic of Latin American *latifundia*[5] push the peasants to migrate massively to the cities (or to join the guerrillas); while the communal, cooperative or collective tenure arrangements fostered by land reforms tend to hold them in the land because of the effect of incentives and controls which improve living conditions, diminish alienation and open up wider vistas of opportunity for the new generations. Consequently, migration towards the cities tends to take place more nearly in response to the increases in the demand for labour in industrial-urban work.

MECHANISATION

There was a time when it made sense to discuss whether to mechanise agriculture or not. The subject, I suspect, owed some of its popularity to the aura that Soviet propaganda conferred upon early tractors, at a time when mechanisation implied the use of heavy equipment for a rather limited number of tasks. Enlightened excerpts of the discussion included mention of the availability of unlimited labour supplies *vis-à-vis* capital scarcity, labour-saving devices *versus* capital-saving devices, and the marginal productivity of capital and labour in farming and outside it. Those times are gone. Modern agricultural technology is a long, complex chain of innovations, which uses in many places mechanised devices that cannot be disentangled from non-mechanised devices.

Whether to develop agriculture *now* or *later* is a valid policy alternative which merits careful analysis. But once it is decided to transform traditional agriculture into modern, high-yield, diversified agriculture, then resort to mechanised inputs in different areas and levels of the productive process becomes unavoidable. For instance, the construction of irrigation dams requires earth-moving equipment, clearing and levelling equipment, generators and so forth. Irrigated lands, in turn, must be used intensively and this implies heavy capital *and* labour inputs in ploughing, fertilisers, fumigation, packaging, refrigeration and transportation. Primitive labour methods alone simply cannot do the job. Assuming modern technology, the substitutability of capital for unskilled labour is very low and obviously without technology development is impossible.

In addition, one must take into account Duesemberry's demonstration effect and realise that, except under extreme conditions of isolation and of capital rationing in the whole economy, the peasants, farmers and politicians of our time have already been exposed to modern means of production, transportation and communication. We must realise that altogether too many people are aware of the magic of motor cars, tractors, trains, diesel engines, mechanical reapers, refrigeration, television, radios and fumigating airplanes. Consequently, the temptation to resort to modern technology in farm operations is strong and the use of machines confers certain prestige upon its users. Once the public or the private sector of a nation succumbs to this temptation, it does not take long to realise that modern agricultural technology comes in ever growing packages, that many parts of the package are mechanised (and soon will be automated) and that the early adoption of the latest innovations often pays handsome dividends, particularly in areas where competition is very keen, such as tropical agriculture.[6]

WATER RESOURCES INCLUDING IRRIGATION

Much of the underdeveloped world needs irrigation, flood control and electrification. Managing water resources requires a construction industry. In the words of Arthur Lewis:

More than half of capital formation consists of work in building and construction. Hence the expansion of capital is a function of the rate at which the building and construction industry can be expanded . . . Hence the question of how rapidly capital formation can be accelerated resolves itself first into the question how rapidly the building industry can be expanded.[7]

The construction of irrigation works and highways is a strategic measure that induces the establishment of a multitude of new productive activities. Albert Hirschman would say that the sequence: irrigation–highways (which in this order is highly complementary) has numerous *backward linkage effects and forward linkage effects*.[8] The development of Mexico provides a good illustration. The land reform initiated in 1917 had a very strong redistributive character. The peasants who received free land grants increased their command over food and, rather than selling it, they ate it immediately; thus corroborating the notion that, at subsistence levels, food shows a high income elasticity. Unhappily for urban dwellers, the sudden unleashing of such a backlog of peasant hunger brought forth acute food shortages. Urban unrest forced the politicians to find measures to secure more food. Since it could not be imported, and the peasants would not surrender their recently acquired rights to a larger share of the agricultural product, agricultural development became imperative.

In a huge semi-desert country, where roads were few and bad, agricultural development meant the construction of irrigation dams and of highways. This required, of course, the establishment of a construction industry – basically cement and steel – which eventually, through import substitution, has turned into a rather diversified, fast-growing industrial sector. Since 1925 Mexico has built dams that irrigate 2·5 million hectares as well as a network of 65,000 kilometres of all-weather highways. Since 1930 agriculture has developed at a sustained average annual rate of 5·4 per cent, and industry at slightly over 6 per cent. A study on the comparative growth of agriculture in twenty-six developing nations shows that from 1948 to 1963 the growth of Mexican agriculture was only exceeded by Israel and Japan.[9] Incidentally, from 1917 to 1942, Mexico had no access to foreign capital because of the nationalisation of land, railroads and petroleum. Therefore, public works were built by resorting to deficit financing, while capital imports were paid for mainly with the export of agricultural products.[10] Rates of inflation have been moderate in Latin American terms.

RURAL INDUSTRIALISATION AND TECHNOLOGY

The agriculture of most developing nations shows high levels of seasonal, disguised and outright unemployment. Ironically such unemployment or 'dead time' often coincides with the presence of large food surpluses. Several ways have been tried to lessen rural unemployment: temporary migration to other nations, migration to industrial-urban centres, diversification and integration of farming and cattle-breeding to absorb more man-days per year and, finally, rural industrialisation. Although all these measures are complementary, the last one seems particularly attractive because at the same time it touches another dramatic problem of our time: the increasing centralisation of industry.

However, there are several trends that effectively countervail rural industrialisation policies. First, in the early stages of industrialisation the economies of agglomeration generated in urban-industrial centres exceed by far its diseconomies; secondly, it has been observed that generally those who leave the farm are endowed with a higher degree of innovational capabilities than those who remain in rural areas who seem to be more tradition-bound; thirdly, concentrating scarce capital and even more scarce personnel to bring about change in a few selected strategic points seems more promising, in the initial stages at any rate, than spreading them over vast rural expanses. However, after the early stages have been successfully by-passed, the possibility of extending employment and industrialisation in rural areas, beyond the industrial activities induced by agriculture and into, say, watch-making, electronics, textiles and certain mechanical industries that require intensive labour inputs, by the spread of the cottage industry, seems to offer a very appealing solution.

RESEARCH

The problem of research is intimately related to the need for massive education and technical training. The returns to investment on research have been studied for the case of the United States and they are so high that they seem to belong in the realm of science fiction: 700 per cent for every dollar invested on hybrid corn research.[11] There is no reason to suppose that returns would be less spectacular in developing countries. In fact, the joint research of the Ministry of Agriculture and the Rockefeller Foundation on hybrid wheat in Mexico has been as spectacular as that of hybrid corn in the United States. Average wheat yields in Mexico increased in less than ten years from 800 kilograms per hectare to 2·4 metric tons per hectare and yields of 8 tons per hectare are not unusual. In ten years Mexico, a traditional wheat-importing country, began to export around one million tons of wheat annually.

The experience of Mexico indicates that the success of a large-scale programme of education can be accelerated by importing technical assistance from abroad and by using the advanced training facilities of foreign universities to train large groups of scientists. However, the process of transplanting modern research and development techniques requires the prevalence of several preconditions. A certain measure of nationalism can avoid a 'brain drain'; fast rates of growth are essential to assure the rapid incorporation to local technical cadres of the technicians trained abroad and, finally, political stability and peace are essential. The Rockefeller Foundation has operated in Mexico and Colombia. We hear constantly of their Mexican success but there is no mention of Colombia. For the last fifteen years Colombia has had a very turbulent history. Large numbers of people have been murdered in rural areas. Under such conditions agricultural research and extension services cannot be easily carried on.

14 · Land Reform

ERICH JACOBY[1]

Land reform and development strategy are very close to each other and it can even be suggested that consideration of land reform is an integrated part of this strategy. If land reform is successful, it will release additional energies for production and initiative and change not only indifferent peasants and those still feudally bound, into active agriculturalists, but also those peasant farmers whose numbers are very great, who are inhibited by customary tenure from achieving a breakthrough from the subsistence level farming now so unnecessarily their lot. In this way land reform could become a measure for the achievement of national economic and social integration.

Land reform is an attempt to bring the institutional framework for agriculture into line with the requirements of social and economic progress. This, however, can only be achieved if the objectives of land reform correspond with the ideas and ideologies of the society concerned.[2] This objective naturally contains a very strong subjective element, and the interpretation of the concept of social and economic progress and of the ideas and ideologies prevalent in the society by the evaluator will necessarily be based on his subjective approach. Every valuation and consequently every land reform programme, therefore, will contain a certain bias – and there is nothing wrong about that. The important point is that the evaluator and planner of land reform demonstrates his bias by establishing the criteria for his approach and giving his concept of the land reform planned and his concept of social and economic progress. The process of evaluation of the cultural and traditional background of the community concerned has to be, of course, a scientific one and should involve the proper selection of facts and their systematic interpretation; but we should be aware of the fact that the cultural features and the whole outlook of the community will be a different one after the process of agrarian reform has been successfully concluded. It will be a community receptive to progress and this – in a very summary way – is the contribution which land reform can make to national development.

It is not the purpose of this paper to develop a programme of land reform and to establish the relationships of its individual parts to the national development. Such an approach would be a piecemeal one and could not reveal the fundamental interrelationships and interdependencies between land reform and economic progress which a basic change in the socio-economic pattern will actually involve, because our vision would be narrowed to details and the whole picture would be fragmented; at the same time the proportions would be distorted and the emphasis changed from land reform as a fully integrated approach to individual structural programmes which under different conditions might mean very different things. All that this paper intends to achieve is to indicate the extent to which land reform as a whole can help to provide the rural basis for national development. In the following sections of this paper we will investigate how land reform can do this and we will give in this context specific attention to the problems of tribal areas.

WHAT CAN LAND REFORM DO?

Land reform in its broadest meaning can:

(*a*) Introduce a change in the land- and income-distribution pattern, which has been marked by outdated tenure conditions and by rural stagnation; in this way it will provide incentives for additional efforts in agricultural production.

(*b*) It can improve the land-use pattern in such a way that it can carry an energetic rural community.

(*c*) It can give human dignity to the peasants, awaken the people to accept education and innovations and open their eyes to the opportunities of economic, social and technical progress; all this will affect productivity favourably.

(*d*) It can help to produce more food with less people and free in this way labour for industrialisation and provide food for urban industrial centres. It can help to establish an efficient agricultural industry with processing factories distributed in rural areas.

(*e*) It can help to settle indigenous nomadic populations and change agricultural tribes into integrated agricultural communities.

Land reform can do all this and it can do only parts of it; but, whatever it will do, it will introduce a change which will have considerable effects on national development, since the climate of a change itself shakes outdated traditions, and makes people ready to accept innovations.

HOW CAN LAND REFORM ACHIEVE ITS OBJECTIVES?

It is today generally accepted that the approach to agrarian reform has to be an integrated one. That means that the planning and implementation has to proceed in various fields in a coordinated manner in order to achieve a global structural improvement. This policy has to be planned and implemented within the framework of the national economic development plan and has to be closely adjusted to its objectives. In a campaign for economic and social progress, isolated measures will not succeed, since positive results can only be obtained by a programme which is interlinked and takes into consideration the interdependencies of all factors concerned. From this point of view land reform by definition will only be successful when it can form the rural basis for national economic development.

A. *Establishment of priorities and institutional surveys*

The governments which are responsible for the determination and definition of structural policies in general and land reform in particular, will have to establish their priorities, within the programme of land reform, with a view to accelerating the achievement of the national development objectives. The selection of the priorities will often be difficult and depend to a considerable extent on the results of a thorough analysis of the existing institutional framework in the country concerned and more specifically on its capacity or lack of capacity to support socio-economic development, agricultural expansion, increased productivity per labour unit, etc. The analysis which could be called an institutional survey and which is required for the design of a successful land reform policy is quite complicated, since it will comprise a thorough appraisal of the so-called ' *non*-economic realities ' which is a precondition for successful institutional planning, including the planning of land reform. A survey of the economic and social conditions which surround the human factor in a definite area is no less required for the planner of land reform programmes than a resource survey for the planner of technical land and water development. It would provide information both on the economic resources of the area in their relation to the people concerned and on the actual availability of, and the access to, the resources for the individual and to the kind of resource types: institutions and creeds which govern availability of and access to resources are equally subject to the survey. An investigation of this type will not only state the actual income distribution and determine the productivity of man and land, but also explain the reason for both. On the strength of the findings of such institutional reviews it will be possible to proceed to the designing of institutions which could support the national development.

It is this type of survey which governments need also for the establishment of priorities in order to achieve the desired short-term and long-term effects of land reform. The placing of the priorities will depend on the kind of deficiencies in the existing agrarian structure and the proper appraisal of their unfavourable impact on the national development policy. The survey will also provide governments with information on retarding factors such as administrative incapacity and potential food-shortages due to lack of management or credit after the introduction of land reform. This will enable the authorities to take preparatory steps in order to avoid or at least to minimise any reduction in production or market deliveries which frequently have been associated with the introduction of agrarian reform programmes at the initial stage.

B. *Land reform as release mechanism for agricultural development and its interdependence with industrial development*

This conference has stated very well the final objective of land reform, by the formulation of the item with which this paper deals: can land reform provide the incentives which will help to create a rural basis for national development?

It is today almost commonplace to say that land reform is the release mechanism for agricultural and economic development, and in using this phrase we think particularly of the close interdependencies of agricultural and industrial development. The contribution which we all expect from land reform is the establishment of specific incentives for additional efforts by the cultivator provided by changes in the tenure system. We have gained the experience in Japan, in Mexico, in Taiwan and also in Cuba, that the implementation of structural reforms has created a new self-consciousness in the peasant and stimulated his interest in new scientific and technological developments in agriculture. In this way, land reform has provided a ready background for education since it has developed the qualities of intellect, commonsense, energy, resourcefulness and prudence – all of which are necessary for the acceptance of technological changes and to make the best use of technological innovations.

We all know that agricultural development requires that farm production should increase at a more rapid rate than total population and much faster than the agricultural work-force. Capital, new technologies, skill and organisation become increasingly important factors in farm production, while land and unskilled labour lose their traditional primacy. Land reform, if properly implemented, will help to achieve all this and will gradually release labour for the building up of an industrial sector and provide the food required for an industrial population. Industrial production can seldom be increased beyond narrow limits except by transferring the necessary manpower from agriculture, by drawing increased supplies of raw materials and food produced by agriculture, and with the help of the expanding market for industrial products provided by a progressive and developing agriculture.

The new industries, in turn, will promote agricultural development while providing wider markets by improved processing methods and by the construction of irrigation and communication projects. After the conscious awakening of the peasants as a result of land reform and the economic opening up of the rural areas by that reform and by the linking of agricultural progress to industrial development, the mutual chain-effect of the growth in both sectors will provide the possibility for industrial decentralisation and for new types of rural industries, organised on a cooperative basis, which would serve the agricultural producer, strengthen the peasant communities and make life in the countryside more meaningful. The increased purchasing power of the cultivator will be of great benefit to developing secondary and tertiary industries.

If agrarian reform has achieved the redistribution of income, it can safely be assumed that the major part of the agricultural income will buy the products and services of the secondary and tertiary industries, since the large incomes which were symptomatic of the feudal societies have been spent partly on economically unproductive purchases. The same argument of course holds good in respect of expenditure incurred in agricultural equipment and material.

SPECIFIC ASPECTS OF TENURE CHANGES AND THEIR RELEVANCY FOR NATIONAL DEVELOPMENT

It might be useful to see a few aspects of land reform programmes in the light of the perspective of this conference. *Security of tenure*, for instance, is one of the most important aspects of any land reform and in many underdeveloped areas of the world the need for security applies both for the owners and for the tenants. The reliable definition of rights in land provided by an efficient *system of surveying and registration* is of immense benefit not only to individual landholders but also to the country as a whole. There is no doubt, for instance, that the vast quantity of boundary conflicts and land litigation in Turkey have a detrimental impact on agricultural productivity and make the establishment of producer cooperatives quite difficult since the harmony of life and work in the village is seriously disturbed. The present defective tenure system in Turkey certainly does not provide the rural basis for development. *Security for the tenant* is essential and can only be provided effectively if it is coordinated with a well-administered rent control system, which is difficult to achieve for under-developed countries. Not less important from a development point of view is that the law should provide for compensation for permanent improvements since otherwise the cultivator will be discouraged from investing capital and labour in order to increase the value of his land.

The great technical advantages of *plantation cultivation* are obvious, particularly from the point of view of large-scale production of export crops which can have a very beneficial impact on the exchange balances of developing countries. Their success can be traced to the low per unit costs of production, to the technological superiority of mass treatment for weeds and pests, the uniformity of the product and the easier quality control. Unfortunately, however, the classical plantation has also great disadvantages, both in the political and in the socio-economic field, and as a type of tenure is no longer acceptable to many developing countries in the world. Therefore, we need to establish a new type of large-scale operation unit which preserves the technical advantages of plantation agriculture without the well-known social and political disadvantages. It should be possible to create large-scale cultivation units based on partnership arrangements between foreign investors and governments which will provide security for both. A promising way seems to be the nucleus plantation schemes in Nigeria which are based on investor–government cooperation. The plantation centre which contains a processing plant, is surrounded by smallholdings, growing mainly the same crop which will be processed in the centre's plant. In this scheme the plantation has lost its controversial features and serves as a demonstration purpose for the development of agriculture and so provides a rural basis for national development.

Another very important contribution which structural policy can make to national development is the change of the tribal concept of land policy to a *national land policy concept*. This type of structural policy, of course, particularly concerns Africa and a very good example of such a change in policy is the land reform programme of Eastern Cameroon which, from the legislative point of view, is one of the most comprehensive undertaken in Africa in recent years. The new law of 1963 sets out the general lines of the reform, according to which land is divided into four categories: land held by communities and individuals by virtue of custom; public property of the state and of local authorities; private property, and the national collective patrimony. The latter is a particular innovation of the new law and comprises all land except land in the possession of communities, land held under the registration system, the Civil Code Rules or under title granted as a result of adjudication procedure, and public and private land. It is significant that a clear distinction has been made between the national collective patrimony and state land proper. It is envisaged that the state will proceed to redistribute the patrimony in furtherance of the aims of social and economic development. It can be expected and hoped that the land policy in Eastern Cameroon will serve as an example for overcoming narrow tribal concepts, for we should not forget that there will be no African nations in the real meaning of the word if they do not have a national land policy. This is one of the reasons why I feel that enclosure measures should not be introduced into under-populated tribal areas, as they may prejudice a future national land policy which has to compromise between densely and less populated areas.

Another interesting feature of agrarian policy with possible great effect on national development is the establishment of *rural development zones* which have been carried out in Madagascar and Tunisia. These zones, the so-called '*Aires de mise en valeur rurale* (AMVR)' are clearly defined areas where development works are projected and on which peasants are settled and introduced, under expert supervision, to modern farm techniques. An essential feature of this system is that each occupier of land within these zones is required to fit in with a rational plan of exploitation regarding, for example, the cultivation calendar and choice of seeds. This applies both to the original inhabitants and to new occupiers. No subdivision of holdings is permitted and in the case of the death of an occupier his heirs must, within three months, designate a representative who will be responsible for all development activities. Any changes of ownership other than through inheritance have to be authorised in advance by the administration. The new legislation provides for the limitation of the size of individual holdings and excess land will be expropriated against compensation. Where fragmentation is excessive the law provides for the consolidation of small parcels of land. The general law on irrigation zones enables the State to require landowners to join what are called 'compulsory agricultural water groups'. The impact of these development zones, particularly in Tunisia, has been very favourable for national economic development.

The success of the adjudication and consolidation schemes in Kenya is well known. They have enabled African agriculture in the Kikuyu areas to develop and to make their contribution to the progress of the country. The enclosure measure, which was the most material factor in the operations, was successful from a general development point of view since the areas were very densely populated. Of more actual interest, however, is the new land settlement which has been carried out in the white highlands of Kenya, the economic benefits of which are regarded as being very considerable.[3] Indirectly the settlement has contributed to the continual functioning of the remaining large-scale farms in that the market for land and for important moveable assets, such as grade cattle, has been maintained. In addition the settlement has relieved some of the land pressure in the former African land units thereby making them more suitable for development, while at the same time lowering land prices to more realistic levels because of the decreased demand. Further, it has to be emphasised that there are strong indications that the settlement has brought about a much larger input of labour relative to other factors of production; that is to say, a substitution of labour for capital which is of great importance in a land such as Kenya where there exists an oversupply of labour and limited sources of development capital.

The final and maybe decisive factor of importance, however, is the reduction of the foreign exchange component within the farming sector. The value of imported factors of production per 1,000 acres of settlement land is about one half or one third of that in the large scale farming areas – the difference being mainly due to lower imports of machinery.

CONCLUSIONS

The close interrelationship and interdependency of land reform and structural policies with general economic progress is an established fact. We economists and development technicians are inclined to emphasise these facts very strongly and provide colourful illustrations of this interdependency. This short paper has followed this tradition, but I feel I would not be fair to land reform if I did not stress at the same time the great contribution which land reform as an integrated part of development makes to *national integration*.

The awakening of the masses of the people by structural policies and land reform in particular, by the changes introduced by them in the course of their implementation; the ever increasing scale of contacts and communications both between isolated communities and between agricultural communities and the administrative and urban centres; the intensification of education and the improvement of administration – all of these make their contribution to more than economic and social progress. They are integral elements in the making of a nation. This is the reason why we should not overdo the protection policy in favour of fragmentary population groups but help to link them to the process of national integration and development. In my view this is one of the ultimate objectives of land policy in developing countries.

4 THE ROLE OF GOVERNMENT

15 · Mobilising Internal Resources through Taxation
STANLEY PLEASE[1]

INTRODUCTION

Of all the obstacles to economic development, the lack of financial resources for building up the stock of productive assets in a country is, of course, of paramount importance. This stock includes not only machines, factories, irrigation facilities, transport, etc., but less tangible assets such as human skills, and the one common ingredient to all these is that they require financial resources to be made available if their supply is to be augmented. It is through their own national efforts to raise their domestic rates of saving that the major contribution to augmenting their stocks of capital must be made. Furthermore, lending agencies, including the World Bank, determine the extent and type of external financial assistance given to a country on the basis of the country's own efforts to overcome the internal obstacles to its development. In part this stems from the moral judgement that external lenders should only concern themselves with a country's development if the country itself shows visible signs of being concerned by the pursuit of policies aimed at reducing the internal barriers to its development. Secondly, however, it stems from mere economic considerations. It has come to be recognised that the ability of a country to service external debt is essentially dependent upon two general considerations: first, its ability to use investible resources in a productive manner so that real national product increases over time and secondly, upon its willingness and ability to save a growing proportion of this increment to its national income. If the domestic performance of a country is good in these two crucial respects then the growth of its external debt burden gives far less cause for alarm.

For a variety of reasons, most economists have argued that a major increase in domestic savings can only be accomplished by direct government action to reduce personal consumption compulsorily, either by increased direct taxes to reduce personal disposable incomes, and/or by increase in direct taxes to reduce the real value of a given level of disposable monetary income. The scope for such action can be broadened to include, in particular, policy measures operating through public enterprises, thus using the prices of public services as para-fiscal means by which personal consumption in real terms can be reduced.

The basis for the widespread acceptance of this strategy for the domestic savings effort is to be found in what appear to be reasonably plausible assumptions regarding the difficulties of raising the level of voluntary savings – the low level of income of the majority of the population, the international demonstration effect upon desired levels of personal consumption, the fear of price increases undermining the real value of savings, political misgivings, etc. Nurkse's work [2] is probably the most quoted in support of this strategy. His analysis of the crucial role played by compulsory savings generated through the tax system in the early stages of Japan's economic development has been the favourite example paraded before developing countries wishing to emulate her success.

To these doubts regarding the possibility that voluntary savings alone could provide the increased flow of domestic savings is frequently added the assertion that public savings are in any case to be preferred to private savings. This assertion is based on the argument that whilst the financing of investment out of tax revenue creates no prior claims on future increases in output, private savers will hold such claims in the form of bonds and other savings media. The future servicing of this internal debt puts a constraint upon the government's revenue and expenditure policy.

PUBLIC SAVINGS PERFORMANCE

As a result of the widespread acceptance of this strategy aimed at raising the level of domestic savings through budgetary policy, we have witnessed, over the past decade and a half, an immense effort at the national and international level to raise the levels of taxation in the developing countries. Major internal enquiries such as that by the Indian Taxation Enquiry Commission have been undertaken, independent reports by tax consultants have been solicited, and the I.M.F. and the World Bank place considerable emphasis on this aspect of a country's economic policy in appraising its economic performance. So significant is this in the eyes of many people and institutions interested in economic development that the ratio of tax revenue to G.N.P. and movements in this ratio over time are treated as major yardsticks of aid and credit-worthiness and growth-potential.

All this effort has not lacked results. Column (i) of the appended table (see p. 171) shows the changes in tax revenue as a percentage of G.N.P. which have occurred for a random selection of less developed countries in recent years. Certainly in most of the countries with which I have been more directly concerned, I have been impressed by the high degree of political discipline which governments have shown in introducing new tax measures and by the considerable administrative capacity in executing these measures, though perhaps not always sufficient capacity to enable one to be completely content that the tax impositions were being fairly and universally applied. In India, for instance, Union Government tax revenue has increased at a rate of 10 per cent per annum since the beginning of the country's programme of planned development in 1951 and by 20 per cent per annum during the Third Plan period which commenced in 1961. As a result of this effort, tax revenue (Union and States combined) in 1965 represented around 12 per cent of G.N.P. as compared with a proportion of around 7 per cent in 1951. Likewise, in Ceylon, tax revenue in 1965 represented 23 per cent of G.N.P. as compared with 20 per cent in 1960. The same is true for many Latin American countries. In Peru, for instance, in 1965 public revenues accounted for 20 per cent of G.N.P. as compared with 15·5 per cent in 1960, and in Brazil, the percentage rose from 20 per cent in 1956 and 23 per cent in 1960 to 27·5 per cent in 1964. There are, of course, exceptions to the generalisation regarding the trend of public revenues. In Argentina, for instance, revenues have fallen from around 22 per cent of G.N.P. in the 1950s to around 18 per cent in the 1960s. Nevertheless, the general impression left by this review is that governments have rarely lacked willingness and ability to extend control over an increasing proportion of their national economic resources.

To the extent that the motive force behind this effort has been the recognition of the need to channel an ever-increasing proportion of domestic resources into investment in economic development, there is some cause for alarm in the record. This record is presented in column (ii) of the table. For the individual countries to which I have referred in the previous paragraph, the record is certainly depressing. In India, the Union Government has increased its income by Rs.9,000 million since 1960–1, yet, out of this increase, less than 5 per cent (Rs.440 million) has been channelled to augment the flow of investible resources. Whilst the Rs.9,000 million represent about 5 per cent of G.N.P., in fact the tax effort of the Union Government has resulted in an increase in the flow of savings, which represents a mere 0·6 per cent of G.N.P. In Ceylon, the situation in this regard has been even more depressing, with the increase in the tax effort since 1959 having been matched by an almost persistent decline in government savings, which in 1963–4 were insufficient to cover the losses generated by government enterprises, thus resulting in net dis-saving by the government sector as a whole. In Peru, the increased tax effort has been matched by a 30 per cent decline in the absolute level of public saving and in relative terms from 4 per cent of G.N.P. to 1·4 per cent. Once again, it must be emphasised that these examples have not been selected because they truly reflect a more general pattern but simply because the author has encountered these cases most directly. However, they do appear to typify a fairly general pattern.

There is nothing novel in this finding. The growth of government current expenditure in the less developed countries which, of course, is the general cause of the disappointing behaviour of public savings in spite of impressive records in terms of tax performance, is a phenomenon which is widely recognised. In 1960, for instance, an unpublished study by the World Bank relating to the financing of public investment in nineteen less-developed countries presented as one of its major findings the fact that ' the proportion of public investment financed by public savings tended to diminish during the 1950s' and that the ' main reason was that the rate of public savings [i.e. as a percentage of G.N.P.] declined in 14 countries and, in a few cases, even a substantial fall of public savings in absolute terms occurred during the period '.[3] Furthermore, the United Nations Economic Commission for Asia and the Far East subsequently drew attention to the same phenomenon in its 1961 Economic Survey. It emphasised that

in spite of the fact that virtually every government in the region has expressed itself in favour of increasing the share of government participation in programmes for economic growth, only in mainland China has government saving risen substantially. In mainland China, practically the whole of annual investment was financed by government saving, and the fact that the public sector was able to generate a level of saving not matched by any other country of the region can be explained primarily in terms of the much greater restraint which the government was able and prepared to impose both upon itself and upon the community.[4]

Most recently Dr Enke, in his paper to the Rehovoth Conference on Fiscal and Monetary Problems in Developing States, has asserted that ' Official pronouncements often make it seem that extra tax yields will be " saved " and invested. The truth, though, is that four-fifths or more of extra tax receipts usually go to extra operating expenses of government and not to what might be termed " investment ".'

Faced with this pattern of events, consultant economists, international institutions, etc., have, in general, advocated that even more emphasis be given in national economic policy to raising the level of taxation in order to provide an adequate flow of internally generated investible funds. Despite the impressive record in this regard, it is still possible to read an article by the best-known of these consultant economists in the tax field which is inappropriately entitled ' Will Underdeveloped Countries Learn to Tax? '.[5] Richard Goode of the I.M.F. in his recent paper prepared for the Rehovoth Conference on Fiscal and Monetary Problems in Developing States argues that ' An underdeveloped country that is determined to avoid both stagnation and inflation will have to find ways of raising large and growing amounts of tax revenue.' Likewise, at the most general level, both Prest and Tripathy, in their identically titled books (*Public Finance in Underdeveloped Countries*),[6] give overwhelming emphasis to the need for an increasing tax effort in the developing countries. Certainly the Bank itself places immense importance in appraising the development plans of its member countries upon the feasible increase in tax revenue which can be expected from them. Judgements are made about a country's ' taxable capacity ', with all the difficulties this involves, as though it were axiomatic that tax policy should exploit the gap between current tax rates and this capacity level.

This attitude and advice are relevant to the development problem providing it is assumed that government current spending and government revenue generation are independently determined. Then, of course, any increase in revenue reduces a public dis-saving or increases public saving. Because this assumption is so crucial to the judgement which must be made upon the whole strategy of development, which relies heavily on compulsory saving through the fiscal system, it seems to me that the factors bearing on its validity ought to be examined.

THE DETERMINATION OF PUBLIC CURRENT EXPENDITURE

The conventional attitude towards public expenditure policy which is taken by economists in the public finance fields is to take it as given and to limit their analysis to its implications for public revenue policy. This is, in fact, Prest's position. He accepts the assertion of Richard Musgrave that the pattern and total of public expenditure are 'fundamentally of a political rather than an economic character'. To the extent that this implies that they are determined aside from *any* economic considerations, it is, of course, patently not true. Political decisions must, however vaguely, take into consideration the ability of the country to undertake increased expenditure on defence, education, etc. This ability can be judged either in relation to the total resources of the country and to the annual flow of income from these resources (some measure of national production) or to a narrower magnitude, reflecting the government's ability and willingness to gain control over the use of national production. It is the first of these two criteria of ability which Prest and others must have in mind when they talk about government expenditure being 'politically determined'. Such aggregative thinking on the part of policy-makers might be highly desirable, but I would respectfully suggest that the narrower magnitude is probably more influential in many instances. However complicated budget accounts might be, they are, nevertheless, likely to be more intelligible to the non-economist policy-maker than even the simplest form of national accounts, the understanding of which implies a recognition of the basic nature of income flows. Money flowing into the exchequer has a reality and significance to the non-economist which is unlikely to be matched by the flows of money against goods and services in the economy as a whole. However, if this is true, then the independence of the two magnitudes (government expenditure and revenue) will be undermined, with the consequent danger which this implies to a development strategy which aims to raise the total flow of domestic savings through increased taxation and other revenue-producing policies.

However, in addition to these considerations, most writers seem to accept the much more dangerous argument that the rise in public expenditure must be almost unconditionally accepted and the whole burden of increasing public savings thrown on to taxation, despite the evidence that this is abortive in many instances. Kaldor states: 'Whatever the prevailing ideology or political colour of a particular government, it must steadily expand a whole host of non-revenue-yielding services as a prerequisite for the country's economic and cultural development.' Goode refers to the need to 'limit private spending in order to allow resources to be diverted to high-priority uses in the public sector', and to the 'main task of fiscal policy in a developing state being to finance large and growing government expenditures'. Whilst he warns of the dangers of 'investment in splendid buildings, luxury housing and inefficient industries' he is at pains to emphasise that 'a well-balanced development programme must include substantial expenditures for education, research, health and other services that improve people's productive capacity and add to knowledge'. Prest argues the justification in terms of population growth and the growth of local and world opinion for increased political action to improve social conditions in the developing countries.

It is one of the tragedies of the emotionally packed environment in which economists discuss their problems that one has misgivings at suggesting or even hinting that this might not be altogether true – that possibly some part, and in some countries, some large part of public expenditure and the annual increment thereto might be of lower priority than other calls on a country's resources. Such scepticism certainly invites the charge of being a reactionary, but on these matters at the personal level one can merely ask to be judged by the record. In any case, the charge is no answer to what appears to be a major developmental problem in many countries.

It is, of course, apparent to all that much public expenditure is of high priority. There are, however, two grounds for questioning whether this should automatically take precedence in the utilisation of resources. First, some of this expenditure is almost completely unrelated to developmental purposes (e.g., defence is the most obvious case but, in addition, expenditure on lavish public buildings, consumer subsidies, unduly high salary levels of officials, etc.). For some countries this expenditure absorbs a large part of both total government expenditure and a large part of the increment to public expenditure. Secondly, within sectors which in general have a developmental element (e.g., education, health, housing, etc.), there is still a non-developmental element in expenditure and even within the developmental element, a question of alternatives forgone.

The more fundamental concern, however, is to judge whether the generation of increased public revenue for the purpose of augmenting the flow of domestic savings for development in fact weakens the administrative and, above all, the political discipline over government current expenditure. Is it possible to resist a political or popular clamour for increased defence expenditure, non-priority social expenditure, salary increases for public officials, etc., when it is known that the money is ' in the kitty '? The ability to understand even simple economic analysis is not so widespread that the justification for increased tax revenue to finance a budget surplus for developmental purposes can be readily understood, let alone accepted. It would obviously be foolish to dogmatise on this matter. No doubt many exceptions could be cited. Nevertheless, the gloomy record of increased tax performance over the years, related to poor public savings performance, cannot but suggest that those who argued for a development strategy based on increased compulsory savings underestimated and, more frequently, ignored the effect that this might have on public consumption. Policy recommendations to increase taxation in these circumstances are chasing a mirage. In the face of the record, it is difficult to be sure or even to hope that in any future year the level of public current expenditure associated with a rate of tax of, say, 18 per cent of G.N.P. would be the same or even very little more than that which would have been associated with a rate of tax of, say, 15 per cent of G.N.P. Yet, essentially, this is what all such recommendations assume.

POLICY IMPLICATIONS

At the most platitudinous level, it is easy to urge that governments in the less developed countries must be more disciplined in relation to the spending of public revenue. Such discipline must apply both to the efficiency with which any given policy is executed and to the legislating of policies which carry with them both present and future commitments out of public funds. There would be little dispute regarding the first of these aspects of expenditure control; everyone interested in economic development must, almost by definition, be interested in greater efficiency in the use of economic resources, including greater efficiency in the implementation of government policies. Where dispute would arise would be in suggesting that insufficient discipline has been shown in relation to policy measures.

In the first place, many would claim that, in some sense, expenditure on defence has overriding importance and thus the question of greater discipline in terms of policy does not arise. It would, furthermore, be strongly represented that this is an area of decision-making which is entirely of national concern. I must refrain from commenting on these highly sensitive issues, but would merely emphasise that, at some point, the requirements of national defence are likely to conflict with those of economic development and that if a country gives such inviolate priority to defence expenditure, it must be prepared to suffer the obstacle to its economic development which this decision implies.

As regards social expenditure on education, health, housing, etc., there is, first, the notorious statistical problem that must be mentioned that, although most (though not all) expenditure under these heads is classified as current expenditure in government budgets, some increased proportion should, in principle, rank as capital expenditure. This would embrace those elements which in fact increase the ability of the economy to produce more goods and services in the future. The financing of this expenditure, therefore, should rank as a contribution to the aggregate flow of domestic savings and, to this extent, public savings figures are underestimated. Whilst this is correct, there are two comments which need to be made. First, that the acceptance of the principle must not give *carte blanche* to the acceptance of all social service expenditure as investment expenditure. Secondly, that even if the investment element as an item of social welfare expenditure is accepted, its priority in terms of the economic return to the expenditure must still be judged in relation to the return on alternative investment outlets.

Linked to this final point, and pervading the whole field of discussion of social expenditure, is the almost universal acceptance of the fact that this expenditure, judged *in vacuo*, is ' good '. Everyone believes in the desirability of an educated rather than an ignorant population, a healthy rather than a sick population, etc. It becomes particularly difficult, therefore, to argue that expenditure on such desirable objectives is itself undesirably high or rising at an undesirably high rate. What this all reduces to, however, is a recognition of the simple economic fact that the process of economic development entails the denial of desirable things in the present for the sake of a higher level of satisfaction of individual and social desires in the future. The more rapidly this process is undertaken, the greater must be the present costs in terms of forgone public and private consumption. The only way in which these costs can be reduced is by a willingness on the part of the developed countries to make development funds available in increased amounts. If the latter are taken as given, however, then only increased domestic saving through, *inter alia*, increased discipline in terms of public expenditure policy can provide the resources which development requires.

Whilst the existence or non-existence of this will to restrain public consumption is the crucial factor, institutional or procedural changes can possibly reinforce where the will exists, but in insufficient strength. I have in mind, in particular, in this regard the institutional arrangements which determine the extent to which public funds are earmarked in such a manner that they are more closely linked to a development use. Economists have widely argued that earmarking of public revenues is an undesirable procedure. The optimum pattern of public expenditure, so it is argued, is attained when marginal social returns are equalised in all sectors of public expenditure. This requires that the government should be free to determine the use to which all revenues are put. Earmarking prevents this by relating in a more or less fixed manner, given items of expenditure to given items of revenue.

Undoubtedly such constraints are undesirable in principle. However, if the argument of this paper is accepted, there would seem to be an *a priori* case for earmarking certain revenues for developmental purposes rather than leaving governments free to allocate the total flow of public revenue between public current consumption needs and the supplementing of domestic savings.

For instance, it seems to me that it is probably undesirable to siphon off into general tax revenue the surpluses generated by public enterprises, if by so doing an increase in government consumption is thereby stimulated. Such mobilisation of financial resources by the government for the general exchequer can take the form of a direct transfer of revenue surpluses through institutional arrangements such as when the enterprise is organised on a departmental basis or through statutory obligations imposed on more autonomous enterprises to remit all or part of their surplus revenue to the government. Alternatively, the siphoning can be achieved by the imposition of an excise tax on sales which is an effective alternative to a simple rise in the price charged for the commodity or service, except that the revenue received by the enterprise is changed. The state tax on electricity consumption in India is an obvious example of the latter.

Furthermore, experience in Britain would suggest that it is probably desirable to treat gasoline taxes, etc., as user charges to which the level of investment in the road system is related. The abolition of the so-called Road Fund is, in general, regarded as a sensible fiscal measure by economists on the grounds that it merely represented a meaningless accountancy fiction. It would be a brave man, however, who would not attribute at least part of the responsibility for the pathetic delay in modernising British roads to the abolition of this ' meaningless fiction '. I would merely suggest that, in fact, the total flow of investible funds has itself probably been reduced by the abolition of this earmarking device; that, in general, it might be better to accept a less than optimum allocation of investible funds if, as a result, the total flow of such funds is increased.

Apart from administrative devices of this nature, it might be appropriate, furthermore, to question the strategy of domestic financial mobilisation based on an increased tax performance itself. I do this hesitantly and, in part, to stimulate discussion. The record, however, cannot be overlooked and, faced with this widespread failure of the tax weapon to raise domestic savings levels, it might be more appropriate to put greater emphasis on alternative strategies.

Emphasis upon public saving, as already noted, has stemmed from the strength attributed to factors which undermine the willingness of the private sector in less developed countries to make an ever-increasing contribution to the flow of domestically available savings – the international demonstration effect, political uncertainty, fear of inflation, etc. There is undoubted validity in this attitude, though, for certain countries, the marginal propensity to consume of the public sector appears to be such that total savings are likely to have been increased if taxation has been reduced and private disposable income thereby increased. However, even if the strength of these factors which weigh against private saving is fully admitted, it does not follow that the only solution is to rely upon publicly generated saving. A more effective solution, or at least a solution which could be given far more emphasis in developmental strategy than it is generally accorded, is to provide the necessary antidotes to the factors which deter private saving.

These antidotes would take the form of an appropriate pattern of terms offered to savers through the securities, insurance policies, savings deposits, and other financial assets which they hold. There is, however, no guarantee, except by coincidence, that this pattern of terms will correspond to the pattern which is required by private borrowers – private firms, etc. – to finance their activities. In these circumstances, it is possible for the terms of the securities which constitute the national debt to be adapted in such a manner that the supply of private saving is stimulated. In effect, the government acts as the bridge between the terms under which the ultimate users of borrowed funds need or wish to borrow and the terms under which lenders are willing to lend. Particularly in less developed countries, where capital markets are relatively underdeveloped and this bridge is not supplied by specialist financial institutions, the need for government action in this respect is vital. Of course, this assumes the acceptance by the government of the proposition that the government should be prepared to use both the volume and the structure of the national debt as an instrument of economic policy rather than as the reflection of the narrower financial interests of the government as a debtor.

The simplest and most obvious change in the terms savers receive would be a straightforward increase in the structure of interest rates. This, however, is an unselective measure. If it is apparent to the government that specific factors are operating to reduce private saving or domestically available private saving (i.e. allowing for capital exports), it is likely that specific terms in a financial asset to take care of the adverse effect on savings of these factors would be preferable. In particular, for instance, it is possible to give savers guarantees against rising prices undermining the real value of their savings, by the issue of bonds or other savings media, the value of which and/or the return on which is linked to some measure of the change in the internal value of money. Furthermore, some form of international guarantee to holders of domestic bonds might allay the fears of savers that they will be the victims of political action.

This paper is not the place in which an extended discussion of such devices can be undertaken, but some experience with the use of the value-linking device by governments is already available – notably in Israel,

Finland and France. These experiences seem to me to be instructive, both regarding the positive advantages of value-linking upon savings and regarding the problems to which such linking gives rise.

It might be argued that a change in the orientation of policy in this way, so that more emphasis came to be given to the encouragement of private saving through enlarging the role of the national debt and less emphasis to the generation of compulsory saving through budgetary surpluses, would still channel funds into the hands of the government which it can then use to finance an increasing volume of current expenditure. This of course is true, but it merely reflects the fact which I have already emphasised, that if a government intends, come what may, to undertake a given level of expenditure, then no administrative or institutional device will prevent it from doing so; even to the extent of unduly augmenting the money supply and forcing up prices. I would once again suggest, however, that governments do not always, except in emergencies, act as free agents but are in part the unknowing victims of institutional forces. If this is the case, the change in the balance between revenue receipts and capital receipts is of significance in terms of the attitude towards financing increased current expenditure. By increasing the government's deficit ' on current account ', or (in terms of the less strict British conventions) the deficit ' above the line ', such a change generates more resistance administratively and politically to increasing public current expenditure.

CONCLUSION

In effect, what this paper has argued is that there appear to be dangers in the assumption of the highly rational government making decisions on behalf of present members of society as well as on behalf of members of society yet unborn. The nineteenth century saw the dominance in policy-making of the idea of economic man as the decision-taker; a man who is forever visualised as weighing incremental gains against incremental costs in all his decisions relating to consumption, saving, working, etc. We now seem to be dominated in our thinking on policy-making by the idea of the economic government and this domination of our thinking is by no means the monopoly of people and institutions which explicitly accept a socialist ideology. The acceptance of the idea of the all-rational government was, in part, based on the notion that the government is a timeless institution, and thus, the telescopic faculty which it would bring to bear on the decisions of society to defer consumption today in order to increase consumption in the future, would be one which would counter the individual's time-preference for present consumption. The evidence is that this counter-force, even to the extent that it has operated at all, has been weak; that the pressures on governments to spend have been irresistible and in some cases, it must be added, understandable. In particular, the pressures to spend are made less resistible when it is apparent to everyone that the funds are immediately available to the government in the exchequer. If this thesis is accepted, the subsequent contribution of this paper has been to indicate administrative devices which might possibly alleviate the problem. These cannot be fool-proof for the very obvious reasons that governments, in the end, are sovereign within their borders and subject only to the ultimate constraint of the basic and universal economic laws which stem from the scarcity of resources. However, they can be assisted in keeping to the path of virtue from the point of view of development policy, if temptations to take easier and politically more popular decisions are removed.

Table 1   *Taxation and government savings in selected countries*

		Taxation as percentage of G.N.P. (i)	Government saving as percentage of G.N.P. (ii)
Ecuador	1959	15	5·3
	1963	16	5·2
Panama	1951	11	1·2
	1958	12	1·5
	1962	14	0·8
Venezuela	1957	22	12·0
	1960	23	8·0
	1964	23	9·0
U.A.R.	1957	13	—
	1962	13	−2·7
	1963	15	−2·4
Nigeria	1950	6	2·7
	1957	10	2·3
	1961	14	3·1
Pakistan	1959	6	0·1
	1964	9	4·4
Morocco	1960	20	1·1
	1964	20	−0·9
Burma	1953	14	3·9
	1961	14	2·0
	1963	14	1·6
Colombia	1955	12	4·7
	1959	12	5·2
	1962	10	1·9
Costa Rica	1953	18	6·3
	1959	17	5·0
	1962	17	2·8
Jamaica	1953	11	2·4
	1959	15	3·5
	1961	15	3·8
Japan	1950	22	8·9
	1959	19	6·5
	1963	21	8·2

16 · Does 'Kaldorian Fiscalism' Work?[1]
CAMBRIDGE CONFERENCE REPORT

Developing countries for ten years past have followed a strategy of what might be called 'Kaldorian fiscalism' to mobilise their internal financial resources. There are many good reasons why national savings for investment should have been organised chiefly by raising more taxes and increasing revenues. Where private banking and insurance is in its infancy, what other choice is there? Action through the fiscal system gives the state control of scarce economic resources and the power to direct them to the highest economic priorities; and only the state can invest savings in the infrastructure and public services required for economic growth, so it must be provided with the means to do so. What is more, the advantage of this sort of fiscalism is that government is enabled to divert the wealth of the rich from private luxury consumption to the benefit of the commonwealth and at the same time to re-distribute it more evenly. The theory indeed has been presented so attractively that those who believe that what is needed is more private enterprise and less state control ask whether it is not too good to be true.

The charge of the 'private enterprisers' is not so much a criticism of Kaldorian theory as of its practical results. In practice most governments have adopted the policy of progressively higher taxes with the idea of transferring more and more resources via the fiscal system into the public sector. They have certainly succeeded. Unfortunately the transfer in itself is no guarantee of productive investment. Statistics show that normally the proportion of increased revenues invested in economic projects that raise the gross national product has not increased. It has remained minute. In other words, the expenses of state seem to have fattened on the increase of revenue, leaving little or nothing over for payable economic growth. If this is true, then obviously the strategy is not achieving its main purpose. Is the Kaldorian plea for higher and higher taxation, then, mistaken? Perhaps the level of taxation should not be progressively raised? The more money government takes into the 'kitty', the more it spends on economically unproductive things, while the extra tax burden reduces investment in the private sector where it might have contributed more to production.

A proposition was put to the conference in this sense: that 'despite higher tax yields, non-developmental expenditures have generally risen faster than developmental expenditures. Therefore the yields of certain sources of revenue should be earmarked for specific developmental purposes, and future increases in government revenues should come from higher savings on expenditure rather than from higher taxation.'

The statistics behind the idea that governments have spent, rather than invested, the extra public savings were first examined. As an Indian speaker put it, ' The fact is that a flat charge has been made in this proposition – and I think that it should be established. I do not think that it has been anywhere near established.'

On the question of whether the charge was factually founded or not, the crux of our debate was to define what could or could not be regarded as expenditure on 'development'. A speaker from Latin America was generally supported when he said that the figures on which the proposition was founded assumed that ' current ' expenditure is generally non-developmental; whereas ' capital ' expenditure is developmental. But ' there are many capital expenditures that are clearly not " developmental " – for example, fortifications. On the other hand, there are many current expenditures that could be regarded as " developmental "; for example, the salaries of doctors and teachers. Surely the large expenses on social infrastructure in developing countries' budgets could be regarded as " developmental "? ' To say the least, the interpretation of the figures is complicated, and they need to be more closely examined in particular cases. ' Data was required on the large expenditure on social services which were probably in the long run productive economically, and on defence and officials' salaries which were probably unproductive from that standpoint.'

Nobody in fact disputed that current expenditure on social overheads was essential to development. It was agreed nevertheless that there is a good deal of waste in government spending and that the amount of it invested directly in the production of wealth is much too low, even though not all capital expenditure is developmental and not all current expense is non-developmental. The proponents of the charge went on to point out, moreover, that it is not enough to go on blithely assuming that all expenditure on social or public services contributes in some way or other to economic growth. Much of it might be classified as luxury consumption in so far as it is not tightly geared up to priority needs in the economic development plan. In education, for example, much of the expenditure on schools and universities is not producing the skilled technicians, managers and small farmers required in the economy. And although everybody would agree in another context that all education is a good thing, humanly speaking, and that you cannot have too much of it, in the economic context, and in view of the scarcity of resources, expenditure that is not strictly devoted to the needs for manpower in the economy, is a luxury that developing countries cannot at present afford.

An international civil servant put the point thus:

There is an urgent need to direct public expenditure much more exactly to the purposes of specifically economic growth, and especially in education, health and social services generally, to scrutinise its productivity from the standpoint of what it will contribute to the gross national product. If it does contribute, then that expenditure can be classed as 'developmental'; if it does not, then under our existing definitions of growth, it cannot be. Even then it remains to be decided whether the money to be put into social services would not make a much bigger contribution to wealth if it were invested instead in specifically economic enterprises. It is the habit of neglecting this crucial test that is responsible for too much luxury spending of tax revenue and too little production of economic wealth to support those services or to use the output of them in the economy. There is a danger of self-deception in this. Naturally governments like to be popular and genuinely want to make their peoples healthier, wiser, better; and it is easy to justify too much luxury spending on these objects by saying that in general and in the end it is essential to the progress of the economy. It may be or it may not be. But here and now, whether it is or not is a definite question of allocating scarce resources among tight priorities. If the economic priorities are consistently ignored on grounds of welfare, developing countries ought not to be surprised that they have gone in for more social services than their economies can well afford for the time being; that their rate of economic growth is not reaching the desired level, and that the reason for it is given as the misdirection of internal financial resources away from the higher economic priorities.

CAUSES OF RISING CURRENT EXPENDITURE

The need for the strictest economy and the allocation of public revenue to the highest economic priorities is obvious. In defence of the performance of developing countries, however, a number of legitimate reasons were admitted why rising current expenditure is unavoidable. Every development project brings with it consequent increases in current expense, so that one would normally expect 'non-developmental' accounts to increase. And this tendency is intensified by the drift of population into cities where the cost in public services of keeping a man healthy and happy is many times what it would have been in the countryside. Because of the crisis of great expectations, political leaders are pressed irresistibly by electors to provide more public services; civil services are powerful and increases in their salaries are naturally not unpopular; and nothing binds the ties of national unity or oils the wheels of political cooperation so much as patronage in the form of current expenditure. Inevitably, that account is also bound to rise because of the need to pay increased debt charges and repay loan capital. When these reasons for rising public expenditure are considered, as one speaker observed, it becomes increasingly hard to distinguish 'developmental' from 'non-developmental'.

I do not quite know how this distinction is going to be made in practice. It clearly cannot be a division between capital and recurrent expenditures. There is no point in building a school and leaving it empty. What parts of the budget cannot be called 'developmental' for one reason or another? One part of it is paying interest on debt . . . There is no sense in saying 'we will have to cut it down'. You will have to pay and that is a result of your past activities. I suppose you will find that what you are thinking of as 'non-developmental' is a certain amount of administrative expenditure – on police, civil servants, armed forces. Be as economical as you can. But even here, can you have development without police and civil servants?

Or indeed, without political unity and political goodwill? 'So one's demand for strict economy should not be directed exclusively to current expenditure on the assumption that it is "non-developmental". The fact is that developing countries generally are just short of money.'

THE REMEDY

Obviously, public expenditure must be strictly pruned to release a higher proportion of public savings for economically productive investment and budgets are already being judged by this criterion. But obviously it is impossible to apply this rule simply by cutting current accounts and inflating capital accounts. It can only be enforced by scrutinising all items of expense in the light of the highest priorities for allocating exceedingly scarce economic resources.

The idea in the proposition of going further and earmarking certain tax revenues to be invested automatically in specific economic developments, found little favour with the conference. It seemed unlikely, and even unnecessary, for governments to tie their hands behind their backs in this way. Conceivably, it might sometimes have the disastrous effect of forcing them to spend public money on objectives of a lower priority than they otherwise would have done. We concluded therefore that earmarking had more disadvantages than advantages. The device seemed too inflexible for the purpose of diverting more public savings into producing more wealth. Hypothecating revenue in this way would introduce regrettable rigidities into planning.

The remedy that one side of the argument preferred was to increase tax revenues progressively to provide more sinews for economic growth and curb 'the luxurious waste of private men defrauding the common wealth'. What the other side preferred was to end the increase of taxation at some point so as to leave more resources in the hands of private enterprise; and to use more public expenditure to stimulate incentive in the private sector. At one point in our discussion the proposition here was formulated thus: that 'Government revenue for expenditure in the public sector of development should come from savings in its "non-developmental" expenditure and not from increased taxation.' But the weight of opinion seemed to be against this principle. 'This proposition', it was said,

I find strange. It seems to be 'agin the government' on principle. It would mean in practice that governments should progressively reduce taxes, because otherwise as the economy grows, tax yields will grow with it. If the government is to have no more money coming in, how are we going to get any development at all? I find this proposition very inadequate in that it ignores the need for more taxation, for a more equal division of burdens between different classes of taxpayer and between the modern and the agricultural sectors.

Foreign aid already bears between a fifth and a quarter of developing countries' development expenditure. It cannot be expected to pay half; and therefore progressively increased taxation to increase domestic savings is the only practicable alternative. The speaker regretted that the proposal had diverted attention from this sixty-four thousand dollar question to that of economy in public expenditure. What the more socially minded contributors wanted was to direct more money from unproductive private consumption into the production of wealth by raising the tax revenue itself to higher and higher levels. The case for this is given in the words of its most eminent advocate:

As far as I can see, the view in the proposition is that where governments are likely to spend their money wastefully and not usefully – because they are likely to do this, we must be chary of giving them more resources and more money to spend. I think this brings up a number of vital issues.

I would certainly not disagree with the general proposition that governments can be bad as well as good. As a matter of fact I was asked by students recently why some countries are prosperous and some are very poor. I would say that it is not natural resources, it is not the propensity of the population to save or to accumulate, it is not indeed their ability, it is really the existence of good or bad governments.

It is turning things upside down to say that because governments are bad let us not give them any money, or let us not give them any chance to improve. This amounts to saying that these countries are merely getting what they deserve and therefore there is no problem of development. Let them be where they are – let them stew in their own juice.

It seems pretty clear to me that whereas governments do not necessarily spend their money usefully – an awful lot of it is spent on palaces and battleships and other status symbols – yet there is no short cut from the point of view of development – from developing those public services which are an essential precondition and prerequisite of the country's development. These cannot be privately provided. It is ridiculous to expect that the countries of either Latin America or of Africa, so to speak, could do without governments; or with as little government as possible. They would not develop like this, I am quite convinced, without governments making great efforts in developing those infrastructures which are prerequisites for development.

In many underdeveloped countries, side by side with extreme poverty there is a ruling class which is small in number but which holds in its hands the economic development within their own society, far more than any British or American tycoon or millionaire. In these societies I submit that it would be difficult to contend that any item of public expenditure, however wasteful it may appear, would have a lower social priority than say, the sixteenth Cadillac of a Latin American millionaire. Yet, in these countries, not only does a high proportion of the national income accrue to a minority of wealthy individuals but, unlike the wealthy individuals in developed countries, they have a very high propensity to consume their wealth and a very large proportion of their wealth is not productively invested, but is spent on private consumption.

Reference has been made to the wasteful use of government money on rice subsidies in one country where rice subsidies are very prominent. Now you may say that rice subsidies are extremely wasteful. But at least it enables a large number of people to eat more rice, people who would otherwise go hungry. You may say that this is not quite such a high priority as some vital technical school for economic development. But I would say it is socially of a higher priority than the sixteenth Cadillac. The question is entirely where the money is drawn from and what would have been the alternative use of resources.

The problem is not really that governments should refrain. Obviously we must try to make governments better – to improve governments, to make them more rational, more idealistic, less like the sheikhs of Arabia and more like the socialist that Mr Nehru was. But due to the fact that we must try to improve governments, we must find ways of putting more resources into the hands of governments.

Here I think the great difficulty arises because it is not a question of whether the taxable capacity of these countries is large or small. The true taxable capacity is hardly ever tapped. Because the very ruling classes in these countries which hold all the reins of power, and which in a sense are highly responsible for preventing development, are also succeeding in preventing the development of administrative procedures which would enable an effective system of progressive taxation. This is the problem before us. It is far too naïve to place a question this way – is it a good thing or a bad thing to put more money in the hands of the government? There is no alternative. Otherwise we put paid to all hopes of economic development. I am not saying whether governments are good, bad or indifferent – they are on the whole bad in my opinion – but it is still true generally speaking that however bad the government, the social utility of every unit of money spent by public authorities is greater than when it is left in private hands. There is very little private saving in the vast under-developed areas.

Whether this case stands or falls depends largely on the degree of potential for economic development in private sectors in particular countries; and whether more money is wasted if it comes into public hands instead of being left with private citizens, is a question that requires deeper research. Opinion on this question was divided between the two poles. Admittedly, very few governments have investigated, let alone taken fully into account, the depressing effects of increased taxation upon private investment. But the private enterprisers by no means accepted the socialist assertion that money left in private hands was less likely to be put into economic development than if it was taken into the hands of the public authority. Government, moreover, had not taken enough trouble to find out why money in the private sector was not invested in economic priorities.

MORE SAVINGS THROUGH TAXATION

Whether we were for more private or more public investment, the conference as a whole accepted the case for progressively increasing taxation, and so we turned to more mechanical questions of how national savings might be increased by improving the tax system. There seem to be plenty of opportunities in the way of better tax collection, higher tax rates, widening the tax net and inventing new taxes.

In many developing countries the assessment of taxes of all kinds is very difficult.

(*a*) Many businesses and the self-employed keep very poor accounts, or none at all, so that it is difficult to establish their tax liability.

(*b*) Where accounts do exist the officials of the tax administration are sometimes not sufficiently competent to fully determine the tax liability.

(*c*) Even when it is possible to assess tax liability, it may be difficult to collect the taxes due. Great emphasis was placed upon the widespread existence of tax evasion by socially, politically or economically powerful groups and individuals. Tax collectors at all levels from village to capital are often unable or afraid to collect the full tax liability of powerful people. Often the tax officials are unable to obtain the support of their political chiefs since the latter may condone the evasion and may refuse permission to prosecute offenders.

In the case of direct taxes, especially income taxes, it was agreed that a large degree of voluntary compliance is essential for efficiency, as the taxpayer himself supplies much of the information about income and allowances that determines his liability. This voluntary compliance is not often forthcoming.

While it was agreed that company taxation is a major and successful source of revenue, less satisfaction was expressed about personal income taxation. An apparently progressive tax system may take a low proportion (relative to ability to pay) from the rich, whose influence and prestige make evasion much easier than for the poor, whose tax is deducted at source.

In the case of indirect taxes levied on goods, it was argued that substantial increases in revenue could not be expected, owing to political factors deriving from the fact that indirect taxes tended to be regressive (expenditure on goods forms a higher percentage of the income of the poor than of the rich). Against this, it was argued that the discriminatory taxation of luxuries is always possible. Indeed, the under-taxation of the rich through the direct-tax system could be balanced by heavy taxation on goods which only the rich can afford.

On the administrative side, it was agreed that taxes on foreign trade are much better than taxes on goods sold within the country (excise duties), since it is much easier to levy taxes on goods entering or leaving a country, the value and volume of which are readily identifiable, than on the basis of inadequate domestic traders' accounts.

However, it was emphasised that as economies develop and diversify, and as the ratio of foreign to national product falls, excise taxes will have to become much more important. The experience of India, where a considerable sum had been spent improving the tax administration, showed that excise taxes could become a major source of revenue.

The collection of taxes, other than in kind, requires that the taxpayer has access to money with which to meet his liability; but a large proportion of the population in developing countries is engaged in subsistence, rather than cash-crop agriculture. While there was disagreement about whether anybody in the subsistence sector really has any cash at all, there was agreement that the imposition of a tax did induce peasant farmers to exchange crops or labour for cash with which to pay their tax. Thus, the taxation of peasant farmers is both possible and is an instrument for extending the monetary economy.

CONCLUSION

Despite the considerable problems impeding assessment and collection of taxes in developing countries, there was unanimous agreement that money spent on improving the tax administration would more than pay for itself. More and better-trained officials would increase the yield of all taxes. In this, the developed countries had a major role to play in sending highly qualified officials to work with, and to train, officials in the developing countries: indeed, the International Monetary Fund has initiated a service for providing officials to developing countries requiring them.

It was agreed that the fundamental requirement is the full support of the political leaders, both effectively to penalise evasion and to improve the system in general.

Higher taxation of a kind that would penalise large landowners who left vast tracts of fertile land uncultivated on their estates was suggested for some countries. The question of raising more tax from peasant smallholders was also considered, as a means of monetising the rural economy and stimulating greater efficiency in land use. But in areas such as India where the land was supersaturated with people, it was pointed out that increased tax would reduce the peasant's real income dangerously, without stimulating his production.

MOBILISING SAVINGS IN THE PRIVATE SECTOR

There was time only for the most cursory examination of the problem of drawing private savings into the work of development and of ways of improving the extension of credit in the private sector. Idle saving, such as hoarding, the holding of idle land or cattle are natural in countries where the money economy and social security system are underdeveloped. Hoarding indeed may even benefit the economy during an inflation. Attractive channels have to be set up to mobilise these idle, private savings for productive investment. Private savings do exist but they are often used for unproductive purposes. Commercial banks have an important part to play in all this, but it was alleged – and denied – that they showed an excessive zeal for liquidity and security, as lenders. Gaping holes in the overall organisation of deposit facilities and credit-giving remain to be filled. Life insurance and pension schemes also need extending for this purpose, and, although experience with them had been discouraging, cooperative credit societies.

The provision of agricultural credit is probably the most vital and intractable problem of all. The sheer administration problem of organising immense numbers of small loans to peasants unused to credit operations is frightful. International and commercial credit agencies refuse to deal with the need for large numbers of tiny loans and a new approach to the entire problem is needed. It was not enough to extend the operation of government agricultural credit services. Loans to peasant farmers are of little use unless they are closely associated with managerial and technical advice on the proper use of them. Credit should be backed with technical assistance. Advice is not much use without the finance required to carry it out. Even when he is offered both as an incentive to get better crop yields, the small farmer may refuse to venture if he is worried about the price he will get at sale or whether he will have enough food. To remove these obstacles to higher yields in agriculture, it may yet be necessary to guarantee him both food supplies and a fixed level of income.

17 · Administrative Obstacles to Development
RASHID IBRAHIM[1]

EMERGENCE OF ADMINISTRATIVE OBSTACLES

Administrative obstacles to development could be considered with reference to development effort in (*a*) the private sector and (*b*) the public sector, and in relation to stages of the development process, namely, (1) planning and sector-programming, (2) project preparation, (3) project appraisal and approval, (4) project execution, and (5) progress review and evaluation. In a *laissez-faire* economy, the development effort would be mainly in the private sector, but developing countries of the present era have almost invariably decided to plan and promote development, and even where they believe in free enterprise and propound no socialist doctrines, they undertake large-scale public sector programmes and regulate private sector activities in a large way.[2] Government machinery and its operations are, therefore, of the greatest consequence in developing countries, and the success or failure of the development effort may hinge on the effectiveness, efficiency and responsiveness of public administration. Administrative obstacles to economic growth emerge, and sometimes in a very serious form, because governments either are not conscious of the relationship between planned development and public administration, or adopt an ostrich-like policy with regard to administration while assuming development burdens. It is true that, in order to avoid inconsistency in economic policies and to mobilise national resources on an accelerated basis, as also to absorb foreign aid which is a dominant feature of present-era development effort, some planning and coordination is essential. But it would be worth while if a country, before deciding upon the size of its public sector operations and the degree of government regulation of the private sector, would first assess its administrative capacity and resources.

PLANNING AND SECTOR-PROGRAMMING

In the planning stage, government functionaries presume to think and adjudicate both for the public and private sectors – they determine the overall size of a period plan and the national objectives to be met, the sector allocations and contents, the physical and financial targets within each sector, the infrastructure and other activities which the public sector should undertake, the level and the manner in which private investments should proceed, and the need and size of foreign assistance. Within the framework of the period plan, they formulate the annual programmes for the public and the private sectors. All this is a truly Herculean task, and may itself constitute a major administrative obstacle. The distinction with 'centrally planned economies' is, or should be, that this planning is done by government officials not in isolation, but in association with the private sector – with well-informed businessmen, farmers, economists and other intellectuals, with the press and the public at large, as well as any research and technical institutions available. The quality of the period plans/annual programmes would depend upon this interaction between official and non-official opinion, the harmony between theory of development and the realities of the situation, and the consistency of economic, social and political objectives. To make sense of the converging schemes, ideas, ambitions, there has to be a central planning organisation. To ensure that it does not create more confusion than it resolves, this organisation should have an adequate structure, it should be manned with qualified personnel,[3] its procedure should be well-defined and well-understood, it should command the attention and respect of government ministries and departments as well as the private sector, and it should have effective political support (one obvious method is that the head of government should be its chief). After this organisation has formulated its plans, they must be reflected in the annual budgets, and there should be no significant departures from the plans without consultation with this organisation. Further, its functions should not be confined to the compilation of an investment programme (including foreign aid of course) and the indication of appropriate economic measures, but it should be continually associated with individual ministries in the evolution of broad economic policies and formulation of vital economic decisions, through representation on standing committees or consultations at staff or other similar level. Conflict and confusion of objectives must be avoided and all policies of the government must be so moulded as to favour and promote the development effort. On its part, the planning organisation should realise its own limitations and should not chew more than it can digest. For instance, it should avoid dabbling in the actual preparation or implementation of development projects or other executive operations which do not properly fall within its sphere (although in order to fill the sector programmes it could help to sponsor pre-investment and feasibility surveys in uncovered or inadequately covered fields). Ideally, the planning organisation ought to be independent of normal ministries, but in smaller countries with inadequate resources of personnel or countries with limited planning objectives, it could be part of the ministry of finance or economic affairs, though its head should have access to the head of government.

Two subsidiary obstacles at the planning stage are the absence (or weakness) of planning machinery at lower levels, and the inadequacy of statistics. The central planning organisation cannot do detailed planning for all ministries/departments or the private sector and, for economic plans to have full meaning, planning from the bottom and from the top should merge into an harmonious whole. Accordingly, planning units of appropriate size ought to be available in the ministries/departments (and in a federation, also in the provincial or state governments). In the private sector, chambers of commerce and industry could be organised and encouraged to do similar thinking, and advisory panels could be set up for each sector and field. As for statistics, which are a prerequisite for any worth-while planning (and later for review and evaluation), adequate staff and organisation need to be established at all levels and in all fields for collection and initial compilation work. The central statistical organisation needs to be properly staffed and should preferably be independent of – though very closely linked with – the central planning organisation.

Pakistan's experience as a typical developing country would be relevant.[4]

Its central planning organisation has grown from a weak unit (Development Board) of part-time officials in 1950, into a well-knit body (Planning Commission) today of whole-time members with the President of Pakistan as Chairman and a minister as Deputy Chairman, with a large complement of well-qualified and trained staff. The provincial planning departments are also now sizeable and effective (headed by Additional Chief Secretaries), and the larger ministries and departments have their own planning cells. The planning process has progressed from a loose stringing together of hurriedly made-up schemes (Development Programme 1951–7) to a well-conceived and integrated Third Five-Year Plan (1965–70) prepared recently. Over 150 survey/research studies were organised to provide a reliable base for the Third Plan. Foreign aid and technical assistance are now fully linked with and integrated into the plans; actual negotiations are handled by an Economic Affairs Division, the minister in charge of which is Deputy Chairman of the Planning Commission, so that there can be no pulling apart of the Plan thinking and the aid utilisation. Similarly, the planning technique has gradually become more sophisticated (and possibly more simplified) and lucid forms and procedures have been laid down for the formulation of Five-Year Plans, the compilation of annual development programmes within the Plan framework, for consideration and approval of individual projects and the review and evaluation of progress made (these are intended to be incorporated in a development manual). Planning is now in the context of a twenty-year perspective; a Plan framework is prepared in the light of pre-determined objectives; investment programmes are tied up with economic policies, and cost–benefit ratios and inputs–outputs are kept in sight throughout. The supreme economic body is the National Economic Council consisting of central and provincial representatives at the highest political level (with the President of Pakistan as chairman) – it accords government approval to the period plans and annual programmes and decides all major issues of economic policy. There is also an economic coordination committee at ministerial level to ensure consistency in policies on an operational level. What is most important is that the President of Pakistan is dedicated to the cause of development so that all roads are made to lead into the avenue of development.

PROJECT APPRAISAL AND APPROVAL

The stage of project appraisal and approval, which is in between project preparation and project execution, can be a serious administrative bottleneck. The government generally wants to scrutinise and give formal clearance after the implementation agencies, whether public sector bodies or private entrepreneurs, have formulated a concrete project. The relevant ministry, the Ministry of Finance, and appropriately the planning organisation also, are involved in this scrutiny and final clearance may be accorded by the council of ministers or a cabinet committee or other ministerial body authorised for the purpose. Where the project falls within the provincial jurisdiction, corresponding provincial agencies are also involved. Although the project may be within the Plan framework and part of the annual development programme (and budget), this individual scrutiny and clearance takes months because there is a criss-cross of comments, clarifications and consultations. Not infrequently delays are due to lack of expertise to scrutinise and assess the project, and yet the ministries wish to contribute! In-service training is needed for all relevant officials, in the technique of project appraisal, from the technical, economic and financial angles.

In Pakistan, a system of development working parties (provincial and central) has been evolved to simplify the process of project approval. These working parties comprise representatives of all ministries/agencies concerned, meet once in two months (convened by the provincial/central planning organisation) and are expected to record their final views on the very first occasion. Thus there is simultaneous rather than successive consideration of the projects. Government approval is accorded by an Executive Committee of the National Economic Council on which the central and provincial governments are represented at ministerial level. In the case of private sector projects, individual scrutiny and clearance has been left to the credit institutions within the limits of 'Industrial Investment Schedules' which are formulated from time to time by the government Investment Promotion Bureau in consultation with the planning organisation and other relevant agencies within the framework of the Plan.

PROJECT PREPARATION AND PROJECT EXECUTION – PUBLIC SECTOR

It is in the stages of project preparation and execution that the administrative obstacles are most glaring. In most countries, public sector development has earned a bad name because projects are often not well prepared – technical feasibility is not studied properly, economic and financial soundness is not checked, benefits are over-estimated and costs are under-estimated (often deliberately), requirements and repercussions in other sectors are not taken into account, arrangements for making full use of the project on completion are not made in advance, and future maintenance requirements are not assessed. In relation to the sector as a whole, an adequate number of properly prepared projects are not available to meet the sector targets, projects listed up initially are changed from time to time, and priorities are altered. While some flexibility is understandable, 'adhocism' and reshuffling can go too far. Actual execution of projects also is often unsatisfactory – requirements of personnel, equipment, land, water supply, transport, etc., are not well coordinated, clearance for matters of detail or for new problems arising during execution is not easily forthcoming, difficulties arise with other government departments, implementation takes much longer than estimated, and so on. The dimension of time is vital in the developing perspective; prices of imported equipment as well as indigenous wages and materials keep on rising and delay in production involves a big cost in itself, and yet time schedules are not fulfilled.

Basically, the responsibility for implementation of public sector projects is that of ministries/departments of the central/provincial governments. But normal government machinery, with its regulatory rather than developmental bias, its long line of command and divided responsibility, cumbersome procedures, administrative rigidities and financial controls, is ill suited for development business. Governments have, therefore, increasingly resorted to the establishment of autonomous corporations subject to overall government control.[5] There is no doubt that where operations in a particular field lend themselves to 'commercial' handling and are large enough in size, autonomous agencies provide the answer. Such agencies are not inhibited by the vast body of constrictive regulations of government departments and are able to arrange their own recruitment, purchases, construction and other services. They are worried more about results than about procedure. Their charters generally enable them to cut across departmental spheres and central/provincial jurisdictions, and, if necessary, they can associate with and benefit from private enterprise. However, since they have such large powers and responsibilities, it is important that members of their boards and their managing directors should be men of known integrity, competence and drive. As qualified personnel are usually in short supply, too many corporations should not be created, or inefficiency and waste might only be worsened.

Not all governmental operations lend themselves to 'commercial' handling and must therefore continue to be the direct responsibility of conventional ministries and departments. Efficiency and speed need to be increased there, too. Whatever can be done [6] to streamline procedure and provide operational flexibility, give greater responsibility and power to departmental functionaries, promote initiative, reward performance and penalise inefficiency should be done. Common service agencies for recruitment (Public Service Commission), promotion (Central Selection Board), construction (Public Works Department), purchase (Supply Department), etc., create the worst bottlenecks. The agency for financial advice (Ministry of Finance) is another. Their procedures should be simplified or decentralised or both. 'Over-centralisation is an ineffective and in fact a spurious form of coordination. It exhibits itself in time-consuming energy-wasting and patience-exhausting checks and counterchecks, references and cross-references, conferences and consultations, often at wrong levels and about unimportant matters.'[7] Specialisation should be encouraged and specialists and technicians should be shown greater respect so that they may be encouraged to show initiative and stimulated to get things done. The administrative heads should be retained in the same position long enough to develop identity of interest with the organisation (or project) and pride in its achievement. In short, business concepts and businesslike methods should be introduced as far as is feasible. O. & M. (Organisation and Methods) machinery should be established as soon as resources permit and O. & M. studies undertaken of departments concerned with the implementation of public projects (or regulation of private enterprise). Administrative inadequacy is most noticeable in the field of agriculture where, despite allocation of resources, targets are seldom achieved. Special attention is, therefore, required in respect of the organisation, procedures and personnel related to agriculture.

The employment of foreign consultants for project preparation and foreign contractors for project execution, sometimes on a turn-key basis, has been done in several countries with notable results. Employment of consultants is often necessary because skills for project preparation, particularly in the more sophisticated fields, are not available, and also because foreign aid is almost invariably dependent upon the submission of a project report by a consultant acceptable to the aid-giving agency. However, too many foreign consultants, some of them with more attractive stationery than experience, have appeared on the scene, and developing countries must guard against injudicious selection. They must also try to establish and foster indigenous consultancy organisations as far as possible.[8] Similar considerations apply to foreign contractors.

Under technical assistance programmes, experts can be obtained quite easily, and they may be used where indigenous 'expertise' is not available. However, they can be employed only in a limited number of senior positions and often can function only as advisers (although the United Nations has sought to meet this difficulty through the 'Opex' cadre and by the World Bank through their Development Advisory Service). Such experts are useful but are understandably not familiar with local conditions and problems, and cannot inspire full confidence. The only remedy is the speedy development of local talent and skills and the undertaking of large-scale training programmes for this purpose. In any case, whenever foreign experts are employed, 'counterpart' local understudies must be attached to them so that their need is liquidated in due course.

A major bottleneck in project execution is the process of allocation, negotiation, commitment and utilisation of foreign aid. Foreign aid is available to the developing countries, but it is seldom offered as a general addition to a country's resources, and is linked with specific programmes and projects. Each project has to be submitted in great detail and justified with all sorts of data. An aid-giving country not only wants to tie up assistance with supplies and equipment made within its own boundaries, but wishes to have even the feasibility and project reports prepared by its own consultants. Thus, if one aid country drops a project for any reason the process has to begin all over again. The aid procedures are quite complicated and time-consuming, and considerable expertise is needed to understand them and keep abreast of the changes that occur. The developing countries have to develop this expertise as well as adequate organisational arrangements to process the aid as quickly and effectively as possible. Coordination is needed of all aid available from donor countries as well as international agencies so that there is no duplication and confusion, and procedures need to be evolved jointly to simplify both the commitment and utilisation of aid to the fullest feasible extent. While negotiations up to the commitment stage ought to be conducted by a single government agency, all implementation agencies are necessarily involved in actual utilisation. The responsibilities of the latter and the procedures affecting them should be clearly spelt out in comprehensive form (manuals, etc.) and, if necessary, short training courses arranged.

PROJECT PREPARATION AND PROJECT EXECUTION – PRIVATE SECTOR

While the private sector has its own measure of internal difficulties, its main headache in developing countries is government controls and regulations. Indeed, in certain countries the establishment of a new enterprise, in the face of all bureaucratic restrictions, procedures and attitudes, is nothing short of a miracle. The concept of planned development, which seeks to achieve a different allocation of scarce resources from that which would take place under free market operations, does involve discipline for the private sector, but the question is how far and in what manner should this discipline be enforced. Governments of underdeveloped countries are usually control-minded, and observers might well say in certain situations that ' the least government is the best government '! Whatever the reason for the imposition of direct controls, they do create obstacles and bottlenecks – the administrative capacity to administer them and to issue permits, licences, certificates, is inadequate. The intentions may be good, but in actual practice controls seldom serve their objective. As executive weapons, they are ineffective, inefficient and self-multiplying. In particular, price controls encourage consumption and discourage production, particularly in the field of agriculture. While higher bureaucratic levels may view them not as sources of patronage but as instruments of planning, for the lower officials they are means of aggrandisement and, frequently, of illegal gain. Controls consume considerable administrative resources for their enforcement, and further reduce the administrative capacity required for the development effort.

It would be helpful if the concrete example of Pakistan is described. The following main controls have existed in Pakistan:

control over investment in industry and other fields, and over location of industries;

control over establishment of companies beyond a certain size, and over association of foreign capital and employment of foreigners;

control over foreign exchange earning and utilisation;

control over imports, and over exports;

control over credit expansion and credit utilisation (through the central bank);

control over prices, and over distribution of essential producer and consumer goods including foodstuffs;

control over production of certain crops and commodities; and

control over labour wages, working conditions and facilities.

The basic purpose of these controls was to allocate scarce resources to planned priority needs and indeed to facilitate the meeting of such needs. Of course, certain political and social objectives were superimposed, e.g. reducing concentration of wealth, removing disparities between different areas, providing certain goods and services at artificially low prices. Since 1959, Pakistan has consistently tried to get away from direct controls and to use the indirect method of fiscal, tariff, monetary and other incentives and disincentives to achieve the same purpose. Procurement of foodstuffs at prescribed prices, and rationing, have been given up. A large section of imports has been placed on 'free list' and 'open general licence'. Taxation and credit patterns have been so adjusted as to attract investment in priority industries and areas. Other concessions, subsidies and facilities have been provided to promote private enterprise in selected fields. Considerable success has thus been achieved in decontrolling the economy. Partly, this has been possible because over the years the economy has become more sophisticated and sensitive to indirect 'influencing' measures. The lesson is that direct controls should be avoided as far as possible and that, in situations where there is a large gap between resources and priority needs, every effort should be made to use the market and price mechanism by employing indirect means to achieve the desired result. Another lesson is that conflict between 'growth' and 'welfare' objectives should be resolved as a matter of policy, otherwise conflicting controls might defeat both objectives.

Some type and degree of direct controls may, however, continue to be necessary. Improvement and simplification of the administrative machinery concerned with such direct controls is, therefore, imperative. The procedure for securing licences or permits should be as lucid and as simple as possible and continuous thought should be given to cutting out unintended and unnecessary 'red-tape'. More important than that, the officials operating the controls should be made development-minded rather than control-minded, i.e. their success should be judged by the manner in which they have helped the applicants in steering through the bureaucratic maze rather than how strictly they have applied the regulations. Wherever feasible, the agencies administering the day-to-day controls should be delegated large operational powers on a semi-autonomous basis, and only broad policy control should be retained by government ministries themselves.[9] To repeat, the government must assess, before imposing or extending any controls, its administrative capacity to enforce the controls with success and with benefit to those for whom the controls are meant.

PROGRESS REVIEW AND EVALUATION

Review of day-to-day progress in relation to the time schedule, cost and other estimates given in the project report as approved, is the concern of implementation agencies, or individual entrepreneurs, and of the relevant ministries and departments. It is also basically their responsibility to locate bottlenecks and ensure their removal at the project level or elsewhere. On the other hand, the evaluation of overall performance of the implementation agencies themselves (and possibly the more important projects in the public sector), the assessment of progress in each sector as a whole, the study of repercussions in other sectors, and the drawing of lessons for future planning, can be better undertaken by the planning organisation. Inter-departmental disputes and difficulties also need to be resolved, and corrective action for any planning mistakes committed has to be suggested. Some countries have found it more useful to have an independent evaluation unit, though working closely with the planning organisations. Instead of having a large body of lower grade officials, it may be better to have a few high-powered officers who have knowledge and experience, may visit projects, are able to establish contacts at the proper level, and report directly to the head of the planning organisation (or the head of government). Evaluation is most important in the case of semi-government autonomous institutions which are subject neither to the strict control of government departments nor to the penalty of losses of the private entrepreneur. Evaluation of the private sector activities is also useful and important, in view of the large concessions and incentives provided by the government and the vital role of the private sector in fulfilling planned targets. Private enterprise is not always as efficient as it is reputed to be, particularly in the developing countries.

The main problem in progress review and evaluation is the defective preparation of progress reports by implementation agencies, or non-submission altogether. An adequate and effective reporting system is a prerequisite; in certain cases special reports on critical aspects may be needed in addition to routine periodical reports. In all cases, completion reports and one or two post-completion operation reports are worthwhile. If possible, the concept of 'performance budgeting' should be introduced so that some evaluation is built into the budgetary process. The correct and timely compilation of government accounts, and reliable and prompt statistical operations, are essential tools for purposes of review and evaluation of progress.

Pakistan's experience of review and evaluation is not as comprehensive as that of some other countries. It is a weak link in an otherwise strong chain of organisational arrangements. A Projects (Evaluation) Division existed in the Planning Commission at one time, and it is proposed to revive it. Review units are available with the Provincial Planning Departments. But the submission of progress reports and their study and utilisation need considerable improvement. It is understood [10] that Iran has an effective independent unit, which not only evaluates and compares the performance of different projects and enterprises but also helps to locate and solve administrative bottlenecks during implementation. It has been given considerable statutory powers during the Seven-Year Plan Law, and may not only initiate disciplinary proceedings against inefficient and irresponsible implementation agencies but also may transfer the project to another agency for execution. It is expected to cover all projects by physical inspection once a quarter (a rather formidable assignment) and to publish reports on both a projectwise and a functional basis. The unit pinpoints all deficiencies of the implementation agency, the project officer, the consultant, the contractor and others concerned, and also brings out the defects in planning, whether technical, or financial and administrative. It also suggests modifications while the project is under way. Another useful function of the unit is the evolution of standards and yardsticks, both for measurement of performance and preparation of future projects.

CONCLUSION

The normal administrative machinery in developing countries was geared for peace-keeping, revenue collection, and limited public works functions. Even then, in most colonial countries, senior positions and key appointments were held by foreigners, most of whom left at the time of independence. The extent of administrative association, and the degree of development of indigenous educational and training institutions, varied with different colonial governments, but in all cases it was inadequate for the responsibilities to come. The ' natives ' were expected to go to the imperial country for higher studies and almost invariably had a ' liberal ' rather than a technical education. When these countries saddled themselves with large-scale public sector development programmes and also large-scale regulation of the private sector, inevitably delays and dislocations emerged. The administrative framework was found inadequate, and therefore also the ' absorptive capacity ' for foreign aid. The more obvious administrative bottlenecks have been described in the preceding paragraphs. It is accordingly essential that in line with the enlarged scale of development effort, government organisation should be expanded and re-ordered,[11] procedures reviewed and simplified.

personnel trained and reorientated, and ancillary facilities like proper office accommodation, telephones, office gadgets and other working aids provided. However, generally public administration is taken for granted. The foremost need for developing countries, therefore, is allocation of adequate attention and resources for developing administration itself. When a development plan is formulated, it ought to include an assessment of the administrative resources required and the means for their acquisition including pre-service education, and on-entry and in-service training, research in administrative organisation and techniques suited to local conditions, evolution of appropriate personnel policies, etc. Frequently, the cost of staff and administrative overheads is regarded as non-development expenditure to be avoided as far as possible. To undertake enlarged development activities, however, more staff will obviously be needed, and there has to be a reasonable relationship between the size of a development plan and the size of the administrative machinery.

Most important is the development of administrative personnel and their skills and attitudes. An adequate number of training institutions need to be established to cater for the administrative hierarchy at all levels and all stages of service. If possible, a computation should be made of the trained manpower – administrative and technical – needed over a Plan period, and training arrangements planned accordingly. This is a field in which foreign aid and technical assistance could be used profitably, though the syllabi and methods of instruction must be based on indigenous needs and problems. While training is being imparted, the officials need to be 'brain-washed' and reorientated from being law and order, static functionaries to being development-minded dynamic instruments of change. The old concept of 'generalists' flitting from post to post should be replaced by a premium on 'specialists' who are associated with policy-making as well as project implementation. The resistance to change, usual with bureaucrats, must be overcome. And the tendency to shift responsibility horizontally, or vertically (up and down), or nowhere (committees and conferences) should be discouraged. As far as feasible, businesslike approach and methods should be inculcated. The senior officials need to be turned into 'managers' who can take decisions, assume responsibility, delegate authority and yet control performance.

The developing countries cannot do without enlightened personnel policies to build up a contented civil service (e.g. proper conditions of service, emoluments, welfare, etc.) and which would egg on civil servants to greater effort (e.g. incentives and rewards for extra performance). The structure of the civil service and its handling may require reorganisation so that merit and not birth or date of birth (seniority) are the basis of promotion. 'Positive steps will have to be taken to provide equitable avenues of advance to all branches of the public service, strictly on considerations of merit, quality of performance and suitability for the job, eliminating the wide disparities in career prospects now observable among different classes of public servants.'[12] Only then will all public officials be motivated to do their best, to improve themselves as well as their organisations, and to contribute to increased production and productivity. All administrative obstacles to growth may be finally traced to public servants, and measures to improve their quality are, therefore, fundamental.

Appendix 1   *Planning organisation in Pakistan*

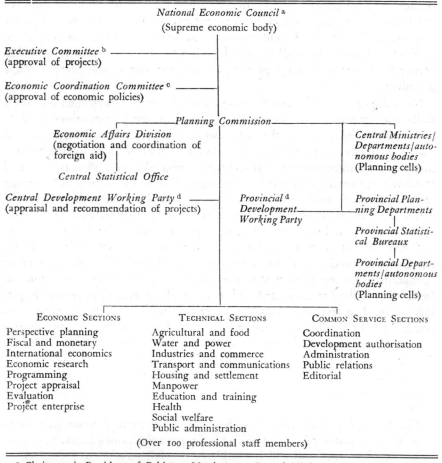

National Economic Council [a]
(Supreme economic body)

Executive Committee [b] ———————
(approval of projects)

Economic Coordination Committee [c] ———
(approval of economic policies)

——————*Planning Commission*——————

Economic Affairs Division
(negotiation and coordination of foreign aid)

Central Statistical Office

Central Development Working Party [d] ———
(appraisal and recommendation of projects)

Provincial [d]
*Development
Working Party*

*Central Ministries/
Departments/auto-
nomous bodies*
(Planning cells)

*Provincial Plan-
ning Departments*

*Provincial Statisti-
cal Bureaux*

*Provincial Depart-
ments/autonomous
bodies*
(Planning cells)

ECONOMIC SECTIONS	TECHNICAL SECTIONS	COMMON SERVICE SECTIONS
Perspective planning	Agricultural and food	Coordination
Fiscal and monetary	Water and power	Development authorisation
International economics	Industries and commerce	Administration
Economic research	Transport and communications	Public relations
Programming	Housing and settlement	Editorial
Project appraisal	Manpower	
Evaluation	Education and training	
Project enterprise	Health	
	Social welfare	
	Public administration	

(Over 100 professional staff members)

[a] Chairman is President of Pakistan. Members are Central Ministers of economic ministries including Deputy Chairman of Planning Commission, and Provincial Governors and Ministers of Planning and of Finance.
[b] Ministerial level. Deputy Chairman of Planning Commission is a member.
[c] Chairman is President of Pakistan. In addition to Deputy Chairman of Cabinet rank, there are two whole-time Members.
[d] Secretary of Planning Commission is chairman of Central D.W.P., and additional Chief Secretaries of the Provincial Governments are chairmen of Provincial D.W.P.s.

Important Standing Committees on which Planning Commission is represented :

1. Exchange Control Committee
2. Import Policy Committee
3. Industrial Advisory Committee
4. Central Permission Committee
5. Indus Basin Development Board
6. Food and Agriculture Council
7. Standing Committee on Agricultural Primary Commodities
8. Family Planning Council
9. Standing Labour Committee
10. National Manpower Council
11. National Administrative Training Council
12. National Statistical Council
13. Budget Reforms Committee

Appendix 2 *Public corporations in Pakistan (and other autonomous bodies responsible for project execution)*

Field	Centre	West Pakistan	East Pakistan
(a) Industry and fuel	Oil and Gas Development Corporation	West Pakistan Industrial Development Corporation	East Pakistan Industrial Development Corporation
	Wah Ordnance Board		East Pakistan Small Industries Corporation
			Forest Industries Development Corporation
			Fisheries Development Corporation
(b) Water and power	Atomic Energy Commission	Water and Power Development Authority	Water and Power Development Authority
		Karachi Electric Supply Corporation	
(c) Transport and communications	Pakistan International Airlines Corporation	Railway Board	Railway Board
	Karachi Port Trust		Inland Water Transport Authority
	Chittagong Port Trust		East Pakistan Shipping Corporation
	National Shipping Corporation		
(d) Agriculture		Agricultural Development Corporation	Agricultural Development Corporation

Appendix 2—*continued*.

Field	Centre	West Pakistan	East Pakistan
(e) Regional development	Capital Development Authority	Karachi Development Authority	Dacca Improvement Trust
		Thal Development Authority	Chittagong Development Authority
		Lahore Improvement Trust	
		Rawalpindi and Hazara Hill Tracts Improvement Trust	
(f) Credit	Industrial Development Bank of Pakistan		
	Pakistan Industrial Credit and Investment Corporation		
	Agricultural Development Bank		
	House Building Finance Corporation		
(g) Miscellaneous	Pakistan Corporation	Cooperative Development Board	
		Soil Reclamation Board	

18 · Difficulties in Public Administration[1]
CAMBRIDGE CONFERENCE REPORT

Economic progress has been held back in recent years by cruelly unfavourable external trading conditions, population explosions, and perhaps also, by the Parkinsonian tendency of governments to spend increasing national savings on increasing administrative and social services, instead of investing them directly to produce more wealth. Shortfalls in meeting targets of production are also due to over-sophisticated and over-optimistic plans that are beyond the existing executive, managerial and technical capacities of these countries to carry into effect.

Obviously an economic plan is not worth the paper it is written on unless it is matched with a corresponding plan for expanding and reorganising executive capacity, both in the public and private sectors.

Whether one holds that disappointing economic results are to be blamed on too much state interference with market mechanisms and too little scope for private enterprise or not, everyone agrees that shortage of executive capacity is a major obstacle to economic advance. For example, the Planning Board in Pakistan forecast in its first Five-Year Plan that: 'the inadequacies of . . . administrative machinery will operate as the most serious single impediment to the maximum economical use of the country's financial and material resources . . . the pace of implementation of economic and social programmes is likely to be governed . . . more by the capabilities of the nation's administrative and technical organisation [than by] the magnitude of resources.'[2] In every country in the world, but especially in developing countries, such forecasts are the safest bets in the book.

Most experienced administrators stressed 'the importance of executive and managerial resources, even more than the fiscal' in the success of economic plans. There is too much economic theory in planning and too little operational pragmatism, according to those who have to carry them out. As a speaker from Africa put it: 'Economic progress does not depend upon plans and planning in the final analysis. Given actual or potential effective demand, development depends upon the presence and behaviour of the agents of production and distribution, whether in the public or private sectors.' The administration itself may sometimes be the obstacle. But shortages of executive capacity will always be a problem because they enlarge with the development process. They are not something that can be solved once for all through some dramatic reorganisation recommended in the diagrammatic blue-prints of organisation experts. As another contributor said:

Administrative resources are always going to be short in every country. If I may refer to the developing country that I know best – the United Kingdom – there has never been a greater scarcity of administrative and technical resources than at present . . . the Government, believe it or not, has now gone out to industry and said: 'can you lend us seventy people for two years to do the jobs in our administrative class – we cannot get enough of them'.

Three kinds of thing can be done about this perennial shortage of executive capacity. In countries with comparatively advanced private sectors, governments can save administrative capacity by attempting to manage and control less of the economy, and leave more to market mechanisms and private management. In other words, the state should wherever possible rely on providing incentives for private men to do desirable economic things rather than trying to do everything itself. However efficient, however huge the administration can make itself, it can never move all the 'centipede' economy's hundred feet for it. The only alternative is to provide incentives to persuade the centipede itself to move them. That this approach is less practicable for Africa than for Asia and Latin America was accepted.

Secondly, 'much more specific attention must be given to operational planning than hitherto. Economic plans should be systematically " tailored " to existing and prospective executive, managerial and technological capacities.'

' Thirdly, the expansion of all these capacities should be planned systematically on a long-term basis in the same fashion as the economic plan to provide its operational requirements.' The formulation of a distinguished Indian member which was generally agreed may be quoted here:

Executive capacity includes all the executive agencies, authorities and processes involved in implementing the development plan; the governmental *cadres*, central and local; other public agencies and managerial *cadres* in state and private enterprises and all scientific, technological, technical, clerical and semi-skilled manpower.

The processes of development planning and of plan implementation intermesh at crucial points in all their phases. Therefore the quality and content of the development plan, on the one hand, and the executive capacity on the other, continuously limit each other.

Since this is so: (1) Development planning and the planning of executive capacity must be continuously matched throughout the processes of planning and the execution of the plan. (2) Executive capacity must be the subject of survey and review and the operational plans should be an integral part of the overall economic and social development plan. (3) The expansion of executive capacity should be planned in detail and specifically, in sectoral, macro and micro programmes and projects. (4) Operational planning, no less than economic planning, should be the direct responsibility of the head of government, assisted by commissions of officials and non-officials from industry and labour who should review continuously the progress of executive resources.

These are doubtless counsels of perfection. In the less advanced countries, admittedly, this is asking for the moon. So much programming would absorb more executive resources than they could spare. Here, a study group reported,

Early plans can only achieve rough estimates to be adjusted by a 'roll-over' process successively shifting the horizon forward. A general survey of manpower should precede the plan but projections of executive capacity are bound to be tentative. There is nothing for it but to go ahead in the dark at first, discovering and correcting shortages by trial and error. It is probably true to say that given the opportunity, there is more native talent than might be expected.

In the more advanced countries of Asia and Latin America, with years of development planning behind them, it should be possible to

estimate manpower requirements in the light of earlier experience and plan expansion in conjunction with the increase of educational and training facilities. Even in their sophisticated sectoral plans no specific calculations of the executive manpower required to reach targets set, seem to have been included, and this defect is particularly acute on the technical side. Therefore, highly specific operational plans are needed to indicate how much of a particular kind of executive manpower will be needed and how all the work is to be carried out.

It is here unhappily – at the critical point where operational plans are needed to carry economic plans into action – that almost all national development is at its weakest.

IMPROVING OPERATIONAL PLANS

At the same time we were warned not to go too far in the opposite direction. Administrators tend to look at executive capacity as a precondition, economists, as a product, of development; and obviously both statements are true. Operational capacity 'reflects the traditions, politics, education economics and sense of national identity of the people of each country. In the long run, it improves as these fundamental determinants alter and the people advance.' For this reason, some economic advisers doubted whether, in fact, lack of operational capability is an obstacle to growth of the same order as shortages of economic resources. To some extent it can be assumed to expand as development proceeds all round. Existing executive resources can be 'stretched' by planning. An important rider to the propositions quoted above was added from this standpoint. Admittedly, we do not like the existing state of affairs in which too often elaborate economic plans without specific operational arrangements for carrying them out, are then thrown on to administrators' desks to do what they can. The general administrator's protest against this practice was earnestly made:

Now I do say it is a good thing to assume capability and that it will respond to opportunity . . . At the same time, one has no sooner digested one highly sophisticated economic plan and begun to work out ways of executing it, than one gets another. Every new inhabitant of the planning unit produces a new model. He must do it – it is his brainchild! It is difficult to keep pace with this model-building over-sophistication – and if I may say so as a pretty ancient administrator – this seeming sophistication conceals a lot of ignorance about practical possibilities.

'A report of the Pan-American Union concluded: "Most economic and social development plans are made upon an unrealistic basis . . . usually lacking is an evaluation of the operative capacity of the administrative machinery to accomplish that part of the plan that is the responsibility of the public sector ".' [3] More specific operational planning is therefore necessary. At the same time, economic planners warned us not to go to the other extreme where a development plan would consist chiefly of schemes for more and more administrative agencies to expand operational capacity and divert still more public savings to unproductive purposes. It was agreed, however, that, in itself, more specific operational planning would help stretch capability by setting targets of productivity. 'One of the most valuable by-products of operational planning is that it provides targets for each branch of the executive to aim at, and standards against which actual performance and responsibility can be tested. If these targets are set higher than seems practicable, capability will be stretched, although of course there is " a last straw ".'

IMPROVING OPERATIONAL CAPACITY

We went on to consider suggestions for improving operational capacity, chiefly in the public sector. Red tape, buck-passing, status-seeking, snobbery, dilatoriness, anti-intellectual rules of thumb, obsolete accounting procedures, inter-service feuding, the bureaucratic disease that mistakes the passing of paper for getting things done and the means for the end – these are the unamiable faults of ' Prufrockery ' around the world. Needless to say we are against administrative ' sin ', and for training, re-training, education, ' stream-lining ' organisation, importing technical assistance to fill gaps, better political leadership, better communications within the administration and with the nation as a whole.

But speakers were wary of suggesting that anything sudden, radical or spectacular could be done for ' virtue '. Since the administration is an organic part of society, ' it is unrealistic to try to transplant systems and devices from one social environment to another, without careful adaptation '. The complaint here was this:

A country wants to increase its food production: so they send the permanent secretary, the agricultural chief and several others to see how they do it in another country. They are driven round at a furious rate, seeing all the sights and come back full of wonderful new concepts. What happens on their return? The civil servant gets back to a desk piled with files about the budget, official misdemeanours, leave, someone is screaming his head off for an important document missing for a Cabinet meeting. In the midst of all this bedlam, the administrator is expected to adapt to the conditions of his own country the very complex social, economic and technological concept that his masters have supposedly picked up, and then to carry it out!

Too frequent and too radical alterations of administrative structure have been shown by experience to produce not more capability but more chaos.[4] What is needed usually is continuous, piecemeal application of ' quite elementary remedies to elementary problems ' of coordination. The crucial task is not to introduce ' correct ' forms of organisation (of which there are many) but ' to establish effective working relationships between those whose responsibility it is to take decisions and execute them '.[5] It is often not a question of raising big new battalions but of getting the right man who is already available into the right job; of opening the ' general administrative ' grade to men of proven technological or managerial ability; of promoting men according to their ability to get things done, instead of by seniority, purely academic qualifications, purity of accent or elegance of manners. Little co-ordination is possible if economic planners talk only to planners – and general administrators talk only with God. 'In the short term, the critical operational bottleneck lies probably in making better use of existing capacity, rather than in planning and expanding it. Much higher priority must be given to day-to-day economic management in the administration than it has received in the past.' As one expert said : 'Developing countries have got to put a much greater emphasis on people who can get results, be they in the public or private sector. A capacity to get economic things done rather than a capacity to acquire knowledge is what is wanted. People with degrees are not necessarily the best people for this.' 'What is necessary is to bring into the administration the kind of manpower that in developed countries is habitually found in the private sector – men who can design and manage economic projects.' Serious middle-level manpower shortages in administration had to be filled in some countries. Obsolete general and financial procedures have to be cut through. More elementary decision-making should be delegated to lower levels. Everywhere the need is to apply more intelligence, vision and 'development-mindedness' to the muscles of executive capacity.

A number of possible ways of generating these reforms continuously inside the administration was discussed. Officials should be subjected to the full glare of public criticism. An 'Ombudsman' to investigate and punish administrative faults might help; or an impartial 'Institute of Productivity' might be set up to report on the efficiency of economic management in the public sector. A unit to keep the action of administration under review and report to the highest authority was also recommended, either within the planning agency or elsewhere. This might concentrate on the working of major structural relations or upon areas of administration vital to the economic plan. It was suggested that the plan agency should keep in reserve a team of 'high-powered, trouble-shooting' executives to smash serious administrative bottlenecks as they occurred.

USES OF SEMI-AUTONOMOUS PUBLIC ECONOMIC AGENCIES

In countries where the private sector is comparatively weak, the state cannot avoid stepping into the vacuum, to manage public utilities, start up new industries and undertake major projects which are partly public utility and partly commercial, of the Tennessee Valley Authority type.

A common way of dealing with these tasks of economic management and initiative in the public sector that are outside the range of normal administration, is to hive them off on to different kinds of public or development corporation. These semi-autonomous bodies have obvious advantages. They expand managerial capacity by recruiting a wide range of talents that is neglected in normal selection for the public service; they offer the advantage of specialisation in economic tasks; and they reduce the amount of administrative machinery involved in reaching economic decisions. 'A corporation for a special purpose is created, hived off from the administrative leviathan and left to sort things out for itself.' This is one way of achieving 'creative decentralisation'. And when some at least of these enterprises had been set up, proved viable, gained experience and efficiency, they can, if need be, be sold out to private enterprise. 'This can have very useful by-products in developing capital markets, training managerial talent, establishing banks and strengthening the financial system and private sector in a country.'

There was no cavil at this opinion, so far as public utilities, such as railways and power, are concerned. Nevertheless, for other purposes, semi-autonomous public agencies have their disadvantages. Maybe to plant a massive set of public corporations in what is hoped will become the private sector is not the quickest way of encouraging private enterprise? It certainly creates powerful state vested interests that are not easily transferred. The advantages may be nullified and costs increased if excessive proliferation occurs and the hived-off corporations spawn their own subsidiaries and special agencies. They may draw off skilled technical and managerial manpower from the general administration; they may duplicate resources already existing within the government's own technical services; they can camouflage for a time the need of central administrative reforms; they may stand in the way of an early decision on the proper scope of the private sector; and the more of these semi-autonomous bodies there are, the more complicated and arduous the problem of accounting for their expenditure and controlling their operations becomes for the central authority. Big losses are made before the central administration is able to stop them. As with almost all attractive administrative solutions, so with semi-autonomous bodies, what is won at first on the swings turns out in the end to be more than lost on the roundabouts. 'Decentralisation', a Latin American contributor pointed out, 'is like inflation. It helps in the beginning but it is very difficult to stop; and if it isn't stopped, it's fatal.'

PROVINCIAL AND LOCAL AGENCIES

It cannot be said too often that another major factor determining executive capacities for development is the extent to which a government is able to explain itself to, call forth and harness the ordinary people to its purposes. Maybe this is primarily a political function to be carried out by political parties; but it is also an administrative function often neglected by civil services whose directors live and work in the enclaves of modern living. Such neglect has obvious political dangers in areas where centralised political parties are weak and local and regional cooperation depends upon administrative linkages with central government. More than that, the comparative weakness of operational capacity in the traditionalist rural sector is partly responsible for the economic lag in agricultural production. This is where the centipede economy has most of its legs and where it is hardest to get them to move and to coordinate them. And this is where services must be improved, where more small businesses, cottage industry, and intermediate technology are needed to keep people on the land. The point of action in developing agriculture which is the foundation of all other forms of economic growth, is at the 'grass roots' in provinces and districts.

In order to execute plans more effectively at these lower levels, we regard the following as essential: better coordination of the various central government agencies operating at these levels, and between them and local authorities, voluntary agencies and local branches of political parties. This is a particular case of that horizontal coordination that is needed at all levels; more trained, better paid, experienced, local staffs; more funds for local agencies; better informed leadership in local government and other local agencies; and more community development. Plans will go by default unless the cooperation of the people is obtained and this involves taking account of the wishes of local communities as well as explaining the meaning of 'development' to them.

The statement that the participation of the people is essential for national development through the institutional forms of local government, supplemented by informal organisations and community development, did not go unchallenged. In Africa at least there are 'local authorities' and local authorities. The larger, richer, more experienced are able to work effectively to organise the production of more wealth: but these are few compared to the majority which are too small, poor and incompetent to do much more than get in the way and waste the time of the central officials. 'Now if in ordinary life', the critic went on,

you encounter an obstacle in your path, you don't try and remove it, or climb over it if you can get round it; and that I think is the solution in terms of development to this problem of the multiplicity of small, inefficient local authorities. They are for this purpose, best ignored.

The only qualification I would make is that, if, as in India, local authorities are integrated with community development (instead of the two things being in separate departments as in Africa), then the problem takes on another aspect. But in the parts of Africa that I know, there are often these two private empires – one concerned with local government and the other with community development – without sufficient professional or technical talent and finance between them to make either effective.

If by 'development' is meant contributions to agricultural and industrial enterprise, it is hard to think of anything significant that African local authorities have contributed, and hard to think what the majority of them *could* contribute. As for the richer local authorities, they spend most of their budgets on social services, leaving an infinitesimal fraction to be spent on development in this sense.

From an economic planner's point of view, decentralised local government is a spending rather than an investing agency and deconcentrated forms of central government may be preferred, and so it is a question once more of whether at the local, as at the central level, too much savings are not diverted from investment in producing more wealth. This was, however, a minority view. The majority preferred to define 'development' in a broader social sense, including not only enterprises producing more wealth but also those improving social services. The majority also preferred a policy of developing decentralised local authorities, instead of one of 'deconcentrated' central government at local level, not least because of the more flexible political linkages that it provides in the fabric of national unity between central government and local, tribal and sectional particularism. Although most local authorities may not be able to embark upon economic enterprise as yet, it was concluded, they should provide the local social services; the wealthier local authorities could well go in for large schemes of economic development.

STRUCTURAL OBSTACLES

A. *Lack of effective machinery for coordinating local development*

For effective development, provision must be made for administrative machinery to (*a*) coordinate the work of:

   (i) agencies of central/national government;
   (ii) agencies of provincial/regional/state government;
   (iii) agencies of district government and local authorities;
   (iv) non-statutory or voluntary associations.

   (*b*) provide a channel whereby information may flow from the people in local communities upwards to the central planning authority so it can be kept continuously informed of the needs and reactions of the people.

   To ensure this coordination and communication between all of these, a three-tiered form of administrative organisation has proven effective in a number of countries. For example, at the *local* level, provision is made for regular meetings of representatives of the local authority (elected councillors), voluntary agencies and any other prominent leaders in the local community. Questions and ideas formulated at these meetings are passed on by its chairman (a member of the local authority) to the district/division development team. This team is headed by the senior civil servant in the district and includes representatives of government agencies working at the district level, local authorities and voluntary associations in the district. Problems and suggestions formulated by this group are in turn transmitted to the region/provincial/state team which has a similar composition. The chairman of the provincial team is frequently in Africa a political figure appointed by the President/Prime Minister. The provincial team approves or rejects proposals made by the local and district teams within the framework of the national development plan and certain financial limits contained in it. Finally, the chairmen of the provincial team join with representatives of national government agencies to form the national team under the chairmanship of a senior politician, e.g. a cabinet minister.

Both the provincial and district teams serve to coordinate and supervise the execution of approved development projects which may involve more than one of the agencies represented on the teams. They are also responsible for continuously reviewing development projects so that adjustments may be made where necessary.

Through the operations of this structure of teams/committees, all of the participating agencies are kept continuously informed of the progress of all development projects. They are thus able fully to comprehend their part in the national plan. Such teams also provide a vitally important means for the people of the local community, through their chosen representatives, to understand the process of national development.

This illustrative outline is adaptable to any given national political structure and form of local government, but its principles are felt to be valid over a wide range of circumstances.

B. *Lack of administrative capacity in local authorities*

Development is frequently impeded by (*a*) the lack of trained and experienced staff to carry out the directives of the local authority, (*b*) the absence of effective supervision and control of the various local government officers, and (*c*) the failure of the newly-elected councillors fully to comprehend their functions in relation to council officials.

The recruitment of high-calibre staff to the local authority service has in many countries suffered because of its uncertain prospects and unattractive image. This situation should be remedied by (*a*) the establishment of salary scales no less favourable than those pertaining to posts of equivalent responsibility in the civil service, (*b*) the creation of a career pattern through which candidates may look to posts of increasing responsibility as they gain experience and complete a series of training courses and examinations. The content of these courses and examinations should be specifically related to the realities of local government service in the country concerned.

Funds should be set aside in all development plans to establish and then maintain a centre within the country for the training of senior officials of local authorities, possibly in conjunction with the training of central government administrative staff. Other officials and councillors may be instructed at regional centres or through visiting teams providing short courses or seminars on the spot.

Special importance is attached to the establishment of a Local Government Service Board responsible for all matters affecting the recruitment, promotion and discipline of local government officials. The Board consists of representatives of the local authorities, under the guidance of an experienced and impartial chairman, e.g. a retired senior civil servant.

The temporary secondment of central government staff may be resorted to in cases of specific and critical staff shortages in local authorities.

c. *Lack of adequate control and supervision of local government officials in the implementing of council decisions*

At the present time many local authorities suffer a fundamental weakness – the lack of positive executive powers to ensure the effective carrying out of decisions made by the local authority. It is suggested that the powers of the clerk of the council or chief officer be reviewed and extended to enable him to direct the activities of other subordinate officials. It was also argued by some that he must be a manager rather than merely a servant of council, but there was no general agreement on this point, except when a central government official was acting as chief clerk.

D. *Unproductive relationships between the field staff of central government agencies (e.g. health and education) and the counterpart officials of the local authority*

This obstacle occurs in many countries especially where the central government official is more qualified than the employee of the local authority. The problem will be reduced as local authorities are able to recruit more highly qualified staff. It might only be perpetuated if permanent allocation of duties and responsibilities are made on the basis of currently available staff. This is a dynamic situation dependent in part on the personalities of the officers involved and should be recognised as such and treated flexibly.

In one case, the local government official is directly supervised by the central government officer, with a clear division of duties between them. However, the possibility of conflict between horizontal and vertical forces of local and central government authorities is a continual danger. Specific cases of conflict might be resolved by an appeal to the district team as mediator. (A similar approach can be effective in resolving inter-departmental strife whose ultimate arbiter, in cases of special difficulty, might be the resident minister (political) in charge of the province or region.)

E. *Inappropriate administrative boundaries in relation to the distribution of people and their occupations*

For historical reasons, present district and other boundaries are in many cases related to ethnic groupings or other matters and not to population distribution and economic activity. This situation can create obstacles to development where it is best carried out on a regional basis, or where substantial population movements have occurred. As data are provided by modern demographic surveys and as new occupations become important, administrative boundaries should be reviewed and revised as part of planning for national and regional development.

FINANCIAL OBSTACLES

A. *Lack of revenue for local authority operations*

In many countries, local authorities are inadequately financed or depend too heavily upon subventions from the central government. Unless the local authority draws a substantial proportion of its revenue from local sources, it cannot operate effectively as an agency to provide the basic services which form a prerequisite for further development.

The following methods may be used to increase local revenue:

   (*a*) provision of high-calibre tax collectors through improved recruitment, training, supervision, salary scale and position in the local authority;
   (*b*) use of the full range of revenue sources, including such new items as motor fishing boats;
   (*c*) active entry into revenue-producing schemes, e.g. public markets, tourism, etc.;
   (*d*) negotiation of matching grants with central government;
   (*e*) providing for equitable assessment of all property owners through the selection and training of competent tax assessors and the use of an impartial system of appeals to correct injustices.

B. *Misdirection of expenditures by local authorities*

Frequently funds are misspent through the employment of unnecessary staff at a low level when one competent person could perform the same duties at a lower total cost. In other cases, local authorities become involved in expenditures on prestige projects at the expense of extending badly needed essential services.

Other means to reduce expenditure involve the participation of the people through Community Development techniques to provide labour for otherwise excessively expensive projects and the provision of matching grants to local sub-groups who wish to carry out small-scale projects.

HUMAN OBSTACLES

A. *Failure of newly-elected councillors to appreciate fully their role in local government*

This problem manifests itself in three ways: (*a*) misunderstandings which arise between councillors and local government officials who often suffer undue and direct interference in the performance of their duties, (*b*) lack of appreciation of the important role of local government in providing services for the people of the area from local resources, and (c) failure to understand the relationship between central and local government.

To overcome this situation, priority must be given to the provision of training courses of a practical nature on a regional basis. The content of the course should include the points noted above and some training in council procedure. A centralised training course for the elected chairmen of rural councils might be provided to enable additional instruction and the opportunity to exchange practical experience with men from other areas.

B. *Failure by the public to realise what can be achieved by community effort*

In many cases, considerable potentials await development but no action is taken by the people because (a) they do not understand the opportunities which exist, (b) they lack confidence to venture into new activities, and (c) their traditional leaders frequently fail to see that they have any function to guide and inspire their people in these matters.

Particularly in the immediate post-independence era, great possibilities exist to channel a powerful stream of human energy and goodwill into constructive projects. Through a process of education, using C.D. techniques, people can gain the knowledge and confidence required to bring about various kinds of social and economic development. Some areas in which public education is needed include literacy training and the functions of local government. The traditional leaders can come to appreciate their new role in local and national progress in a similar way.

In every society, some traditional social attitudes militate against development (e.g. excessive individualism) while others provide a positive or stabilising force (e.g. attachment to land). Community development workers can lead the people to identify their problems, to view them constructively in the light of selected traditional values, and to work together for a more satisfactory life.

5 AID

19 · Effectiveness of Foreign Assistance[1]

HOLLIS B. CHENERY[2]

Programmes of public assistance to less developed countries have increased rapidly over the decade 1956–66 in the United States and Western Europe. Since private investment has stagnated during this period, public grants and loans in 1965–6 provided $6 billion of the total of $8–9 billion of capital transferred. For most underdeveloped countries, foreign assistance is already a critical source of development finance and one of the main hopes for accelerated growth in the future.

Foreign aid programmes differ in their objectives, in the types and sources of resources furnished, and in the performance required of the recipient. The resource flow from the members of the O.E.C.D. to the underdeveloped world in the mid-nineteen sixties took four principal forms:[3]

(a) grants, primarily for budgetary subsidies to ex-colonies and military allies (40 per cent);
(b) loans for capital projects (25 per cent);
(c) loans for general support of development (15 per cent);
(d) transfer of surplus agricultural commodities against loans repayable in local currency (15 per cent).

The mechanisms for allocating and controlling assistance are largely bilateral. Although perhaps half of the total flow is subject to some form of international coordination, only 15 per cent is supplied directly by way of international institutions.

The several types of public assistance have evolved in response to a variety of post-war political and economic developments: (a) the increasing political importance of the newly independent, underdeveloped countries: (b) the need to replace budgetary support under the colonial system with other forms of resource transfer: (c) the relative stagnation of private foreign investment in most of the underdeveloped countries, due largely to political uncertainty. The system that has developed is fragmented, donor-oriented, and relatively inefficient as an instrument for supporting development.

The purpose of this paper is to suggest ways in which the assistance mechanism can be made more effective. I take it as given that the common purpose of foreign assistance programmes is to accelerate the development of the recipient countries, although there may be a variety of political and economic motives for seeking this development. The role of external assistance in an efficient system of international development is discussed in section I. Proposals for improving the present system are outlined in sections II and III.

I. THE ROLE OF EXTERNAL ASSISTANCE IN DEVELOPMENT

The main defects in the present approaches to foreign aid stem from the narrow view that is usually taken of the role of external resources in the development process. The existing bases for international loans derive largely from private banking criteria and focus almost entirely on the direct effects of investment. The present analysis starts from an assessment of the effects of the total resource transfer over time in order to bring out the indirect effects of assistance. From evaluations of the effectiveness of past aid programmes, it has become clear that these indirect effects have been the decisive factors in determining their success and that they should be more fully taken into account in the allocation process.

A. *Accelerating the rate of growth*

The transformation of a poor and stagnant country into one capable of sustained growth at a fairly rapid rate is the core of the development problem. Its solution requires an improvement in the quality of human resources, a rapid increase in the capital stock, substantial changes in the composition of output, and accompanying changes in attitudes and institutions. Without external assistance or private foreign investment, a developing country would need to provide for all of these requirements from its own resources, including only such imports as can be financed by export earnings.

A country's failure to develop is more often attributable to its inability to bring about these changes in a sufficiently coordinated way than to any single factor. The limits to development at any moment are more likely to be bottlenecks in the supply of skills, particular commodities, or productive capacity in particular sectors than general shortages of resources. This limited flexibility reflects the imperfect functioning of market mechanisms which is one of the distinguishing features of underdeveloped economies.

By relieving potential bottlenecks, external resources can make the requirements for coordinated changes in the economy less stringent and permit fuller use to be made of domestic resources. They contribute to supplies of skills, importable commodities, and savings. The value of additional imports in a situation of bottlenecks and under-utilised capacity derives from their flexibility; they can supplement whatever commodities are in short supply. For example, three dollars of additional imports may permit the production of ten dollars of additional G.N.P. from domestic resources that would otherwise remain unused. In this case, an annual resource inflow costing one dollar will have a marginal productivity of 3·3 measured by the resulting increase in G.N.P.

While in many countries the main contribution of external resources is to offset the imbalance between the structure of supply and the structure of demand, in others their primary function is to finance additional investment. Since no income is generated by the receipt of external assistance, it should normally be possible for a country to increase investment by the entire amount of the resource transfer, whatever the form of the additional commodities supplied.[4] The productivity of aid in these circumstances is equal to the marginal productivity of additional capital. It is typically lower than the productivity of assistance when there is a balance of payments bottleneck.

In order to present these ideas more systematically, it is useful to distinguish three 'phases' or types of situations, identified by the scarce factor that is more restrictive to growth:

(*a*) Skill-limited growth.
(*b*) Savings-limited growth.
(*c*) Import-limited growth.

While external capital – public or private – increases the supply of each of these scarce factors, the effect of additional resources will depend primarily on their effectiveness in offsetting the bottleneck which is most restrictive. If growth is limited mainly by lack of managerial talent and skilled labour, for example, a million dollars spent on adding to the supply of these factors will be more productive than an equal amount of additional capital goods or other commodities. A similar distinction can be made between the form of assistance that is appropriate when the principal need is to raise the level of investment and the appropriate form when there is a shortage of specific imports.

Assuming that external resources – accompanied by reallocation of other available foreign exchange – are provided in such a way as to increase the supply of the limiting factor, the short-run effects of aid can be measured by the contribution of that factor to additional output. This contribution is likely to be higher in the bottleneck situations of skill or import limitations than when aggregate savings and investment provide the limit to growth. In each case, however, it is the availability of under-utilised natural resources, labour, or physical plant which determines the productivity of the complementary resources supplied from abroad.

B. *Long-term effects of external assistance*

In assessing the effectiveness of aid over a longer period, we must consider the alternative growth paths made possible by varying assistance streams rather than merely the effects of incremental resources at a given moment. The effect of aid on growth over a period of ten or twenty years will depend on the productive uses that are made of the increments it produces in G.N.P. in addition to the short-term effects just described. The long-term productivity of aid therefore consists of two parts:

(*a*) the initial increment in G.N.P. resulting directly from the additional resources provided;

(*b*) indirect effects on growth resulting from the productive use made of this initial increment.

The increments in G.N.P. can be used to reduce any or all of the three types of restrictions to further growth. Appropriate uses include labour training in the skill-limited phase; additional savings and taxes in the savings-limited phase; and import-substitution or additional exports in the import-limited phase. To measure the long-run productivity of assistance, we must therefore specify the use to be made of the stream of added production in promoting further growth.[5]

In studies of Greece, Israel, and Pakistan,[6] my collaborators and I have calculated the long-term productivity of assistance by comparing alternative growth paths determined from econometric models. From the analysis of Greek development over the period 1950–61, it was estimated that the marginal productivity of assistance – as measured by the ratio of the cumulative increment in G.N.P. over the period to the corresponding increment in capital inflow – was of the order of 2·5. Similar estimates for Israel are as high and projections for Pakistan are higher.[7]

The relative importance of the indirect effects of assistance in determining the total outcome is illustrated by the case of Greece, where the savings limitation was estimated to have been predominant over the period studied. Of the total increase in G.N.P. since 1950, 15 per cent would have been achieved without assistance at the estimated savings rate; 35 per cent represented the direct effect of the assistance provided; and 50 per cent is attributable to the indirect effects of aid. As a result of the relatively high marginal savings rate of 22 per cent maintained by Greece, additional savings out of the aid-induced increase in G.N.P. have financed a higher proportion of additional investment than the aid itself even though aid was exceptionally large. If the marginal savings rate had been lower, the long-run effectiveness of aid would have been substantially less even if the direct short-run effects had been the same. Much the same conclusion can be drawn from the successful aid experiences of Israel, Taiwan, and the Philippines, and from current projections for Pakistan, India, and other countries.

To generalise from this experience, the productivity of external resources can be measured in a simpler way by the increase in G.N.P. ten or twenty years hence per unit of aid needed to achieve it. The following formulae for this measure can be derived from simple aggregate growth models:[8]

(a) *Savings limited case* : $\dfrac{dVn}{d(\Sigma Ft)} = \dfrac{1}{k - a^{1}\beta}$

(b) *Import limited case* : $\dfrac{dVn}{d(\Sigma Ft)} = \dfrac{1}{\mu^{1}\beta}$

where k is the marginal capital–output ratio
  a^{1} is the marginal propensity to save
  μ is the marginal ratio of required imports to increased G.N.P.
  Vn is the G.N.P. at the end of the period
  ΣFt is the total capital inflow during the period
  β is a constant which increases with the time period considered.

Over longer periods of time, the savings limit should predominate if good development policies are followed. On this assumption the importance of variation in the indirect effects of aid can be shown by taking different values for the marginal savings rate, which represents a country's ability to channel additional income into investment by fiscal measures or otherwise.[9] A variation in the marginal savings rate from 0·10 to 0·30 with marginal capital–output ratios of 3·0 to 4·0 produces the following variation in the marginal productivity of external assistance:

Productivity of external assistance

Marginal savings rate	Over ten years		Over twenty years	
	$k=4\cdot0$	$k=3\cdot0$	$k=4\cdot0$	$k=3\cdot0$
0·10	0·28	0·38	0·30	0·44
0·20	0·31	0·45	0·38	0·63
0·30	0·35	0·54	0·53	1·11

From this example, it is clear that variation in the indirect effects of assistance is likely to be the dominant element in the total productivity of aid when a longer time period is considered. Differences in savings rates and balance of payments policies can easily outweigh substantial variations in the direct effects.[10] This fact is largely ignored in existing procedures for aid allocation and control, which are discussed in section II.

c. *Achieving self-sustaining growth*

Virtually all recipients of aid are attempting to establish a process of growth which can continue in the future without further assistance. The possibilities for success depend on the country's ability to change its economic structure as it develops. Unless there is a rise in the savings rate or an improvement in the efficiency with which capital and human resources are used, the growth rate after aid has terminated will revert to the growth rate existing when it started, no matter how much aid and growth there has been in the intervening period. In other words, the prospects for achieving self-sustaining growth depend entirely on the indirect effects of assistance in changing the structure of the economy.

The structural changes that must be brought about in order to achieve self-sustaining growth at a given target rate may be summed up as follows:

(a) *Investment* must be raised until it equals the share of G.N.P. required by the target growth rate (r) and the capital–output ratio. For a 5 per cent growth target and a typical k of 3·0 to 4·0, investment must increase more rapidly than 5 per cent per year until it reaches the required share of 15–20 per cent of G.N.P.

(b) *The marginal savings rate* (α') must exceed the required investment ratio (kr) in order eventually to eliminate the need for external capital.

(c) *Trade criteria* : If the ratio of imports to G.N.P. is constant, exports must increase more rapidly than the target growth in G.N.P. in order to close the trade gap. Cutting the marginal import ratio in half through import substitution lowers the required export growth to 4 per cent to close the gap with a 5 per cent growth of G.N.P.[11]

An A.I.D. study [12] gives some estimates of the extent to which recent performance of aid-receiving countries meets these requirements of self-sustaining growth. Of the twenty-six countries for which these measures could be obtained for the period 1957–62, the performance of eleven satisfied all three criteria for ultimately attaining self-sustaining growth of 5 per cent or more. Five countries satisfied neither the savings nor the trade criteria, and the remainder were deficient in at least one of the three.

Although experience with attempts to accelerate growth through aid is still limited, the comparative analysis that has been made throws considerable light on the relative difficulty of overcoming the several obstacles to further growth. Almost all of the fifty countries for which data was analysed by A.I.D. showed a substantial ability to increase investment rates; the median rate of investment growth for the whole group for 1957–62 was over 10 per cent per year. These substantial increases in productive investment suggest that absorptive capacity may be less of an obstacle to raising the growth rate than is often supposed, except in the most primitive countries.[13] If past rates of increase are continued, investment can be raised in most countries to the levels required to sustain growth rates of 5–6 per cent in G.N.P. within ten to fifteen years.

Of the several potential limits, the most serious obstacle to achieving self-sustaining growth at rates of 5 per cent or more is currently the balance of payments. It seems to be easier to increase the savings rate rapidly enough to prevent indefinite dependence on external aid than to follow trade policies that will eventually reduce the payments gap. Of the countries in which both savings and trade performance have been disappointing – many of which are in Latin America – there is strong evidence that a primary cause has been the sluggish performance of exports and the widening trade gap. The receipt of increased aid to fill the trade gap, unaccompanied by a rise in investment, implies a diversion of potential savings into consumption and a lack of effective demand for higher investment. Such a sequence seems to have occurred in Bolivia, Brazil, Chile, Colombia, Costa Rica, and other countries with falling savings rates in the recent past.

The key role of exports in achieving progress toward self-sustaining growth is also demonstrated by an analysis of the countries which are currently succeeding in this effort. In almost all cases, the trade criterion has been met by an export expansion of 5 per cent or more. Although Brazil, Colombia, Turkey, India and a number of other countries have attempted to limit the need for external capital primarily through import substitution rather than export expansion, none of them has succeeded in avoiding severe balance of payments difficulties in the long run.

Projections for the future based on the experience of the recent past point to the increasing importance of structural deficits in the balance of payments as determinants of future aid requirements.[14] Aid is increasingly being provided not to accelerate investment and growth but to offset the growing imbalance between the structure of production and the structure of demand. Despite the success of a number of countries in raising rates of growth in G.N.P., an increase in capital inflow to all less developed countries of at least 5 per cent per year will probably be required to sustain the existing growth rates of slightly over 4 per cent. To raise the growth rate of the underdeveloped world to 5 per cent or more would probably require an annual increase in assistance of 10 per cent even with some improvement over past performance.[15] The difficulty of securing such increases in aid or private investment emphasises the importance of making more effective use of the funds that are available.[16]

The above discussion has omitted any explicit consideration of the effects of education, skills and technological advance. Athough studies of advanced countries usually attribute half of the increase in output to factors other than the increase in factor inputs, we do not yet have estimates of production functions in underdeveloped countries that would be useful in predicting the effects of future improvements. A considerable amount of technological improvement is implied by the demonstrated ability of many countries to raise investment rates substantially without a significant fall in the marginal productivity of capital and is incorporated in projections based on this experience.

It seems unlikely that in the next decade or so the less developed countries will be able to lower the capital requirements for further growth significantly even if there is much greater concentration on technical assistance. Although increasing the amount and effectiveness of technical assistance deserves the highest priority in aid efforts, it does not follow that external capital requirements are going to be reduced as a result.

II. ALLOCATION AND CONTROL

Unlike private capital, public assistance funds are allocated among countries in accordance with predetermined criteria. Any attempt to evaluate the effects of public assistance must therefore examine the bases for its allocation and control. Starting from the objectives of assistance, a strong case can be made for a rapid increase in the amounts made available and for larger allocations to countries that perform well. From the working of the existing control system, however, it is often alleged that additional funds cannot be effectively absorbed under present criteria. The control system is therefore a key element in any discussion of future aid policy.

An ideal system of aid administration would include:

(a) an explicit statement of objectives;

(b) a set of criteria for allocating aid based on these objectives;

(c) a mechanism for controlling the form and amount of resources to be transferred to each country.

Existing systems vary greatly in the relative emphasis given to these elements. For countries to which it is politically important to secure an adequate flow of resources, the allocation tends to be made regardless of development objectives or controls which are normally applied in other cases. In the absence of political urgency, however, the control aspect of the administrative mechanism tends to dominate; allocation by country tends to become a by-product of project review and other partial controls.

In order to improve the present system, there should be a clearer separation of its allocation and control elements and greater attention to the incentive aspects of each. Proposals to this effect will be developed from an evaluation of how the present aid mechanisms perform.

A. *Objectives of assistance*

Among recipients of economic assistance, there is a general consensus that its primary objective is long-term economic and social development, however defined. For the aid providers, the statement of objectives is more complicated: it involves both a choice among recipients and a balancing of benefits to the recipients against costs and secondary gains to the donor. The main purposes considered by donor countries and lending agencies include:

(a) the long-term development of the recipient;

(*b*) maintenance of minimum income levels and political stability in the recipient;

(*c*) political advantages to the donor, including the strengthening of one country instead of another;

(*d*) economic advantages to the donor.

The first three donor objectives require a specific country allocation as part of the administrative process. This is particularly important for the less viable economies, which would have immediate economic and political reactions to a reduction in aid. The allocative aspect appears less important in some of the aid programmes designed to produce development in the underdeveloped world as a whole, such as I.B.R.D. project lending or the distribution of P.L. 480 commodities.

There are two types of country to which aid is currently allocated in amounts designed to secure specific objectives:

(*a*) *Non-viable economies* – notably Korea, Vietnam, Laos, Jordan, the Congo, and some other former colonies – which need a minimum of external support to prevent economic and political deterioration.

(*b*) *Countries with relatively effective development programmes* – such as India, Pakistan, Turkey, Chile, Nigeria, Tunisia – which have been judged capable of utilising substantial amounts of assistance to increase their rates of growth.

For these two groups of countries, efforts are made by the principal bilateral donor or by an international coordinating group to secure a flow of assistance adequate to meet the primary objective.

Donor objectives are less well defined for countries which are not near the top of the list in either political urgency or development performance. Allocation in this large middle group tends to be more the result of the piecemeal working of the control system than of conscious decisions based on country performance and need.

B. *Efficiency criteria*

Although it is impossible to set out unambiguous criteria for evaluating an allocation system having multiple and ill-defined objectives, some partial tests can be deduced from the assumption that long-term development is the primary reason for the transfer of public capital. These tests are based to a large extent on the preceding analysis of the role of assistance in the development process.

(*a*) *The allocation system should be explicitly related to the principal objective of long-term development.* In practice, this implies looking more at indirect effects and considering longer time periods than is usually done.

(*b*) *The allocation and control system should provide an incentive to improved performance by the recipient.* Country allocation on the basis of development performance will tend to improve the effectiveness of total resource use, while country allocation on political criteria may actually reduce economic incentives and overall efficiency.

(*c*) *Excessive avoidance of risk*. Some types of aid administration allocate funds to activities and countries primarily because the risk of failure is low. Examples are the preference of the I.B.R.D. and A.I.D. for power and transport projects. However, minimising the risk of individual projects may not be consistent with maximising the prospects for development of the country as a whole. Use of this principle may also distort the allocation of aid among countries.

(*d*) *Costs of donor benefits*. Each condition attached to aid by the donor in order to secure some economic or political advantage is likely to have a cost to the recipient in comparison to an unrestricted loan or grant. These opportunity costs should be weighed against the gains to the donor and the attempt abandoned where the costs are excessive.

(*e*) *Effects on development strategy*. In addition to partial tests of efficiency, the combined effects of all controls on a country's choice of development strategy should be considered.

The significance of these criteria will be brought out in subsequent discussion of the alternative forms and conditions of aid.

c. *Project versus programme controls*

The most important difference among methods of aid administration lies in the choice between individual projects or overall programmes as the basis for allocating and controlling aid. The *project approach* takes a single plant or other unit of investment as the basis for analysis and aid decisions. The *programme approach* is based on the analysis and needs of the whole economy. While combinations of the two are possible, it is easier to compare them initially in a relatively pure form.

Under the project approach capital loans provide the imports required by individual investment projects. The commodities supplied are typically the investment goods to be used in executing the project, although an allowance may be made for the indirect imports needed elsewhere in the economy for producing investment goods or satisfying the increased consumer demand that results. Control of disbursements of aid funds is related to the importation of the specific commodities used in the project and is typically spread over three to five years. The allocation of assistance among countries is largely a by-product under this system, although limits to the amounts of project aid going to any one country are often imposed by the lending agencies.

The programme approach permits controls of aid to be applied on the resources needed to carry out a given set of development policies designed to achieve specified goals. These goals and the means to accomplish them are usually set out in a development programme prepared by the recipient government. The elements of performance most commonly considered in determining aid requirements are the country's allocation of investment by sectors, its fiscal and balance of payments policies, and its recent experience in carrying out investment and mobilising savings.

The programme approach permits controls of aid to be applied on the basis of the end results – an increased investment, output, and use of income – rather than being limited to the aid-financed imports. While it is customary to use non-project assistance primarily to finance producer goods imports, this is a relatively meaningless form of control.

The project system of aid administration may provide some benefit to the recipient countries through its effect on their own systems of budgetary review and control. While this enforced emphasis on better project preparation is often beneficial, its opportunity cost may be very high. Since all the major lending agencies combined can only process a few hundred loan applications per year, the system contains incentives to both donors and recipients to select large projects with a high import content in order to minimise administrative requirements and maximise the aid received. These criteria often conflict with the priorities of a well-conceived development programme if project aid is offered in any quantity.[17]

In terms of the five criteria suggested above, the programme approach is likely to be superior on all counts in countries where sufficient political stability and adequate information exist to apply it.[18]

The main arguments in its favour are:

(*a*) The programme approach relates the amount and form of aid to the objectives and performance of the recipient country.

(*b*) The programme approach can be more readily administered to provide incentives to improved performance by the recipient.

(*c*) Since the project approach focuses on individual projects and sectors, it gives less attention to overall development policies.

Apart from uncertainty and inadequate information, the main reasons for the persistence of the project approach lie in its suitability to other donor interests. Probably the most important of these is the fact that furnishing aid on a project-by-project basis allows the donor to remain uncommitted. Since project approval involves a complex of technical and economic judgements, it is quite feasible to increase or decrease aid for political reasons without appearing to do so. In the course of accepting a certain proportion of the projects proposed, a donor country can apply whatever additional political or economic criteria it chooses without being liable to a charge of discrimination. This is more difficult under the programme approach, where the conditions for qualifying for aid are more explicitly set out. The project approach also provides a convenient basis for limiting aid on the grounds that the recipient countries cannot prepare and submit a larger number of acceptable projects.

The disadvantages of the project system can be mitigated by combining it with elements of country analysis and the programme approach. This trend is apparent in both the I.B.R.D. and A.I.D. procedures for project selection and review. However, the programme approach requires a certain amount of continuity in policy and information for economic analysis, which currently exist only in a fairly small number of underdeveloped countries.

D. *Secondary objectives and donor benefits*

A large proportion of the apparatus for controlling aid is designed to achieve trade or other benefits for the donors rather than to promote the interests of the recipients. For this purpose, aid is limited to commodities supplied by the donor ('tied aid') or even more narrowly to commodities for which the donor would like to establish export markets.

The costs to the recipients of these donor benefits are of three types:

(*a*) overvaluation of the amount of aid and increased loan repayments;
(*b*) reduction in the total assistance provided;
(*c*) distortion of resource allocation of the recipient.

Aid is overvalued when commodities are exported at prices above the world market. This overvaluation occurs not only with P.L. 480 surpluses but also with steel, machinery, vehicles and other commodities when competition is reduced. Overvaluation is not of any great importance to the recipient in the cases of grants or loans repayable in local currency (which covers the bulk of P.L. 480). For other loans, the extra cost due to tying must be absorbed by the purchaser and reduces the element of subsidy in the loan. Part of the popularity of the project approach among bilateral donors derives from the fact that it normally requires the procurement of the whole range of inputs for the project from the donor country, regardless of relative prices.

Procurement controls may lead to distortion of the recipient's allocation of resources when the choice of aid-financed commodities is too limited. The leading examples are agricultural surpluses and machinery tied to projects. To absorb this type of aid in substantial amounts may require the country to inhibit domestic production which would otherwise be economical if aid were not so restricted in form.

The cost of the resulting distortion in investment allocation can only be ascertained on a case-by-case basis. In the larger countries, such as India, Pakistan, Brazil and Turkey, where the development of machinery and metal working industries is consistent with their long-run comparative advantage, excessive reliance on the project approach would force the country to inhibit the development of these sectors and limit the total aid that they could receive.[19] The same is true of agricultural aid in other cases, where the distortion of resource allocation must be weighed against the value to the recipient of the additional assistance.

Considering the differences in opportunity cost to the donors, there may be more justification for tying aid to agricultural commodities than to machinery, since the political and economic problems of continuing excess capacity are more acute in the former. The cost of the present system would be clarified and the worst abuses prevented if all aid commodities were charged at competitive world prices, with a separate accounting for the subsidy to exporters such as now exists for P.L. 480 commodities.

E. *Effects of multiple controls*

The full effects of the present set of controls can only be seen when they are examined together as a system. Perhaps a quarter of all aid is supplied in a form that is sufficiently flexible to meet the general import needs of the country, and this type of assistance is limited to relatively few countries. The remainder is available in the form of certain commodities or for certain types of projects. Recipients must try to match up the portions of their development plans with the criteria of the various donors, while donors often have to search for suitable projects.

The most serious disadvantages of this system are:

(*a*) The incentives it gives to aid recipients relate more to the technique of project preparation and good book-keeping than to good development policy.

(*b*) The availability of unused funds for certain purposes gives a false impression of limited absorptive capacity, which in many cases is merely a product of the control system itself.

(*c*) Too much of the scarce administrative talent of the underdeveloped countries has to be devoted to making the system function rather than being available for more important tasks of development policy.

It is almost impossible to estimate the quantitative significance of these factors in any scientific way, but I would hazard a guess that the present volume of aid would contribute 40 per cent to 50 per cent more to development if the control system were designed to operate entirely for the benefit of the recipient countries. If this order of magnitude is correct, it seems much too high a price to pay for the political support of special interest groups and the very limited real economic advantages gained by the donors. As in the case of tariffs and export subsidies, aid tying and other restrictive measures become largely self-defeating when everybody adopts them.

III. INCREASING THE EFFECTIVENESS OF ASSISTANCE

Three main conclusions emerge from the preceding analysis:

(*a*) Foreign assistance can be a powerful mechanism for securing rapid development when supplied in adequate amounts to governments able to mobilise resources with reasonable effectiveness.

(*b*) The aid mechanism is operating far below its full potential because it is not sufficiently focused on the goal of development. The attempt by donors to secure secondary economic benefits for themselves involves a variety of controls that do not contribute to development and often inhibit it.

(*c*) Since the major donors compete for these secondary benefits, their efforts are largely offsetting. There is a substantial cost to the recipient in the system of source and use controls without any significant gain to the donors as a group.

Proposals for improving this situation must take account of the dominant position of the donor countries, their mixed motives in providing assistance, and the nature of existing international institutions. It is therefore not realistic to consider the abolition of all controls – nor would it be likely to yield as good results as a purposive combination of incentives and controls.

The following set of proposals is suggested as being both desirable for the aid recipients and within the realm of imaginative diplomacy for the aid providers.

(*a*) *Objectives of assistance*. There should be general agreement that long-term development of the recipient country is the overriding objective of economic assistance. It is not necessary to eliminate the variation in donor preferences for individual countries so long as the criteria for amounts and forms of aid are based on developmental considerations. International – or at least Free World – agreement on this subject would strengthen the hands of recipient governments interested in the welfare of their people and reduce the temptation to seek aid by playing off donors against each other. With development established as the primary objective of public capital movements, a substantial redesign of the present system of conflicting incentives and piecemeal controls should be possible.

(*b*) *Incentive programming*. Since the amount of aid required to achieve any given developmental objective depends largely on the use that a country makes of its added output, aid allocation should be designed to improve the indirect effects of growth and not concentrate only on the efficient use of aid-financed commodities. To vary aid in accordance with performance, it is necessary to carry out an overall analysis of the economy. This procedure can be followed to some extent even when aid is being controlled on a project basis.

The potential effects of an incentive programming system can only be determined after the major donors have made it clear that better performance will lead to more aid when it is warranted rather than to cutting down assistance. While the United States has taken the first steps to establish this principle in its major support countries,[20] the correlation between changes in performance and variation in aid is not yet high enough to be very persuasive. Endorsement and use of this principle by the major bilateral and multilateral aid providers would make it much more effective.[21] The success of the I.M.F. in securing acceptance of standards of balance of payments performance – even if one does not agree with their applications in every case – is suggestive of what could be accomplished in the aid field.

(c) *More purposive controls.* The control mechanism should be redesigned with the economic development of the recipient country as its primary objective. As information on performance improves, it should be possible to shift increasingly from project control to a programme type of control. The greater economic validity and better incentives that result from programme controls have already been discussed.

With growing information, it should be possible to establish usable measures of savings, investment, and balance of payments performance that would provide an adequate basis for control. For example, a country which had been performing well – investing productively and saving 20–25 per cent of the resulting increase in national income [22] – could be safely provided whatever assistance it needed to achieve growth rates of up to perhaps 7 per cent.[23] So long as this performance was maintained, additional aid could only accelerate the rate of growth and reduce the total amount of assistance ultimately needed to attain self-sustaining growth.[24]

On tests such as this, the number of countries having access to international assistance without excessive controls might be increased from half a dozen to a dozen or more. The resulting incentive to others to try to achieve better performance should be substantial.

(d) *Broadening the project approach.* To implement the preceding suggestions, the project approach should be redesigned to retain only the features which contribute effectively to development. Two changes are particularly needed: (i) consideration of projects in an overall framework of country analysis; (ii) weakening or abolishing the link between aid allocation and project approval, which tends to remove the incentive for better performance in other aspects of development policy.

The example of countries where some of these conditions have been met – usually because of their political importance to particular donors – suggests that effective use of aid has not depended on detailed project-type controls. The most successful post-war examples of the use of aid to transform underdeveloped economies – Taiwan, Greece, the Philippines, Israel, Pakistan, etc. – have been supported largely by programme assistance. It is very doubtful that anything approaching the volume of resources transferred to these countries could have taken place under present project procedures.[25] Furthermore, any estimate of absorptive capacity or development potential based on the project approach would have proven to be much too pessimistic.

(*e*) *Donor coordination.* To carry out the country programming approach outlined above, the donors need a common evaluation of recipient needs and performance. Here again the analogy of I.M.F. reviews as a basis for agreed action comes to mind. Several organisations – the I.B.R.D., the D.A.C., the O.A.S. – have taken on some of the comparable aid-coordinating functions, but a great deal more is needed.

(*f*) *More adequate aid levels.* With the preceding examples in mind, I am very sceptical of the conclusion that levels of aid should not be substantially raised because a shortage of projects would limit the recipient's ability to use it effectively. The ability to prepare projects is only one of the requirements for successful development, and probably not the most important one. Since the marginal savings rate and the marginal productivity of capital are of equal importance in determining the future rate of growth, it would be just as logical to measure absorptive capacity by the external capital flow that could be absorbed without depressing the savings rate. If absorptive capacity is to have any operational meaning, it should be identified with the total productivity of assistance, not just with one of its components.

The most important change that is needed is to aim at rapid growth rather than aiming at maximum efficiency in the use of aid. In all the countries that have 'graduated' from the category of aid dependents, one of the keys to success seems to have been the accomplishment of high levels of investment and rates of growth of G.N.P. of 6 per cent or more. It is not at all clear that the marginal productivity of investment was particularly high in Greece, Taiwan, or Israel in the early 1950s. What is clear is that the rapid growth of output has facilitated the structural changes in taxes and savings rates, in export potential, and in import requirements that were needed to make growth self-sustaining. In countries where additional aid can be used to get growth started, it is likely to turn out to have been very productive in the long run even if the short-run productivity of investment seems low.

20 · Criteria for Allocating Aid[1]
CAMBRIDGE CONFERENCE REPORT

If donors are to make aid more effective, they should direct less of it into military expenditure and political subventions, more of it into economic development. But opinion was divided about the method. Nothing clarified our thinking about the meaning and purposes of aid as much as the practical question of how to allocate a limited quantity of it so as to get the best results. Aid is scarce and there is not enough to go round, which inevitably sets the question of priorities between different objectives, all desirable in an ideal world of plenty, but not attainable all at once. Practicably we must decide that some purposes are more constructive than others, that aid can achieve more in some countries than in others. How should we allocate what aid there is? What are the proper criteria?

Allocation hitherto has been to some extent haphazard, 'a mixture of short-term expedients and political accidents'. But development is a long-term process and, to contribute effectively, foreign assistance must be planned in a longer perspective. Aid has been distributed in the past fairly evenly but thinly over all developing countries, according to their sentimental or historical ties, strategic and political importance, and humanitarian appeal to different donors. There is little doubt that the wider the scatter of aid the less effective it becomes. Concentration is needed to produce demonstrable economic results without which donor countries get discouraged from giving. To be effective, aid must be directed to the places where its multiplier and catalytic power generates maximum economic growth. The conference felt that so far too little attention had been paid to this long-term economic criterion, too much attention to short-term political, strategic and humanitarian considerations. The result has not been exactly waste, but we have not got as much economic advance out of the resources as we could have done if we had allocated on specifically economic criteria based on the recipients' long-term growth prospects. It was said that aid handed out for short-term political or commercial reasons with little reference to this economic criterion probably does more harm than good to the recipient's development. For example, this kind of assistance easily gets absorbed into his revenues and deprives him of incentive to raise taxes and increase internal savings. Again, aid given to tide a recipient over a balance of payments crisis actually rewards him for poor economic performance and bad planning. Hence a 'hard-boiled' school of thought argued at the conference: if aid is not allocated on objective, economic criteria its incentive effect on recipients to work harder and better at their economic tasks is lost. What is more, the multiplier effects of aid would be four or five times greater than they are if it were aimed more specifically at energising the recipient economy by promoting structural changes. The idea of aid as a political dole or human birthright perhaps has been carried too far.

What the so-called hard-nosed school proposed on the lines suggested in Professor Chenery's paper therefore was this: to move away from the concept of aid as an indiscriminate palliative for re-distributing a small fraction of the world's income for a variety of military, political, relief and social welfare purposes, towards a policy of aid as a means of transferring scarce resources to the places where they have the maximum catalytic and multiplier effects specifically on economic productivity. In other words, the recipient countries which proved by their economic performance and policies that they could use aid best would get most aid. Good performers would get more, bad performers would get less. Such a policy, it was argued, would give them greater incentive to do better economically, reward them when they succeeded and so greatly increase the effectiveness of assistance. The World Bank, it was said, had used this incentive successfully to encourage improved fiscal and external payments policies and economic planning in recipient countries. It should be added that advocates of strictly economic criteria for allocation did not wish to abolish aid expenditure for relief and welfare purposes altogether. On the contrary, they would maintain it at present levels; but they gave this kind of aid a low priority for increases in future.

There were, of course, heated objections and cool qualifications to this tough line from the rest of the conference. Several speakers feared that the policy proposed would mean too much interference by donors in the internal affairs of developing countries; but, it was replied, no more than the discipline international bankers apply to advanced countries when they ask for loans to tide over balance of payments crises. Other speakers objected that to distribute aid rigidly according to an econometric yardstick based on cost–benefit analysis might be appropriate for large corporations and military logistics; but it would outrage the sentimental, internationalist and humanitarian feelings that inspired and supported the giving of aid in donor countries. If it were attempted it might lead to a decline in the total of foreign assistance; in any case politicians who decide these things and habitually think in terms of politics rather than economics, probably would not be persuaded to apply strict economic criteria to the allocation of aid between countries. Societies, it was well said, are moved to act by simplifications. If this is true it is unlikely that anything as complicated as performance criteria will survive the passage through the sausage-machine of political decision-making.

The argument turns, however, on the tests of economic prospects and performance to be applied. They would obviously be based on available statistics; and for the purpose of forecasting the multiplier and catalytic effects of possible aid, they would have to be based on one or other of several possible econometric models, the choice of which other economists might dispute. Experience has not always been that any of these models work well in practice, perhaps because they exclude the social, cultural and political factors that affect economic behaviour in incalculable ways as much as calculable economic factors. To be reliable, therefore, the tests would somehow have to be qualitative as well as quantitative. What is more, there would have to be a different model for each recipient country, which makes comparison of their individual performances somewhat more difficult. More than that, analysis of economic behaviour over a number of years would be necessary before each model could be regarded as at all reliable; and aid is needed now. Considering all this some speakers wondered whether the criterion of economic performance was as objective as its advocates claimed or whether it was not just a statistical wrapper for a great many of the same old subjective guesses.

Whatever the practical difficulties, most of the conference agreed that some sort of economic performance criteria were essential if aid is to be allocated more rationally and employed more effectively. Policy could swing with advantage much further in this direction. In other words, more aid should take a form, analogous to 'matching' grants from central government to local authorities, that proportions the amount given to the quality and quantity of the recipient's own economic efforts to bring about growth. One speaker put the general feeling thus:

I started with the feeling that what is proposed is incredibly difficult but basically in the right direction because there is really no other direction in which we can move to improve things. There has been an alternative proposal that donors should add up all the aid requirements of recipient countries' development programmes and then raise the level of their aid to the amount needed to foot the bill. I think that is one of the more unrealistic propositions that could be put forward. If every donor contributed four or five per cent of his national income to aid instead of under one per cent as at present, the question of priority in allocation would practically disappear. But, for the present and forseeable future, aid is short, and as long as it is so, donors have to decide how much to put into economic priorities, how much into welfare and political priorities, how much to give to one country instead of another. Now how can we try and distribute this limited amount in a way which, if it were done right – and that is a big question mark – would make it more productive? A donor sends his officials to a consultative group to evaluate with the recipient's officials and those of other donors the pros and cons of his development plans and past performance. They not only apply econometric criteria but also try and consider all the circumstances of the country. If they think the proposed plan is good and the recipient's policy realistic, they go home and recommend that their government's aid should be as generous as possible and specify the right mixture of different kinds of aid needed. If they do not believe the policies are good enough in another country, it gets less aid allocated to it. Now you may say that their judgements are subjective or unreliable. You may complain that they are imposing on the country a judgement on questions to which nobody knows the answers with certainty. But one has got to take these decisions and try to take them on some intelligent criterion – unless you try, you will never get a more effective and rationalised allocation than you have got at the moment. And I should have thought that developing countries might like it if they got more aid for something called better performance, if we can measure it. The difficulty of matching aid is not all on the recipient's side. If donors promise to match aid to performance they will have to commit more aid in advance which they are reluctant to do at the moment. I see all the difficulties in the way of this proposal but we must go in this direction of allocating more aid on the test of economic productivity or the cause of aid may be lost in a catalogue of frustrating failures.

The crucial tests in distributing aid should be, first, will it produce more economic effect in this country rather than that; and secondly, does it transfer the right resources to help bring it about? Admittedly this is an ideal. The difficulty in practice is that aid is not homogeneous. It is rather a curious mixture of a variety of things given from different motives; and politically the strongest motive in donor countries is still a genuine elymosinary concern to do something to improve the lot of the poorest of fellow-men. It is this that interests churches, trade unions, women's leagues and internationalist organisations most; and to insist on distributing assistance mainly to good economic performers who are inevitably not the neediest from the standpoint of social welfare may be regarded as unethical or inhuman. Politically, ' to him that hath, it shall be given; from him that hath not, even that which he hath shall be taken away ' is a poor slogan for aid. For this, among other reasons, the conference agreed that the criteria for allocating aid in practice must strike a balance between objectives of human welfare and economic growth. But the balance of compromise should be shifted heavily on to the economic side.

There was an alternative proposal which opposes the humanistic to the hard-faced economic point of view. Aid, it was argued, should not be distributed on a country basis according to economic yardsticks at all but concentrated on solving on a world basis some of humanity's crying distresses in whatever poor country; for example, the malnutrition of children, disease and illiteracy; or on regional projects such as a comprehensive road system. The case for this ' Oxfam ' type of approach is that its appeal to the heart of donor countries might bring a spectacular flood of money into aid coffers. On the other hand the hard-headed part of the conference wondered whether the limits of sentimental giving had not already been reached so far as the ordinary taxpayer is concerned, and preferred the view that economic advance would be the surest cure of social distress in the end.

There is in the process of aid an ineradicable conflict between economics and humanity; and whether the one or the other governs its distribution makes a tremendous difference in practice. The single consolation is that each can only be served by the other.

Everybody agreed that one of the most valuable ways of making aid more effective is to rationalise the criteria on which it is allocated and to allot much more of it to specific economic development. A distinguished ambassador probed its complexities thus:

Now let us look at this question of criteria for allocating aid again. So far as I know, nothing whatsoever is being done to make the allocation more rational. There are some people who talk about it. I have doubts whether it is a worthwhile project anyway, because the allocation is what it is for a whole variety of reasons, most of them quite special. There are people who suggest any one of five possible approaches to this question, and I ask you if you really think that in practice any of them should really be used to the exclusion of the others. Aid might be distributed for example on a *per capita* population basis. On this measure some African countries get the highest aid *per caput* in the world. Is this wrong?

Then there is this criterion of need, that is to say, let's give most aid to the poorest countries to bring them up to the minimum standard of living that we think is fit for human beings. I never heard the case for this strongly supported except in the case of famine and similar human catastrophes. Food Aid to India is an example and it goes on regardless of situations in other developing countries because it is desperately needed there. But need is certainly something that has to be taken into account. I have seen tabulations of aid *per capita*. I don't know what sense that makes unless one wants to prove that India should get more aid. Nevertheless it is sometimes used to compare the aid requirements of one country with those of another.

We have heard about the criterion of 'economic performance'. And we all know the difficulties about measuring and comparing that. There is the theory of the 'big push' which proposes that we should pick the eight or ten recipients with the best economic performance and focus all aid on them and really put them over the top, and then take the next eight and do the same in their turn. Instead of giving all developing countries a little push, let's give the most promising few a really powerful shove. But somehow nobody in politics will dare to pick out those eight countries and ignore all the rest until later.

There is a theory that aid ought to be given to countries which are coming closest to *self-sustaining growth*; that doesn't mean a high level, that means that their structure is such that they have got an export balance of a sort so that they can move into the capital markets and obtain their own capital. Well, there is even *the Marshall Plan idea*, which was just, let us fix a figure and say to all the undeveloped countries, You get together and argue out how much you should get, and come back and tell us. I just wonder if we have reached a point where that is workable. It was workable in Europe, but this was perhaps because they were told a specific amount, and because they were countries which talked in very much the same general economic language.

On the allocation of aid on a world basis, I think Professor Chenery can talk about the fact that we could by a rational application achieve a greater result. But I challenge you to find any of these rational bases, and I wonder whether after all, the pressures aren't such that, by and large, the fact that the French historically aid this area, and the British concentrate on that and the Japanese concentrate on that, is not to a considerable extent balanced out by the Germans, the Americans and the multilateral agencies. Multilateral agencies have their own political pressures, they have got to do something for everybody, and therefore this tends to even out the process.

In the end, therefore, we qualified our insistence on the criteria of economic performance in allocating aid in various ways. The economic standards of sound policies, good, payable economic projects must be observed far more than they have been. But these factors should be measured qualitatively as well as quantitatively. Considerations of comparative poverty and welfare cannot be excluded, however, nor is it possible to dismiss political considerations in assessing economic prospects and performance for the purpose of allocation. The economic criterion must also be qualified with reference to the size and stage of development reached in each recipient country if their economic performance is to be compared realistically. Inevitably the principles on which allocation is based in practice can only be compromises.

A study group submitted the following propositions in this sense:

(1) The overall criterion should be economic performance but our interpretation of this differs somewhat from that in Professor Chenery's paper. It should not be applied rigidly or absolutely. A past setback with economic performance may have been due to excessive expectations in a country's development plan rather than an absolute failure and, in such a case, too rigid a reading of performance could be misleading about future prospects. (2) Plainly the recipient's relative ability to absorb more capital profitably in future must also be taken into account as well as his past performance. (3) Allocation criteria must also be related to the qualitative problems of individual recipients. They are not homogeneous and so aid cannot be distributed among them according to a common, comparative, market allocation model in terms of the marginal productivity of aid. (4) Lastly, the quantitative indices suggested by Professor Chenery seem more appropriate for the purpose of evaluating a single country's performance over time than for that of making comparisons between the performance of different recipients, the entire circumstances of each of which are unique. (5) It is important that recipient countries should be brought in to all discussions in which the criteria for allocating aid internationally are applied.

21 · Bilateral Aid

LORD BALOGH[1]

A sensible appreciation of the role, implications and future of bilateral aid necessitates a brief review of the problems which are encountered in the field of the relations of the less to the more fully developed countries. Only in the light of these problems, including psychological problems, can we make sensible decisions about the way in which aid is to be channelled, its distribution and its economic pattern.

Opinion on matters of political economy usually moves in violent swings much like fashions in the length of ladies' dresses. The problem of foreign aid is not exempt from this fluctuation in conventional wisdom. Just at the moment, and for reasons which are quite comprehensible, bilateral aid has come under obloquy and attack, having had its apogee at the time of Marshall Aid – an apogee perhaps better justified than the present disfavour.

THE ATTACK ON BILATERAL AID

The fear that bilateral aid might lead or contribute to eventual military involvement or undue political influence, has been used by high-minded people of great goodwill as an argument for its root and branch condemnation, without due enquiry into potential advantages. Nor have the potential, or even the actual, drawbacks of the alternative, the use of multilateral channels, been explored and suggestions made for its improvement. This failure is the stranger, since an improvement of the organisations responsible for the direction of multilateral aid would considerably strengthen the case for internationalising national aid. However, in my view, even an improvement in multilateral aid would not weaken the political argument in favour of bilateral action, i.e. from nation to nation.

The political and economic arguments in favour of a multilateral approach to the problem of world inequality are powerful. It is true that bilateral aid has often been based on irrelevant criteria, aimed at political ends, subject to changes and interruptions from Budget to Budget, and thus has been an unsatisfactory basis for a steady and unrelenting pressure to eliminate or at least mitigate inequality in the world. Moreover, there has always been an element of what we might, perhaps somewhat unjustly, call ostentation (or, more euphemistically, the need to show the extent of generosity) in bilateral aid. This has resulted in the tendency for bilateral aid to be tied to grandiose projects when an equal, or greater, need was for general aid to overall programmes of development. Even from the donors' point of view, bilateral aid very often misfired. It created more tensions, more hostility, more impatience and was more liable to associate, or even identify, donor countries with a *status quo* which was often abhorrent to a majority, or at least a very large minority, of the population concerned. The forceful maintenance of such a *status quo*, moreover, was often facilitated by the aid given.

Whatever the disadvantages of bilateral aid, however, I feel that this fashion of denigrating it has gone too far. Some important advantages of bilateral aid are beginning to be overlooked and the balance of judgement is thus being distorted. As Senator Fulbright said : [2]

Extended in the wrong way, generosity can be perceived by its intended beneficiary as insulting and contemptuous.

The problem of bilateralism is psychological and political rather than managerial. It is a problem of pride, self-respect and independency, which have everything to do with a country's will and capacity to foster its own development. There is an inescapable element of charity and paternalism in bilateral aid – even when it is aid in the form of loans at high rates of interest – and charity, over a long period of time, has a debilitating effect on both its intended beneficiary and its provider; it fosters attitudes of cranky dependence or simple anger on the part of the recipient and of self-righteous frustration on the part of the donor, attitudes which, once formed, feed destructively upon each other.

I can see Senator Fulbright's reasons for so uncompromising a stand, even if perhaps I differ from him in causal analysis. I am more sceptical, however, when I come to some of his positive proposals.

He says:

Foreign aid can indeed be a powerful means toward the renewal of strained partnerships, toward the reconciliation of national animosities, and above all toward the economic growth of the world's poor countries under conditions that foster dignity as well as development. To accomplish these ends we will have greatly to increase our aid programme and to transform it from an instrument of national policy to a community programme for international development.

And how is this miraculous transformation to be accomplished?

I propose, therefore, the internationalisation and expansion of foreign aid. I propose its conversion from an instrument of national foreign policy to an international programme for the limited transfer of wealth from rich countries to poor countries in accordance with the same principle of community responsibility that in our own country underlies progressive taxation, social welfare programmes, and the effective transfer of wealth from the rich States to the poor States through programmes of Federal aid. The time has come to start thinking of foreign aid as part of a limited international fiscal system through which the wealthy members of a world community would act sensibly and in their own interests to meet an obligation towards the poor members of the community.

So great a transformation in the character and conduct of aid cannot be achieved all at once. At present, however, virtually no progress is being made toward the internationalisation of aid. The implementation of the Foreign Relations Committee's amendment to the foreign economic aid bill requiring the channelling of 15 per cent of the Development Loan Fund through the World Bank and its affiliated agencies would be an encouraging but, in itself, inadequate step forward. A more significant advance would be a favourable American response to the request of Mr George Woods, the President of the World Bank, for greatly increased contributions to the International Development Association, the Bank's soft-loan affiliate.

What steps can be taken toward the development of an international system for the limited redistribution of income between rich countries and poor countries? First, the aid-providing countries of the world should terminate bilateral programmes and channel their development lending through the World Bank and its affiliated agencies, especially the International Development Association. Second, the Bank and its affiliates should be authorised to dispense the increased development funds that would be at their disposal as they now dispense limited amounts – that is, according to social needs and strict economic principles. Third, the Bank and its affiliates should execute aid programmes through an expanded corps of highly trained international civil servants, encouraging objectivity by the assignments of field personnel, so far as possible, to countries and regions other than their own. Fourth, the Bank and its affiliates should be authorised to recommend amounts to be contributed each year by member countries to an international development pool; contributions should be progressive, with the main burden falling on the rich countries, but, in keeping with the principle of a community responsibility, with even the poorest countries making token contributions.

It sounds simple. I fear it is not. It is merely the yearning of a man of great goodwill for a good solution without adequate analysis of its implications in the future. If entered upon without due enquiry and reform it can only lead to further disillusionment and reaction. It contrasts strangely with the violent criticism which has been and is being voiced of the policy of the very institutions which the Senator favours in the most articulate of the countries receiving aid through this channel.

NEW CAUSES OF FAILURE

What are the problems which the world is facing in this vital matter?

We are clearly approaching a crisis in our effort to achieve cooperative development of the miserable, tradition-ridden areas of the world towards self-sustaining progress, which could lead to a better balance between the poor and the rich, the industrialised and educated and the primary producers and the neglected. It would be wearisome to repeat the quantitative evidence which demonstrates that international inequality has increased. This has occurred although nearly a whole generation has passed since purposive international redistribution of resources and knowledge started, at the end of the Second World War, to mitigate this evil. We are now at the beginning of the second half of what has been officially designated the 'International Development Decade'. Not only has there been a slowing down in the absolute rate of expansion of more poor countries well below the rate achieved a decade ago and appreciably below that of the rich areas, there has also been a frightening acceleration in the rate of increase of the population, an acceleration which has yet to be brought under control.[3] The fact that the rate of economic expansion in the rich industrialised countries has also declined is a vital and almost certainly causal factor to which utmost attention must be paid.

There is an increasing degree of agreement about the reasons for this disappointing turn after the brave optimism of the early fifties:

(*a*) the most important cause, as we have already mentioned, was the population explosion. Unlike the acceleration of the rate of increase in the population of those countries the industrial development of which was successfully accomplished in the nineteenth century, this explosion is not an organic consequence of the increase in wealth, i.e. of the capacity to provide sanitation, education and health services; it is a result of the chemical revolution imported from abroad in the treatment of disease and has no link with the autochthonous evolution in the poorer areas; in addition the attraction (and at the same time stimuli to more advanced techniques) which the existence of large, empty, yet potentially exceedingly rich, areas represented for Europe of the nineteenth century has disappeared; in contrast to this

(*b*) there has been little success in increasing the output of traditional agriculture, though the means in terms of existing technical knowledge and even in resources are available for a self-accelerating breakthrough based on new educational techniques and administrative arrangements; as a result—

(*c*) a cumulative progress in industrialisation in these countries was also impossible, partly because of a lack of markets, itself due to the poverty of agriculture, and partly because

(*d*) domestic savings have not shown sufficient increase, despite the frightening (and often increasing) inequality in income and wealth within the poor areas; and

(*e*) such investment as was undertaken seems, as time went on, to have been rather less effective in bringing about an expansion of income, in spite of the planning and analysis that has been undertaken with the reinforced help of richer areas as well as international agencies;[4] this was to some extent, but by no means completely, due to the partitioning of South-East Asia, the Middle East, Africa and Latin America into small independent countries, each of which is unable to sustain efficient industrial units; it was also due to the fact that both technical and institutional development is dominated by the highly industrialised countries[5] so that neither the methods of production nor the socio-economic institutions [6] are adapted to the needs of small, weak and poor countries; [7] the gravity of this failure has been increased by the fact that

(*f*) the increase in the value of exports from the poor countries has been far more sluggish than those from prosperous areas and this further limited their import capacity; [8]

(*g*) this failure can be explained by the *inability of primary producers*, for reasons deeply embedded in their social structure, and aggravated by their poverty itself, to obtain for their *exports* an equivalent to the continuous increase in the price of essential manufactures; [9] this was further aggravated by the *rapid development of production techniques* in the fully developed areas which *saved* raw materials and *created new materials* often superior to and cheaper than the natural product : both cumulatively thus cut the demand for the latter; the *slowing down of the expansion* of the fully industrialised countries was an additional grave cause of the lopsided pressure on primary products : this was partly due to the misguided utilisation of monetary policy to repress inflation mainly caused by rising costs (e.g. wages), and partly to the increasing pressure on international liquidity. Thus, even where a plan for a conscious and balanced development of a country existed, the means were lacking. While this cannot be taken as a ' natural law ' (any more than the opposite, the ' permanent' worsening of the terms of trade of industrial countries said to be due to the ' law ' of decreasing returns, so sedulously propagated a decade or so ago as after the First World War), only a reversal of Soviet policy is likely to change it in the shorter run; [10] in addition the existence of trade and financial ties themselves deter industrial development, thus clamping an *unequal partnership* on the poor countries; [11] this has been further

(*h*) aggravated by the consequential increasing burden of international debt and direct investments made in the less developed by the industrialised countries. This is caused to some extent by the systems of taxation in the rich countries which enable domestic borrowers to offset interest charges against (high) direct taxes; finally,

(*i*) progress is further retarded by the acute shortage of skilled manpower especially in the vital rural sphere, again an interacting consequence of poverty, but also connected with

(*j*) tribal, feudal or religious attitudes, incompatible with collective and individual social responsibility, cohesion and economic incentives or orderly planning and administration.

The institutions which are at the root of the past sharp limitation of the spread of economic prosperity and social betterment since the eighteenth century have also come to be regarded with increasing clarity as an impediment to development. Indeed the apologists of the ebbing effort of the rich countries of the non-Soviet orbit have, with increasing self-righteousness, used the concept of ' limited absorptive capacity ', the inability of the poor areas to make ' effective ' use of aid as an excuse for, indeed as an argument in favour of, the cut in technical and resource assistance.

Yet in a great many cases (and especially in the pre-Kennedy Era) it was the influence of the contributing countries which prevented the change in institutions needed to liberate the domestic forces for progress and to create the social framework in which development is practicable.

It is clear from this condensed sketch of the interrelationship of factors making for the ebbing of economic development towards a self-sustaining expansion that we are faced in the most populous part of the world with a deep-seated economic malaise which defies monolithic explanations and easy solutions. They are embodied in the social structure and motivation patterns of the population together with the impact of the advanced countries' influence on institutional arrangements as well as the sheer competitive process on the economic plane. Thus there is no reason to believe that a practical increase of investment financed partly or wholly by a rise in aid will overcome the crisis. Any measure, on the other hand, which is likely to diminish aid would be injurious, and might be fatally injurious, to the interests of the poor countries. For success, however, far more is required, including resolute encouragement of reforms of institutional arrangements and attitudes and education at all levels in order to make economic policy more effective in these countries. More especially, it is essential to evolve such a link between these countries as would permit the rise of viable industries through cooperative planning in wide enough sub-regions to sustain them. Apart from certain regions of Latin America, and even there success is as yet elusive, little if any progress has been made towards this goal. Indeed, links forged during the colonial régimes, in a number of regions, including Indo-China and Africa, have been broken in the fierce post-liberation troubles.

A new approach is more than overdue. It must rest on a ruthless re-examination of past policies in order to lay bare the mistakes committed both in the contributing industrial and the recipient underdeveloped countries by both bilateral and multilateral agencies and their policies. A mere condemnation of bilateral aid, such as we have quoted, however comprehensible it is, does not really meet the point. We must realise that there are good grounds to believe that a *concentration on multilateral aid would tend to diminish total aid*, not so much because of *balance of payments reasons* – though this objection is not unimportant – as because of political reasons. There are, moreover, some grounds for believing that *bilateral aid*, if duly reformed, could *make a specific contribution to increasing the effectiveness of aid*, which multilateral agencies, as they are at present, cannot achieve.

THE OBJECTIONS RECONSIDERED

Let us first, then, take the objections against bilateral aid on the political level.

In the first group, there is the obvious objection against bilateral aid being continued by the erstwhile colonial power in the newly independent territories. It is said that this represents neo-colonialism and the continuation by other means, as it were, of the previous domination. This is hardly less objectionable in the eyes of the critics in Latin America which was under the (mainly economic) domination of the United States (in the Caribbean area, of course, her political dominance was the rule in the early part of this century) than in the dissolved great empires of the European powers.[12] From a slightly different angle, this type of objection is extended to the cold war aspect of bilateral political aid.[13] It is said that politically motivated aid is both less effective and more objectionable, that a number of recipient countries would in fact be unwilling to accept it, and that if accepted, it would create resentment rather than gratitude. The experience in a number of aid-receiving countries bears this out.

I have no doubt that this line of attack on bilateral aid and the favouring of multilateral aid is perhaps the strongest as yet made, far stronger as we shall see than the attack on the ground of the ineffectiveness of the former or excessive emphasis on technical excellence. In a number of areas there is ambivalence to, if not distrust and hatred of, the erstwhile colonial administration. The replacement of the citizens of the erstwhile colonial power by local men of indifferent qualifications cannot altogether be attributed to the comprehensible haste to occupy positions of high status and income nor to the justifiable criticism of these colonial administrators as hardly fit to create a new positive welfare state. It has also been due to the understandable desire to rid the country of the tangible remains and memories of past domination.

Nor can there be any doubt that the cold war rivalry has in a number of countries bounced back on the contributing countries, especially in those cases where the cold war resulted in the propping up of corrupt, and administratively bankrupt, régimes which wasted, or worse, the resources provided. It is equally obvious that no international organisation will distribute aid in the *ad hoc* political fashion as both East and West have done until now. Thus one might go far in accepting this line of criticism of the aid-giving process and its motivation in the bilateral field.

What is far more questionable, however, is

(*a*) whether a switch from bilateral to multilateral aid would in all circumstances mitigate these shortcomings, and

(*b*) whether the total amount of aid could be expected to remain unaltered and whether the switch towards multilateral channels would increase the effectiveness of aid.

The size of the aid can hardly be expected to remain on the same scale if it were switched from bilateral to multilateral channels. Thus its effectiveness would have to increase more than the volume decreased if the switch is to be favourable to the mitigation of international inequality. As we shall see this is, as yet, doubtful. The volume of aid thus becomes decisive – at any rate in the short run.

Even political motivations in giving aid must therefore not be condemned out of hand. If Britain, for example, exerts itself to support almost exclusively Commonwealth countries, this is a perfectly understandable, and morally admirable decision. Britain has, as in the case of India, decisively influenced the development and has even been responsible for the creation of some other Commonwealth countries. This responsibility has gone so far as to embrace in some cases, e.g. in the Caribbean, even the basic composition of their population. Therefore, Britain has a special moral responsibility for setting them on the way towards self-sustaining growth. This Commonwealth responsibility also creates a political will, because of the moral obligation felt, to make sacrifices which otherwise would not be made. *Thus, bilateral aid in many circumstances represents an addition to what otherwise would be forthcoming* on a multilateral basis where much vaguer and looser moral considerations apply, however important and admirable such general aims or feelings are. A reduction in the magnitude of aid at the present juncture would be inimical to the interests of the poor countries. It is significant that the contribution of those countries which are actuated by past political responsibilities, e.g. France, has been higher relative to their income per head than those which are making their contribution in a spirit of altruistic disinterestedness.

Now it is unquestionable that some aspects of the use of the power inherent in bilateral aid to influence the pattern of development plans were mischievous and not consistent with the interest of the developing countries, so that the effectiveness of the aid was reduced. Ideological aims, the hostility to what were termed 'socialist' institutions, such as cooperatives (despite the fact that they flourish in the U.S.), a dogmatic push towards commercial liberalisation and monetary manipulation, protests against even mild direct taxation of foreign and therefore also of domestic investors – such are the economic counterparts of the political mischief caused by the propping up of régimes incompatible with accelerated growth and greater social justice. In addition the tying of aid to certain conspicuous projects or to domestic supplies from the contributing countries reduces the effective as compared with the nominal value of the aid. Thus it is argued that even a cut would be preferable if the reduced amount were channelled multilaterally.

There are, however, a number of powerful arguments which support the contention that it is a *reform of bilateral* rather than an *unconditional switch towards multilateral aid* that is required.

The first argument is that the effective decision-making in the international agencies – as against formal responsibility or national distribution of recruitment – is to a very large extent concentrated in the hands of the same nationals against whom the protest against bilateral aid was in fact directed. This is not surprising. The large highly developed countries, most of which have had an imperial past, are the main reservoir of skilled manpower and, more particularly, of the skilled manpower familiar with the technical and administrative problems of the areas which were formerly dependent on them. The only large-scale exception to this is the United States, and one of the impact effects of the cold war and associated hot sub-conflicts such as Vietnam and Cuba has been to make the impartiality and disinterestedness of U.S. experts perhaps even less credible (however unjust this may have been in a great – indeed overwhelming – number of cases) than those of the former colonial powers. The fact that members of the international agencies are often subject to security clearance and liable to be exposed to general, if not organised and specifically official, pressure by their national Governments has at least tended to sharpen this problem. If bilateral aid is largely replaced by multilateral, is this tendency not bound to increase sharply?

Then, in the second place, it is not to be supposed that the mere fact that an international agency is not national will *ipso facto* endow its principles and modes of operation with efficiency, wisdom and charity.

The financial and monetary criteria underlying the operations and influence of the multilateral financial agencies in particular do not seem to have given satisfaction or proven invariably successful especially in the vast underdeveloped areas of the world. These agencies, and not only the International Bank, are in close contact with those Governmental and semi-Governmental organs, like Treasuries and Central Banks, that are necessarily not the most expansionist in economic policy. Moreover, they have to rely on the capital markets of the highly industrialised countries which remain most closely under conservative banking dominance even in countries where the Governments are progressive. They have to take into account the reactions of these circles to the criteria by which they judge requests for resource aid. No such limitation is imposed on bilateral Governmental contributions.

This objection does not apply to the same extent in respect to multilateral agencies which rely on the outright contributions of member Governments, such as the Technical Assistance Board and the Special Fund. Yet technical assistance and the limited activities in pre-investment exploration are frustrating unless they can be carried forward to full fruition through investment. There is thus a grave danger, which has not altogether been eliminated by the successive liberalisation of the international financial institutions, e.g. by the creation of the I.D.A., that very narrow and largely irrelevant principles will be applied by them in judging and in influencing economic development plans.

It is yet to be seen whether an increase of the specifically public, member-Government contributions to their resources would alter the *esprit de corps* of these institutions. While it should be emphasised that under the new management both international financial institutions have made surprisingly rapid progress towards truly progressive international attitudes, Senator Fulbright's vision seems to be too much influenced by his revulsion against certain aspects of U.S. policy which obscures important and difficult problems in planning and stimulating development, liable to produce unfortunate effects even in multilaterally channelled aid.

Hardly less important from the viewpoint of the progress of less developed areas is the efficiency of and coordination between multilateral agencies in helping to establish sensible development plans and assisting in organising their execution.

Here again the objections against the present bilateral régime are more justified than the confidence that all criticised aspects will change automatically with the change in the methods of channelling aid. The yearly budget struggle in securing allocations for bilateral aid, the favour extended to spectacular single projects proclaiming the ' donor's ' prowess or might while general aid is starved and existing capacity is kept idle, have all come in for just criticism.

What has been less discussed is the problem posed by multiplicity of and overlap if not conflict between multilateral agencies, their efforts at building up empires, their comprehensible but one-sided and unfortunate technocratic approach [14] to the problems of development, dominated by the ill-fitting and mostly irrelevant experiences and traditions which have crystallised in the fully developed countries whose wealth is long established. In the new post-Second World War international agencies (and the survivals of the inter-war ones) we have potent sources of unbalance and hindrance. Before I discuss certain suggestions for the improvement of bilateral aid, I shall therefore briefly discuss the reforms of multilateral aid needed if we are to shift responsibility decisively towards the latter.

THE REFORM OF MULTILATERAL AGENCIES IS A CONDITION OF SUCCESS

The multiplicity of multilateral agencies leads to the overlap of their duties. This in turn has objectionable results, especially when combined with the – inevitable – restriction on the degree of positive initiative which they can take.[15] All this seems to reduce the effectiveness of multilateral agencies because it makes them liable to *compete for projects* rather than *planning help for development programmes* in the most effective way.

The dearth of coordinating planning staff in this framework is a further important factor at the bottom of much of the failure. If the best way by which a country representative of a single multilateral 'special' agency can achieve success is to increase the programmes of his own agency within the total technical assistance available for that country, if he is not versed in economics and absolutely convinced that only a coordinated planning of all aspects of development can lead to success, he will hardly resist temptation; especially if political leaders in that country are pressing hard for large, if not altogether well-thought-out, projects. His expert critical faculties, even if he had had any, are liable to get blunted. As a diplomat he will know where his bread is buttered irrespective of the long-run interests in terms of real income and social integration of the recipient country.

If, thus, a request by the recipient Government is needed before aid can be given, the marginal importance and expansion of the specialised agency will to a considerable extent depend on the compliance of the head of the local mission with such requests, whether sensible or not. This must influence the quality of the advice tendered. If in addition there is no strong coordinating and evaluating team (as contrasted with technical back-stops) at headquarters the tendency will be strengthened. These factors are not present to the same degree in bilateral relationships, where increases in aid are watched with a hostile eye by powerful financial departments. Only a powerful over-all control, capable of overriding the autonomy of individual agencies and having organs which can gather detailed knowledge of requirements, could provide a hopeful framework. This does not exist: the recent linking of the Special Fund and of the Technical Assistance Board might provide the nucleus of such an organ.

In the second place, there is more possibility in bilateral relationships of influencing the use of resources than there is in the case of aid through multilateral agencies. This is because the directors of multilateral agencies are subject to pressures by the receiving countries from which the officials of the contributing countries are rather freer in bilateral relationships. The fact that this capacity for bilateral pressure is liable to abuse – and has been abused in the past – is not a justifiable argument against it. One can imagine bilateral relationships animated by unswerving desire to increase the aid as much as possible and make it as productive as possible irrespective of political considerations. Even from the viewpoint of the Governments of recipient countries influence from abroad might be welcome, as blame for unpopular measures could be shifted. Nor can we assume that all developing countries can adequately judge the most effective way of using aid irrespective of local political or even personal considerations.

For effectiveness and efficiency a concentration of decision-making in aid allocation between all agencies and of the control of operations at country level is essential; only in this way can rational development planning supersede competitive bidding. On the other hand the process of establishing plans should preferably be decentralised to regions or sub-regions.

One of the most vexed problems created by multilateral aid is the choice and training of personnel. Recruitment policy is bedevilled by the strong (and comprehensible) pressure of national delegations to secure an 'equitable' distribution of what in most cases represents employment of unparalleled affluence. In many cases technical assistance is nothing more than a reciprocal recruitment of nationals to be exchanged with one another at high salaries. Some developing countries have actually lost more trained personnel than they gained. In the absence of a competitive examination system this pressure tends to result in the acceptance of unsuitable personnel.

There is a further problem arising from the desire of national administrations to move people into international agencies who were proven failures or 'awkward' in the member countries. While on occasion the latter prove excellent acquisitions, this is not always the case with the more numerous first category. A qualifying examination and the organisation of a staff college seem the essential preconditions of success. Geographic distribution of employment must be qualified by proof of suitability. The awkward problem in maintaining balance between the various nationalities is perhaps not as acute in the case of 'field-experts' as in the case of permanent appointments at headquarters, but it is troublesome even there. Recruitment, moreover, seems even more haphazard.

The representative of the specialised agency in a recipient country is usually the most senior expert in that country of the agency concerned. There is, of course, no reason why a specialised expert should be able to represent his agency adequately and have the diplomatic skill, political sense or general economic knowledge that are necessary if his advice on general programming questions is to be valuable. On the other hand, it is difficult to find experts capable of serious scrutiny, from a general developmental viewpoint, of the proposals of – not to say of evolving and submitting coherent plans to – the recipient Governments, who at the same time understand the problems dealt with by the special agency they represent and capable of persuasive diplomatic action. Yet no effective effort has been devoted to organising training. It would be quite impossible to fill the requirements of a multiplicity of agencies satisfactorily if they all wanted to have their own representatives. Planning staffs and U.N. representation in member countries must be combined.

It would seem to be essential therefore that the representation of the whole U.N. family of agencies in each recipient country should be in the hands of one man, trained for the job, having both diplomatic capabilities and a general knowledge of political, economic and social issues, and more especially, able to give advice to the Regional Offices and Headquarters of U.N. and specialised agencies on general programme questions. This would be preferable even from the narrowest point of view of the specialised agencies: in this manner these agencies would be able to get past the specialised ministries, to which they are now confined (e.g. F.A.O. to the Ministry of Agriculture, I.L.O. to the Ministry of Labour, etc.). They would be able to perform their work more satisfactorily if they could enter into direct contact with the ministries which are responsible for finance and economic programming, and therefore have power over specialised fields. This might not be essential on the regional planning level. It certainly is vital in the national framework where the ultimate execution has to be carried through.

Thus the organisation scheme for each international agency would comprise a Headquarters Programming Department, consisting mainly of trained economists who would be in touch with their own separate Regional Offices, and single common Resident Country Representatives of all agencies in each country. It would be advisable, if possible, that Regional Offices of the various international agencies should be located near enough to one another for close contact.[16] In some continents it would be essential to organise such agencies on a sub-regional basis.[17]

In order to increase the expertise, and the intimacy of collaboration, staff college courses ought to be organised so that these common Multilateral Agency Country Representatives are made aware of modern economic and social thinking and the approach of each specialised agency. Their job is a very exacting one and they need all help that can be made available. They have to combine diplomacy with some general ability to carry out general social and economic analyses.

It would be advisable to hold periodic (sub-)regional economic conferences at which the approach of various agencies can be discussed in confidence and with the utmost frankness and attempts made to coordinate operations and iron out differences. It would be equally important to obtain the view of experts of varied shades of opinion within the region. In this respect, again, the Regional Economic Commissions of the U.N., with their specialist economic staff, might play an essential role. Unfortunately only some of these Commissions have devoted time and resources to the problems of single national economies, and their relations with Technical Aid have not been as close as they should be.

If this approach were to be accepted, certain safeguards would have to be introduced to make the U.N. Technical Assistance Resident Country Representative genuinely representative of all specialised agencies, i.e. prevent his being entirely dependent on and partial to any single one among them.

If the work of the U.N. Country Resident Representative expanded too much to be manageable by one person, specialised agencies with special interests or much activity could appoint attaches joined to his office. In order to avoid a recurrence of competitive agency exclusiveness, however, all communications ought to be channelled through the common Resident Country Representative.

In order to provide an effective representation of sufficient standing of the special agencies at country level, important negotiations with countries might well be entrusted to the regional representative of the specialised agency (as contrasted with the country attache). Their standing and effectiveness is far greater than that of the present Specialist Agency Country Representatives, and they could safeguard the interest, if need arose, much more effectively. In that case, however, Regional Offices must be suitably strengthened with good economists in close touch with the U.N. Regional Economic Commission research departments and the specialised agencies' Headquarters Programme Department. They should keep Headquarters and field staff currently informed. The recent reform of the Technical Assistance Board has gone some way to redefine the relations of its head with the heads of the various agencies concerned, to give him greater powers to resolve differences.

One of the gravest defects of international aid is the lack of knowledge of the manpower requirements of the plans and lack of coordination in planning the training and recruitment. Three inter-related problems are involved:

(*a*) The training and briefing of experts from advanced countries who are to give advice and/or man the training and educational establishments created in underdeveloped areas. Without adequate training of these experts the danger is great that they will give technocratic advice and education which would be sociologically or politically irrelevant and might be economically totally wrong. Much harm has been done because such unsuitable advice has aroused hostility or contempt. The results of a large amount of work are pigeon-holed and wasted.

(*b*) The training of experts from underdeveloped areas in institutions of highly developed countries. The problems created by the influx of large student bodies in foreign countries are difficult and often result in hostility rather than gratitude being engendered.

(*c*) The establishment of large-scale training and educational institutions in the underdeveloped areas. Unfortunately, very little attention has been given in highly developed areas to discovering the best way of meeting this need.

Apart from the all-important choice of personnel and of the organisation of the planning staff in multilateral agencies there is the even more important problem of securing an adequate chain of responsibility for democratic accountability, which is conspicuously lacking at present.

The heads of international agencies, once they are elected, are autocrats provided they obtain majority – i.e. in fact the receiving countries' governmental approval and hence effective democratic or expert control over the technical administration is not feasible. Indeed, it has happened in some United Nations' agencies that criticism has led to a blacklisting of the critical writer. This is a severe deterrent to criticism in the specialised field in which they operate. A corporate organisation of management might in this respect present distinct advantages.

The control over these agencies by the various organs of the U.N. Assembly and the superior bodies of the specialised agencies does not correspond to parliamentary control; there is no opposition party trying to criticise programmes (including those of the national Governments) from the point of view of the ultimate recipients. The international bureaucracy is only controlled by the national ones and the political element is superimposed and mostly dominated by high international policy rather than technical considerations. Control over the Special Fund and the Bretton Woods institutions is still more tenuous. Before the U.N. and even more the Bank could be entrusted with a monopoly or even a considerable share in directing foreign aid resources, as Senator Fulbright suggests, far more direct representation of a democratic character would have to be secured, perhaps akin to the parliamentary organs of the various Western European institutions.

All this does not mean that one should be in favour of switching aid from multilateral to bilateral channels. Bilateral aid is still far bigger than multilateral aid and I am thoroughly convinced that this discrepancy should be decreased, not increased.

I feel, however, that bilateral aid has had too much abuse, much of it unjustified, and that before multilateral aid is lavished on the basis of general political or moral considerations, however well-meant, a much closer scrutiny and critique ought to be exercised over the way in which multilateral aid is channelled and controlled than has been the case hitherto. What it does mean is that we should try to strengthen the sub-regional planning of multilateral agencies and use them for the coordination of a reformed and coordinated bilateral system of aid while all the while shifting towards multilateral channels as they in their turn improve in quality.

REFORM OF BILATERAL AID

I think in dealing with bilateral programmes Britain can claim to have made three extremely important innovations since Mr Wilson formed his administration. These should commend themselves generally but have not as yet attracted due attention.

A. *The creation of a Ministry of Overseas Development*

The first of these was the creation of a separate Department for the administration of aid for Overseas Development, the Head of which is in the Cabinet. Through this separation, on equal footing, of aid administration from the departments charged with foreign policy, recognition was given to aid as an end in itself in contrast to aid for political ends or in conjunction with consideration of defence policy. This is a momentous decision, and, in my opinion, will in future play an important, indeed decisive part in transforming ' aid ' into a true international social service given as of ' right '.

The fact that in creating this department the government endowed it with a powerful planning unit is a typical but none-the-less pathbreaking and welcome development. The organisation of staff whose attention is devoted entirely to making aid effective – i.e. viewing it from the standpoint of the recipient country – is the first step towards the international reorganisation of the aid-giving process and towards the fitting of national administrations in the contributing industrial countries for their future duties in an effort at multilateral sub-regional planning. The change from the classical administration and quasi-diplomat towards the expert in development planning is a decisive break with misguided tradition of the past. We are yet to see the full consequences especially in terms of policies affecting population-control, agriculture and education as well as the evolution of new techniques in industrial development.

B. *The organisation of training*

The second and hardly less important (but closely interrelated reform) was the organisation of an Institute of Development Studies. In this country too little attention even, not to say effort, was exerted to make administrators (or even technical experts) fit to do the vital jobs with which they were entrusted. In the foreign service (especially as far as economic intelligence and technical assistance was concerned) this was if possible even more neglected than in the home departments. Indeed the need for such training and preparation would have been repudiated by the wrongly ' superior ' approach of the dilettante. Our academic organisations were not much better in this particular field. This explains the lamentable failures experienced especially in Africa. In most other countries, it must be said the position was no better,[18] and the U.N. agencies, as we have mentioned, never filled the gap.

Thus there is now the prospect of Britain being able to

(*a*) train experts – from her own overseas services, for the U.N. and its agencies and for overseas Governments, and

(*b*) help to develop new techniques (both of policy and production including new implements) for the use of less developed countries.

This is a most satisfactory development.

c. *Interest-free loans*

The last important innovation in our system of bilateral aid was the provision of interest-free loans. On balance the provision of aid in terms of loans rather than grants is preferable and this for several reasons.[19] In the first place, loans do call attention to the need for more careful planning and husbanding of investment. On the other hand the contemporary trend towards high rates of interest (mainly due to the fact that domestic interest payments can be offset in fully developed countries against direct taxation) has produced calamitous conditions for commercial debtors who are unable to do this, among which the less developed countries are prominent. Unless a halt can be called to this race towards economically unjustifiable levels of interest, defaults (equivalent to an increase in outright aid) will be inevitable. The British initiative therefore is doubly welcome.

D. *Some pseudo-problems*

In contrast, I could never become over-excited about the tying of aid to the supplies of the contributing country. If satisfactory international monetary arrangements were arrived at, with some of the increase in international liquidity being channelled towards aid, there would be no justification for tying aid. There is little hope of reaching this situation just now. Until we reach it, the alternative to tying aid is cutting it. I prefer tying. On the other hand the tying of aid to specific projects can be exceedingly wasteful and should be avoided, except if the aid is additional, and a result of unemployment in the contributing country.

Far too much has been made also of the differences and conflicts between so-called programme and project aid. The real difference is between sensible and foolish allocation of aid. It is not really possible to pick sensible projects without having some idea of the overall, economic and social aims, without a ' plan '. Over-elaborate plans based on econometric models (derived mainly from static neo-classical assumptions), on the other hand, are mostly nonsense. This is the result partly of the lack of data, partly of simplification of extremely complex social phenomena in order to make them determinate and quantifiable. They do not give even as much guidance as commonsense, however fallible that may be.

E. *The urgent need for coordination and training*

The partitioning of Africa, South America, the Middle East and South-East Asia effectively prevents a sensible large-scale industrialisation and development in the areas most in need and defeats the end of aid. The most urgent task is to secure an effective coordination of multi and bilateral aid. Pressure should be applied to secure compliance of both types of agencies with an overall plan elaborated sub-regionally. Equally necessary is an extension of training of personnel and a sensible and sociologically oriented planning of national and international contributions.

CONCLUSIONS

After the first phase of high-minded optimism, we seem to be in a slough of despond. There is little more justification for the latter than for the former. What we need is hard-headed, socially conscious and morally animated professional planning and skilful education. What we need is a strict coordination of bilateral and multilateral aid on the basis of sub-regional plans in which the political and moral impulses in both contributing and receiving countries are fully mobilised. In fact, we need both bilateral and multilateral channels because we need far greater and far more effective action.

APPENDIX. THE PEARSON AND JACKSON REPORTS [20]

(Lord Balogh, 1970)

The Pearson and Jackson reports of 1969 (*Partners in Development,* Pall Mall Press; U.N. Capacity Study, 2 vols, United Nations) together with the F.A.O. indicative plan and the Tinbergen report – the latter still to come – represent the result of the wave of questioning and disillusionment of 1965–6 when the previous paper was written. This was caused by the depression at the suspected failure of the Development Decade begun with such fanfares. This in turn was due to the economic commentators' invariable custom of basing their statements on global figures and their predictions on a few observations of the immediate past. In these aggregates India and South-East Asia have a very heavy weighting. Thus the unfavourable weather cycle in that area had a discouraging effect on the global performance. In that depressing atmosphere the willingness to extend aid was going sour. The donors, to ease their troubled conscience, pointed to the malfeasances of recipients and the lack of capacity of multilateral agencies. This was not altogether without advantages. As a result, a feverish reforming zeal overtook the United Nations. There was the committee of the three wise men on the organisation of the U.N. headquarters, the F.A.O. reorganisation committee, the U.N.D.P. (Sir Robert Jackson) committee on the capacity of the U.N. in promoting aid, the Woods-Pearson commission and the Tinbergen committee on the second Development Decade.

All this frenetic activity so far did little good. Such reorganisation of the U.N. headquarters and of the F.A.O. as was undertaken further swelled the rise of the bureaucracy without, in my opinion, contributing to efficiency. Indeed, in the case of F.A.O., it aggravated an already grievously top heavy system by adding geographically oriented departments without sufficient technical knowledge or economic understanding.

It is against this background that we have to judge the two reports, Pearson and Jackson, which have recently appeared in quick succession. To anticipate the conclusions, Pearson should be viewed exclusively as an act of authoritative persuasion and prodding of the governments of industrialised countries to greater efforts. For this reason it tries to dissipate most misgivings felt today in the rich countries about the consequences of increased aid contributions to their balance of payments and internal prospects; about the way in which aid was used and thus the consequences of increased aid on recipient countries. It is a persuasive document of little, if any, serious analytical content. The acclaim it had in this country, the sharp increase in aid promised, shows that it has served its purpose, that it was pitched in exactly the way it needed to be to have the desired political impact. Its authors must be congratulated on their political perspicacity.

The Jackson report is on a different scale and level. It is centred on one simple question, the reform of the U.N. structure to enable it to play a fresh, more effective role in devising development programmes and channelling aid. It provides a definitive textbook on the role of the U.N. organisation in this capacity in the past. Its proposals, which would effectively integrate development planning on the multilateral plane, are as much to the point as they are bound to arouse the rage of the great feudal chieftains of the U.N. bureaucracy. They have slid into a position of virtual independence on the backs of the specialised ministries composing their governing bodies and the votes of recipient countries now in a vast majority in the membership. Their unregulated and unarticulated Parkinsonian triumph was completed through the divisive impact of the cold war which prevented collaboration between the super-powers and their partisans.

For its implementation, the Jackson report will need the closest possible collaboration of member countries. It is to be hoped that the 'good' which rose effectively to sponsor and defend Pearson will be 'clever' enough to see that if Jackson is implemented (with some modifications), a new era could open, and the multilateral channels would become capable of playing a much greater role in the total effort.

The Pearson report, true to its determination to allay doubts and fears, paints a roseate picture of the potentialities for aid. A neat analysis of the balance of payments implications of aid shows that an all-round simultaneous untying of aid would increase the value of aid to the recipients without burdening the balance of payments of any one contributor. The return of foreign aid is shown to be satisfactory. In particular, the food problem which was so acutely worrying in recent years is, according to the report, well on its way to solution through the 'green revolution', the continuance and widening scope of which are taken to be accomplished facts. If aid proper is increased to 0·7 per cent of the gross national product of the 'rich' countries and provided only that the population explosion can

be controlled, a self-perpetuation of general world development with beneficent consequences to poor and rich alike could be taken for granted.

Private investment should be encouraged because it brings into the traditional societies technical and managerial knowhow, so essential to change in
structure and attitudes (in their turn an indispensable condition of progress).
Multilateral aid should take a more prominent part. To make it even more
effective, the U.N. should call a conference of its 'family' of international
organisations and secure coordination between their activities.

The middle of the sixties was dominated by the spectre of famine. This
was due to the population explosion and the insufficiency and ineffectiveness of aid, especially on the agricultural front. Only with the help of the
U.S. food supplies was this threat successfully met. This was the time when
President Woods was thinking of appointing a committee in order to
reinforce his hand. American aid was beginning to be affected by the Vietnam war. The Germans, who became the chief world creditors, were
hesitant in giving official aid; their contribution was mostly private and
mostly commercial credits. The deepening economic difficulties of the U.K.
were a further adverse element in the picture.

The first important fact to realise is that the Pearson commission had to
address not merely a hesitant if not hostile Congress but also a group of
non-Anglo-Saxon contributors – Japan, Germany and France (being herself
under pressure) as well as the smaller but intensely conservative continentals
such as Holland and Belgium.

Private investment

This, at least partly, explains the commission's unqualified enthusiasm for
private investment. Yet as I have demonstrated (*Economics of poverty : The
mechanism of neo-colonialism*, London, 1966, Ch. 2), private investment and
consequential capital infrastructure implies artificial stimulus to the export of
primary products and the import of manufactures. This follows from the
fact that not only the transport system but the general capital market and
structure will come to represent a channel for the movement of exports and
imports rather than fostering development within the country by using and
linking up domestic resources. The capital market for imports and exports
will be conducted on the basis of relatively low rates of interest while
domestic entrepreneurial finance will be dear (20–5 per cent a year) and
peasant credit much dearer (50–120 per cent a year).

This also explains their silence about the grave political problems – not
least, corruption – which have burgeoned in the receiving countries. They
rightly play down the consequential waste of resources. From the viewpoint
of immediate politics, they admirably stress the inefficiency and waste arising
from defects in the policies and institutions of donors – for example, tying
of aid, refusal to shoulder local costs; yearly budgeting without longer term

commitments; the absence of an international corps of technical assistance personnel with adequate career opportunities. (The problems of recruitment posed by the national original regulations in respect to the U.N. established staff is not discussed.) Finally, they stress the hope that on the basis of a large, further effort the problem could be finally solved.

The green revolution

In this effort to persuade conservative political opinion in rich countries of the worth-whileness of the aid effort and its liberalisation, the Pearson commission has taken on board a number of unproven hopes. Much the most important among these is the so-called green revolution, the magic wand of investment in improved seeds (and techniques), which has, in their view, completely transformed the outlook for the developing world.

Now there is no doubt that real advances have been made in a number of countries in rice (among them the Philippines, Ceylon, Taiwan) and in wheat (parts of Pakistan and India and Mexico). The whole phenomenon is, however, exceedingly patchy even within countries and among countries. It is also likely to give rise to very awkward ' second generation ' problems which have been highlighted by Robert McNamara's speech to the governors of the World Bank last September. Indeed this speech is from the viewpoint of balance and strategic sense a far superior product than the lengthy but ' discreet ' disquisitions of the Pearson commission.

In the best circumstances it seems that the ' green revolution ' means progress for the advanced (large) peasant and a maximisation of the surplus rather than the maximisation of food crop per acre and family nutrition. If a fall in rural employment should ensue and were followed by a similar retardation of the increase in employment in industry – because of parallel increases in industrial efficiency – a revolutionary situation of the severest kind would have been created by the lack of social engineering and economic control measures.

The absence of social awareness is perhaps most patently demonstrated in the passages on education and research. Like the respective U.N. special agencies, the Pearson report wishes to stimulate, not a reconsideration, but a broadening of the conventional type of education; Robert McNamara shows in this vital respect greater awareness: he wants to divert expenditure from bricks and mortar. What is needed is a modification and not an uncritical transplantation of modern agricultural (and industrial) knowledge into an environment of traditional primitive agriculture. A new strategy is needed of which Pearson has no inkling.

It seems obvious that the committee's sane recommendations for liberalisation and favouring of trade, because they impose burdens on the most sensitive and backward segments of the rich countries' economies, will not be heeded. Thus, here too a conflict arises between those who want to exert the maximum effort to change the unsatisfactory situation, and those who wish to avert conflict and find the second best solution. I feel that the Pearson exhortation to perfectionism will be nugatory.

I have always been very puzzled by the uncritical acceptance by progressive pro-aid experts of the 1 per cent target. The target represents a proportional international income tax. For internal politics all modern progressive parties from their inception favoured a progressive and not a proportional income tax. Somehow or other they were mesmerised by their low-sounding (but in absolute terms large) proportion and accepted a proportional income tax in international aid. How silly it is can be demonstrated by the Pearson calculations themselves. These demand that the Japanese by 1975 should disburse some $2,000 million while the Germans can satisfy their criterion by contributing only $1,200 million. Now the Germans will have a national income which (even in 1975) will be perhaps twice as high per head as the Japanese. Nevertheless the Japanese as a nation are to pay almost twice as much.

As countries get richer, new ones ought to come into the aid-giving process, but they ought to enter in an orderly, gradual fashion. This can only be achieved if a certain basic level of national income per head (say $400) is exempt from contribution while the rest is made liable to contribute at a considerably higher rate, say, 2 per cent. (We are told by Sir Robert Jackson that the 1 per cent was invented by the sinister figure of Harry White, the author of the so-called Morgenthau plan for pastoralising Germany.)

The Jackson report

The very existence of a number of independent, overlapping (and mostly ill-chosen) committees and panels inhibited the Pearson team from coming to grips with the problem of reorganising the U.N. machinery charged with aid for development. They only made the rather lame recommendation (p. 229) that the president of the World Bank should call a conference of heads of U.N. agencies to discuss 'the creation of improved machinery of coordination'. Yet there is no time to lose. Far from progressing towards a more rational solution, the impetus is away from streamlining. The F.A.O. wishes to appoint separate 'ambassadors' (resident representatives) to most developing nations, thus duplicating the role of the U.N. resident representatives.

This plan was sharply and courageously opposed by the U.K. but seems to proceed, incredibly enough, with the blessing of the head of U.N.D.P.

Under these circumstances the courage of Sir Robert Jackson and his collaborators (especially Miss Joan Anstee) must be highly commended. They have faced up to their hard and displeasing task. They have produced a very notable document.

The advantages of channelling aid through multilateral agencies are now generally accepted. They were often offset or even turned into disadvantage by the incapacity of the U.N. agencies to coordinate their activities, get a coherent and consistent development plan adopted and acted on. The cause of this failure was that specialisation on the one hand, and the dependence of their secretaries and directors general on the mass-votes of the developing countries on the other, prevented a rational approach. There were numerous efforts to centralise planning. The establishment of the technical assistance board and the special fund are examples. But all failed. The specialised agencies fiercely resisted all efforts. They had been created in a period when cooperation between equals was regarded as the real aim of the U.N. For that task they were of course quite well fitted. And their reliance on the specialised ministries was an advantage in that respect. The development and eradication of poverty in the less privileged areas was a new concept to which they have yet to be adapted.

The recruiting and training of resident representatives was defective. Yet they would have been the obvious people to assure continuity and coherence. Thus, though much valuable work has been done, and programmes evolved,

the lack of effective coordination in most poor countries, of effective implementation and follow-up, the diffuse organisational pattern at country, regional and headquarters level . . . inhibits both central policy direction of the programme and an adequate degree of decentralisation at the field level, channelled through one focal point.

The report rightly points to the absolute need for reorganising and centralising the planning, that is, the allocation of aid to the various agencies. This still is shown to be done in a completely unscientific manner by 'shares'. The U.N.D.P. and the bank together should take charge to 'centralise all policy decisions affecting technical cooperation and pre-investment activities on U.N.D.P., and, secondly, to decentralise as much operational authority as possible to the country level, in the interests of the realistic preparation and expeditious delivery of programmes. Here, the resident representatives must play the same central role as U.N.D.P. itself at the headquarters level and their position must be strengthened accordingly.'

It is here that I feel certain misgivings. The report centres the basic planning on the *country* level. It is inconceivable that up to 80 people competent to do this job can be recruited. Now it can be argued that there are only about fifteen to twenty countries that matter; and that excellent experts could be obtained for these. This argument overlooks the fact that it is precisely the small, poor countries which pose the most difficult problems. It is there that the lack of indigenous trained manpower is greatest. It is there that the status demands of sovereignty are the most exigent, relative to resources. It is there that the problems of national consciousness clash most acutely with the imperative of regional coordination for a sensible regional or sub-regional division of labour.

In one word, the continued enforced neglect of these countries will further contribute to the polarisation of fate between success and failure, not only between the rich and the poor but between the poor themselves. This polarisation through the success of new agricultural techniques now threatens to invade the countryside.

Unless there is an overall coordination counteracting this, the task of rural development will pose social and political problems even more acute than those raised by the prosperity of urban minorities; and they are quite enough on any count.

Coordination and planning must therefore take place on the basis of (large) *sub-regions*, reporting to the U.N.D.P./I.B.D.R. coordinating committee which in its turn must have an expert planning staff. Subsequently, a further decentralisation might take place – subject to overall coordination. That time is not yet.

The Jackson report, commendably, does not shirk the problem of personnel:

. . . a career U.N. development service is proposed, specially designed to reflect the needs of an operational programme, as distinct from those of a secretariat. It should be based entirely on merit and ensure adequate geographical distribution through proper selection and training of first entrants. The service would have its own salary structure and a promotion pattern enabling the most outstanding members to aspire to the top posts in the organisation. A staff college is also envisaged. The calibre of resident representatives must be raised and their conditions of service improved. Political patronage must be eliminated. As regards project personnel, a number of suggestions are made for improving and speeding up recruitment, notably by greater use of sub-contracting and by enlisting the cooperation of member governments and private organisations and firms. More systematic briefing of project personnel is also recommended, preferably through a central briefing service organised by the staff college.

The report also ' advocates a more liberal approach towards the employment of government counterpart staff, and the introduction of new techniques for training and fellowship programmes '.

This is indeed courageous, and it is right.

While the Pearson report has had a commendable success in restoring the morale of aid giving, the Jackson report has, for the first time, grappled with the mounting problems posed by the stultifying bureaucratisation of multilateral aid channels. It will depend on the main contributing countries whether this unexpected chance will be fully taken. The British government machine is notable for having concentrated its aid processing in one ministry concerned with development as such, and ended the fractioning of motives between the usual specialist ministries each pursuing its own narrow interest. It is to be hoped that it will take a courageous stand and try energetically to end the existing confusion in the multilateral machine – not the least in U.N.D.P. itself. The occasion has been created.

22 · Roles of Bilateral and Multilateral Aid[1]
CAMBRIDGE CONFERENCE REPORT

Theoretically, all these teasing problems in aid strategy would solve themselves if only the volume of assistance could be sufficiently increased. Unfortunately, this easiest solution is the hardest from the standpoint of the donors' politics and external payments problem. Most of us had no great expectations of it for the time being. As a speaker put it: 'aid is not going to leap to two or three or four or five per cent of the donors' national income in the near future. If it increases at all it will be a slow, painful creep.' And so the conference concentrated on finding ways of getting the maximum impact from a gradually increasing aid flow.

There seem to be four main methods of doing this: to improve the allocation; to improve the forms in which foreign assistance is given; to coordinate the activities of donors and recipients better; and to persuade recipients to use it more effectively.

BILATERAL AND MULTILATERAL AID

A crucial issue of form is that of multilateral versus bilateral aid. How much foreign assistance should be distributed through multilateral, how much through bilateral, channels to achieve the optimum effect? Every conference to begin with pretends to be too sophisticated to indulge in the usual dog-fights about the theoretical merits of the two, and ends with members singing the praises of their own agency and decrying the vices of the others. We had fun playing this traditional game. We also tried to evaluate the advantages and disadvantages of the two methods of giving in order to get an idea of which jobs the one does better than the other. Both kinds, of course, are paid for by the donor taxpayer; but the channels to the recipients are different. The multilateral kind passes indirectly through international institutions, the bilateral sort, from one government to another directly.

COMPARATIVE ADVANTAGES AND DISADVANTAGES

Recently (1966), between 85 and 90 per cent of total aid has been transferred bilaterally. From the donors' point of view there seem several good reasons why, although, as will be seen later, some of them may be illusory. First, virtually all bilateral aid is tied to the donors' national exports whereas multilateral aid is normally untied. Donors prefer to give bilaterally partly because this seems to them to ensure that the commercial fringe benefits of assistance come back to them instead of to some other nation. It also ensures that they are giving what they have in surplus; and it is thought to safeguard their external payments balance. Secondly, when the donor gives bilaterally, he retains operational control of his aid; if he gives through international institutions, he loses it. This means that bilaterally the donor can direct his aid to particular countries which for historic, strategic or commercial reasons are of special concern to his electorate or his foreign policy. Contributed to international agencies, his assistance may be helping a country in which his taxpayers have no interest whatsoever. The appeal of aiding recipients with traditional connections to particular donors, such as that of Commonwealth countries to Britain, of South American countries to the United States, should not be under-estimated. For this appeal to donors' electorates plays a crucial part in persuading them to give; it is probably the reason why they can be persuaded far more easily to give bilaterally than multilaterally; and, more than any other factor, it probably decides the amount of aid that a donor is prepared to contribute. Hence the third and supreme advantage of bilateral aid is that taxpayers will give so much more of it. They take more pride in what they can see they are doing as a nation bilaterally than in what they cannot so easily see they are contributing to a collective multilateral effort. Sentiment and a sense of historic responsibility open the aid purse widest. This fact of life has to be accepted whether we like it or not. Fourthly, bilateral aid, it was argued, is carried into effect more speedily, easily and at less administrative cost than the multilateral kind, especially in the field of technical assistance. Speakers from international agencies questioned this, and everybody agreed that examples of inefficiency might be found in both kinds of operations. Nevertheless, particularly in the case of former colonial connections, a donor and a recipient with a common historic and cultural background often find it easier to communicate and cooperate with each other to get things done quickly, than they do working through a polyglot, international institution.

Conversely many of the advantages of bilateral aid to the donors are disadvantages to the recipient. For example, aid-tying often prevents him from buying his imports in the cheapest market and adds considerably to the costs of development. Moreover, he naturally resents the fact that bilateral assistance makes interference in his domestic politics easier. Recipients, therefore, generally much prefer multilateral aid. But in the face of donor electorates' preferences, recipients would rather have more bilateral aid than no increase of aid at all. Unhappily it is true that the interests in foreign assistance of recipients, donors and international agencies by no means exactly coincide. Happily the issue of which channels it flows through is marginal enough not to impair their fundamental community of interest.

Multilateral aid has big advantages from every point of view, except that it is very hard to get. It is normally untied. It is more acceptable politically to recipients; and to a large extent it takes the national politics out of foreign assistance that often perplexes bilateral operations. International organisations such as the World Bank, the regional banks, the International Development Association, the United Nations Development Programme and Special Agencies claim to be, and to a large extent are, politically neutral. At least their politics – for all aid-giving impinges upon politics whether deliberately or not – are supra-national rather than national. Hence the multi-lateral medium tends to eliminate the donor's national political and strategic objectives from the aid given and directs it more specifically to the recipient's economic and social objectives. In other words, these channels are governed more by technocratic than by political considerations. What is more, recipients as well as donors are represented and share in controlling these multilateral agencies; and they are bound by common rules and procedures that are collectively enforced. In bilateral negotiations, on the other hand, a weak recipient faces a single powerful donor. He may do better, he may do worse as a result, but he stands alone. The international aid-giving authorities are thus peculiarly well placed to arbitrate fairly between individual donors and recipients, to exert powerful, admonitory pressure upon them to adopt sound economic policies and observe good standards of performance, and to coordinate their individual activities into comprehensive operations for international, regional and national economic cooperation. Lastly, multilateral aid is obviously the best answer for many smaller donor countries whose effort is too small to justify a bilateral programme of their own. It goes without saying that the capacity of the international services to arbitrate, coordinate and persuade depends upon the amount of multilateral aid placed at their disposal.

When the advantages and disadvantages of the two types of operation are considered, it is plainly foolish to state the issue as one of bilateral versus multilateral aid. For one thing, our freedom of choice between the two is marginal so long as taxpayers in donor countries vote for bilateral but not multilateral assistance; for another, their roles are not interchangeable. Some things are better done multilaterally, some, bilaterally; some can be done equally well in both ways if things are well managed; and there are some things such as arbitrating and coordinating that only multilateral aid can do. Inevitably the total aid programme therefore must be a mixture of bilateral and multilateral aid with the proportion heavily weighted on the bilateral side, in which each is allotted sufficient resources to perform the roles that it does best.

The conference agreed that it is essential not to place the two forms of assistance in opposition to each other. It is not an 'either or' question. The world programme should incorporate the best elements of both. It has become fashionable in some quarters to denigrate bilateral aid, perhaps in the hope of getting more multilateral contributions from donors. We felt that this tactic endangers foreign assistance as a whole. As a distinguished economic adviser from a donor country put it:

One ought not to decry bilateral aid which is based on political – that is to say – non-economic motives. If they are altogether eliminated it is very doubtful whether present levels of aid will be maintained. And any diminution would have catastrophic results. Everybody should be terribly careful before they attack bilateral aid simply because it has political overtones. 'Political' in international aid circles seems to be a dirty word. But what I mean by it is a moral conviction of indebtedness to your past, to history, to your historic responsibilities. If history has left a donor country a concern, a sympathy with a particular recipient people, the voters are prepared to give more aid to it. They feel involved in it. I do not feel the passionate concern for example, for San Salvador that I feel say for a Commonwealth country. I know that San Salvador has very great problems; I know that as human beings we ought to feel concerned about San Salvador. But this is unsaleable as a political appeal to taxpayers in Britain. For this reason I should warn that if people, because of certain general objections against bilateral aid, go too far in denigrating it and create a feeling in contributing countries that somehow or other it stinks, you are not going to get an increase in multi-lateral aid. You will get cuts in bilateral aid of alarming proportions.

Or, as an economic adviser from a recipient country said:

It seems to me that when we discuss whether multilateral or bilateral is better we are indulging in a little bit of shadow-boxing. The difference, if there is any, is only one of degree and in all cases the advantages are not all on one side. Take any of the claims made for multilateral aid – for example that it is politically more acceptable to the recipient. It is true up to a point but not beyond. The interference of an international agency in a recipient's affairs even if for the soundest of economic reasons, is just as likely to be resented as that of individual donors for political reasons. International agencies which specialise technocratically in economics are just as likely to make political mistakes in recipient countries as individual donors with political axes to grind are likely to make economic mistakes. The difference between bilateral and multilateral aid is usually one of marginal advantages and small degrees according to the circumstances of each particular case. If it is agreed that in any case there is not likely to be much increase in multilateral aid in the near future, or that proportionately at any rate, the increase will not be much, I personally feel that the question of which of the two is better is not worth very heated debate.

It is, indeed, unfruitful to compare the merits of the two methods of giving aid theoretically, and easy to say that they should not compete with one another. But so long as the volume of aid remains relatively static, they do compete in practice for the limited amounts of money in the aid budgets of donors; and although the freedom of choice is marginal because of electoral attitudes, that marginal choice should be exercised. At this point donors have necessarily to fix priorities between bilateral or multilateral channels and decide according to their view of what most needs doing in the next quinquennium to make aid more effective, and which medium would do it best, whether funds should be diverted from the one form into the other.

NEED FOR MORE MULTILATERAL AID

We decided that the proportion of aid given multilaterally needs to be increased urgently for several reasons. First, the pressing debt-servicing problems facing many recipient governments arc best dealt with by international agencies, since the rc-scheduling of debts requires the agreement of all the donors involved. Hence multilateral are more suitable than bilateral contributions for this purpose. Similarly, multilateral agencies are probably the best means of bringing international aid and trade policies more into complementarity with each other. We were deeply impressed with the need to use aid as one component in a coherent world commercial policy so as to improve its efficiency. Secondly, the commitments of many international agencies will have to be curtailed unless more multilateral resources are put into them, because they have increased their activities beyond their available finance. Thirdly, and most important of all, more multilateral aid must be given to the international institutions to empower them to strengthen the frame of coordination and cooperation at regional and national levels which is vital to improve the efficiency of bilateral aid. It was said that if multilateral contributions could be expanded from 15 to 20 per cent of total aid the remaining 80 per cent of bilateral aid could be made much more effective. If this be so, it would be penny wise and pound foolish not to expand multilateral aid to the limit at which it might begin to endanger public support for aid politically.

Admittedly most of these problems could be tackled by agreements between individual donors and recipients to coordinate their policies without the intervention of multilateral agencies. For example, bilateral donors and recipients could come together and agree on revised debt settlements for recipients without increasing their contribution to a multilateral agency for the purpose. On the other hand, agreement would probably be reached more justly and surely if a multilateral institution arbitrated and managed the negotiation. And so multilateral intervention is necessary to solve these problems. So is improved cooperation between bilateral donors. We agreed that the best solution for this purpose is bilateral aid working in a stronger framework of multilateral organisation to coordinate it. 'The absence of strong international institutions', it was argued, 'is a major bottleneck preventing us from getting together to promote the common prosperity, so let us use aid to strengthen these institutions. More multilateral assistance is therefore essential. But let us not make multilateral a rival of bilateral assistance. We can get the best advantages of both if we give more bilateral aid within a stronger multilateral framework.'

Increased multilateral assistance is vital. Considering the attitudes of donor public opinion and other reasons, however, we do not think it wise to try and achieve the increase at the expense of existing bilateral aid. The conference hoped rather that this would be sustained at existing levels. They proposed (what they hoped would prove a realistic compromise) that to the largest possible extent the increment in total aid for the next few years should be placed at the disposal of multilateral agencies. The principle of burden-sharing should be observed specifically in multilateral contributions to encourage donors to give more.

It was further agreed that

to coordinate better the activities of dozens of different donors and recipients operating at international, regional and national levels so that confusion and waste are prevented, requires an enormous expansion of the managerial roles of the international agencies. A blanket proposal for indiscriminate expansion however, without specifying which particular institutions need more money to do which things, would not be a sufficient basis for practical decisions.

First priority in allocating multilateral aid should be given to replenishing the International Development Association and progressively increasing the resources at its disposal. For this is the institution best fitted to persuade donors and recipients to cooperate in solving the debt-servicing problems that increasingly perplex the development of many recipients. This is also the agency that must supply the World Bank with the funds and thus the influence to set up more consortia and consultative groups to coordinate bilateral aid to individual recipients. It was said that the Bank must put up about 20 per cent of the capital aid handled by each consultative group to acquire sufficient influence to 'manage' its bilateral activities, and I.D.A. and the Regional Banks are the agencies which can best deploy more funds to influence recipients to cooperate in developing regional economies. Many tributes were paid to the work of the World Bank in improving the allocation, efficiency and coordination of the world aid effort, although a few speakers from recipient countries complained that its methods were too commercial. Good as it is, however, the I.D.A. and World Bank cannot do everything. The regional development banks – the Inter-American, the Asian and the African – need funds badly and they are in some respects best suited to promote regional plans without which much aid is wasted through duplication. What is needed badly to improve the quality of aid and to allocate it more efficiently, is more powerful international machinery to exert more rationalising and coordinating influence on donors and recipients. The United Nations Development Programme must be built up considerably because it is best fitted to rationalise and coordinate technical assistance and pre-investment work, and the activities of the U.N. specialised agencies. Lastly, better international arrangements should be set up to supply recipients with short-term credit. Their past reliance on supplier credit and short-term borrowing is partly responsible for their present difficulties with external payments. They should be given access to multilateral aid for short-term borrowing through compensatory finance from the International Monetary Fund.

23 · The Case for Economic Aid[1]
RONALD ROBINSON

PERSPECTIVE

Potentially, foreign aid is the most promising innovation in international affairs for several centuries. In the history of relations between industrial and under-developed countries, it is a striking novelty. Up to the 1950s economic resources were selected and transferred from one to the other mainly by private enterprise for private profit. Since 1960, transfers have been organised mostly by governments and international agencies in the public interest. The risks and costs as a result fall less on private business, more on the taxpayer in donor and recipient countries. In 1966 member countries of O.E.C.D. contributed between six and seven thousand million dollars of official aid – at no noticeable sacrifice to themselves. Insufficient as it was, this made up two-thirds of all the foreign capital invested in developing countries. Private, foreign investment, on the other hand, contributed one-third only. Hence aid is transforming the relation of the first and second worlds with the third in a way that would have scandalised Adam Smith and delighted John Maynard Keynes. But the full import is not widely understood. Aid is popularly supposed in donor countries to be pure philanthropy, in recipient countries, neo-colonialism. Is it a good thing?

This conference had no doubt. The growth of a system based largely on official aid, in which private enterprise still plays an important role, is an enormous stride forward in world history. It offers the first chance of international cooperation to organise the mutual economic and political interests of developed and underdeveloped countries rationally and constructively. For the next two decades at least, aid of the right kinds, effectively used, is indispensable to growth in the international economy and stability in world order. Experience of the former dispensation at least, suggests that this conviction is probably correct.

It is commonplace that the industrial revolution brought about the most profound transformation of human life in recorded history. Beginning in Britain in the 1790s, the manufactory and railway by 1900 had conquered Europe and the Eastern United States, thrusting tentacles of European trade, colonisation and investment deeply into the comparatively empty lands of the Americas and Australasia, the ancient empires of Asia and Africa, to relieve the surfeits and feed the appetites of machines. What is remarkable is the spontaneity of this original movement. In an era of *laissez-faire* policy it was not essentially the outcome of official initiative. Governments neither planned nor controlled it. The process stemmed rather from the proliferating activities of thousands of manufacturers, merchants, bankers, investors and colonists. Thus haphazardly the underdeveloped regions were first harnessed to the industrial chariot.

The absence of system served Europe well up to a point. Progressively throughout the nineteenth century, European energies generated complementary economies in other continents supplying more cheap minerals, food stuffs and raw materials, buying more manufactures to sustain industrial growth in Europe.

By and large, however, the success stories were limited to societies of European origin which provided adept commercial collaborators, and to India, already under European control, where expatriate officials and entrepreneurs made good the lack of indigenous cooperation. Normally in the Americas and Australia the expansive process worked constructively. It proved economically and politically creative. In the course of time most of these countries graduated from the status of economic satellites of Europe into the stage of self-generating growth and either maintained or achieved a corresponding political independence.

In Asia and Africa, on the other hand, the invasion from Europe disrupted the economics and politics of a vast range of societies held together on very different principles. Japan was the unique exception. But in the Chinese and Ottoman empires, in Egypt, Tunis, Algeria and Morocco, in the kingdoms and confederacies of tropical Africa, the uncontrolled activity of private European traders and investors sooner or later worked chaos.

In the beginning most of these countries refused commercial partnerships on European terms. Obviously the intruders threatened to subvert traditional order. Their importunate fire power commanded agreement. By 1850 unwilling hosts had been forced to dismantle tariffs and monopolies, grant concessions of their natural resources, beg loans, admit foreigners under privileged protection and lay their economies open without reservation to the invasion of free trade.

Originally it was the advanced countries that imposed the international economy on the underdeveloped societies. It would be almost indecent therefore for the advanced countries to reject their historic responsibility for making the enforced relationship work constructively today.

Free trade proved profitable enough for European private business but eventually it threw many underdeveloped economies and states into bankruptcy – among others, Tunis in the 1860s, Egypt and the Ottoman Empire in the 1870s, the Chinese empire in the 1890s. For they imported European manufactures and capital by mortgaging their revenues and natural resources, but failed to invest them in producing enough exports to pay their debts. As their balance of payments fell into chronic deficit they depended increasingly on foreign loans with political strings, bowed under the sway of European governments and became pawns in European power politics. Impotent to protect their subjects from foreign exploitation, these régimes were now vulnerable to civil disaffections – some xenophobic and reactionary, others proto-nationalist and modernising. The vast Taiping and Boxer upheavals in China, the Arabi revolution in Egypt, the series of abortive *coups* by old and young Turks at Constantinople were all more or less reactions to European intrusion. Desperately endeavouring to raise more revenue from landlord and peasant to repay foreign creditors, the old régimes succeeded only in provoking rebellions. And so step by step they paid for their economic failure in political disintegration and lost independence.

It is easy, from a vantage point in the second half of the twentieth century, to see why these first essays in economic development failed. A large proportion of the resources transferred by private foreign enterprise were not of a kind to increase production. Imports of military equipment or prestigious luxuries made no real contribution. Manufactured textiles and hardware merely knocked out native handicraft industry. It was no business of unenlightened nineteenth-century private enterprise to develop these economies as a whole, but merely the export–import sector that supplemented European growth profitably.

Neither the European nor the Afro-Asian governments had much idea of what they were about economically. They had no comprehensive plans for economic progress – if they had, they had not the cadres of officials and entrepreneurs necessary to carry them out; they felt no passionate desire to increase the prosperity of their peoples through revolutionary innovations that in reaction might sweep them from office. Foreign treaties had deprived them of the right to control the selection of economic resources to be imported or their allocation to particular purposes; and consequently foreigners took over the ownership of their most valuable commercial assets.

One by one these régimes corroded and cracked because they lacked the social infrastructure required to put foreign enterprise and imported resources to work creatively.

By the 1870s they were paying heavily for their compulsory ineptitude, and their loss was by no means Europe's gain. Her investors lost not a little capital, her merchants much prospective trade and her manufacturers' hopes of bigger markets turned into ludicrous pipe dreams. But the crushing penalty paid universally for the industrial countries' failure to organise the transfer of resources and institutions to Asia and Africa so as to strengthen the recipients' political economies, was military and political. Eventually it necessitated, directly or indirectly, between 1881 and 1914 the occupation of Tunis, Egypt, Morocco, the partitions of Africa, China and Asiatic Turkey and intensified great power rivalry at enormous cost to the international economy and hazard to peace. Imperialism was to be the price of the chaotic egocentricities of free trade during the previous three-quarters of the century.

Up to about 1880 imperialism in the sense of annexing and ruling Afro-Asian countries was regarded in Europe as the one mode of expansion to be avoided. Far from being Europe's original sin, imperialism was obviously the most unpopular, expensive, arduous and dangerous method of protecting a nation's strategic and commercial stakes abroad. Everybody realised that these were best secured by means of diplomatic influence and commercial partnerships with independent governments. This was normal European policy wherever and whenever it proved at all practicable. Successful collaboration, however, depended first on the existence of viable, cooperative governments in the underdeveloped regions; secondly, on the partnerships strengthening their political economies. Diplomatically perhaps Europe, during the first three-quarters of the nineteenth century, had done its best to protect the integrity and buttress the authority of these Afro-Asian régimes. Economically it had done nothing to direct European capital and enterprise into the tasks of indigenous development nor had it permitted, let alone helped, indigenous governments to control them. Increasingly after 1880, as a result, the preferred method of working with independent governments cracked. As one by one the traditionalist empires reached the critical point of actual or anticipated collapse, the European Powers were compelled to protect their strategic and commercial interests by other means. They became bitter rivals for advantage under the new arrangements. A set of internal Afro-Asian crises cajoled them into securing interests against each other by means of military intervention, spheres of influence, annexations or colonial rule, and helped embroil them in the imperial rivalry that led to Fashoda, Agadir, and contributed eventually to the First World War. The original failure to organise economic relations between industrial and underdeveloped countries constructively to the benefit of both was a prime cause of the dramatic imperial advances at the end of the nineteenth century. There seemed to be no alternative to imperialism. Is there a moral here for the twentieth century? It is not in the least improbable that for the next two decades increased aid to help developing countries make a success of their political economies is the only alternative to more internal crises, more flash-points of neo-colonialist rivalry and a revival of imperialism in new forms. Perhaps the choice is between more aid and a high risk of more Vietnams? Foreign aid is not, as it is often suspected to be in recipient countries, neo-colonialism. But it may well be the only alternative to it.

Everybody now agrees that the twentieth-century colonial empires were certainly not the best possible solution to relations between developed and underdeveloped societies. Improvised originally out of local emergencies, they were rationalised later into proud national institutions. But military, administrative and social cost to subjects if not to rulers proved high compared with the dividends in terms of economic growth and social progress. Alien administrators, like traditional rulers, rarely embarked upon revolutionary innovations. They were too wary of provoking rebellion. Deliberately or involuntarily, nevertheless under colonial rule developing countries began erecting the modern governmental institutions and other social infrastructure, lack of which had made them unable to cope with international trade on European terms and helped to bring the imperialist catastrophe upon them. Indigenous official, commercial and political elites emerged under the foreign yoke to awake and unite their peoples, achieve independence and organise the popular will to modernise their nations. Their task of fulfilling popular demand for better living standards and social services is tremendous; the price of failure a military coup, a revolution, civil war and national disintegration. And yet there is now, as there never was in the nineteenth century, a national leadership, a national will to modernise these countries and reconstruct their economies. Consequently the social and political conditions necessary to constructive economic cooperation with developed countries have never been better. Ironically it is just now that the private sectors of rich countries feel least incentive to invest in their economic development.

Paradoxically, during the nineteenth century when the industrial countries most needed to develop the underdeveloped economies of Afro-Asia, traditionalist governments and social orders resisted and baffled cooperation. Now that they have nationalist régimes eager to modernise society the private enterprise of industrial countries no longer feels much need to develop them. Sufficient private foreign capital no longer flows into the third world.

Since 1939 the economic relation of rich to poor countries has altered radically from what it was in the century previously. The small-scale industrial economies of nineteenth-century Europe required for their own growth a much higher complementary development of food and raw material production in the backward regions than is required by the large-scale, more self-sufficient economies of the United States, the European Common Market and the Soviet *bloc* today. What is more, the industrial countries have vastly expanded their agricultural production and so import less food from the third world; and extended use of synthetic materials also diminishes the demand for raw material. Secondly, the industrial technology of the twentieth century retains much more capital in advanced countries and yields higher returns there than did the unsophisticated industrial technology of the nineteenth century. From 1850 to 1929 the surplus capital of industrial countries tended to flow to underdeveloped regions because its productivity and profits were higher there where it was scarce than at home where it was abundant. Since 1950 this classical mechanism no longer operates to transfer sufficient capital. The direction of capital investment is no longer governed primarily by conditions of scarcity and abundance. Its productivity and profits are determined by the extent of a country's technological advance. Since it is now more profitable to invest in rich countries than poor ones, a higher proportion of capital stays at home in the industrial countries.

Thirdly, the social and fiscal policies adopted in advanced countries to equalise the internal distribution of wealth and social services have impeded the accumulation of private capital. And lastly, the end of empire, the advent of independent national governments with quasi-socialist ideologies have shaken the confidence of the foreign private investor in the security and profitability of investment in many underdeveloped countries. As a result, the world's private capital is now concentrating more than ever before in already industrialised regions. And so the rich countries are getting comparatively richer and the poorer countries poorer.

It would be wrong to conclude from this either that backward countries have little hope of progress, or that it does not matter to the advanced nations whether they do or not. The total foreign investment in underdeveloped regions accumulated over the years is considerable. Absolutely, if not proportionately, capital continues to flow into them annually at a rate that exceeds anything the nineteenth century ever saw. The volume of foreign trade with poorer countries grows every year. So also does their national product. Most important of all, their internal savings and domestic investment since independence have risen steeply – a solid proof that national governments are better than colonial régimes at mobilising their subjects' energies. Of the total capital invested in developing countries in 1966, their own internal savings contributed more than three-quarters, foreign aid and foreign private investment together, something between one-quarter and one-fifth.

At last after a century and a half of economic egoism and imperialist cajolery on the one hand, resistance and incapacity on the other, the necessary conditions for rich and poor countries to collaborate in developing the international economy are coming into being. There is no doubt that the underdeveloped countries are beginning to advance. There is no doubt that the more they succeed, the more the developed countries will profit from the success; and the more they fail, the more, in one way or another, the rich countries will lose by the failure.

THE CASE FOR DEVELOPMENT AID

Success, however, cannot be won without maintaining and increasing official aid, for that is the master lever necessary to make all other factors in the political economy work together, work constructively and work fast. It supplies the missing elements without which other factors tend towards disruption. Without it the blunders of the past are likely to be repeated.

Why then is aid vital? Why cannot the developing countries succeed by their own effort with the help of foreign trade and private foreign investment? Perhaps with excruciating effort a few of them could, but it would take decades, and the risks of political disintegration in doing it the hard way for so long would be high. Most of them could not. For whatever sacrifices they make, their internal savings and domestic investment cannot earn them anything like enough foreign exchange, nor with the decline of the classical mechanism of capital transfer, will the private foreign investor supply the lack. Normally he will not invest in many kinds of agricultural and industrial development and social infrastructure that are vital to balanced economic growth but costly in foreign exchange; and he cannot invest in some vital sectors until governments have built up the social infrastructure to make his investment profitable. Private foreign investment, moreover, concentrates in the export–import sector, chiefly in producing and processing raw materials, and especially in oil and minerals. On the other hand, what developing countries most need for maximum growth is to diversify their production, advance the domestic and public sectors, particularly in agriculture and service industries, and integrate their already over-developed export sector into a truly national economy. If they are not helped to do more than expand their exports of primary commodities, they not only run unnecessary political risks from top-heavy economies and maldistribution of wealth, they are standing in danger of glutting world markets, bringing down world prices, earning less foreign exchange and competing for dead laurels in a race towards mutual impoverishment.

These are some of the reasons why the unaided efforts of developing countries with the help of world trade and private foreign investment alone cannot work the trick. Without aid, these factors do not provide enough foreign exchange. They do not transfer the resources most needed to erect social infrastructure, expand the public sector and rationalise the domestic economy. Essential as they are, they cannot be expected by themselves to bring about the internal structural changes required for swifter and more balanced growth. Even if the world agreed tomorrow, which is most improbable, to give the poorer countries preferences and higher than world prices for their primary exports as recommended by U.N.C.T.A.D., trade alone would still not bring the necessary structural changes about. To leave all to the blind play of world economic forces upon these countries would be to repeat the follies that led to chaos in the nineteenth century.

The role of official aid is simply to do as many of the tasks necessary for economic growth as these other factors for the time being cannot do or are not doing. It is not of course a substitute for internal savings, foreign trade or private investment, but the essential complement of them. It is needed to attract and generate more of them and provide the missing links between them until eventually it works itself out of a job.

In the first place, aid is needed to bridge the gap between the amount of foreign exchange developing countries gain from foreign trade and private investment and the amount they need to pay their foreign debts and achieve a reasonable rate of growth. This need is increasing; and if the bridge is not maintained consistently, development grinds to a halt, the countries' own efforts are frustrated and their political stability is imperilled.

Secondly, official aid is needed to fill gaps in economic and social infrastructure until it works with enough impetus to attract sufficient private investment. The expansion of public services such as power, transport, communications, banking, credit and marketing facilities, technical and professional education, agricultural and administrative services exerts a powerful, if incalculable, multiplier effect on economic growth. They expand a country's capacity to absorb capital profitably but until they are advanced to a certain point their profits are too slow to mature and too diffuse to attract much private investment. In addition to heavy local costs, large expenditure of foreign exchange on imported capital equipment and technical know-how is necessary to strengthen infrastructures, and, of their very nature, these are tasks mainly for the public sector. More official aid here is indispensable and here perhaps it plays its most important role. For expanded public services and public works must promote the advances in peasant agriculture, domestic markets, the linkages between rural and industrial, domestic and export sectors, full employment and a more equal distribution of wealth on which the bringing into production of unused domestic resources depends and which private enterprise cannot plan comprehensively or invest in profitably.

Thirdly, aid, particularly in the form of technical assistance, is essential to strengthen the administrative, technical and managerial cadres of recipient governments and improve their capacity to plan, coordinate and control the complicated internal and external factors that govern their economic fate. More than that aid is essential to sustain and expand the international institutions and services needed to rationalise the hitherto chaotic economic relations between developed and underdeveloped sectors of the world economy. The World Bank, United Nations Development Programme, Regional Banks and Economic Commissions, and Overseas Development Ministries of donor countries, so far as they rise above national considerations, exert considerable influence on donors and recipients to adopt and cooperate in constructive policies. They can also persuade neighbouring recipients to recognise their mutual advantage in developing a regional economy. The more aid is placed at the disposal of these international economic institutions, the greater their influence in these directions becomes. As an investment in international economic organisation aid saves far more resources from being wasted than it costs.

Fourthly, official aid, so far as it contributes to the integration of national economies effectively, contributes at the same time to national unification and political stability. Recently there have been one or two glaring examples of what appears to be the opposite effect; but circumstances have been exceptional. It is true that virulent political strife may rend a nation however advanced its economy. Politics are not only determined by economics. It is also true that the structural changes which the developing countries are striving for tend to disturb their politics. The stabilising effect of economic and social construction in the long term is nevertheless certain. If the history of advanced countries is a guide, national unity gradually increases as more wealth is more evenly distributed and the interests of localities, provinces, classes and peoples become bound up more closely with one another commercially. What is not in doubt is that aid makes a vital contribution to economic development in helping to bridge the foreign exchange gap, raise living standards, improve public works and services, provide more opportunities of employment, to equalise the distribution of wealth and integrate national and regional economies. These things are far more likely to assure stable politics in the future than the shock of foreign exchange crises and bankruptcies, revolution and reaction, foreign invasion and occupation that have characterised the past.

Fifthly, economic aid is a sensible insurance against neo-colonialist rivalry, the revival of imperialism and its risks to international peace. There is of course no cast-iron guarantee and other forms of insurance are also necessary. But if in the past internal crises in developing countries arising from flagrant mismanagement of their relations with the international economy have frequently invited Juggernauts to clash and intervene, it is cheaper and better to prevent these occasions arising again by helping economic and social construction. As Reginald Prentice put it, the intelligent thing to do from this standpoint would be to divert money from developed countries' defence budgets into foreign aid where in the long term it will prove a much cheaper and better protection for most of their foreign interests than military expenditure.

Sixthly, economic aid acts as a multiplier, albeit a marginal one, in the growth of a world economy. Although foreign aid helps a donor to subsidise his exports, get rid of some of his surplus manufactures, relieve his distressed areas and keep up full employment, these effects are minute by comparison with the century before 1939. Their importance varies from donor to donor but generally the advanced countries do not at present depend directly for their prosperity on further development in backward regions to any great extent. They may do so again in the future, however, when industrial technology produces such surpluses that there will be nothing for it but to transfer more of them to the third world on hire-purchase terms. And who can doubt that when two-thirds of the world's population are fully employed and its unused resources are brought into production, the donor countries' prosperity will multiply? The 'Welfare' state shows this effect on the national scale. Similar effects are possible universally.

Lastly, official aid is vital to the cause of humanity – to relieve famine and suffering, to raise up some societies to the minimum standards of life and health tolerable in a humanistic world. There are moral objections as well as political dangers in deliberately doing nothing to redistribute the world's wealth creatively, when two-thirds of humanity are getting poorer and one-third richer. We acknowledge the humanitarian role of aid and the generous international idealism that inspires public support for it in donor countries. But for us the case for more aid is not essentially philanthropic nor is it – as recipient opinion suspects sometimes – neo-colonialist; it is enlightened self-interest in international cooperation to a host of invaluable mutual benefits.

THE RIGHT KIND OF AID

So far we have discussed aid as if it were a homogeneous commodity. In practice it is of many different kinds designed to serve a variety of purposes – a few pernicious, some misguided, most beneficent. Its nature is in fact so curiously complicated that this conference had difficulty in defining it. A comparatively small proportion takes the form of gifts for the relief of famine and suffering; about 40 per cent is contributed by way of subventions to developing countries' budgets which may cover anything from golden hand-shakes for ex-colonial officials to subsidising a new university or re-equipping a navy. And the remainder is given in hard or soft loans, repayable with interest which, although below market rate, costs the recipients a good deal. Too little aid is directed to 'economic' or 'development' assistance, to particular economic projects and overall development plans. Too much of it is designed to subsidise the donors' exports or serve his diplomatic, strategic or military purposes abroad. These different varieties of aid should not be tarred with the same brush. The pity is that they often are in discussion of the pros and cons. For example, there is a tendency for donor opinion to blame recipient countries for the disappointing fact that military and famine assistance do little to encourage economic growth. It is absurd to judge the effectiveness of one kind of aid by results only to be expected of another. On the same principle there is no case for aid in general regardless of its form, purpose and usefulness to the recipient. None of the beneficial effects that aid promises can actually be produced unless it is of the right kind to be effective; and effectiveness depends above all on the recipient's cooperation, for no objective can be achieved without it. Hence we arrived at the conclusion that the only effective kind of aid is that which serves agreeably the coincident interests of both parties.

The conference on this premise adopted one of the main theses in Professor Chenery's paper. In the past donors have spent far too much aid on attempts at winning political influence and swaying the diplomatic and military alignments of recipient countries. We appreciated that this is a naughty world and that states are bound to protect their interests abroad playing power politics. But this is not a field in which donors' and recipients' interests often coincide; so that according to our first principle, aid as a direct instrument of foreign policy will not achieve its objects. Experience shows that this kind of politically-inspired aid is often wasted. When a donor uses aid to play politics, the recipient's policies and politics naturally react. He begins to bite the hand that feeds him most, exploits international rivalry to diversify his sources of assistance and so protects his independence. Although the original donor's aid has not assisted his economic growth the recipient is nevertheless accused of wasting aid and being ungrateful for it. The model may be crude but it is only too familiar. Obviously this is not the right kind of aid. Ultimately it proves self-defeating. The use of aid to play politics then is the worst way to win friends and influence people in developing countries. It exacerbates instead of ameliorating international rivalries, provokes xenophobic reactions, disturbs internal political stability, hinders national unification and does little for economic development, except distort it.

Historically the necessity for great powers to intervene imperialistically as rivals in the internal affairs of underdeveloped states has arisen more often from the latters' internal weakness and collapse than from the nature of the formers' interests in them. Today similarly, advanced countries' interests are at risk from foreign intervention and Great Power rivalry so long as underdeveloped states remain economically and politically weak. In the light of history, therefore, the best method for advanced states to secure their interests is not to use aid to play politics against each other. This merely weakens the recipient more and so raises the risk to foreign interests. The best method is to use aid to strengthen his economy and government. The highest risk to foreign interests arises from economic failure and consequent political instability on the part of the recipient. It is far safer to direct aid to removing these risks now, than to wait and gamble high diplomatic and military stakes that they will not eventually precipitate major international interventions and crises in one part or other of the third world in the future.

In the long term, donors will safeguard their legitimate commercial and diplomatic aims best by directing their aid to helping recipients achieve the highest rate of balanced economic growth. This is also the best way of insinuating political unity and stability. We believe that, if the aid used misguidedly hitherto to promote the donors' individual strategic and commercial interests directly, were used specifically to develop the recipients' economy, these interests would be much better served than they have been. In future much less military and political aid, much more 'development' or 'economic' aid should be given.

Appendix I Regional Growth of Gross Domestic Product in Constant Prices, Population, and Gross Domestic Product per Capita, 1950–67 (Per cent per year)[1]

Area	1950–60	1960–7	1950–67
Developing countries [a]			
G.D.P.	4·6	5·0	4·8
Population	2·2	2·5	2·3
G.D.P. per capita	2·3	2·5	2·4
Africa			
G.D.P.	4·0	4·0	4·0
Population	2·3	2·4	2·3
G.D.P. per capita	1·7	1·6	1·7
South Asia			
G.D.P.	3·6	4·1	3·8
Population	1·9	2·4	2·1
G.D.P. per capita	1·7	1·7	1·7
East Asia			
G.D.P.	4·7	5·6	5·1
Population	2·5	2·7	2·6
G.D.P. per capita	2·1	2·8	2·4
Southern Europe			
G.D.P.	5·2	7·1	6·0
Population	1·4	1·4	1·4
G.D.P. per capita	3·7	5·6	4·5
Latin America			
G.D.P.	5·0	4·5	4·8
Population	2·8	2·9	2·9
G.D.P. per capita	2·1	1·6	1·8
Middle East			
G.D.P.	6·0	7·2	6·5
Population	3·0	2·9	3·0
G.D.P. per capita	2·9	4·2	3·4
Industrialised countries [b]			
G.D.P.	4·0	4·8	4·3
Population	1·2	1·2	1·2
G.D.P. per capita	2·8	3·6	3·1

[a] Eighty developing countries covering approximately 97 per cent of G.D.P. of all developing countries. The countries included are:

Africa: Algeria, Angola, Cameroon, Congo (K), Ethiopia, Gabon, Ghana, Ivory Coast, Kenya, Libya, Malagasy Republic, Malawi, Mali, Mauritius, Morocco, Niger, Nigeria, Rhodesia, Senegal, Sierra Leone, Sudan, Tanzania, Togo, Tunisia, Uganda, U.A.R., Upper Volta, and Zambia. (Coverage: 92 per cent of the aggregate G.D.P. of the region.)

South Asia: Burma, Ceylon, India, and Pakistan. (Coverage: 100 per cent.)

East Asia: Cambodia, China (Taiwan), Hong Kong, Indonesia, South Korea, Malaysia, Papua and New Guinea, Philippines, Singapore, Thailand, and South Vietnam. (Coverage: 94 per cent.)

Southern Europe: Cyprus, Greece, Portugal, Spain, Turkey, and Yugoslavia. (Coverage: 100 per cent.)

Latin America: Argentina, Barbados, Bolivia, Brazil, British Honduras, Chile, Colombia, Costa Rica, Dominican Republic, Ecuador, El Salvador, Guatemala, Guyana, Haiti, Honduras, Jamaica, Mexico, Nicaragua, Panama, Paraguay, Peru, Surinam, Trinidad and Tobago, Uruguay, and Venezuela. (Coverage: 99 per cent.)

Middle East: Iran, Iraq, Israel, Jordan, Lebanon, and Syria. (Coverage: 78 per cent.)

[b] The countries included are Canada, United States, Austria, Belgium, Denmark, Finland, France, Federal Republic of Germany, Italy, Netherlands, Norway, Sweden, Switzerland, United Kingdom, Ireland, Iceland, Luxembourg, Australia, Japan, New Zealand, and South Africa.

Source: World Bank.

Appendix II   Agriculture and Industry as Per Cent of Gross Domestic Product in Selected Developing Countries, 1953 and 1966[1]

Country	Agriculture [a]		Industry [a]	
	1953	1966	1953	1966
Latin America				
Argentina	20	15	28	37
Brazil	29	30 [b]	24	27 [b]
Chile	14	9 [b]	23	40 [b]
Colombia	38	32 [b]	18	22 [b]
Costa Rica	41	26	12	18
Ecuador	40	35	18	18
Guatemala	n.a.	29	n.a.	16
Jamaica	21	12	17	26
Mexico	21	16 [b]	28	33 [b]
Nicaragua	42	32	13	15
Paraguay	45	35	17	16
Peru	34	22 [b]	18	22 [b]
Africa				
Algeria	30	19	19	n.a.
Congo (K)	29	26	35	n.a.
Ivory Coast	53 [b]	41	8 [b]	12
Kenya	47 [b]	36	10 [b]	14
Malawi	67 [b]	56 [b]	5 [b]	8 [b]
Morocco	34	33 [b]	17	22 [b]
Nigeria	65	66	5	12
Sudan	61	54	5	6
Tanzania	62 [b]	54	10 [b]	8
Tunisia	25 [b]	18	18 [b]	21
Uganda	72 [b]	60 [b]	5 [b]	10 [b]
U.A.R.	32	28	9	23
Zambia	11 [b]	10	62 [b]	46
East and South-East Asia				
Burma	34	34 [b]	8	10 [b]
China (Taiwan)	38	26	14	23
South Korea	49	35 [b]	9	20 [b]
Philippines	34	33 [b]	18	20 [b]
Thailand	43	31 [b]	13	16 [b]
South and West Asia				
Ceylon	47 [b]	41	5 [b]	7
India	51 [b]	50	14 [b]	14
Iran	31 [b]	28 [b]	27 [b]	29 [b]
Israel	12	8	23	24
Jordan	18 [b]	19	7 [b]	12
Pakistan	53	50	9	10
Turkey	48	37	11	37

[a] Agriculture includes forestry, hunting, and fishing. Industry includes mining.
[b] Chile, Mexico, Burma, South Korea, Philippines, Thailand, 1967; Uganda, 1954–67; Malawi, 1954–65; India, 1960; Kenya, Tanzania, Zambia, 1954; Ivory Coast, Tunisia, 1960; Ceylon, 1958; Brazil, Colombia, Morocco, 1965; Jordan, 1959; Peru, 1963; Iran, 1959–65.
Sources: United Nations, *Statistical Yearbook*, various issues; World Bank.

Appendix III Net flow of Official Bilateral and Multilateral Aid and Private Investment to less developed countries 1956–68

Table 1 *Net flow of financial resources by category to less developed countries and multilateral agencies : 1956–68.*[1] *(In millions of U.S. dollars)*

Disbursements	1956	1957	1958	1959	1960	1961	1962	1963	1964	1965	1966	1967	1968
Official disbursements [a]	3,260	3,856	4,387	4,311	4,927	6,099	5,990	6,054	5,889	6,290	6,585	6,988	6,910
Official development assistance [a]													
Multilateral	n.a.	421	367	333	548	536	539	305	382	439	477	717	661
Bilateral	n.a.	3,435	4,020	3,978	4,138	4,629	4,996	5,504	5,570	5,618	5,802	5,897	5,768
Other official [a]					241	934	455	185	−63	233	306	374	481
Private investment and lending	2,998	3,779	2,917	2,820	3,148	3,998	2,497	2,511	3,192	4,170	3,841	4,181	5,843
Direct investment [b]	2,350	2,724	1,970	1,782	1,969	1,986	1,528	1,710	1,910	2,702	2,355	2,102	2,775
Bilateral portfolio [b]	190	601	733	691	437	453	153	200	290	467	282	698	730
Multilateral portfolio					205	90	239	−33	141	248	15	306	605
Export credits [a, c]	458	454	214	347	537	569	577	634	851	753	1,189	1,075	1,734
Total flow	6,258	7,655	7,304	7,131	8,075	9,197	8,487	8,565	9,080	10,461	10,426	11,169	12,753

[a] A new system of classifying official flows was introduced by the D.A.C. in 1969. This involved reporting 'official development assistance' (flows which are concessional and primarily intended for development) separately from 'other official' and including in the latter export credits extended by independent governmental institutions (previously classified as 'private' in some cases). This classification is only available for 1960–8, and for this reason figures for export credits and official flows in that period are not directly comparable with those in 1956–9.

[b] Figures for direct investment include U.K. and Italian bilateral portfolio investment.

[c] The coverage of non-guaranteed export credits is not complete.

Sources: O.E.C.D., D.A.C., *Statistical Tables for the 1969 Annual Aid Review, Efforts and Policies of the Members of the Development Assistance Committee; The Flow of Financial Resources to Less Developed Countries, 1961–5;* O.E.C.D. Secretariat.

Table 2 *Net flow of total official and private financial resources classified by donor countries to less developed countries and multilateral agencies :* 1957–68.² *(In millions of U.S. dollars)*

Country	1957	1958	1959	1960	1961	1962	1963	1964	1965	1966	1967	1968
Australia	(45·0)	(52·0)	(50·0)	(58·9)	(70·9)	(73·8)	96·8	118·8	136·6	148·1	192·2	187·2
Austria	−4·8	6·6	−1·3	5·7	20·2	31·0	5·9	21·3	47·3	49·3	47·8	73·9
Belgium	36·5	111·9	167·8	182·2	163·9	118·2	174·7	164·3	221·1	178·0	164·4	243·0
Canada	131·6	155·1	82·3	144·7	87·0	109·6	130·5	141·8	169·3	266·7	253·9	306·4
Denmark	2·1	5·2	(21·2)	37·9	33·3	14·7	(10·5)	31·8	15·2	21·3	24·8	73·7
France	1,228·7	1,337·4	1,171·7	1,325·1	1,406·3	1,395·2	1,242·0	1,360·4	1,229·4	1,319·7	1,341·3	1,482·9
Germany	522·5	510·5	866·3	624·7	839·0	650·0	604·5	707·2	726·7	737·5	1,140·2	1,634·9
Italy	208·6	154·8	149·2	298·3	257·5	390·4	321·1	236·8	265·5	631·6	287·3	505·2
Japan	(110·5)	(314·8)	(190·2)	246·1	381·4	286·2	267·4	289·8	485·5	625·1	797·5	1,049·3
Netherlands	145·1	193·5	208·7	238·6	200·3	114·2	134·4	118·4	239·1	254·1	228·2	276·1
Norway	9·2	3·1	6·9	10·2	26·9	6·8	21·5	23·0	38·4	17·1	30·2	57·7
Sweden	25·2	26·7	45·0	46·6	51·9	37·3	53·4	67·2	72·7	108·0	120·7	127·0
Switzerland	114·2	78·7	112·8	156·8	210·6	161·1	202·8	110·1	191·9	110·2	133·7	214·7
United Kingdom	960·5	668·2	843·6	880·8	899·0	743·9	720·8	918·8	1,027·7	939·2	841·4	845·6
United States	4,099·7	3,685·0	3,276·1	3,818·2	4,548·7	4,354·5	4,578·6	4,770·3	5,524·3	5,019·9	5,565·4	5,675·7
Total	7,634·6	7,303·5	7,130·5	8,074·8	9,196·9	8,486·9	8,565·0	9,080·0	10,460·7	10,425·8	11,169·0	12,753·3

Note: Parentheses indicate estimates.
Source: O.E.C.D., D.A.C., *Statistical Tables for the 1969 Annual Aid Review.*

Notes

CHAPTER 1

1 *African Development Planning : Impressions and Papers of the Cambridge Conference, 1963* (ed. Ronald Robinson), Cambridge University Overseas Studies Committee, 1964, p. 9.

2 *Industrial Developments in Asia and the Far East*, Vol. 1. U.N. Publication No. 66.I.B.19, New York, pp. 12–13.

3 See below, p. 104.

4 See below, pp. 98–9.

5 *Ibid.*

6 See below, p. 19.

7 P. 25.

8 From his review of R. F. Mikesell's 'The Economics of Foreign Aid' in *Economic Journal*, June 1969, p. 386. Paul Streeten gave a paper to the 1965 conference hinting at this view. See also G. Myrdal, *Asian Drama, An Inquiry into the Poverty of Nations*, III, p. 1889, also Appendices 3–5.

9 M. Lipton, 'Strategy for Agriculture: Urban Bias and Rural Planning', in P. Streeten and M. Lipton, *The Crisis of Indian Planning*, Oxford, 1968, Ch. 4.

10 *The Rural Base for National Development : Papers and Impressions of the Sixth Cambridge Conference, 1968*, Cambridge University Overseas Studies Committee, 1968, p. 65.

11 *Ibid.* p. 2.

12 *Ibid.* pp. 49–50: see also M. Yudelman, 'Planning the Rural Sector', *ibid.* pp. 102–8; and E. M. Godfrey, 'Personal Impressions of Conference Discussions', *ibid.* pp. 52–3.

13 *Ibid.* p. 47.

14 See below, pp. 153–6; also, E. Flores, 'From Land Reform to Industrial Revolution: The Meexican Case', *The Developing Economies*, March 1969, Vol. VII, No. 1.

15 E. M. Godfrey, 'Personal Impressions of Conference Discussions', *The Rural Base for National Development*, pp. 52–3.

16 *Ibid.* p. 52.

17 See M. Lipton, 'Strategy for Agriculture', in *The Crisis of Indian Planning*.

18 Godfrey, 'Personal Impressions of Conference Discussions', *op. cit.* p. 52.

19 S. P. Huntington, *Political Order in Changing Societies*, New Haven, 1968, pp. 91–2.

20 See below, p. 176.

21 See below, p. 196.

22 A. Waterston, 'Administrative Obstacles to Planning', *Economica Latinoamericana*, July 1964.

23 J. LaPalombara, 'An Over-view of Bureaucracy and Political Development', in J. LaPalombara (ed.), *Bureaucracy and Political Development*, Princeton, 1963, pp. 127–31.

24 See below, pp. 176–7.
25 *International Cooperation in Aid, Papers and Impressions of the Fifth Cambridge Conference, 1966* (ed. Ronald Robinson), Cambridge University Overseas Studies Committee, 1968.
26 Huntington, *Political Order in Changing Societies*, pp. 91–2.
27 See also *Politics and Change in Developing Countries : Studies in the Theory and Practice of Development* (ed. Colin Leys), Cambridge, 1969, pp. 1–12, 13–34, 247 ff.

CHAPTER 2

1 Gerald M. Meier, Professor of International Economics at Stanford University, presented this paper to the Cambridge Conference, September 1965, on 'Overcoming Obstacles to Development'.
2 See pp. 33–5.
3 See p. 34.
4 See pp. 135–6.
5 *Ibid.*
6 See p. 37.

CHAPTER 3

1 Reprinted from the Report of Cambridge Conference, *Overcoming Obstacles to Development* (ed. Ronald Robinson), Cambridge University Overseas Studies Committee, 1966, pp. 4–10.

CHAPTER 4

1 The views expressed in this paper are those of the author in his personal capacity. The paper was presented to the Cambridge Conference on 'Industrialisation in Developing Countries', in September 1964, when Dr Ikram was working in the Perspective Planning Section of the Planning Commission of Pakistan.
2 A crore of rupees = Rs.10 million and is roughly equivalent to £750,000 at the current exchange rate.
3 Most of the figures quoted are still only provisional, pending the completion of detailed sectoral studies. The broad strategy, however, is clear and the Third Five-Year Plan is being drawn up in accordance with it.
4 Mahbub ul Haq, 'Problems of Formulating a Development Strategy for Pakistan's Third Plan' (paper presented to the O.E.C.D. conference, Berlin, 1963). The preceding point is also discussed in this paper.
5 Moreover, I am informed by a number of industries using imported second-hand machinery that one very great drawback is that the older equipment produces output of an inferior quality to that produced by more modern methods. The implications of this for international competition should be clear.
6 F.A.O., 'Agricultural Commodities – Projections for 1970', Rome, 1962; E.C.A.F.E. Secretariat, 'Projections of Foreign Trade of the E.C.A.F.E. Region up to 1980', Bangkok, 1963 (mimeo).

7 The arguments against relying heavily on the manufacture of consumer goods and trading these for foreign capital goods have been discussed above.

8 If that motley aggregate, ' services ', is broken down into its component activities.

CHAPTER 5

1 The author was Chief Economic Adviser to the Indian Ministry of Finance and this paper was presented to the Cambridge Conference on Industrialisation in Developing Countries in September 1964.

CHAPTER 6

1 Reprinted from the Report of the Third Cambridge Conference, *Industrialisation in Developing Countries* (ed. Ronald Robinson), Cambridge University Overseas Studies Committee, 1965, pp. 5-20.

2 Professor Arthur Lewis, *Report on Industrialisation in the Gold Coast*, 1953.

3 J. M. Bairoch, *Révolution Industrielle et Sous-Développement*, 1963.

4 See above, Khalid Ikram, ' The Role of Industry in Pakistan's Development Plan '.

5 *African Development Planning*; Report of the 1963 Cambridge Conference (ed. Ronald Robinson), p. 17.

CHAPTER 7

1 Dr C. F. Schumacher, Chief Economic Adviser to the British National Coal Board, presented this paper to the Cambridge Conference on ' Industrialisation in Developing Countries ' in September 1964. The views which he expresses are personal.

CHAPTER 8

1 Reprinted from the Report of the Conference on *Industrialisation in Developing Countries* (ed. Ronald Robinson), Cambridge University Overseas Studies Committee, 1965, pp. 24-31, 50-3.

2 Dr Kaldor.

CHAPTER 9

1 The following notes were prepared as comments on two Agenda items while the Conference on Industrialisation in Developing Countries of September 1964 was going on. Though they were revised afterwards, it seemed advisable to keep their impromptu character unchanged. The views expressed are those of the author in his personal capacity.

2 At the time of writing, the author was Director, Joint U.N. Economic Commission for Latin America, Latin American Institute for Economic and Social Planning.

3 Real *per capita* income, according to E.C.L.A.'s provisional estimates, was about 400 dollars for the whole region (excluding Cuba, for which no data are available).

4 *The economic development of Latin America in the post-war period*, United Nations publication, Sales No.: 64.II.G.6, Part I, Ch. 1, p. 1.

5 *Ibid.* Part III; and *Latin America and the United Nations Conference on Trade and Development* (E/CN.12/693), 1964.

6 On its own account, or in the tertiary sector that grows with industry.

7 *The economic development of Latin America in the post-war period*, Part III, Ch. 3.

8 *Ibid.*

9 In the twofold sense of restriction of consumption and pressure on the capacity to import. On the one hand, the standards of living of broad population strata do not exceed minimum subsistence levels. On the other, how far the savings corresponding to this higher rate of capital formation can be really converted into capital goods, a large proportion of which still have to be imported, depends upon the very limited possibilities opened up by the generally unfavourable evolution of the external sector.

10 See the paper presented at this Conference by Dr Khalid Ikram, Ch. 4.

11 *The economic development of Latin America in the post-war period*, Part II, Ch. 3; see also 'Changes in employment structure in Latin America, 1945–55', *Economic Bulletin for Latin America*, Vol. II, No. 1, Santiago, Chile, February 1957.

12 This influence is likely to be greater in a more indirect sense, i.e. in so far as the strategy chosen brings about changes in certain unfavourable structural factors, with the corresponding acceleration of the overall rate of development.

13 Redistribution not only of personal income but also by geographical areas (i.e. among the different parts of each country).

14 See *Selection of techniques and manpower absorption* (S.T./E.C.L.A./CONF.11/L.3), document prepared by the E.C.L.A. secretariat for the Seminar on Industrial Programming held at São Paulo, Brazil in March 1963, p. 4.

15 See *Theoretical and practical problems of economic growth* (E/CN.12/221), Ch. III, p. 47.

16 See *Selection of techniques and manpower absorption*, p. 5.

17 The same saving clause applies to the use of second-hand techniques and equipment.

18 *Problemas y perspectivas del desarrollo industrial latinamericano* (E/CN.12/664), 1963, Ch. I.

19 *Ibid.* Ch. I, section 3.

CHAPTER 10

1 Sir Joseph Hutchinson, Draper's Professor of Agriculture in the University of Cambridge, presented this paper to the Sixth Cambridge Conference on 'The Rural Base for National Development', 1968.

2 W. Allan, *The African Husbandman*, Edinburgh, 1965.

3 J. W. F. Hill, *Tudor and Stuart Lincoln*, Cambridge, 1956.

4 B. H. Farmer, *Pioneer Peasant Colonisation in Ceylon*, Oxford, 1957.

CHAPTER 11

1 Dr Busia, at the time of writing Chairman of the Political Committee, Ghana, is now Prime Minister of Ghana, and presented this paper to the Sixth Cambridge Conference on 'The Rural Base for National Development' in 1968.

CHAPTER 12

1 Tarlok Singh, lately a member of the Planning Commission of India, presented this paper to the Sixth Cambridge Conference on 'The Rural Base for National Development', 1968.

2 As, for instance, in the recent *Brochure on Revised Series of National Product for 1960–1 to 1964–5*, August 1967, Central Statistical Organisation, Government of India.

3 For instance, the Indian Fourth Plan Outline of August 1966 was drawn up against the following estimates of demand for 1970–1 and 1975–6 [1 Lakh = 100,000]. See also *Agricultural Commodities – Projections for 1975 and 1985*, Food and Agricultural Organisation, 1967, and P. V. Sukhatme, *Feeding India's Growing Millions*, Asia, 1965.

4 See *Yardsticks of Additional Production of Certain Foodgrains, Commercial and Oilseed Crops*, Institute of Agricultural Research Statistics, Indian Council of Agricultural Research, 1964.

5 National Council of Applied Economic Research, *All India Rural Household Survey : Saving, income and investment*, Vol. II, 1965.

CHAPTER 13

1 Professor Flores of the School of Economics, University of Mexico, presented this paper to the Cambridge Conference on 'The Rural Base for National Development', 1968.

2 Theodore W. Schultz, *Transforming Traditional Agriculture*, New Haven, 1964; see particularly Ch. 8, 'Farm size, control and incentives', p. 111.

3 Folke Dovring, 'The Share of Agriculture in a Growing Population', in *Agriculture in Economic Development*, Eicher and Witt (eds.), 1964.

4 Georgescu-Roegen, 'Economic Theory and Agrarian Economics', *op. cit.*

5 Solon Barraclough and Arthur Domike, 'Agrarian Structure in Seven Latin American Countries', *Land Economics*, Vol. XLII, No. 4, November 1966.

6 Wyn Owen, 'The Double Development Squeeze on Agriculture', *The American Economic Review*, Vol. LVI, No. 1, March 1966.

7 W. Arthur Lewis, *The Theory of Economic Growth*, London, 1955, pp. 208–9.

8 Albert O. Hirschman, *The Strategy of Economic Development*, New Haven, 1958.

9 United States Department of Agriculture, *Changes in Agriculture in Twenty-Six Developing Nations, 1948 to 1963*. Foreign Agricultural Economic Report No. 27, November 1965.

10 See James R. Himes, 'La formación de capital en México', *El Trimestre Economicó*, Vol. xxxii, Num. 125, Enero–Marzo 1965. Fondo de Cultura Economica.

11 Zvi Griliches, 'Research Costs and Social Returns: Hybrid Corn and Related Innovations' in Eicher and Witt, *Agriculture in Economic Development*.

CHAPTER 14

1 Erich Jacoby, Research Professor at the Institute for Economic Studies, Stockholm, presented this paper to the Cambridge Conference on 'The Rural Base for National Development', 1968.

2 Erich Jacoby, *Evaluation of Agrarian Structures and Agrarian Reform Programmes*, F.A.O., Rome, p. 17.

3 J. W. Maine, 'Kenya: Land Settlement in Kenya', p. 26. Paper submitted to World Land Reform Conference, RU–WLR–C 66/20, Rome, 1966.

CHAPTER 15

1 Mr Please, at the time of writing on the staff of the World Bank, presented this paper to the Cambridge Conference on 'Overcoming Obstacles to Development' in September 1965. The views expressed are personal to the author.

2 Ragnar Nurkse, 'Problems of Capital Formation in Underdeveloped Countries'.

3 I.B.R.D., *Financing of Public Investment in Underdeveloped Countries: An Analysis for Nineteen Less Developed Countries During the 1950s*, September 1960, a study prepared by Marinus van der Mal.

4 United Nations Economic Commission for Asia and the Far East, *Economic Survey of Asia and the Far East, 1961*, Bangkok, 1962, pp. 56–7.

5 Nicholas Kaldor, 'Will Underdeveloped Countries Learn to Tax?', *Foreign Affairs*, No. 41, 1963.

6 Alan R. Prest, *Public Finance in Under-developed Countries*, London, 1962, and R. N. Tripathy, *Public Finance in Underdeveloped Countries*, Calcutta, 1964.

CHAPTER 16

1 Reprinted from the Report of the Fourth Cambridge Conference, *Overcoming Obstacles to Development* (ed. Ronald Robinson), Cambridge University Overseas Studies Committee, 1966, pp. 11–20.

CHAPTER 17

1 Rashid Ibrahim, at the time of writing Financial Adviser, Military Finance, Pakistan, presented this paper to the Cambridge Conference on 'Overcoming Obstacles to Development', September 1965.

2 A comparison of the Indian Plans which are socialistic in approach with the Pakistan Plans which are free-enterprise-oriented would illustrate this:

INDIA

First Plan (1951–6) Rs.31,000 million (public sector 64 per cent).
Second Plan (1956–61) Rs.62,000 million (public sector 61 per cent).
Third Plan (1961–6) Rs.116,000 million (public sector 65 per cent).
Fourth Plan (1966–71) Rs.215,000 million (public sector 67 per cent).

PAKISTAN

Six-year Programme (1951–7) only public sector covered (Rs.2,600 million).
First Plan (1955–60) Rs.10,800 million (public sector 69 per cent).
Second Plan (1960–5) Rs.24,600 million (public sector 66 per cent).
Third Plan (1965–70) Rs.52,000 million (public sector 58 per cent).

3   If qualified personnel are not available in sufficient numbers initially, it may be desirable to have foreign experts as advisers. For instance, Pakistan's Planning Commission has received the assistance of a distinguished group from Harvard University. It helped in preparing the First Plan and was also present when the Second Plan was prepared, but the Third Plan has been prepared by Pakistani personnel.

4   The structure of the planning organisation in Pakistan is briefly given in Appendix 1. The more important standing committees on which the Planning Commission is represented are also listed there.

5   A list of the public corporations established in Pakistan is in Appendix 2.

6   Pakistan has made considerable effort in this field, e.g. it has set up standing committees for simplification of procedures and forms, enlarged the scope of delegated powers, attached financial advisers to ministries/departments so that greater awareness of the problems and practical difficulties is ensured, established a strong O. & M. Division for continual review of organisation and working methods, etc.

7   *First Five-Year Plan 1965–6*, Government of Pakistan.

8   Pakistan has established a semi-official Industrial Advisory Centre, the object of which is to make market studies and prepare feasibility reports and projects, whether required by a government agency or a private entrepreneur. Several private consultants have also emerged, so far mostly in the civil engineering field.

9   For instance, in Pakistan, licences for new investments (Investment Promotion Bureau), operation of export controls (Export Promotion Bureau), administration of foreign exchange control (State Bank of Pakistan), regulation of individual commodities (Jute Board and Cotton Board), have been entrusted to semi-autonomous bodies. Most credit agencies are also semi-autonomous (Industrial Development Bank, Pakistan Industrial Credit and Investment Corporation, Agricultural Development Bank, House Building Finance Corporation), and operate independently, subject to broad government directions.

10   From a statement made at the R.C.D. Colloquium on 'Common Problems of Growth' held at Karachi in June 1965, by Dr Parviz Khabir, Director of Observation, Plan Organisation, Government of Iran.

11 In Pakistan, several committees have been appointed since independence for administrative reorganisation and now there is a Standing Committee on Organisation.

12 *Third Five-Year Plan 1965–70*, Government of Pakistan.

CHAPTER 18

1 Reprinted from the Report of the Fourth Cambridge Conference, *Overcoming Obstacles to Development* (ed. Ronald Robinson), Cambridge University Overseas Studies Committee, 1966, pp. 28–40.

2 *The First Five-Year Plan*, pp. 91–2. Government of Pakistan Planning Board.

3 Quoted in A. Waterston, 'Administrative Obstacles to Planning', *Economica Latinoamericana*, July 1964.

4 *Ibid.* p. 339.

5 *Idem.*

CHAPTER 19

1 This paper, originally presented to the International Economic Association, Conference on Capital Movements and Economic Development (July 1965), was given in revised form to the fifth Cambridge Conference on 'International Cooperation in Aid' held in September 1966.

2 Professor at the Center for International Affairs, Harvard University.

3 The members of the O.E.C.D. accounted for over 90 per cent of the public assistance to less developed countries; most of the remainder comes from the Communist Bloc.

4 This is the assumption made in the conventional national accounts definition of savings as the difference between investment and the import surplus. In some cases, however, the additional resources are distributed in such a way as to subsidise increased consumption. In this case, the investment equivalent of the external aid is less than one, i.e. for every dollar of external aid domestic investment increases by less than one dollar.

5 A similar point has been made by Eckstein in his analysis of the productivity of domestic investment (see 'Investment Criteria for Economic Development and the Theory of Intertemporal Welfare Economics', *Quarterly Journal of Economics*, February 1957).

6 See I. Adelman and H. B. Chenery, 'Foreign Assistance and Economic Development: the Case of Greece', *Review of Economics and Statistics* (forthcoming); H. B. Chenery and M. Bruno, 'Development Alternatives in an Open Economy: the Case of Israel', *Economic Journal*, March 1962.

7 A more satisfactory theoretical concept is the discounted present value of the stream of future increases in G.N.P. divided by the present value of the aid inflow. This ratio is not much affected by benefits more than ten years hence if discount rates of 8–10 per cent are used.

8 The formulae are given in Chenery and Strout ('Foreign Assistance and Economic Development', Discussion Paper, Agency for International Development, 1965). For a growth rate of 5 per cent, $\beta = 1 \cdot 8$ for five years,

3·8 for ten years, and 7·0 for twenty years. Export growth is taken as given and a zero discount rate is used.

9 The median values of the parameters for the thirty-one-country sample studied in Chenery and Strout were: $k = 3.5$, $a = 0.19$, $\mu = 0.21$, initial savings rate $(a'_0) = 0.12$.

10 Variation in k represents the change in the productivity of all investment; the effect of a change in the productivity of the aid-financed portion alone would be considerably less.

11 Necessary conditions for closing the trade gap under other assumptions are given by the formula in *ibid*. pp. 11–15.

12 *Ibid.*

13 The fifty-country sample covers 90 per cent of the G.N.P. in underdeveloped countries, but it includes only thirteen African countries and also omits the most primitive economies in other areas.

14 See Chenery and Strout, 'Foreign Assistance and Economic Development'.

15 A number of alternative projections of the performance of less developed countries and corresponding assistance requirements are given in section II, *ibid*.

16 For 1963–5 the total net flow of resources has remained about constant although it had been growing at about 10 per cent per year prior to 1963.

17 The administrative features of the project aid mechanism limit the maximum amount of aid provided to a country in practice to 10–20 per cent of its total investment.

18 The two systems are compared in more detail in *Principles of Economic Assistance*, A.I.D., Washington, 1963.

19 This reasoning has been accepted by the U.S. Government in its loan policies but not by most other donors.

20 See A.I.D., *Principles of Economic Assistance* and the A.I.D. presentation to Congress for 1966 (see *Proposed Mutual Defense and Development Programs for Fiscal Year 1966*, A.I.D., Washington, 1965).

21 The principle of allocating assistance against performance is implicit in the Charter of Punta del Este, but the agencies of the Alliance for Progress have only taken a few halting steps to apply it.

22 These standards would be met by perhaps a third of the thirty-one countries analysed in Chenery and Strout.

23 Early suggestions along these lines were made by Millikan and Rostow, *A Proposal*, New York, 1957.

24 An upper limit to the growth rate to be supported is suggested to avoid the possible problem of having a few exceptionally good performers receive a high proportion of total aid, but this eventuality seems remote.

25 In each case, the capital inflow exceeded 6 per cent of G.N.P. during its peak years, which is much larger than the 1–2 per cent that can be transferred under existing project procedures. The analysis of optimal growth patterns for Pakistan in Chenery and A. MacEwan, 'Optimal Patterns of Growth and Aid: The Case of Pakistan', *Pakistan Development Review*, Summer 1966, suggests that peak levels of 8–10 per cent of G.N.P. would be desirable with good performance by the recipient.

CHAPTER 20

1 Reprinted from the Report of the Fifth Cambridge Conference, *International Cooperation in Aid* (ed. Ronald Robinson), Cambridge University Overseas Studies Committee, 1968, pp. 21–6.

CHAPTER 21

1 Lord Balogh, Fellow of Balliol College, Oxford, presented this paper to the Fifth Cambridge Conference on 'International Cooperation in Aid', September 1966.

2 *Congressional Record*, Vol. 112, No. 120.

3 Cf., e.g. *Overseas Development : The Work of the New Ministry*, Cmnd. 2736, esp. Ch. 11. Also the statement of the President of the I.B.D.R. See also H. Wilson, *The War on World Poverty*, 1953, esp. Chs x and xi.

4 Cf. *Overseas Development*.

5 Not least through the direct influence on the constitutional set-up exercised by the ex-colonial power.

6 Especially the economic institutions developed through economic and/or political dependence. See T. Balogh, *Economics of Poverty*, London, 1966, section 1, Ch. 2, 'The Mechanism of Neo-Imperialism'.

7 The evolution of a tiny privileged class and its sustenance by the possibility of migration (including migration to international institutions) when the mass of people had no such outlets increases the imbalance.

8 While there is some doubt about the precise quantitative answer, it seems tolerably established that the loss of import capacity caused was greater than the increase in effective aid.

   For a more detailed analysis, see 'The Mechanism of Neo-Imperialism', in T. Balogh, *Economics of Poverty*. In most African countries (as in the Latin Americans before them), industrial development experienced a spurt after liberation on account of their regained freedom to introduce or increase protective measures.

9 Cf. *Economics of Poverty*, Ch. 8, 'Aid versus Trade'.

10 For a more detailed discussion, see *Totalitarian Trade*, 'Unequal Partners', Vol. 11, p. 285/7.

11 Cf. *Economics of Poverty*, section 1, Chs 1 and, especially, 2.

12 As we saw, this objection has been voiced by Senator Fulbright against U.S. aid in territories where that country is dominant even if it was never a major direct colonial power.

13 This has also been taken up, notably by Senator Fulbright.

14 Cf., e.g. the misguided educational drives, the unbalanced plans for industry, agriculture, fisheries and animal husbandry, etc., elaborated by enthusiastic technocrats.

15 They, at least formally, are dependent on requests by recipient member Governments. See *Economics of Poverty*, Chs 9 and 11.

16 It is regrettable that this did not happen even in the case of Africa, where Regional Offices have only recently been organised.

17 E.g. Africa or South America; in the case of both, internal communications are impeded by the nature of the country.
18 In these countries, however, the political background was not conducive to a fully effective action.
19 Repayment of loans and the redirection of the funds so obtained towards the worst-off areas will be of the utmost importance as self-sustaining development gets under way in some less under-privileged areas.
20 Reprinted from *Venture*, January 1970.

CHAPTER 22

1 Reprinted from the Report of the Fifth Cambridge Conference, *International Cooperation in Aid* (ed. Ronald Robinson), Cambridge University Overseas Studies Committee, 1968, pp. 29–34.

CHAPTER 23

1 Ronald Robinson, Argument of the Cambridge Conference, 1966, reprinted from *International Cooperation in Aid*, Cambridge University Overseas Studies Committee, 1968.

APPENDIX I

1 Reprinted from Lester B. Pearson (chr.): *Partners in Development : Report of the Commission on International Development*, New York, Praeger, 1969, pp. 358–9.

APPENDIX II

1 *Ibid.* pp. 362–3.

APPENDIX III

1 *Ibid.* p. 378.
2 *Ibid.* p. 379.

Index